STUDIES IN FRENCH FICTION
IN HONOUR OF VIVIENNE MYLNE

STUDIES IN FRENCH FICTION
IN HONOUR OF
VIVIENNE MYLNE

Edited by
ROBERT GIBSON

GRANT & CUTLER LTD
1 9 8 8

I.S.B.N.: 0-7293-0283-0

Impreso en España
Printed in Spain

I.S.B.N.: 84-599-2419-X
Depósito legal: V. 1.559 - 1988
Artes Gráficas Soler, S.A. - La Olivereta, 28 - 46018 Valencia - 1988

Table of Contents

Foreword

T H E list of contributors to this *Festschrift* is not a wholly accurate measure of the high esteem with which Vivienne Mylne is regarded by her ex-colleagues, former pupils and ever-faithful friends: the number could have been significantly higher. The list of contributions will indicate rather more accurately than the detailed check-list of her writings the formidable range of her interests but even that does not do them full justice. The necessarily brief sketch that follows will, I hope, fill some of the more important gaps and 'give you all the facts' required in any shilling life.

If there is a right royal road to the higher reaches of French studies, then Vivienne Mylne certainly did not follow it. She spent the first five years of her life in mainland China where her father was a Methodist missionary and where she was born on 19 October 1922. Five years later, with the Yunnan natives voicing increasingly anti-Western sentiments, all Europeans were ordered out of the province and the Mylne family returned to England. By the time Yunnan xenophobia had diminished in intensity, her father was adjudged no longer to be well enough for the rigours of foreign service. His activities were confined instead to the comparative calm of the south of England, the peace being broken every three or four years when his superiors bade him take up his crook and seek another flock. So it came to pass that Vivienne's secondary education was completed at East Ham Grammar School (1934-35), then at Southend-on-Sea High School (1935-39) and that most of the 'phoney' war was spent in the Channel Islands. When these were occupied in 1940, she was teaching at the Girls' College in Jersey and her academic ambitions at this time were to become a Classicist: Fate then intervened.

She had not been long in her first teaching post when she was arrested
by the German authorities. They had been sent an anonymous letter (ever
since, assumed by Vivienne to have been sent by a disgruntled rival
candidate) reporting that she still possessed and operated a radio after all
sets had officially been confiscated. She was put on trial, convicted of
'propagating information contrary to the welfare of the Third Reich' and
sentenced to nine months imprisonment in a French jail: it was indeed
called a *centre pénitentiaire*. Two months were cut from this sentence for
good conduct and she was then allowed to return to Jersey. This was
largely thanks to friends in Jersey insisting that her presence in the Girls'
College was vital. For Vivienne, it may well have been vital in a sense
those friends didn't fully realize at the time. After sentence, British
prisoners in France were regularly sent on to some *Stalag* or concentration
camp, so her career might well have ended before it had properly begun.
In the event, Hitler's War brought her mixed fortunes: it permanently
impaired her health; it caused her to neglect the Greek in which she had
once been proficient but so improved her French that a change of
academic direction became inevitable, and the road forward to University,
previously denied to her, was made that much easier by the dramatic
improvement in the student grant-system which came when the war
ended. She went up to Lady Margaret Hall in 1945 and the rest, as the
saying goes, is history . . .

After graduating at Oxford, she moved on to University College,
London where, in 1952, under the supervision of Professor Brian Woledge,
she completed her Ph.D. thesis entitled 'Interjections in the French
Eighteenth Century theatre: a semantic study'. She stayed on at University
College till 1955 as a part-time assistant lecturer then moved to University
College, Swansea, where she spent her next eleven years. In 1966, after
some heart-searching, she accepted an invitation to join the still small but
rapidly expanding French Board at the University of Kent at Canterbury
and from then on, it did not take her long to achieve the professional
status that clearly became her due: she was promoted to a Senior
Lectureship in 1967, to a Readership in 1973 and to a Personal Professor-
ship in 1976. She readily took a (more than) full share of the onerous
administrative duties which are inevitably required within a burgeoning
new University and discharged them without complaint or fuss and
always with exemplary competence. She served as Senior Tutor of Rutherford College from 1967 till 1971 and was Deputy Master of the College
from 1971 till 1976. She was Chairman of the French Board from 1971 till
1973 and Sub-Dean of the Faculty of Humanities from 1974 till 1977. In

addition, she served on a wide array of Faculty and Senate committees and sang regularly at concerts of the University's Music Society. All this while, she was playing a crucial role in the leading learned societies devoted to eighteenth century studies in the wider world beyond.

In 1971, she became a founder-member and first secretary of the British Society for Eighteenth Century Studies and, in 1978 and 1979, served as President. She also served two terms as member of the Executive Committee of the International Society for Eighteenth Century Studies, the federation of the world's national groups. While continuing to shoulder a heavy burden of undergraduate teaching and post-graduate supervising, she accepted invitations to give papers at the annual conference of the Society for French Studies, at the inaugural conference of the British Society for the Study of Comparative Literature, at the University of Rheims and at successive meetings of the International Congress of the Enlightenment: at St Andrews (1967), at Nancy (1971) and at York (in 1975). She was asked to examine doctoral theses by British universities, too many to enumerate here, and, as the following bibliography will reveal, she was commissioned, with growing frequency, to contribute articles to the *Festschriften* of other Professors *Emeriti*, British, American and French. All this while, she continued to publish, with undiminished vigour and exemplary dispatch, books, articles and reviews of marked distinction.

The book which first brought Vivienne Mylne to the notice of the wider academic public was *The Eighteenth-Century French Novel; techniques of illusion*, first published in 1965. The main title is not the most accurate guide to the contents of the work. It does not set out to be a comprehensive study of all the French eighteenth century novelists, concentrating as it so commendably does on those who, in a variety of forms, and principally the memoir, pseudo-memoir or epistolary novel, aimed at verisimilitude, and the analyses of characterization, plot, point of view, general theory and specific practice provide ample evidence of wide and judicious reading of novels English and Spanish. It was deservedly acclaimed by the foremost authorities in the field, for the width and depth of the erudition, for the sense and sensibility of the ideas and the lucidity and vigour with which these were invariably expressed. All these qualities, which are the hall-marks of a Mylne lecture, are very much to the fore in her monographs on *Manon Lescaut* (1972) and on *La Religieuse* (1981) which are object-lessons in how to present to a student readership infinite riches in remarkably little room. Qualities of a rather different order – most particularly clarity of concept, tenacity of purpose and thoroughness

in execution – all characterize her other major work to date, the monumental *Bibliographie du genre romanesque français 1751-1800,* finally
published in 1977 after many long years of patient foraging, checking and
collating. She had been gathering material for quite some time before
discovering that two other scholars (Professors Angus Martin of Macquarie
and Richard Frautschi of North Carolina Universities) were each, inde-
pendently, engaged in an identical enterprise. Their tripartite collaboration has produced a research tool which any eighteenth century literary
specialist would ignore at his peril: the lists include all works of fiction
(romans, contes and *nouvelles)* written in French together with all works
published in France during the period in question. Each title is accompanied by a brief description of its form and content, its availability in major
libraries together with details of subsequent editions. The work is a
triumph of international collaboration and, if Vivienne Mylne's demean-
our is anything to go by, eloquent refutation of the hoary adage that
'Those whom the Gods would destroy, they first turn into bibliographers'.
Scholars will assuredly be heartened to learn that Vivienne is devoting
some of her years of retirement in North Oxford to the preparation of a
companion volume covering the first half of the eighteenth century. She is
also very actively engaged on a general study of 'Dialogue in the Novel', a
work which will range well beyond the eighteenth century and, when
completed, provide yet further proof of her forensic skills and of the
breadth of her interests.

   Those interests made of her that most welcome of colleagues, the one
willing and able, given reasonable (and, sometimes, even unreasonable)
notice to provide a course of lectures on virtually any topic in the French
curriculum. Having written her doctoral thesis on a linguistic topic and,
like any eighteenth century specialist, having had to familiarize herself
with social and political history, with the clash and swirl of ideas, with
aesthetic theory and practice, she was equipped to teach all manner of
courses in addition to the novel. She is equally well informed about the
history of the language, phonetics, stagecraft and musicology, as well, of
course, as of *l'Encyclopédie,* of which she always seemed to her colleagues
and pupils not only a superb exponent but a living example. For all that, a
bluestocking she emphatically was not. While she maintained the very
highest of professional standards, she never flaunted her formidable
erudition and the range of her interests remained refreshingly eclectic. In
the Senior Common Room, she was the most sought-after of conversation-
alists, as ready to discourse on Zen and the art of archery or the finer
points of a championship snooker match televised the previous evening as

to enthuse over her beloved Mozart or dissect the latest specimen of *la nouvelle critique*. Those who know her only through her published writings may perhaps be surprised to learn that she is formidably well-informed about the detective-story, English, American and French, and that she has not given up hope of polishing and publishing a *roman policier* she herself wrote many years ago. To her colleagues and pupils, she was the most generous of hostesses, providing memorable meals which were always spiced with wit and, as often as not, ended with music-making.

One is tempted to end this brief appreciation with a tribute to the dedication and sheer professionalism of a scholar and teacher who achieved all that she did for her University and her discipline while functioning, since her student days, with only one lung. But that, I know, would not be to Vivienne's liking. '*Affettuoso,* if you absolutely insist', I can hear her remonstrating, '*ma non troppo...*' Better, therefore, to conclude with two vignettes from her music-making at Canterbury. The first is of an end-of-term Common Room review when, appearing as Britannia, and equipped with burnished helmet, dustbin lid and pitchfork, she led us all in a spirited rendition of 'Land of Hope and Glory'. The second is of her preparations for a performance of *H. M. S. Pinafore* when, due to appear as Buttercup, so great was her desire for verisimilitude that she furnished her provision-basket with a real chicken. After several weeks of rehearsal, this had grown sufficiently gamey for the University Surveyor's department to begin eyeing the theatre's drains with increasingly darker doubts. Given that Diderot's *Paradoxe sur le comédien* was, deservedly, one of her most popular lectures, there is an irony about this technique of illusion not lost on her pupils or herself. It might help explain why one can say of Vivienne Mylne what one cannot, alas, say of every academic: that she is remembered with affection as well as with respect, not least because, like Falstaff, she is not only witty in herself but the cause that wit is in others.

R. G.

Bibliography of writings by Vivienne Mylne

David J. Shaw : University of Kent

1944

1. Music criticism, under the pen-name 'Orpheus', in the monthly journal *Jersey Forum,* June-December.

1946

2. Three poems in *Spring Harvest,* Oxford University Author-Critic Club.

1956

3. 'Par exemple', *Archivum Linguisticum,* 8, pp. 38-50.

1957

4. 'Notes on eighteenth-century interjections', *Modern Language Review,* 52, pp. 28-34.

1961

5. 'Structure and symbolism in *Gil Blas', French Studies,* 15, pp. 134-45.

1962

6. 'Truth and illusion in the 'Préface-Annexe' to Diderot's *La Religieuse', Modern Language Review,* 57, pp. 350-57.

1963

7. 'Changing attitudes towards truth in fiction', *Renaissance and Modern Studies,* 7, pp. 53-77.
8. Review of: *La Littérature narrative d'imagination. Des genres littéraires aux techniques d'expression,* 1961. In: *French Studies,* 17, p. 300.

1964

9. Review of: Georges May, *Le Dilemme du roman au XVIIIᵉ siècle. Etude sur les rapports du roman et la critique (1715-1761),* 1963. In: *French Studies,* 18, p. 382.

1965

10. *The eighteenth-century French novel: techniques of illusion,* Manchester University Press.

1966

11. 'Illusion and the novel', *British Journal of Aesthetics,* 6, pp. 142-151.
12. Review of: James A. Leith, *The idea of art as propaganda in France, 1750-1799,* 1965. In: *British Journal of Aesthetics,* 6, p. 207.
13. Review of: Rémy G. Saisselin, *Taste in eighteenth-century France,* 1965. In: *British Journal of Aesthetics,* 6, p. 207.
14. Review of: Charles Dédéyan, *Lesage et 'Gil Blas',* 1965. In: *French Studies,* 20, pp. 298-99.
15. Review of: *L'Abbé Prévost, Actes du Colloque d'Aix-en-Provence, 20 et 21 décembre 1963,* 1965. In: *French Studies,* 20, p. 409.

1967

16. 'Reading and re-reading novels', *British Journal of Aesthetics,* 7, pp. 67-75.
17. 'Literary techniques and methods in Voltaire's *contes philosophiques'*. In: *Studies on Voltaire and the eighteenth century,* 57, Geneva, pp. 1055-80.
18. Review of: William Mead, *Jean-Jacques Rousseau ou Le romancier enchaîné. Etude de 'La Nouvelle Héloïse',* 1966. In: *French Studies,* 21, p. 349.

1968

19. 'Select bibliography of French publications on aesthetics', *British Journal of Aesthetics*, 8, pp. 295-97.
20. 'Sensibility and the novel'. In: *French literature and its background*, ed. J. Cruickshank. III: *The eighteenth century*, Oxford University Press.
21. Review of: Alice M. Laborde, *L'Œuvre de Madame de Genlis*, 1966. In: *French Studies*, 22, pp. 165-66.
22. Review of: Alexander A. Parker, *Literature and the delinquent. The picaresque novel in Spain and Europe, 1599-1753*, 1967. In: *French Studies*, 22, pp. 245-46.
23. Review of: Charles A. Porter, *Restif's novels or An autobiography in search of an author*, 1967. In: *French Studies*, 22, pp. 253-54.

1969

24. 'Beaumarchais, *Le Mariage de Figaro*, Act V, Scene 3'. In: P. H. Nurse (ed.), *The art of criticism*. Edinburgh University Press, pp. 155-167.
25. French publications on aesthetics. In: 'Selective current bibliography for aesthetics and related fields, January 1, 1968-December 31, 1968', *The Journal of Aesthetics and Art Criticism*, 27.
26. Review of: Henri Coulet, *Le Roman jusqu'à la Révolution*. Tome I: *Histoire du roman en France*, 1967. Tome II: *Anthologie*, 1968. In: *French Studies*, 23, pp. 178-80.
27. Review of: Frédéric Deloffre, *La Nouvelle en France à l'âge classique*, 1967. In: *Modern Language Review*, 64, p. 174.

1970

28. Translation of: Tzvetan Todorov 'The fantastic in fiction'. In: *Twentieth-century studies*, 4, pp. 76-92.
29. Review of: Philip Stewart, *Imitation and illusion in the French memoir-novel, 1700-1750*, 1969. In: *British Journal of Aesthetics*, 10, p. 295.

1971

30. With Janet Osborne, 'Diderot's early fiction: *Les Bijoux indiscrets* and *L'Oiseau blanc*', *Diderot Studies*, 14, pp. 143-66.

31. Review of: Peter Brooks, *The novel of worldliness: Crébillon, Marivaux, Laclos, Stendhal*, 1969. In: *French Studies*, 25, pp. 464-65.

1972

32. *Prévost: 'Manon Lescaut'*, London, Edward Arnold.
33. Translation of: Julia Kristeva, 'The ruin of a poetics'. In: *Twentieth-century studies*, 7, pp. 102-19.
34. Review of: René Godenne, *Histoire de la nouvelle française aux XVIIe et XVIIIe siècles*, 1970. In: *French Studies*, 26, pp. 75-76.
35. Review of: Philip Stewart, *Imitation and illusion in the French memoir-novel, 1700-1750*, 1969. In: *French Studies*, 26, pp. 77-78.
36. Review of: Raymond Joly, *Deux études sur la préhistoire du réalisme: Diderot, Rétif de la Bretonne*, 1969. In: *French Studies*, 26, p. 80.
37. Review of: Charles Duclos, *Les Confessions du Comte de****, ed. Laurent Versini, 1969. In: *French Studies*, 26, pp. 206-207.
38. Review of: Rétif de la Bretonne, *La Vie de mon père*, ed. Gilbert Rouger, 1970. In: *French Studies*, 26, p. 207.
39. Review of: Philip Thody, *Laclos: 'Les Liaisons dangereuses'*, 1970. In: *French Studies*, 26, p. 208.
40. Review of: Robert Lancelot Myers, *Rémond de Saint-Mard, a study of his major works*, 1970. In: *Modern Language Review*, 67, p. 893.
41. Review of: Theodore Besterman (ed.), *Studies on Voltaire and the eighteenth century*, 73, 1970. In: *French Studies*, 26, pp. 335-36.

1973

42. Letter on 'The epistolary novel'. In: *Times Literary Supplement*, p. 153.
43. Review of: Francis Pruner, *L'Unité secrète de 'Jacques le fataliste'*, 1970. In: *French Studies*, 27, pp. 72-73.
44. Review of: Jeanne R. Monty, *Les Romans de l'abbé Prévost: procédés littéraires et pensée morale*, 1970. In: *French Studies*, 27, pp. 330-331.
45. Review of: Fougeret de Monbron, *Le Cosmopolite ou Le citoyen du monde, suivi de La capitale des Gaules ou La nouvelle Babylone*, ed. Raymond Trousson. In: *French Studies*, 27, pp. 337-38.

1974

46. Review of: Lawrence J. Forno, *Robert Challe: Intimations of the Enlightenment,* 1972. In: *Modern Language Review,* 69, p. 870.

1975

47. 'Dialogue as narrative in eighteenth-century French fiction'. In: J. H. Fox, M. H. Waddicor & D. A. Watts (eds), *Studies in eighteenth-century French literature presented to Robert Niklaus,* University of Exeter, p. 173-193.
48. Review of: Christine Belcikowski, *Poétique des 'Liaisons dangereuses',* 1972. In: *French Studies,* 29, pp. 333-334.
49. Review of: Madeleine B. Therrien, *'Les Liaisons dangereuses': une interprétation psychologique,* 1973. In: *Modern Language Review,* 70, p. 905.

1976

50. 'Scriblerus Redivivus', *British Society for Eighteenth-Century Studies Newsletter,* 10, pp. 1-6.
51. Review of: Odile A. Kory, *Subjectivity and sensitivity in the novels of the Abbé Prévost,* 1972. In: *French Studies,* 30, pp. 66-67.
52. Review of: Peter V. Conroy, Jr, *Crébillon fils: techniques of the novel,* 1972. In: *French Studies,* 30, pp. 216-17.
53. Review of: Henri Blanc, *'Les Liaisons dangereuses' de Choderlos de Laclos,* 1972. In: *French Studies,* 30, pp. 219-20.
54. Review of: Katharine Whitman Carson, *Aspects of contemporary society in 'Gil Blas',* 1973. In: *French Studies,* 30, pp. 466-67.
55. Review of: Henri Coulet, *Marivaux romancier. Essai sur l'esprit et le cœur dans les romans de Marivaux,* 1975. In: *French Studies,* 30, pp. 467-68.
56. Review of: English Showalter, Jr, *The evolution of the French novel, 1641-1782,* 1973. In: *Modern Language Review,* 71, p. 167.
57. Review of: Guilleragues, *Chansons et bons mots, Valentins, Lettres portugaises,* ed. Frédéric Deloffre and Jacques Rougeot, 1972. In: *Modern Language Review,* 71, p. 168.
58. Review of: René Démoris, *Le Roman à la première personne,* In: *Times Literary Supplement,* p. 460.

1977

59. With Angus Martin and Richard Frautschi: *Bibliographie du genre romanesque français (1751-1800),* London, Mansell and Paris, France Expansion.
60. 'Ancient Greece and neo-classicism in eighteenth-century French fiction'. In: H.T. Barnwell, A. H. Diverres, G. F. Evans, F. W. A. George, Vivienne Mylne (eds), *The classical tradition in French literature: Essays presented to R. C. Knight.* London, Grant and Cutler, pp. 156-166.
61. 'Social realism in the dialogue of eighteenth-century French fiction'. In: Ronald C. Rosbottom (ed.), *Studies in eighteenth-century culture,* University of Wisconsin Press, pp. 265-84.
62. Review of: Philip Stewart, *Le Masque et la parole. Le langage de l'amour au XVIIIᵉ siècle,* 1973. In: *French Studies,* 31, pp. 73-74.
63. Review of: Bette Gross Silverblatt, *The maxims in the novels of Duclos,* 1972. In: *French Studies,* 31, pp. 76-77.
64. Review of: Stephen Werner, *Diderot's great scroll: Narrative art in Jacques le fataliste,* 1975. In: *Modern Language Review,* 72, p. 692.
65. Review of: Josephine Grieder, *Translations of French sentimental prose fiction in late eighteenth-century England: The history of a literary vogue,* 1975. In: *Modern Language Review,* 72, p. 912.

1978

66. 'Re-editions as a guide to the assessment of public taste in fiction'. In: *Studies in the French eighteenth century presented to John Lough,* University of Durham, pp. 128-40.
67. Review of: Jean-François Marmontel, *Correspondance,* ed. J. Renwick, 1974. In: *British Journal for Eighteenth-Century Studies,* 1, pp. 138-39.
68. Review of: Marie-Thérèse Hipp, *Mythes et réalités: Enquête sur le roman et les mémoires (1600-1700),* 1976. In: *Modern Language Review,* 73, p. 183.
69. Review of: Douglas A. Bonneville, *Voltaire and the form of the novel,* 1976. In: *Modern Language Review,* 73, p. 188.
70. Review of: Donna Kuizenga, *Narrative strategies in La Princesse de Clèves,* 1976. In: *Revue d'Histoire Littéraire de la France,* 78, p. 826.

1979

71. 'The *Bibliothèque universelle des dames* (1785-97)'. In: Eva Jacobs, W. H. Barber, Jean H. Bloch, F. W. Leakey, Eileen Le Breton (eds), *Woman and society in eighteenth-century France. Essays in honour of John Stephenson Spink,* Athlone Press, pp. 123-36.

72. 'A Picara in *Candide:* Paquette', *College Literature,* 6, pp. 205-10.

73. 'The punctuation of dialogue in eighteenth-century French and English fiction', *The Library,* sixth series, 1, pp. 43-61.

74. Review of: Robert Challe, *Journal d'un voyage fait aux Indes Orientales,* ed. F. Deloffre and M. Menemencioglu, 1979. In: *British Journal for Eighteenth-Century Studies,* 2, pp. 174-75.

75. Review of: René Godenne, *La Nouvelle française,* 1974. In: *French Studies,* 33, pp. 116-117.

76. Review of: Ronald C. Rosbottom, *Marivaux's novels. Theme and function in early eighteenth-century narrative.* In: *French Studies,* 33, pp. 725-26.

77. Review of: *Les Paradoxes du romancier: les 'Egarements' de Crébillon,* par un collectif de chercheurs des Universités de Grenoble, Lyon et Saint-Etienne, 1975. In: *French Studies,* 33, pp. 758-59.

78. Review of: Joan Hinde Stewart, *The novels of Mme Riccoboni,* 1976. In: *French Studies,* 33, pp. 765-66.

79. Review of: Robert L. Dawson, *Baculard d'Arnaud: Life and prose fiction.* I-II, 1976. In: *French Studies,* 33, pp. 778-79.

80. Review of: Jean-Pierre Claris de Florian, *Nouvelles,* ed. R. Godenne, 1974. In: *French Studies,* 33, pp. 786-87.

81. Review of: Roger Poirier, *La 'Bibliothèque universelle des romans'. Rédacteurs, textes, public,* 1977. In: *French Studies,* 33, pp. 794-95.

82. Review of: René Démoris, *Le Roman à la première personne. Du Classicisme aux Lumières,* 1975. In: *French Studies,* 33, pp. 952-53.

83. Review of: Yves Giraud, *Bibliographie du roman épistolaire en France des origines à 1842,* 1977. In: *French Studies,* 33, p. 954.

84. Review of: Pierre Testud, *Rétif de la Bretonne et la création littéraire,* 1977. In: *Modern Language Review,* 74, p. 462.

85. Review of: Pierre Testud, *Rétif de la Bretonne et la création littéraire,* 1977. In: *Revue d'Histoire Littéraire de la France,* 79, p. 524.

1980

86. Review of: Restif de la Bretonne, *Le Paysan perverti,* ed. François Jost, 1977. In: *French Studies,* 34, pp. 78-79.
87. Review of: Pierre Choderlos de Laclos, *Œuvres complètes,* ed. Laurent Versini, 1979. In: *French Studies,* 34, pp. 456-57.
88. Review of: Suellen Diaconoff, *Eros and power in 'Les Liaisons dangereuses'. A study in evil,* 1979. In: *French Studies,* 34, pp. 456-57.
89. Review of: Bernadette Fort, *Le Langage de l'ambiguité dans l'œuvre de Crébillon fils,* 1978. In: *Modern Language Review,* 75, p. 890.

1981

90. *Diderot: 'La Religieuse',* London, Grant & Cutler.
91. *The eighteenth-century French novel: techniques of illusion,* second edition, Cambridge University Press.

1982

92. 'Le parler des personnages dans *Les Liaisons dangereuses',* *Revue d'Histoire Littéraire de la France,* 82, pp. 575-87.
93. 'What Suzanne knew: lesbianism and *La Religieuse',* in: *Studies on Voltaire and the eighteenth century,* 208, pp. 167-173.
94. 'R. S. Wolper and Voltaire's *contes'.* In: *Studies on Voltaire and the eighteenth century,* 212, pp. 318-327.
95. Review of: Laurent Versini, *Le Roman épistolaire,* 1979. In: *French Studies,* 36, pp. 333-34.
96. Review of: Jean Lombard, *Courtilz de Sandras et la crise du roman à la fin du grand siècle,* 1980. In: *Modern Language Review,* 77, p. 451.
97. Review of: Jacques Proust, *L'Objet et le texte. Pour une poétique de la prose française au XVIIIe siècle,* 1980. In: *Revue d'Histoire Littéraire de la France,* 82, p. 664.

1983

98. Review of: Madame Riccoboni, *Lettres de Mistriss Fanni Butlerd,* ed. Joan Hinde Stewart, 1979. In: *French Studies,* 37, pp. 84-85.
99. Review of: Jacques Rustin, *Le Vice à la mode. Etude sur le roman français du XVIIIe siècle de 'Manon Lescaut' à l'apparition de 'La*

Nouvelle Héloïse' (1731-1761), 1979. In: *French Studies*, 37, pp. 343-344.

100. Review of: Jean Fabre, *Idées sur le roman de Madame de Lafayette au marquis de Sade*, 1979. In: *French Studies*, 37, p. 465.

101. Review of: Jacques Barchilon and Peter Flinders, *Charles Perrault*, 1981. In: *Modern Language Review*, 78, p. 185.

102. Review of: Marian Hobson, *The object of art: The theory of illusion in eighteenth-century France*, 1982. In: *Modern Language Review*, 78, p. 921.

103. Review of: Choderlos de Laclos, *Les Liaisons dangereuses*, ed. René Pomeau, 1981. In: *Revue d'Histoire Littéraire de la France*, 83, p. 128.

104. Review of: Jean Rousset, *Leurs yeux se rencontrèrent*, 1981. In: *Revue d'Histoire Littéraire de la France*, 83, p. 314.

1984

105. 'Le dialogue dans *Les Illustres Françaises'*, *Saggi e ricerche di letteratura francese*, 23, pp. 235-75.

106. 'Le droit du seigneur in *Le Mariage de Figaro'*, *French Studies Bulletin*, 11, pp. 3-5.

107. 'Prévost and *Manon Lescaut'*. In: *Manon: Massenet*, John Calder, Opera Guide 25, pp. 29-38.

108. Review of: Janet Todd, *Women's friendship in literature*, 1980. In: *French Studies*, 38, pp. 68-69.

109. Review of: François Pétis de la Croix, *Les milles et un jours, contes persans*, ed. Paul Sebag, 1980. In: *French Studies*, 38, p. 346.

110. Review of: Michael Cardy, *The literary doctrines of Jean-François Marmontel*, 1982. In: *Modern Language Review*, 79, p. 940.

1985

111. 'The Use of accents in French', *French Studies Bulletin*, 16, pp. 1-4.

112. Review of: Philip Stewart, *Rereadings. Eight early French novels*, 1984. In: *French Studies*, 39, p. 341.

113. Review of: Clifton Cherpack, *Logos in mythos: ideas and early French narrative*, 1983. In: *Modern Language Review*, 80, p. 165.

1986

114. 'Prévost's translation of dialogue in Richardson's *Clarissa', Franco-British Studies,* 1, pp. 1-11.
115. Review of: Raymond Trousson, *Le Tison et le flambeau: Victor Hugo devant Voltaire et Rousseau,* 1985. In: *French Studies,* 40, p. 85.

1987

116. 'The uses of dialogue in Hugo's early fiction', *French Studies,* 41, pp. 408-420.
117. Review of *Cahiers Prévost d'Exiles. 2. Le Miroir brisé d'Héléna: réflexions sur les Mémoires pour servir à l'histoire de Malte,* 1985. Ibid, pp. 459-460.

'Un pauvre diable': the blind beggar in *Madame Bovary*

Sheila Bell : University of Kent

T H E 'mendiant' or 'cul-de-jatte', as he is first referred to in Flaubert's *scénarios,* is a late addition to the dramatis personae of *Madame Bovary* and his appearances are brief, occupying a total of barely four pages of text. Though the character's function in the plot seems peripheral, a *fioriture* rather than a supporting column, his value as a symbol has appeared to many inversely great. Most readings of *Madame Bovary* have included comment on the significance of the figure and some critics have singled him out as particularly worthy of attention.[1] Murray Sachs attributes this degree of attention to the association of the blind beggar with the novel's climactic moment, namely the heroine's death: his role is 'brief but intense'.[2] It is also no doubt due to the fact that, as Sachs points out, critics have tended to read the figure in rather different ways, ranging from Thibaudet's 'démon', who gives Emma's death 'une figure de damnation', through Demorest's 'incarnation de Némésis' and Levin's *'memento mori'* to Alison Fairlie's 'menace of the grotesque behind all human pretentions'.[3] In an attempt to rescue interpretation of the blind beggar from polarization into two categories, 'the supernatural and the human',[4] Murray Sachs argues for a reading which sees the blind beggar as standing for reality: 'In limited, specific terms he represents the ugly truth of life in Rouen, after Emma's romantic illusions about it have been stripped away. By extension, he can symbolize the hard reality of life anywhere.'[5] Sachs's reading redirects attention to the scene for which the figure was originally invented, Emma's return journey from Rouen. He equally stresses the scene in which Homais encounters the beggar, as supplying an alternative perspective to that of Emma: the figure of the beggar allows us to contrast the reactions of Homais with those of Emma and proves 'a revealing touchstone of character and destiny'.[6]

P. M. Wetherill likewise stresses the importance of the scenes involving
the beggar other than that of Emma's death and goes further than Sachs in
arguing for the relativization of the symbol: Hivert, as well as Homais,
challenges Emma's view of the blind man: 'The Blind Man, far from being
an absolute symbol of anything, therefore, merely reinforces that impression of meaningless experience which typifies the majority of Flaubert's
works'.[7] Such an argument firmly – and rightly – reintegrates the figure of
the blind beggar into the ambivalent and ironic perspective of the
Flaubertian text. The blind man, like other figures in the landscape of
Yonville and its environs, serves as an objective correlative of Emma's
feelings, but the reactions of others make it clear to us that these are
nonetheless subjective feelings, that they are Emma's alone.

While an acceptable reading of the figure of the blind beggar must
indeed depend upon an awareness of his symbolic value as relative, it is
also true that, as we devalue Emma's perceptions, we risk losing some of
the figure's impact. In returning to the first scene in which the beggar
appears, as the proper point of departure for a reading of the figure, Sachs
seems to imply that notions prompted by the death scene are to be treated
with suspicion:

> While the beggar's role in the death scene may well inspire such notions
> as the devil, damnation, degradation or death in the reader's mind, no
> such extension of his core symbolic meaning seems needed for the scene
> in Chapter V which was the occasion for his original creation by
> Flaubert.[8]

P. M. Wetherill suggests that we are dealing with 'something infinitely
more subtle than the vulgar and rather clumsy symbol of death and
damnation ... some critics have thought the Blind Man to be'.[9] We wish
to return to the text of *Madame Bovary* and re-examine, in the light of
these discussions as well as more recent commentaries, the grounds, on
which notions of death and damnation might properly be entertained by
the reader, and the function of such notions in the strategy of the fiction.
We shall want to argue that the blind beggar does indeed act as a *memento
mori* figure, for the reader as well as for Emma, and that he also plays the
role of the devil, though Flaubert's intention in that respect must be seen
as more ironic than Thibaudet allowed.

A number of critics have traced the network of associations established
in the text between the figure of the blind beggar and Emma herself. Such
links provide an ironic commentary on Emma's concerns and aspirations

and point to the more general theme of the deterioration and corruption of
the flesh, which ends ultimately in death. The blind beggar is, according
to Harry Levin, 'linked by a grotesque affinity with Emma herself'. [10]
Most immediately obvious among the links are those between the beggar's
song, his only articulated utterance in the novel (his exchanges with
Homais are conveyed to us through reported speech), and Emma's past
life. The song, as quoted and paraphrased on its first mention, conjures up
for the reader and, we may suppose by virtue of her reactions, for Emma
herself, the emotional climax of her life, the *promenade à cheval* with
Rodolphe:

> Souvent la chaleur d'un beau jour
> Fait rêver fillette à l'amour.
>
> Et il y avait dans tout le reste des oiseaux, du soleil et du feuillage. [11]

The details refer us back to the scene in the wood but their summary
character and the dismissive turn of phrase ('Et il y avait dans tout le
reste . . .') turn the exceptional, unique event into a trivial and familiar
pattern of behaviour. The actual lines quoted reduce Emma's emotional
experience to a physical impulse of frequent occurrence ('Souvent . . .').
Thus the possession of a lover becomes the subject of an ironical ditty and
is further degraded by association with the singer's pitiful physical state
and his lowly social status. The effect is largely dependent on the contrast
between, on the one hand, the physical charm and elegance of Emma, so
recently conveyed to us from the perspective of Léon ('Jamais il n'avait
rencontré cette grâce de langage, cette réserve du vêtement, ces poses de
colombe assoupie', p. 270), and on the other, the horrific appearance of
the beggar. Later in the novel, links emerge between his appearance and
that of Emma; here perhaps a first hint of these is already to be found.
Sterling Haig, in his study of the colour blue in *Madame Bovary*, [12] points
to the use in the first description of the beggar of a term which has
been – and continues to be – associated above all with Emma and with her
dreams: 'bleuâtre'. The climax of the description concerns the rolling
eye-balls of the beggar: 'ses prunelles bleuâtres'. This refers us back to the
promenade à cheval, to the description of Emma's face under her veil, 'on
distinguait son visage dans une transparence bleuâtre, comme si elle eût
nagé sous des flots d'azur' (p. 164), and to Emma's ensuing vision of the
life with Rodolphe which lies before her: "Elle allait donc posséder enfin
ces joies de l'amour, cette fièvre du bonheur dont elle avait désespéré. Elle
entrait dans quelque chose de merveilleux où tout serait passion, extase,

délire; une immensité bleuâtre l'entourait . . .' (p. 167). A number of
similarities between Flaubert's description of the dying Emma and the
earlier ones of the blind beggar have been pointed out by Claudine Gothot-
Mersch: 'celle qui était la séduction même devient semblable à l'être le
plus repoussant du livre'.[13] Rolling eyes, projecting tongue, head thrown
back, all these recall the beggar and the link is further stressed by the
correspondence between the 'face hideuse' of the beggar (p. 332) and the
'face cadavéreuse' of Emma (p. 327). More recently, Jean Starobinski, in
his analysis of references to hot and cold in *Madame Bovary*,[14] has
pursued the same line more exhaustively, finding in the death scene a
number of leitmotifs which recall the figure of the beggar, thus preparing
us for his appearance in advance of its actual occurrence. The perspective
is that of the (re)reader, embracing and surpassing that of Emma herself.

The blind beggar is not the first figure in the novel to connote
mortality. Emma is, of course, preceded by another Madame Bovary, who
dies to make way for her: 'Elle était morte! Quel étonnement!' (p. 21). This
death takes place with almost unseemly haste and lack of ceremony.
Flaubert is at pains not to engage our sympathies with Charles's first wife
or to detract from the long drawn-out death of the second. It is also the
case that this rapid demise, followed by the parallelism of the two wedding
bouquets, suggests an ironic perspective on Emma's hopes and dreams.
Emma's marriage to Charles provokes, in her father's mind, fond memories of his own dead wife as she was on her wedding-day: 'sa petite mine
rosée qui souriait silencieusement, sous la plaque d'or de son bonnet'
(p. 32). However, the figure whose function is most similar to that of the
beggar is the Duc de Laverdière, whom Emma sees at the ball at La
Vaubyessard. The beggar is, one might argue, a reincarnation of the
aristocrat – the same figure *en plus noir* – and the variations are themselves of interest. Flaubert is careful to show us the Duke from Emma's
perspective. We know only what Emma might reasonably be supposed to
know.[15] For Emma, the figure belongs to that glamorous world of which
she herself is at this moment briefly part, and he is an object of
wonderment on account of his extravagant career. She sees 'l'amant de la
reine Marie-Antoinette': 'Il avait vécu à la Cour et couché dans le lit des
reines!' (p. 50). The reader however is free – and is likely – to focus on the
present figure, bereft of his glorious past, and see an old man who sits bent
over his plate at the dinner-table, 'laissant tomber de sa bouche des gouttes
de sauce' (p. 50). Thus at the château, in counterpoise to the select group
of aristocratic young men ('Ils avaient le teint de la richesse, ce teint blanc
que rehaussent la pâleur des porcelaines, les moires du satin, le vernis des

beaux meubles, et qu'entretient dans sa santé un régime discret de nourritures exquises', p. 52), who talk of their travels in Italy and their horses' exploits, there is also an image of the future which awaits them, the end of all human endeavour, graceless old age, 'sans teeth, sans eyes, sans taste, sans everything'. The Duke has not yet been wholly overtaken by the seventh age and he focuses his few remaining energies on food. Pointing to dishes whose names he can no longer properly articulate, he parodies Emma's appetite for living, so evident in this particular episode. Her own life, subsequently, becomes a kind of parody of the Duke's past career: 'Il avait mené une vie bruyante de débauches, pleine de duels ['As-tu tes pistolets?', p. 174], de paris, de femmes enlevées, avait dévoré sa fortune et effrayé toute sa famille' (p. 50). For Emma, the ball is a moment when reality and dream appear to meet and it confirms her in her belief that there are indeed 'certains lieux sur la terre' (p. 42), where the kind of life she wants is to be found. The reader, however, is aware that in this world too lurks eventual disillusionment: the sugar only *seems* whiter and finer than elsewhere. The figure of the aristocratic lover, glamorous to Emma, is associated for us with decay and senility; the appetite for living is rendered grotesque by being associated with mortality.

With the blind beggar, we are transported into the real circumstances of Emma's own life; he is both more mundane and more horrific. He impinges on Emma in a way the Duke did not. Although his appearances are rare and the segments of text concerning him are brief, it is stressed that he is, in this latter stage of Emma's life, a constant accompaniment, a regularly reappearing figure. The first scene is narrated in the imperfect tense: the blind beggar is one element in the pattern of the Thursday visits to Rouen. The second passage, though it deals with the particular encounter of the beggar and Homais – in preparation for the particular appearance of the former at the moment of Emma's death – reminds us at the outset that the blind beggar's presence is no unusual occurrence: 'quand l'Aveugle, comme d'habitude, apparut au bas de la côte' (p. 305). The capital letter underlines his status as familiar character. Homais only pretends to be seeing him for the first time.

The beggar appears in the text for the first time as Emma travels back to Yonville, having left Léon behind. She notices him and reacts to him in terms of her feelings of desolation. Thus he becomes the embodiment of her despair at parting from Léon, of her bleak horror at the return to Yonville and to Charles. He belongs to a period when the pattern of Emma's love-affair with Léon is well-established, when she goes to Rouen once a week, supposedly for piano lessons, in fact to meet Léon. Her *désarroi,* on parting from Léon, is rendered more acute by a fear that this relationship too will come to an end: 'Tu seras comme les autres' (p. 274). Emma's experience with Rodolphe has made her more aware of reality than she was before. She is also more corrupt. Rouen appears to her 'comme une Babylone où elle entrait'; to find Léon within it, she makes her way through 'les ruelles sombres... le quartier du théâtre, des estaminets et des filles' (p. 269). On leaving him, she has her hair rearranged by a hairdresser in the rue de la Comédie and watches the actors go in at the stage door, 'des hommes à figure blanche et des femmes en toilette fanée' (p. 272). The love affair with Léon begins at the opera; it continues in an increasingly ignoble atmosphere of role-playing and pretence, first to Charles, then to Léon and to herself. The rest of the chapter underlines the increasing disorder of her life in Yonville: her love affair with Léon strengthens the hold which Lheureux has over her, embroils her in a series of lies, and makes her increasingly careless of the lives of others. The next chapter underlines how corruption affects the love affair itself. For Léon, Emma takes on an alien quality which frightens him:

> il y avait sur ce front couvert de gouttes froides, sur ces lèvres balbu-tiantes, dans ces prunelles égarées, dans l'étreinte de ces bras, quelque chose d'extrême, de vague et de lugubre, qui semblait à Léon se glisser entre eux, subtilement, comme pour les séparer. (p. 288)

Satiety is more degrading than abandonment: the point is underlined by the reminiscence of Rodolphe in what has now become Emma's question: 'Mais comment pouvoir s'en débarrasser?' (p. 296). The *bal masqué,* associated in the first instance with the *garçon coiffeur,* who offers her tickets, while he arranges her hair for the journey home (p. 272), offers a debased parallel with the ball at La Vaubyessard when she finally goes there: supper is taken in 'un restaurant des plus médiocres' and in matching company, 'Il y avait un clerc, deux carabins et un commis: quelle société pour elle!' (p. 297). The distance travelled by Emma is measured most strikingly by contrasting references to her father in the context of her two love-affairs. In the context of the affair with Rodolphe, her father's letter – the text of which is supplied in full – causes Emma to repent (and leads to the club-foot operation – since even Emma's repen-tence is self-regarding); here Emma asks Léon to pawn her father's wedding present without, we must assume, hesitation or regret.[16]

Thus in the first instance, the blind beggar expresses what is for Emma the ugliness and desolation of the rest of the week, her life without Léon;

the text however also suggests decay and corruption present in the
love-affair itself and the beggar becomes an expression of that corruption.
He also acts as a reminder of the end term of that process, mortality.
Various elements in the first description of the character suggest a
memento mori figure, such as one finds in depictions of the dance of
death. When his hat is off, 'deux orbites béantes' (p. 272) are revealed; he
appears suddenly behind Emma making her jump or puts his head in
suddenly at the coach window. [17] Alone among the travellers, Emma reacts
with fear and melancholy. It is Hivert in particular, who serves as
counterpoint to Emma's reactions in this first passage. When Emma starts
and utters a cry, Hivert makes fun of the beggar: 'Il l'engageait à prendre
une baraque à la foire Saint-Romain, ou bien lui demandait, en riant,
comment se portait sa bonne amie' (p. 273). When his face at the window
and the sound of his voice induce in Emma 'une mélancolie sans bornes',
Hivert is simply aware of the fact that his coach is unbalanced by the
beggar's weight and knocks him off into the mud with his whip. As P. M.
Wetherill points out, we learn more of Hivert's character thereby and,
what is more, the subjectivity of Emma's feelings regarding the beggar are
made clear to us. [18] It is she, and she alone, who is left 'la mort dans l'âme'.
The melodramatic aspects of the figure are therefore the result of Emma's
perspective upon him. The other people in the coach do not react, it
would appear; we have no reason to suppose that their attitude to the
beggar is other than one of indifference. [19] They fall asleep: 'les uns la
bouche ouverte, les autres le menton baissé, s'appuyant sur l'épaule de
leur voisin, ou bien le bras passé dans la courroie, tout en oscillant
régulièrement au branle de la voiture'. The light of the lantern casts
shadows upon them: 'des ombres sanguinolentes sur tous ces individus
immobiles'. Again the associations with blood are appropriate to Emma's
fevered imagination and convey to us her present mood. The (re)reader
will be aware at this point, however, of patterns of meaning which cannot
be dismissed as melodramatic and which are closer to Emma's vision than
to that of Hivert or of the unconscious passengers. The sleeping passengers
prefigure the image we are given later in the text of Homais and
Bournisien ('il baissa le menton', p. 339) beside the dead body of Emma:

> Ils étaient en face l'un de l'autre, le ventre en avant, la figure bouffie, l'air
> renfrogné, après tant de désaccord se rencontrant enfin dans la même
> faiblesse humaine; et ils ne bougeaient pas plus que le cadavre à côté
> d'eux, qui avait l'air de dormir. (p. 339)

The weakness which makes them sleep is equated with the mortality which sooner or later will reduce them to Emma's present state. Thus, though we are aware that we are entering into Emma's mood by sharing her reactions to the beggar, at the same time, our perceptions – as orchestrated by the text as a whole – are closer to Emma's than they are to those of Hivert or of her sleeping fellow-travellers.

Apart from the content of the blind man's song, the main link with Emma's past experience lies in the sound of his voice. The similarity of the beggar's voice to the cry heard by Emma, when she is in the forest with Rodolphe, has been remarked upon by a number of critics, most recently by Jean Starobinski.[20] With Rodolphe, after she has become his mistress:

> elle entendit tout au loin, au delà du bois, sur les autres collines, un cri vague et prolongé, une voix qui se traînait, et elle l'écoutait silencieusement, se mêlant comme une musique aux dernières vibrations de ses nerfs émus. (pp. 165-66)

Here, a similar sound has a very different effect on Emma:

> Sa voix, faible d'abord et vagissante, devenait aiguë. Elle se traînait dans la nuit, comme l'indistincte lamentation d'une vague détresse; et, à travers la sonnerie des grelots, le murmure des arbres et le ronflement de la boîte creuse, elle avait quelque chose de lointain qui bouleversait Emma. (p. 273)

On both occasions, other participants in the situation react very differently. Rodolphe smokes a cigar and mends a broken bridle: his gestures are those of a sensual and practical man, not an emotional one. Emma's fellow-travellers fall asleep. Emma's awareness and her reactions are a function of her nervous state, but there are grounds for assuming that she perceives – subliminally perhaps – the similarity of the second sound to the first and that this renders more acute her state of melancholy. Both past and present seem mocked by association with the grotesque figure of the beggar. If we may see both voices as disembodied (as the first is, and the second becomes, 'Elle se traînait dans la nuit . . .'), they may also seem to the reader to express the indifference of the world to Emma's passions. The world's echo in response to Emma's feelings might be compared with that heard by Mrs Moore in the Marabar caves: 'whatever is said, the same monotonous noise replies, and quivers up and down the walls until it is absorbed into the roof'.[21] Emma is less reflective than Mrs Moore and, above all, younger, but the immediate effect upon her is similar: 'Cela lui descendait au fond de l'âme comme un tourbillon dans un abîme, et l'emportait parmi les espaces d'une mélancolic sans bornes' (p. 273).

The second scene with the beggar, involving his encounter with Homais, justifies itself in terms of the plot by motivating the beggar's presence at Emma's death ('Je le fais inviter le pauvre à venir le trouver à Yonville pour avoir mon pauvre à la mort d'Emma?').[22] But its function goes considerably further. It relates the beggar to Homais (the blind leading the blind?) as well as to Emma, as both Murray Sachs and P.M. Wetherill emphasize,[23] and therefore to the other principal character of the novel.

It also suggests a pattern, where Emma's own experience is concerned, which prepares for his appearance at the death scene. This second scene with the beggar follows upon Léon's failure to help Emma in her financial trouble. The parallel with the events of the next chapter, leading not to an encounter with the beggar but to her taking arsenic, is striking (though of course the encounter with the beggar does eventually follow). She goes to see Léon at his office, as later she goes to see Rodolphe at La Huchette. In each case, we have a repetition *en noir* of many earlier visits; in each case she is turned away by a polite but recognizable evasion. The parallelism extends to Emma's reaction. She is stunned into a kind of insensibility: 'Emma n'avait plus la force d'aucun sentiment' (p. 304) and: 'Elle resta perdue de stupeur' (p. 319); 'elle fut si accablée, si triste, qu'elle s'appuya contre un mur pour ne pas tomber' (p. 305) and: 'cent pas plus loin, essoufflée, près de tomber, elle s'arrêta' (p. 319). She looks back in one case to 'la rue (. . .) déserte' (pp. 304-05) (a tilbury has just driven by in which she thought she recognized the vicomte), in the other to 'l'impassible château' (p. 319). In the former episode, the figure of Homais, tied comfortably to the present by his local speciality, the *cheminots,* and by his self-satisfaction, shields Emma from the full impact of the blind man. She throws him her last five francs, 'prise de dégoût' (p. 306). In the latter episode, she has no money left; she goes to the pharmacy, but Homais is in the next room having supper and Justin is no match for Emma. Thus, when both Léon and Rodolphe have failed her, she turns to suicide, or, by implication, to the blind beggar. The beggar (or death), as substitute lover, is an underlying theme in the first scene in which he appears. Emma is crying out passionately for Léon: 'Elle sanglotait, appelait Léon, et lui envoyait des paroles tendres et des baisers qui se perdaient au vent' (p. 272). It is the blind beggar who appears, 'Il y avait dans la côte un pauvre diable . . .', with his reminders of another love-affair dead and buried. Equally, at the point of death, it is the blind beggar who appears in the place of 'l'Homme-Dieu', the divine lover for whose arms Emma is being prepared. [24]

Traditionally, the *memento mori* theme has religious implications: the figure of death implies imminent judgment with salvation or damnation to follow. Its depiction is intended to fill the beholder with anxiety and bring the faithful back to the fold. An element of religious reference might be taken to be present in the first scene with the beggar, but it is only implicit. In the death scene, on the other hand, the religious theme is an important element. As befits a 'Madame Bovary', who, from the title onwards, is depicted as a character imprisoned within her social context, Emma – unlike Gervaise – dies with benefit of clergy. The administering of extreme unction by Bournisien is described to us in detail. It occupies the final stage of the death scene, taking us back to Emma after the interruption of Larivière's visit and leading up to the climactic moment which coincides with the arrival of the blind beggar.

Our response to the religious observances at Emma's death is conditioned by much that has preceded them earlier in the novel. Emma's religiosity on the one hand, the church as institution on the other, both are from the beginning treated ironically. In the convent, Emma disappointed the nuns: 'Mademoiselle Rouault semblait échapper à leurs soins' (p. 40). Emotional needs underlie her religious fervour, and her turn of mind, 'positif au milieu de ses enthousiasmes' (p. 40), makes her unresponsive to the central mysteries of the Christian faith. The description of the church at Yonville focuses on the temporal aspects of the building: undistinguished and already dilapidated, despite its relative modernity. The religious images it contains suggest on the one hand superstition, on the other state approval. The bad taste of the statue of the Virgin, 'vêtue d'une robe de satin, coiffée d'un voile de tulle semé d'étoiles d'argent, et tout empourprée aux pommettes comme une idole des îles Sandwich' (p. 73), is matched by the total lack of distinction of the painting above the high altar, 'une copie de la *Sainte Famille, envoi du ministre de l'intérieur*' (p. 73). The décor does not promise much in the way of spiritual comfort. The incumbent is well-meaning enough and sincere, but more comprehending of physical ills than spiritual ones. When Emma goes to him in search of help, Bournisien has nothing to offer. When she returns to reality ('elle avait l'air de quelqu'un qui se réveille d'un songe', p. 117), she sees before her 'un vieillard à soutane', which 'soutane', as we have already been told, is spotted with food and stained with tobacco. When they look at one another at last, 'face à face', they fall silent, having nothing to say. A similar process of disillusionment is experienced by

Emma when she turns to religion during her earlier illness. She takes communion: 'Ce fut en défaillant d'une joie céleste qu'elle avança les lèvres pour accepter le corps du Seigneur qui se présentait' (p. 218). Flaubert's text makes no overtly negative comment but the description of the attendant circumstances makes it clear that Emma is deceived. The curtains on her bed billow out like clouds and the 'deux cierges brûlant sur la commode' seem to her 'des gloires éblouissantes'. The artificiality of the experience is underlined by the stereotyped content of her vision: 'croyant entendre dans les espaces le chant des harpes séraphiques et apercevoir en un ciel d'azur, sur un trône d'or, au milieu des saints tenant des palmes vertes, Dieu le Père tout éclatant de majesté, et qui d'un signe faisait descendre vers la terre des anges aux ailes de flamme pour l'emporter dans leurs bras' (pp. 218-19). The emotion Emma invests in religion subsequently is seen as transferred from Rodolphe and she is left with a feeling of dissatisfaction: 'elle se relevait, les membres fatigués, avec le sentiment vague d'une immense duperie' (p. 220). Once again, the church fails her. Bournisien (understandably) finds her extravagant and the bookseller, whose aid he enlists, embodies, at its most uncaring, society's response to spiritual yearnings. He sends whatever he has to hand in the way of pious literature: 'Le libraire, avec autant d'indifférence que s'il eût expédié de la quincaillerie à des nègres, vous emballa pêle-mêle tout ce qui avait cours pour lors dans le négoce des livres pieux' (p. 219).

Religion and death are again associated – more explicitly still – in the description of Rouen cathedral. Irony is already present in the discrepancy between the building's proper function and its function for Léon and Emma: antechamber to the cab. As Léon waits for Emma, it seems to him as if the cathedral is transformed into 'un boudoir gigantesque' (p. 245). Emma seeks to return the building to its original function but once again, as in the earlier scene with Bournisien, her unspoken request for help meets with no response: 'elle (. . .) prêtait l'oreille au silence de l'église, qui ne faisait qu'accroître le tumulte de son cœur' (p. 246). The official representative of the cathedral, with whom Emma comes into contact, is not a priest but a beadle, anxious to show off his knowledge and to receive a tip. The cathedral he offers is not a place of spiritual comfort but a collection of sights, of 'curiosités' (p. 245). The central Christian message of the Resurrection is an architectural feature on the north doorway, which the beadle recommends to the attention of Emma and Léon: 'Sortez du moins par le portail du nord! (. . .) pour voir la *Résurrection*, le *Jugement dernier*, le *Paradis*, le *Roi David*, et les *Réprouvés* dans les flammes d'enfer' (p. 249). Emma and Léon are too concerned with each other and the pleasures of this world to heed what the beadle says to them and they turn their backs on the cathedral's depiction of heaven and hell. What they and the guide spend most time on, however, in their (reluctant) tour of the cathedral, is the tombstones, which stress the mortality of all men, even the great;[25] the guide draws their attention to the tomb of Louis de Brézé, which portrays him first in his worldly splendour, then stepping into his tomb: 'Il n'est point possible, n'est-ce pas, de voir une plus parfaite représentation du néant?' (p. 247). Death thus occupies the centre of the stage, and resurrection is a detail on the doorway: though Léon and Emma are unconcerned, by the reader the message of the cathedral is to be read thus. In imparting such a message, the cathedral reflects its modest predecessor in the text, the church at Yonville. There, the first aspect drawn to our attention is the cemetery, which is much older than the church itself and very full: 'si bien rempli de tombeaux, que les vieilles pierres à ras du sol font un dallage continu' (p. 73). The same message is implicit in Rouault's thoughts after Emma's wedding. Saddened by memories of his dead wife, 'il eut bien envie un moment d'aller faire un tour du côté de l'église. Comme il eut peur, cependant, que cette vue ne le rendît plus triste encore, il s'en revint tout droit chez lui' (p. 32).

It is against this background that Emma's death scene (pp. 330-33) is played out. The tone does not change. The administering of the sacrament is an important element, but it is portrayed in a way which plays down its religious significance. Bournisien's arrival is made the pretext for another shot in the protracted warfare between himself and Homais: 'Homais, comme il le devait à ses principes, compara les prêtres à des corbeaux qu'attire l'odeur des morts'. The objects he brings with him are rendered banal: 'cinq ou six petites boules de coton dans un plat d'argent, près d'un gros crucifix, entre deux chandeliers qui brûlaient'; his prayers are a rigmarole: 'le prêtre, appuyé sur un genou [not both?], marmottait des paroles basses'. The paragraph which describes the administering of the unction to Emma is one of the most moving in the novel, but it is with the human experience that we are invited to empathize by Flaubert's *effets de style*, not with the religious ceremony. We are moved by the contrast between what Emma was and what she has become, between her appetite for life and her present state: 'et enfin sur la plante des pieds, si rapides autrefois quand elle courait à l'assouvissance de ses désirs, et qui maintenant ne marcheraient plus'. By comparison with the text's eloquence at this point, the role of the priest is woefully inadequate. It is reduced in status by the references to the mundane activity of clearing up afterwards

– Bournisien wipes his fingers and throws the bits of cotton on the fire – and by the trite formality of Bournisien's injunctions to the dying Emma: 'elle devait à présent joindre ses souffrances à celles de Jésus-Christ et s'abandonner à la miséricorde divine'. [26]

Emma's own response is in line with her religious experience earlier in the novel: 'collant ses lèvres sur le corps de l'Homme-Dieu, elle y déposa de toute sa force expirante le plus grand baiser d'amour qu'elle eût jamais donné'. The description implies an analogy with other loves, and the references immediately thereafter to Emma's past life make it clear that this is again to be seen as an extension of Emma's appetite for love in this world rather than as an aspiration towards a different kind of love. When Bournisien gives her a candle to hold, 'symbole des gloires célestes dont elle allait tout à l'heure être environnée', she threatens to drop it when his hand is withdrawn. Her serenity is short-lived: she looks around her, 'comme quelqu'un qui se réveille d'un songe' (the phrase is reminiscent of her earlier and fruitless encounter with Bournisien), and asks for a mirror. She (and we) return to the physical Emma and to the process of dying which is then emphasized: the stretched-out tongue, the rolling eyes, the rasping, rapid breathing. The noise of Emma's breathing and Charles's sobbing is accompanied by the priest's (incomprehensible?) prayers: 'le sourd murmure des syllabes latines, qui tintaient comme un glas de cloche'.

As if announced by the tolling bell comes a noise which dominates all the others, the noise of clogs and a stick on the pavement, and a hoarse singing voice: the blind beggar. He is come of course in search of Homais, but we, for the time being, are focusing on Emma's perceptions of the figure. The effect of his appearance is to create a contrast with the previous scene in a number of ways. For the 'gloires célestes', offered by Bournisien, are substituted the 'ténèbres éternelles', for the *Homme-Dieu*, the *Aveugle*, once more deriding love in his song. The God made man, who is promised, remains on the crucifix. Who comes for Emma instead? Death the reaper, blind because he chooses his victims at random: the associations between the blind man and death have already been established for the reader. When Emma recognizes the figure, she dies. If the symbol is a vulgar one (and soon to be discredited by the revelation of the blind man's mundane motives), it must after all be accessible to Emma. The vulgarity need not invalidate the insights. We have that on good authority: 'comme si la plénitude de l'âme ne débordait pas quelquefois par les métaphores les plus vides . . .' (p. 196). [27]

Does the figure also suggest the devil and damnation? Again the text encourages us to entertain such an interpretation. Emma confronts 'les ténèbres éternelles'; she sits up 'comme un cadavre que l'on galvanise', reminiscent, with her 'cheveux dénoués'[28] and her 'prunelle fixe', of depictions of the 'réprouvés', such as are to be seen on the north doorway of Rouen cathedral. Emma, for whom the song is a taunting reminder of corruption, turns from the prospect of salvation to that of damnation. Perhaps the latter is more real to the person she has become, who reads all night 'des livres extravagants où il y avait des tableaux orgiaques avec des situations sanglantes' (p. 295). It is imperative that, temporarily, we perceive the *aveugle* as Emma does, if we are to register the full impact of her disillusionment. Here, Flaubert submits his heroine to the ultimate irony – thrusting the knife into her heart and turning it there twice, like Joseph K.'s executioner. [29] Hell is mocked, as well as Heaven. The *aveugle,* temporarily transformed into the semblance of a supernatural being, then reverts to the poor victim of Homais's self-advertisement. Lucifer, the fallen angel, is become a blind beggar, 'un pauvre diable vagabondant avec son bâton' (p. 272). This is, ironically it seems in retrospect, the phrase by which the figure is first introduced to us. It is also used of the blind beggar in the scene which involves Homais: 'bien qu'il connût ce pauvre diable, il feignit de le voir pour la première fois' (p. 306), who goes on to accord him a role in his own particular scenario. Though temporarily the blind man fights back against Homais and threatens to discredit his reputation as a pharmacist, his adversary is far too strong for him and has him shut up in an asylum. It is fitting that Homais, with his vulgar scientism, should be the one to cut the devil down to size and even, apparently, to put death in its place. His *bêtise* is indestructible and still flourishing at the end of the novel. The figure signifying death and damnation is still further reduced in status and glamour by being associated through this phrase with two of the most ordinary, mediocre figures in the novel: Charles and Hippolyte. It is in the context of his first appearance in the novel that Charles is identified for us as a 'pauvre diable', when he is being made fun of by the other boys and enjoined by the master in charge of the class to write out twenty times 'ridiculus sum'. Hippolyte is referred to by the same phrase, when he is the victim of Charles's ill-fated surgical experiment and the object of Bournisien's spiritual consolations (p. 257). Thus everything turns to dross for Emma: husband, lover ('elle retrouvait dans l'adultère toutes les platitudes du mariage', p. 296), heaven and hell. The devil becomes 'un pauvre diable'.

At the beginning of the affair with Léon, we find Emma smiling at his efforts to romanticize their encounter: 'Il prétendit avoir été guidé vers elle, au hasard, par un instinct. Elle se mit à sourire . . .' (p. 237). A less transparent lie – that he has spent the morning going round the hotels of Rouen – still deceives her. By contrast, the quality of her laughter at the point of death – 'un rire atroce, frénétique, désespéré' – suggests that all deceptions are now at an end. It is the laughter of one who measures the gap between dream and reality, who perceives the irony represented by the *aveugle*. At the last moment of Emma's life, her perspective and that of her author coincide. [30] For that laugh to convey to us its full *frisson*, we must realize how every aspiration in the novel, every flight beyond the mundane, leads us to the blind beggar: behind Rodolphe and Léon stands the beggar and his ditty, in place of the *Homme-Dieu* comes the beggar, the embodiment of death, and finally the devil himself becomes 'un pauvre diable'. With this final role played by the beggar, *Madame Bovary* completes its self-mocking critique of romanticism. The figure of the Byronic or the Hugolian Satan, 'le père de toute révolte et le type accompli du maudit', [31] becomes the butt of Hivert's jokes and the victim of Homais's pseudo-science. The passage from the *Tentation* to the bourgeois novel is complete.

Notes

[1] See particularly Murray Sachs, 'The Role of the Blind Beggar in *Madame Bovary*', *Symposium*, 22, 1968, pp. 72-80, and P.M. Wetherill, '*Madame Bovary*'s Blind Man: Symbolism in Flaubert', *Romanic Review*, LXI, 1970, pp. 35-42.

[2] op. cit., p. 72.

[3] Albert Thibaudet, *Gustave Flaubert*, Paris, 1935, p. 102; D.L. Demorest, *L'Expression figurée et symbolique dans l'œuvre de Gustave Flaubert*, Paris, 1931, p. 466; Harry Levin, *The Gates of Horn*, New York, 1963, p. 265; Alison Fairlie, *Flaubert: Madame Bovary*, Studies in French Literature, London, 1962, p. 37.

[4] op. cit., p. 73.

[5] ibid., pp. 74-75. A similar line is taken by Andre Vial, in *Le Dictionnaire de Flaubert ou le rire d'Emma Bovary*, Paris, 1974: the beggar is 'l'image même du monde' (p. 92).

[6] ibid., p. 78.

[7] op. cit., p. 42.

[8] op. cit., p. 75.

[9] op. cit., p. 36.

[10] op. cit., p. 265.

[11] *Madame Bovary*, ed. Claudine Gothot-Mersch, Classiques Garnier, Paris, 1971, p. 273.

[12] 'The *Madame Bovary* Blues', *Romanic Review*, LXI, 1970, pp. 27-34.

[13] 'La description des visages dans *Madame Bovary*', *Littérature*, no. 15, 21.

[14] 'L'échelle des températures. Lecture du corps dans *Madame Bovary'*, in *Travail de Flaubert*, Paris, 1983 (article first published 1980), pp. 45-78.

[15] It is interesting to note that Flaubert eliminated from the final version detailed information about the Duke's past, to which Emma would not have access, and thereby made the narratorial voice more neutral:

> Pendant l'émigration, il avait été maître d'armes en Hollande. Il en était revenu à soixante-trois ans passés, exécrant la France et son peuple et la populace, quoiqu'il fut philosophe comme Voltaire et athée même jusque dans la moelle de ses vieux os. Ce qu'il toucha du milliard lui servit alors à remonter sa maison, il maria sa fille, prit une demoiselle à l'opéra et s'acheva une nuit aux Tuileries dans une partie d'écarté. N'ayant donc à present que l'hospitalité de son gendre, assailli d'ennuis, d'infirmités et de souvenirs, ne parlant plus, dormant mal et entendant déjà dans la toux de ses catarrhes clouer son cercueil, il reportait sur son estomac demeuré bon, l'énergie complète de toutes [ses] passions impuissantes.

> (*Madame Bovary*, nouvelle version, textes établis par J. Pommier et G. Leleu, Paris, 1949, p. 206)

[16] The corruption of the context for which the beggar is invented is stressed by the scenario in which he is first mentioned:

> Après les f....ries va se faire coiffer – odeur des fers chauds s'endort – [torpeur sous le peignoir] – bas de la rue Grand-Pont – quelque chose de courtisanesque chez le coiffeur et elle, elle va retourner à la campagne. [-mendiant dans la côte du Boisguillaume.] Emma est très savante en voluptés – Léon se demande d'où cela lui vient. qu'est-ce qui lui a appris.

> (ibid., p. 30. The square brackets indicate an addition to the manuscript).

[17] An earlier phrase, suppressed in the final version, made the connotations of this latter appearance more explicit: 'et c'était comme une tête guillotinée qui se tenait en équilibre sur le bord du vagistas' (Pommier and Leleu, op. cit., p. 532).

[18] op. cit., pp. 38, 41.

[19] Some display of interest on the part of the other passengers, present at an earlier stage, was eliminated from the final version: 'Quand on avait parlé de lui quelque temps, la conversation peu à peu se calmait dans l'*Hirondelle'* (Pommier and Leleu, op. cit., p. 533).

[20] op. cit., p. 62.

[21] E.M. Forster, *A Passage to India*, London, Penguin, 1936, p. 145.

[22] *Correspondance*, IV, Paris, 1927, p. 90.

[23] Cf. also Claudine Gothot-Mersch, 'Homais et le mendiant sont complémentaires: l'un représente tout ce que la société approuve, l'autre tout ce qu'elle rejette', *La Genèse de Madame Bovary*, Paris, 1966, pp. 223-24.

[24] There are reminiscences of the blind beggar in the *croquemort* figure in *L'Assommoir*, Bazouge, 'dit le consolateur des dames' (Paris, Garnier-Flammarion, 1969, p. 445).

[25] The similarity between this passage and that on the family portraits at the château de la Vaubyessard is pointed out by Graham Falconer in 'Création et conservation du sens dans *Madame Bovary'*, in *La Production du sens chez Flaubert*, ed. Claudine Gothot-Mersch, Paris, Coll. 10/18, 1975, pp. 395-429.

[26] The *nouvelle version* of Pommier and Leleu has Bournisien wiping the oil gently – 'doucement' – off Emma's skin (p. 611). The elimination of this one indication of simple humanity on the part of Bournisien reduces the figure here to his religious role, negatively perceived.

[27] The stuffed parrot in *Un Cœur simple* is another such: unless the reader performs the feat of reading this as Félicité reads it, at the same time as he stands apart, the peculiar strength of Flaubert's irony, the power of his 'grotesque triste' is lost. For a discussion of the parrot which argues the importance of entering into Félicité's perspective, see C.H. Wake, 'Flaubert's Search for an Identity: Some Reflections on *Un Cœur simple*', *French Review,* XLIV, Special Issue, no. 2, 1971, pp. 89-96.

[28] The description of Emma here is ironically undercut by a reminiscence of the visit to the opera: Charles, anxious to stay to the end, points to what can be taken as a promising sign of the heroine's future fate: 'Elle a les cheveux dénoués: cela promet d'être tragique' (p. 233).

[29] 'Aber an K.s Gurgel legten sich die Hände des einen Herrn, während der andere das Messer ihm tief ins Herz stiess und zweimal dort drehte' (Franz Kafka, *Der Prozess,* Frankfurt, Fischer Bücherei, 1960, p. 165).

[30] Murray Sachs argues such a coincidence of vision in his article 'La fonction du comique dans *Madame Bovary'* (*Langages de Flaubert,* ed. M. Issacharoff, Coll. Situation, 32, Paris, 1976):

> Ne faut-il pas comprendre que la voix de l'Aveugle, à ce moment suprême, inspire chez Emma une vision-éclair de la réalité qu'elle s'était constamment efforcée de nier, la réalité que sa vie n'aboutit à rien, comme la vie de tout le monde? Son rire marque donc un dernier instant de lucidité, où elle comprend la désolante vérité sur sa vie. A ce moment-là, son sens du comique de la vie est identique à celui de Flaubert lui-même. (p. 180)

André Vial pursues a similar argument, associating Emma's laughter, 'devant la révélation de la force et du néant' (op. cit., p. 122), with that of Yuk, in *Smarh,* and that of the Devil, in the *Tentation* of 1849. Neither critic, however, suggests an awareness of the *aveugle* as substitute devil.

[31] Max Milner, *Le Diable dans la littérature française de Cazotte à Baudelaire 1772-1861,* 2 vols., Paris, 1960, vol. 2, p. 489.

Jean Barois: Le mirage et le moment pathétique*

William Bell : University of Kent

> 'Seal up the mouth of outrage for a while,
> Till we can clear these ambiguities...'
> *(Romeo and Juliet,* Act V, Sc. 3)

S ETTING out from a fragment of text in which the expressions *mirage* and *moment pathétique* figure, I propose to examine some of the ambiguities of the novel – Martin du Gard might have preferred the term 'ironies'. I try to show what sort of balance is struck between the tentative and the partisan, between scepticism and commitment, and to offer various possible accounts of the way in which Barois's tragedy might be thought of as historically determined.

I make no claim to shed new light on the 'philosophy' of the author as mediated by the totality of his writings. It is theoretically possible that new material will lead to a refinement in the understanding of that philosophy. It is however extremely unlikely that our sense of what Martin du Gard stands for – tragic humanism, as defined by Camus in the preface to the Pléiade edition [1] – will change. We know where his sympathies lay, we know which philosophical propositions he was prepared rationally to assent to, we know what difficulties he perceived in grounding his views upon something other than intuition or emotion. Those who are familiar with Martin du Gard scholarship will recognize the landmarks in what follows.

* * *

* A first version of this essay was delivered as a paper at the University of Wales intercollegiate French Colloquium, Gregynog, 1985.

The fragment of text which affords the spring-board occurs in Part III of the novel, in the final section, 'Le Crépuscule'. It is typical both of the form of the book, the *roman dialogué,* and of the content inasmuch as it turns upon questions of the widest general import:

> L'ABBÉ (violence inattendue).–"Et, même si vous pensez que je lui ai offert un mensonge, vous devriez être heureux que j'aie pu, par n'importe quel moyen, lui rendre la paix!"
> LUCE.–"Je ne connais pas deux morales. On doit arriver au bonheur, sans être dupe d'aucun mirage, par la seule vérité."
> Un temps.
> "Ah, nous aurons été un moment pathétique de l'histoire de la science, le moment le plus aigu sans doute de son conflit avec la foi!"
>
> *(Jean Barois.* Troisième Partie. 'Le Crépuscule' IV. Dernière visite de Luce à Barois).[2]

Specifically, the discussion concerns Barois and what he has become. The scene or chapter which immediately precedes has shown Barois, in sickness and old age, gripped by a kind of mystical experience. He is described as happy, confident, and his appearance is glossed as implying faith: 'C'est la grâce, aujourd'hui, qui rayonne sur ces lèvres...' (p. 544). He tries to give some account to the parish priest, the Abbé Lévys, of the illumination which he has undergone, and as he does so, he is led to affirm: '"Oui, l'âme existe!"' (p. 545); '"*Tout a un sens!...*"' (p. 546). He who has walked in the valley of the shadow of death, now feels the presence of the shepherd: '"[J'avais] l'impression de sortir d'un tunnel, de trouver la lumière, de commencer vraiment une nouvelle vie!"' (p. 546).

In extremis, then, Barois is converted. What value is to be placed on the conversion? Is the criterion practical or is it moral, happiness or truth? Is the perspective divine or is it human, God's triumph or Man's defeat? Has there been some supernatural struggle – '"tout en dormant,"' says Barois, '"je ne cessais pas de sentir une lutte au-dessus de moi"' (p. 546) – or have the conflict and its resolution taken place purely on the human level, within the divided self, heart versus head?

Luce knows the answer to these questions. So far as he is concerned: '"[Barois] est méconnaissable... Il ne reste plus rien de son intelligence..."' (p. 549). His verdict is perfectly compatible with Barois's own description of his frame of mind: '"Depuis longtemps je ne croyais plus aux idées . . ."' (p. 548). We remember that the priest, anxious that no chill wind should damage the tender plant of faith, has invited Luce to touch only lightly on certain subjects: '"sans rien qui puisse provoquer un effort cérébral"' (p. 547).

As these indications multiply, testifying to a kind of self-destruction in advance of death, the conversion of Barois seems to be emptied of all meaning. The play of argument and counter-argument, the seeming even-handedness of the narrative, these tend to give way to an unequivocally negative reading of the fictional event. The negative reading is that much more difficult to resist because Martin du Gard has found a means, in the *testament spirituel,* of ensuring that the event comes to us already negated. '"Je proteste d'avance,"' the mature Barois had written, '"avec l'énergie farouche de l'homme que je suis . . . contre la prière agonisante du déchet humain que je puis devenir"' (p. 454). Barois's *testament,* the profession of materialist faith which concludes Part II, is reintroduced in the final scene of Part III, when it is read by wife and priest and destroyed by them. Their sense of what has happened to Barois – dying, as they would wish to believe, *in spe* – is so much affronted by the *testament* that they can think of no response other than to burn it. The clear flame with which the novel ends is then the flame of the Inquisition, and the Church's victory, 'une lugubre victoire' (p. 454). In a letter to Pierre Rain, written in the spring of 1913 just as he is completing the novel, Martin du Gard speaks of 'ce livre où j'ai si violemment attaqué le catholicisme'.[3] A not inappropriate description, it may be thought.

* * *

Copious evidence about Martin du Gard's beliefs, from other sources, serves to confirm these impressions. To state the facts in summary fashion: Martin du Gard belongs to a Catholic family;[4] he stops believing during his teens and stops practising at about the age of twenty; thereafter he engages with religion as an object of enquiry, but having read and reflected, pronounces himself an atheist by temperament and by conviction. The attitude having once been formed, it does not change.

Robidoux's book on the subject remains authoritative.[5] There are two phases to the intellectual career of Martin du Gard: 'L'Etape métaphysique' and 'L'Etape morale'; the shift from one to the other comes with the publication of *Jean Barois.* Within the metaphysical phase, it is possible to distinguish lesser moments: a first stage, when Martin du Gard abandons the family gods; a second, when all philosophical systems, religious and scientific, are grist to his mill; a third, coinciding with the genesis of *Barois,* when conclusions are reached which owe much to the work of the biologist and *publiciste,* Félix Le Dantec.[6] By 1913, the debate concerning the validity of the religious outlook, in which Martin du Gard has engaged for more than a decade, is negatively and definitively resolved. When Gide dies, in 1951, Martin du Gard is moved to protest at the religious rites which accompany the burial. In effect, he reaffirms the point of view which he had earlier ascribed to Barois: '"Aux heures troubles que traverse notre humanité, il n'est rien de plus grave qu'un acte de foi public..."' (p. 447). Over a period of forty years and more, the anti-religious position is maintained.

It is worth stressing the fact that loss of faith, for Martin du Gard, was not the occasion for anguish. His retrospective judgment is that he was never a Catholic in anything other than a formal sense. To Marcel Hébert he writes, in 1910: 'Il y a ... tout un côté des choses qui m'est fermé. Le sentiment religieux, mystique ... m'échappe'.[7] To Henriette Charasson, in 1916: 'J'appartiens à une famille catholique, mais je n'ai jamais eu, moi, la moindre émotion religieuse; je n'ai pour ainsi dire *aucun senti-ment religieux...* '[8] Catholic commentators such as Robidoux and Moe-ller see statements such as these as reflecting – and perhaps promot-ing – the error whereby faith and feeling are equated. But even if his opinion were founded in error, there is no reason to doubt the sincerity with which Martin du Gard presents himself as being, like Le Dantec, his guide, or Dalier, his creature, by mental constitution and from the outset, uncomprehending of religion:

> Or je suis certainement né *incrédule* car j'ai toujours eu beaucoup de peine à croire, n'y ai jamais trouvé aucune véritable satisfaction de ma nature, et ne me sens vivre que depuis ma libération définitive ...[9]

Jean Barois is a novel about religion written by an atheist: that is the gist of the argument so far. The extent to which the author has a point of view is of course disguised by Martin du Gard's preoccupation with objectivity. Nevertheless his own sense was that the work was tendentious and that no sensitive reader could fail to note the tendency. The dedica-tion, to Marcel Hébert, begins: 'Votre sensibilité religieuse ne peut qu'être blessée par certaines tendances de ce livre' (p. 207). When the book is published, in a firm but infinitely courteous letter to his father-in-law, he writes: 'je n'ignore pas le déplaisir que *Jean Barois* va provoquer dans mon entourage...'[10] His own extraneous comments are unequivocal: in no way should Barois's return to the fold be construed as vindicating the religious option. It testifies, not to the truth of religion, merely to its function: to console, to make the intolerable tolerable. 'L'atavisme plus fort que l'éducation': in the cultural dimension of Barois's end, no less than the physiological, we are to see the working of a determinist hypothesis.

* * *

It should not escape us, however, that there is an element of paradox in Martin du Gard's position. He lacks religious sense, he is hostile to religion, but as a writer, and especially as a young writer, he is repeatedly impelled to confront religious subjects. In 1901, *La Chrysalide:* a novel concerned with the tensions provoked in marriage by the attitudes of the conventional *jeune femme bien-pensante.* As he works on the subject, Martin du Gard becomes aware of his incompetence in crucial areas of feminine and religious psychology and he abandons. In 1906, *Une Vie de saint:* the biography of a parish priest – and again he is defeated by a subject which, by definition, lies beyond anything of which he has direct experience. In 1909, *Marise,* of which the surviving fragment, *L'Une de nous* (Grasset, 1910), examines the impact of suffering upon deeply held religious convictions. As Robidoux says:

> Dans presque tous les exercices formels que nous lui connaissons, [les problèmes de fond] concernent, directement ou par quelque biais, la religion . . . [11]

Is this not surprising on the part of a man who considered himself 'non seulement affranchi . . . mais radicalement incrédule'?[12] Reviewing the frame of mind in which Martin du Gard finds himself when he embarks upon *Jean Barois,* Robidoux comments:

> Il est plus que paradoxal, en vérité, de se consacrer à un ouvrage où la crise religieuse tient tant de place, lorsqu'on se déclare incapable de comprendre l'esprit religieux.[13]

The project is perverse in the extent to which Martin du Gard lacks knowledge, cannot present himself as a living witness. But what is paradoxical when viewed in terms of his credentials, is less so when viewed in terms of motive. We should bear in mind that Martin du Gard shares the intensely serious conception of the writer's task which is common to the great novelists of the nineteenth century. This seriousness would combine with a very proper sense that it was in the area of religious speculation that the most difficult problems for the non-scientist (and for the scientist also?) were located. Add to these general arguments – seriousness of mind, profundity of the issues – the *hantise de la mort* which he would seem to have carried with him from an early age. It is in relation to the fact of mortality that religion and its promises take on an urgency which they might otherwise lack.

'La clef secrète de ma vie aura été l'horreur et l'oubli de la mort'; 'J'ai peur de la mort, chère Angèle. – Ne pourrons-nous jamais poser rien hors du temps – que nous ne soyons pas obligés de refaire?' The first is Martin du Gard, *in propria persona;*[14] the second is Gide, in *Paludes, par personnage interposé.*[15] For Martin du Gard and Gide and Proust (and Sartre, in *La Nausée,* when he is influenced by Proust), literature, the construction of the *œuvre,* offers a means of calming the fear. The work of art lives in a world of essence. Immortality is achieved in the work. The ascesis of work and the sense of achievement procured for him by the completion of literary tasks which, by virtue of his method, he rightly perceived as vast and daunting, these are for Martin du Gard the means of exorcizing the fear of death. But in his train of reflection he continually returns to the other, more generally human, more generally available solution which Christianity, with its promise of eternal life, affords. In the long term, it is the pragmatist in Martin du Gard, as much as the philosopher, whose interest is held by religion; as the Abbé Lévys says: ' "La plupart d'entre nous ont bien davantage besoin de paix intérieure que de vérité..." ' (p. 543).

* * *

Jean Barois: the title directs us to a conception of the subject in terms of character. 'Une longue monographie masculine, la destinée d'un homme et l'histoire d'une conscience', such is the description offered by Martin du Gard in *Souvenirs.*[16] Throughout the entire period of composition and indeed almost until printing begins, it is however intended that the work shall be called *S'affranchir!* The original title implies a conception of the subject in terms of ideas: it will be a 'problem' novel, examining the modern conflict between belief and unbelief, science and religion. Early descriptions of the project, in the letters, confirm the importance of ideas. To Jean Fernet:

> Le sujet que je vais aborder est gros de difficultés. Cette fois on pourra y voir posée la question religieuse, *"la question bien froide de l'existence de Dieu"* comme m'a dit Fr. Caillard, de la *Revue du Temps Présent...*[17]

To Marcel Hébert: 'Je prépare quelque chose de très important, un bien beau sujet sur le besoin religieux de la nature humaine...'[18] The latter formulation is interesting in the extent to which it defers to the point of view of Hébert: *beau sujet sur le besoin religieux.* The shift of emphasis does not however alter the fact that both descriptions imply the pursuit, via the novel, of some kind of broadly philosophical enquiry.

The creative method is congruent with this conception of the subject. Martin du Gard devours monographs in the philosophy series published by Alcan and by Flammarion and distils the content of scholarly and popularizing works – those of Le Dantec are especially important – in the intellectual debates which fill the pages. His own sense of the dense, intellectually demanding nature of the book is reflected in ironic and self-deprecating remarks in the correspondence, during the entire period of composition:

> Par moments, l'ensemble de mon sujet apparaît et je chancelle de vertige: c'est pure folie que de vouloir enclore tant de choses dans une œuvre de jeunesse;[19]

> C'est une besogne formidable. J'ai 85 scènes différentes, dont certaines contiennent toute une discussion philosophique, matière à un volume;[20]

> Je me heurte à des difficultés insurmontables. Un sujet immense, dans lequel je suis souvent perdu, noyé; des pensées abstraites qu'il faut transposer, morceler, transformer en actes, en gestes . . .;[21]

> Un sujet d'*idées,* de discussions; l'évolution religieuse d'un bougre contemporain, qui s'évade de son catholicisme, fait l'Affaire Dreyfus, et retombe dans son hérédité . . . environ 600 pages de dialogue . . . Enfoncé, Platon![22]

In its conception then, in its method and explicitly in its dialogues, the novel seeks to establish and maintain itself at the highest level of intellectual seriousness. To what extent does it purport to answer the questions which it raises?

* * *

Le mirage (i)

It would certainly be reasonable to argue that, by the time we reach 'Le Crépuscule' and the *mirage/moment pathétique* text, Martin du Gard's opinion has been conveyed to us. In the pattern of antonyms: truth/falsehood, reality/illusion, religion occupies the negative spaces. Religion is 'un conte de fée', the afterlife 'un mirage'. This judgment comes with a rider, however: if religion is lies, it is also consolation, and as Lévys says: ' "La plupart d'entre nous ont bien davantage besoin de paix intérieure que de vérité . . ." ' (p. 543). One question dominates the final section of the book: is it possible to reconcile truth with happiness? In the extent to which that is difficult to achieve, the solution may seem to lie in a choice between the two. Impossible not to be reminded of the syllogisms which are exchanged by the author-hero and Martin, on the stairway, in *Paludes:*

> *Etre aveugle pour se croire heureux. Croire qu'on y voit clair pour ne pas chercher à y voir puisque:*
> *L'on ne peut se voir que malheureux.*
>
> *Etre heureux de sa cécité. Croire qu'on y voit clair pour ne pas chercher à y voir puisque:*
> *L'on ne peut être que malheureux de se voir.*[23]

The advocate of truth (lucidity) and the advocate of happiness: 'Je' and Martin, Luce and Lévys. We as readers are, of course, no more able than Luce to resist the philosophical imperative: truth before all things. If happiness and truth are really incompatible – something which the serene death of Luce tends subsequently to 'disprove' – then we must opt, as Camus suggests in glossing this passage, for 'le renoncement éclairé au bonheur'.[24]

(ii)

Barois is afraid. The remedy for fear is faith. Reaffirmation of faith on the part of Barois is perceived by the reader as involving a betrayal of the self and an offence against the truth. So much is clear. But the question arises: in the extent to which we can trace a link between opinion and the motives which this or that individual may have for holding an opinion, is it not possible to challenge any set of beliefs? Is the thought of the *libre-penseur* somehow purer than that of the *bien-pensant?* How pure were the thoughts of Anthime, in *Les Caves du Vatican?* Might we not argue that, at every stage in Barois's career, the correlation between his views and what might loosely be defined as his needs is absolute? Thus, for example, the survival of Barois the child, depends upon his preferring the world-view of the father to that of the grand-mother, medicine to mysticism. Similarly, the achievement of Barois the adult, the putting forth of his powers, requires that he escape from the family and the provincial Catholic milieu of Buis:

> "L'atmosphère que tu crées autour de moi, j'y étouffe!... Du fait que tu es là dans ma vie, elle est gâchée, quoi que je fasse!... Tu briseras mes élans, un à un..." (p. 295)

On one view, the ideas determine the act: '"Ce n'est pas moi qui dois les diriger [mes idées], mais elles qui doivent diriger ma vie!"' (p. 299). On another, the ideas are framed with emancipation in mind: 'il cherche... à se faire une doctrine vitale' (p. 295). Jean and Cécile are intellectually incompatible, but when he acknowledges the failure of their relationship, what Jean says is: '"Tu as voulu, en m'épousant, prendre de la vie plus que tu n'en pouvais porter!"' (p. 312). As he inspects the possibility of divorce and its implications,

> il a brusquement senti croître en lui, malgré lui, malgré les mots qu'il dit, une ivresse nouvelle, le goût démesuré d'une liberté toute proche, un furieux appétit de vivre encore! (p. 312)

Is it in the name of truth that Jean leaves Cécile, or in the name of life? 'Ivresse nouvelle... goût démesuré de liberté... furieux appétit de vivre' – the terms employed do not relate to the faculty of intellect. The correlation which we are compelled to notice in the last phase of his life, correlation between opinions and that which makes life possible (makes *life* possible, not death: death is always possible), that correlation has been present at every stage. Men adopt the hypotheses which promote their well-being; health is a stronger determinant of what one thinks than truth: either formulation is consistent with the view expressed in Barois's materialist testament:

> "Les fonctions physiologiques et les fonctions psychiques sont solidaires; et la pensée est une manifestation de la vie organique, au meme titre que les autres fonctions du système nerveux." (p. 454)

It is worth insisting. The propositions of the *testament* have the appearance of truth, first, because they are put to us as the convictions of a healthy man: '"Ce que j'écris aujourd'hui ... en pleine force et en plein équilibre intellectuel ... etc."' (p. 453), second, because they have about them the bleakness which, it is sometimes suggested, is the hallmark of truth (cf. Camus: 'renoncement éclairé au bonheur'). I leave aside the question of whether Barois is indeed, at the moment of writing, 'en pleine force'. I leave aside equally the question of whether he is able to sustain the level of stoic acceptance envisaged in the final paragraph of the *testament* (no sooner is the writing concluded than, 'sa volonté tendue se rompt ... etc.' p. 456). If it is the case that 'la pensée est une manifestation de la vie organique', then it will exhibit all the characteristics of the life of micro-organisms. The characteristics of that life have already been defined by Jean's father in the opening section of the novel:

> "Un corps humain, ça nous paraît harmonieux, ordonné? ... Eh bien, ce n'est qu'un vaste champ de bataille ... Il y a des myriades de cellules qui se heurtent et s'entre-mangent ..." (p. 216)

No more than the life of the body is the life of the mind harmonious, ordered. Scientific materialism does not represent the base on which equilibrium can be achieved, it is one of the parties to the conflict. Thus, the *testament,* which on a first, second, third reading has the appearance of a privileged statement, must in the end take its place in the patterns and strategies of the *doctrine vitale.* It is evidence of Barois's continuing will to live, his appetite for the struggle.

(iii)

'Dupe d'aucun mirage': it is not only with regard to the world and our interpretations of it that the issue of lucidity is raised. Is the self any more accessible to us than God or the universe? What comfortable myths do we entertain about our individual nature, about human nature, about the meaning of history, about our capacity to influence the course of history? We choose, we act, we rationalize our actions in terms of motive and consequence, but do we give a true account, do we achieve either science or prescience? The novel is littered with instances of behaviour on the part of thinking men which the author in the short or long term qualifies as passionate, unselfconscious, misdirected, misdescribed. Is the launching of

Le Semeur a generous initiative, principled, public-spirited, or is it aggressive and sectarian? Are the *dreyfusistes* saints and heroes betrayed by the politicians (Péguy's thesis), or are they naive Utopians whose ultimate discouragement was in the logic of their extravagant hopes and misplaced confidence? Is mental discipline something we can achieve, or is it at best precarious, as the episode of the traffic accident would suggest? Was Barois ever free, or was the 'freedom' of his mature years as uncertain a quality as are the attributes of the Heroic Captive/*Esclave enchaîné?* Is life progress or repetition, line or circle? The novel tends to suggest a process whereby, with time, comfortable illusion gives way to uncomfortable truth. Thus:

> "Je me suis marié comme un imbécile!..." (p. 492);
>
> Il est écrasé par ce qu'il a osé écrire, jadis, *sans savoir*... (p. 497);
>
> "Pendant longtemps, on croit que la vie est une ligne droite... et puis, peu à peu, on découvre que la ligne est coupée..." (p. 464);
>
> "Je laisse des livres, des articles, qui ont eu leur actualité... Mais croyez-vous que je sois leur dupe? que je m'illusionne sur la pauvreté de tout ça?" (p. 526)

Rude awakenings! But what if the waking were itself an illusion? What if the final perspective were no less relative than that at any other point in life's journey? The chapter in which Barois separates from his wife ends with the words: 'Il parle... Mais, au loin, devant lui, il aperçoit – et son regard ne s'en détache plus, – il aperçoit au loin... la trouée lumineuse!' (p. 312). Describing his mystical experience to the Abbé Lévys, Jean speaks of a sense of waking from a long sleep:

> "L'impression de sortir de léthargie après plusieurs années de sommeil...L'impression de sortir d'un tunnel, de trouver la lumière, de commencer vraiment une nouvelle vie!" (p. 546)

Apercevoir la trouée lumineuse; sortir d'un tunnel, trouver la lumière: from the point of view of the seeker after truth, the parallel is not encouraging.

(iv)

'Un conte de fées', 'un mirage': the terms are applied by Luce to a particular element of Christian teaching, namely the resurrection of the body and the life everlasting. The force of the terms is not however confined to this or that item of faith, it is the whole edifice which is condemned. By comparison, what can be achieved on a basis of reason? In his Trocadéro speech, Barois flatly states: '"Le raisonnement est l'opposé de la foi"' (p. 448). Is this the message of the novel? Is it the case that Martin du Gard proposes a simple contrast between stout reason and flawed faith?

We are bound to notice that the terms employed by Luce – 'conte de fées', 'mirage' – have previously been employed at the expense of the point of view which, formally at least, is the very opposite of the religious view. During his lecture on *L'Avenir de l'incroyance,* a point is reached in Barois's relation with his audience when the narrator, for the moment omniscient, remarks:

> [Barois] comprend: après avoir suivi jusqu'au bout sa pensée destructive, ils [les auditeurs] ont soif de quelque mirage, ils attendent, comme des enfants, leur conte de fées. (p. 445)

The appeal is irresistible: 'Il n'a rien préparé, mais il obéit'. Barois then embarks on an unscripted development in which the caveats – '"*l'intelligence est négative*"' – and the promises – '"J'entrevois la possibilité de lois morales, basées sur l'analyse de l'individu et de ses rapports avec ce qui l'entoure"' (p. 445) – jostle for attention. We might argue that his sophisticated atheism stands, to the crude expectations of his audience, in the same relationship as the symbolism of Schertz to *la foi du charbonnier.* But even as he insists that the atheism of the future will have none of the characteristics of a religion, he does so in the tones of an enthusiast: 'Son regard devient lumineux: un sourire de visionnaire joue sur ses lèvres' (p. 445). '"Les temps nouveaux n'ont plus de prophètes"' (p. 446): has he forgotten the inaugural meeting of *Le Semeur* and the epigraph for the new journal, taken from Lamennais, *Paroles d'un croyant:* '"Fils de l'homme! monte sur les hauteurs et annonce ce que tu vois!"' (p. 319)? What does the Trocadéro lecture represent if not the literal enactment – 'Barois gravit lentement les marches de l'estrade. Il est un nain au centre du vaste hémicycle' (p. 441) – of Lamennais's injunction?

Every commentator on the novel recognizes that the convictions of Barois and his friends are based upon intuition. Camus describes the novel as: 'le seul grand roman de l'âge scientiste'; Barois is an adept of 'la religion scientifique ... il trahit au dernier moment cette nouvelle croyance ... [Son] évolution [est celle] d'un homme qui vient à douter de la foi traditionnelle et qui croit trouver une foi plus sûre dans la science ...

etc.'[25] Similarly Robidoux, describing Martin du Gard's debt to Le Dantec, argues that: 'à la base de cette "science", il y avait en fait un postulat fondamental qui ne pouvait s'expliquer que dans l'aveu d'une certaine foi',[26] and he cites Le Dantec in support. Le Dantec acknowledged, according to Raïssa Maritain, '"que du reste le matérialisme est une foi aussi indémontrable que le credo des chrétiens"'.[27] Equally, in Moeller's discussion of *Jean Barois,* we find the expressions: 'mystique scientiste et humanitaire', 'mystique de la science', 'religion laïque', 'élan presque religieux qui anime les apôtres du laïcisme', etc.[28]

The prime exemplar of *la foi nouvelle* is of course the staunch Luce rather than the doubting Barois. In his profession of faith to Lévys, Luce insists upon the rational nature of his hopes and the way in which they correspond to evidence:

> "Mon espérance, à moi, n'exige pas, comme la vôtre, l'abdication de ma raison; au contraire, ma raison l'étaye. Elle me prouve que notre vie n'est [pas] un mouvement à vide . . .; elle me prouve que mes actes collaborent au grand effort universel . . ." (pp. 550-51)

What could proof of such theses possibly consist in? An appeal to experience? But would the countervailing instances not be at least as numerous and readily to hand? If, for example, from the point of view of the reader's confidence in the thesis, the life of Luce constitutes 'proof', do those of Cresteil and Barois not furnish the refutation? Luce is a monist (denying the duality of mind and matter), who believes in progress and the essential goodness of man; monism apart, such beliefs do not coincide with those professed by Barois in his materialist testament. Nor do they appear to be more susceptible of demonstration than articles of Christian faith. They are properly irrational.

When he visits Luce for the last time in Auteuil, Barois challenges him: '"Avouez donc que la croyance au progrès est un postulat optimiste qui est nécessaire à votre équilibre personnel!"' (p. 524). Luce does not concede the point at this stage, but his last sayings, reported by Woldsmuth ('Le Crépuscule', V), acknowledge the link between world-view and temperament. A belief in progress is something which comes 'naturally' to him; it is the luck of the draw, a given fact of his nature:

> "Je suis né avec de la confiance en moi, en l'effort quotidien, en l'avenir des hommes. J'ai eu l'équilibre facile. Mon sort a été celui d'un pommier de bonne terre, qui porte régulièrement ses fruits." (p. 554)

On this account, what we affirm about the world has little to do with any reality other than that of self. And the nature of the self is at the same time random and determined.

(v)

A conflict then, not of reason and unreason but of two faiths, the new and the old, and on either side comfortable illusions: not immortality but progress, not God-man but man-God, not providence but still, evidence of design. '"Partout je vois . . . la science naître de l'erreur, l'harmonie naître du désordre . . ."' (p. 551) – it sounds very much as though the old *objection du mal* which prompted the first doubts of the youthful Barois ('Le Goût de vivre', IV) has been overleapt by Luce as gaily as by his intellectual inferior, the Abbé Joziers.

As we become aware of the symmetries, we are bound to ask whether the position of the scientists does not contain a fundamental incoherence, whether it is not in effect two world-views rather than one: the materialist view, put by Barois in his testament, and a kind of neo-idealism spliced with positivism, rather in the manner of Renan, which is the view expressed by Luce in his confrontation with Lévys? Here is the negative Barois (though he is by no means negative elsewhere):

> "Je nie donc que l'homme puisse en rien influer sur sa destinée. Le bien et le mal sont des distinctions arbitraires . . . etc." (p. 455)

and the positive Luce:

> "Mon espérance, c'est de croire que mes efforts vers le bien sont indestructibles." (p. 550)

How are these statements to be reconciled? If Luce is the complete exponent of scientism, it looks as though he is drawing on two very different philosophical traditions: materialist-determinist and Christian-humanist. All the illusions, the talk of good and bad, derive from the second tradition.

I am aware that my terminology hereabouts is strained. Before we reject the hybrid 'Christian-humanist', we should however reflect that Luce, embodiment of the ideal for Barois and his group, is described as: 'Fils d'un pasteur sans église. A commencé ses études de théologie . . . etc.'

(p. 336); that the epigraph to the journal comes from Lamennais, catholic turned socialist; that the model for the journal Martin du Gard found in the *Cahiers...* of Péguy, socialist turned catholic; that Péguy, on whom Martin du Gard draws heavily for his picture of the *dreyfusiste* milieu, represents *dreyfusisme* as religious in inspiration, a triple *mystique*, Christian, Jewish and Republican. To extend our argument beyond the novel, remember that, while he is writing *Jean Barois,* the moral ideal for Martin du Gard is embodied in Marcel Hébert, the ex-abbé Hébert. Robidoux suggests that the influence of Hébert, 'avocat inlassable de la "conscience"', acts throughout as a counterweight to that of Le Dantec. [29] Casting the net further still, we remember the place which Chadwick accords, in his infinitely subtle analysis of the factors making for secularization in the late nineteenth century, to the Christian conscience:

> Christian conscience was the force which began to make Europe 'secular'; that is, to allow many religions or no religions in a state, and repudiate any kind of pressure upon the man who rejected the accepted and inherited axioms of society. [30]

And again, he writes: 'In western Europe, the ultimate claim of the liberal was religious. Liberal faith rested in origin upon the religious dissenter'. [31] These scholarly claims shed new light on the passage of the novel where Barois tries to confute the intransigent atheism of Dalier ('L'Age critique', I). The text seems to be inviting the judgment that he is soft in the head, so inconsistent are his arguments with any which he has advanced in the past. But is he in fact wrong when he affirms:

> "Le sentiment religieux, il se laïcise déjà, il est partout! . . . Qu'est-ce qui me guide obscurément vers le bien, sinon la permanence en moi d'un sentiment religieux qui a survécu à ma foi?" (p. 502)

If he is not wrong, perhaps the illusions which attach to the new faith are simply variants on the illusions which attached to the old? To borrow the symbolism of Gide's *Thésée,* they are the bones of Œdipe, the bones of the religious man, buried in the city. Perhaps if we were all good intellectual historians, we should see that, at bottom, there is just one 'mirage'.

(vi)

A final thrust: perhaps the greatest mirage in the novel is that created by youth and health. 'When thou wast young, thou girdest thyself and walkest whither thou wouldst; but when thou shalt be old . . .' (John xxi. 18). Martin du Gard would of course be familiar with the scriptural text, but perhaps he would also remember the use which Gide had made of it in *L'Immoraliste,* to stigmatize the blindness of Michel. At the height of the Affair, when the going is at its toughest and spirits fail, Barois comes up with the thought:

> "Oui, je l'accorde, la réalité, en ce moment surtout, est laide, féroce, injuste, incohérente: mais quoi! c'est d'elle pourtant que la beauté finale jaillira un jour!" (p. 403)

The remark is proferred, 'avec un grand éclat de rire, jeune et crâne', and the text goes out of its way to tell us how Barois looks, at this point in time, to the older Luce:

> Luce le dévisage à la lueur d'un bec de gaz: les traits de Barois reflètent une joie de vivre, une confiance, une activité sans bornes: c'est un accumulateur vivant. (p. 402)

'Youth on the prow, and Pleasure at the helm' (Gray) – the image fits not exactly, but it fits. Body mechanisms and the laws of heredity operating, this same proud Barois (same, but not the same) comes to wonder whether, '"de toute éternité, [je n'étais pas] voué à la servitude?"' (p. 538).

* * *

Le moment pathétique (i)

'Moment pathétique': I have isolated the phrase in my title. In the text, it is first qualified: 'moment pathétique de l'histoire de la science', and then a phrase is offered in apposition: 'moment le plus aigu de son conflit avec la foi', by way of indicating where the suffering and pathos are located.

The conflict of Science and Religion: it is legitimate to make fun of a conception of history which implies, with or without the help of capital letters, a war of abstractions. But in this case, the stuff of human beings is not lacking. Luce is not writing history but trying to understand what has happened to Barois. Here is a man in whom intellect and sensibility are at odds. Why is that? Could it have been otherwise? Luce cannot see how it could be otherwise. The axiom which governs the last part of his life is this: it is tradition, sentiment, family ties which make us what we are, not knowledge:

> "Notre conscience morale, dont nous sommes si vaniteux, nous la tenons, par hérédité, de plusieurs centaines de générations mystiques. Comment rejeter un pareil patrimoine?" (p. 549)

It is more than Barois can do, to reject the heritage. *Conscience écartelée, mystique qui ne croit à rien:* if his death throes express 'le summum de la souffrance humaine', it is because to physical suffering there is added mental anguish.

It is that anguish which makes inappropriate a comparison with Renan which might commend itself on other grounds. Renan is the elegiac past:

> Il me semble souvent que j'ai au fond du cœur une ville d'Is qui sonne encore des cloches obstinées à convoquer aux offices sacrés des fidèles qui n'entendent plus. [32]

Barois is the tortured present. In Dalier – '"Chez moi, l'athéisme est inné"' – we have a glimpse of a possible future, when secularism has triumphed, moral anguish is out of fashion and the bells have ceased to chime. Why is he made so unattractive by Martin du Gard, rather as Gletkin is made unattractive, in *Darkness at Noon,* by comparison with Rubashov?

(ii)

What train of thought is suggested if we concentrate all our attention on the one phrase, 'moment pathétique de l'histoire de la science'?

At about the time when *Le Semeur* is launched (1895-96), nineteenth-century confidence in science falters. In France, the intellectual climate has changed from that of Renan's *Avenir de la science* (written in 1848) to that of Brunetière's articles in the *Revue des deux-mondes* (1895). Brunetière's views are interesting not for their power or originality, but as a straw in the wind. Science, he argued, was incapable of shedding light on fundamental questions, 'celles qui touchent à l'origine de l'homme, à la loi de sa conduite, à sa destinée future'. The field of enquiry of the natural sciences was severely limited. The findings of pseudo-science – philology, exegesis, history – left intact the claims of Christianity to truth and the notion of intelligible purpose in the universe. People had begun to realise that this was so; as a result, 'la Science a perdu son prestige; et la Religion a reconquis une partie du sien'.[33]

Assuming that Brunetière was right, Barois's intellectual development in the 1880s and 1890s is the reverse of the norm. He has no inkling of that fact, if fact it is. Absorbed in his teaching and the drama of his marriage, he might not notice what was happening in the larger world. But from the moment when he founds the journal, commits himself to the cause of Dreyfus, becomes a force to be reckoned with, his behaviour implies that he is in tune with history, that he understands it, can adapt to it, can shape it if need be. And then, years after Brunetière had thrown his hat into the ring, in Grenneville and Tillet he encounters the evidence that middle-class intellectuals, *young* middle-class intellectuals, think different-ly from him. Of course he knows about Bergson and Brunetière and Maurras, but it is as if he has not been able to take them seriously until he sees the impact of their teaching on the young. The encounter with Grenneville and Tillet is one of a series of factors which produce, in Barois, a massive loss of confidence.

If intellectual history contributes to Barois's misfortune, if he is 'une victime de notre époque' (p. 549), the most unsettling feature may not be the long-term decline of religion but rather the short-term loss of confi-dence in science. Barois is undermined, we might argue, not by his first apostasy but by his second: doubting religion, he is certain of science; doubting science, he is certain of nothing. Only at that stage does he feel the force of the reproach which the clerical party traditionally directs at the *libre-penseur:* ' "Nous avons été deux semeurs de doutes, mon vieil ami" ' (p. 549).

(iii)

'Moment pathétique': what if the source of Barois's tragedy lay not in the history of the conflict, not in the history of science, but in the history of the Church? It is a possibility which is worth entertaining, even if it is not one which is consistent with Martin du Gard's understanding of his subject.

Charles Moeller, whose discussion of this and other literary works serves a larger purpose, says of *Jean Barois:* '[Cette œuvre] évoque une période déjà ancienne de l'histoire de la pensée religieuse...'[34] It is possible to argue that the problems posed for faith by historical criticism or evolutionary theory were problems not by definition but because the

Church, lacking in intellectual vigour, made them such. 'Churches are institutions concerned with truth,' writes Owen Chadwick:

> not concerned with truth only, but still concerned with truth. When a theory could be shown to be well-founded, they hesitated and cast a rueful glance backward, but they accepted it because it was true and soon were again serene. [35]

The theory seems to me to be correct, even if the practice of adjustment is more often marked by the gnashing of teeth than the casting of rueful glances. How soon is soon? Even if Chadwick is right, the time-scale in respect of these nineteenth-century 'problems' is too short to accommodate Barois. He grows to manhood at a point when the Church's attitude to the modern world seemed to be that defined by the Syllabus (1864); when the mentality of the Catholic community in France was that of the ghetto; when religious apologetics were in lamentable state:

> La crise de Jean Barois n'est qu'un exemple, entre mille, de l'inévitable conflit qui devait opposer une apologétique décadente et un rationalisme triomphant. [36]

Would it have made any difference to Barois, or, to put the question in more sophisticated form, would it have made any difference to the way in which Martin du Gard presented the situation of Barois, had the fate of the Modernists and the career of Hébert been other than they were? In theory, his situation would be very different, but how would Martin du Gard have reacted? Can we be sure? It is clear from his letters that Martin du Gard was no more attracted to the compromise proposed by Hébert than is Barois to the compromise proposed by the fictional analogue of Hébert, the Abbé Schertz. In all probability, Martin du Gard shares the conviction which he attributes to Barois as part of the latter's argument in the Trocadéro lecture. Catholic dogma cannot change:

> "Une doctrine philosophique peut évoluer; elle est composée de pensées *humaines* qui sont groupées dans un ordre arbitraire et, par nature, provisoire. Mais une religion *révélée,* – dont le point de départ n'est pas sujet à correction, mais parfait dès l'origine, immuable par définition, comme l'absolu, – une telle religion ne peut varier sans se détruire elle-même." (p. 443)

On this understanding, the Church's failure to move with the times could not afford a ground for criticism. A Lamennais or a Loisy might deplore the intransigence of the papacy, but a Barois or a Martin du Gard would consider that intransigence and immobilism were the logical consequence of the Church's teaching on the matter of revealed truth. But can this be right? If Scripture were literally true, it would presumably be no part of the Church's task to interpret Scripture. If the Church's teaching were immutable, theology would be a science without a history. So we might reasonably argue that Barois's difficulties stem from the weakness of the Church's teeth and not, as he supposes, from the toughness of the nut which the new knowledge represents.

(iv)

History of a conflict, history of science, history of the Church – is there finally a sense in which Barois's predicament is politically determined, or if not determined, at very least compounded by politics? I have said little about the Dreyfus Affair which dominates the middle section of the novel. Barois is presented as a key figure in *dreyfusisme,* energetic, combative, 'une force qui se rue' (p. 448). We understand what makes him such: a cast of mind, a failed relationship, a conflict with authority. The Affair is in the logic of his passions ... but so are his passions in the logic of the Affair. Even as he tries to shape events, he is shaped by them. They threaten to make of him a sectarian and a hollow man.

It is a commonplace that the Affair had, as one of its consequences, the interruption of any dialogue between the Church and the secular authorities. The policy of the *ralliement* failed (the papal initiative of 1892, whereby French Catholics were encouraged to play a fuller part in the life of the secular state). There occurred a *mouvement de défense républicaine,* with anti-clericalism as the force which bound together politicians whose views on the social question were very different. Anti-clericalism is then translated, under Combes, into a programme of separation of Church and State, political vetting of Army officers, closure of unauthorized religious houses. These various developments are faithfully reflected in the novel: the main function of 'La Fêlure' (the brief opening section of Part III) would seem to be, on the one hand, to advert to them, and on the other to mark the distaste which they provoke in the members of the *Semeur* group.

When the Abbé Joziers reproaches him with the effect, in the curacy of Buis, of *'votre* nouvelle loi des congrégations', Jean is indignant: '"Ce n'est pas ... parce que j'ai combattu l'injustice, que je suis solidaire de tout ce qui se fait en France"' (p. 461). What is the extent of his responsibility? He wanted to carry the fight to the enemy, as Combes has done. In the matter of education, he argued, the state should not be neutral:

> "Neutralité, cela veut dire aujourd'hui: effacement devant la propagande acharnée de l'Eglise ... Prenons franchement notre parti d'une lutte qui est inévitable ... Laissons les prêtres libres d'ouvrir des écoles ... Mais soyons libres, nous aussi, d'ouvrir des écoles où nous aurons le droit de prouver, avec tout l'appui de la raison et de la science, sur quelles inqualifiables crédulités se fonde encore la foi catholique!" (pp. 449-50)

This stance on education ensures that he will experience in the most painful way his relationship with his daughter. Her religious vocation is proof against all argument. In loving her, he loves the enemy. But in what context other than that of the Affair could Marie assume the guise of enemy?

Barois is required to eat his hat. What is worse, in loving Marie he has to make the painful rediscovery of self. All his attention, as an intellectual and a *dreyfusard,* had been given to matters of principle and the public weal. He had no private life, no self, or so it seemed to him: '"Rendez-vous compte: je vis ici, seul, depuis plus de dix ans; je ne vois personne ... Je suis terriblement occupé ..."' (p. 459). It is in 'La Fêlure' that we learn for the first time of Barois's failing health: '"Oui, il paraît que je me détraque ..." (la main sur le cœur) "... par là ..."' (p. 461), but perhaps the title should be construed as an allusion, not to health, but to the gap which is revealed in Part III between the public and the private man. The final phase of Barois's life, when sentiment predominates, represents a kind of revenge of the personal. Reason is overthrown not by faith but by *le moi.*

* * *

What emerges from these remarks? Examination of the ambiguities tends to show that Martin du Gard's scepticism is more radical than has sometimes been supposed. He rejects religion, certainly, but he also pours cold water on humanistic alternatives, on the notion that man is regenerate, or indeed that moral concepts and moral vocabulary correspond to any real order whatsoever. There is life, life equals conflict, and then there is defeat and death, *le trou.* Describing Martin du Gard's achievement, Camus offers the striking phrase: 'Pierre de Craon athée, mais non pas sans foi' (p. xiii). If we try to relate this formulation to *Jean Barois,* we might say that it corresponds to the presence in the novel of Luce, 'athée, mais non pas sans foi'. My account of the *mirage* implies that, so far as this novel is concerned, Martin du Gard's faith is at best a shimmer on a black surface. The final perspective is bleak, closer to that of Cresteil than to Luce:[37]

> Le vapeur, d'un coup, s'éteint. Il était sombre et semé de lumières; il devient blanchâtre et percé de trous noirs, comme une carcasse abandonnée. Il tremblote lourdement au clapotis de l'eau, et le peu de vie qui lui reste s'exhale dans le panache hésitant de sa fumée. (p. 490)

I am reminded of lines from Philip Larkin's second collection of poems, *The Less Deceived:*

> Only one ship is seeking us, a black-
> Sailed unfamiliar, towing at her back
> A huge and birdless silence. In her wake
> No waters breed or break.

As regards the discussion of *moment,* it shows simply how rigorous is Martin du Gard's historical imagination. Whatever facet of the historical conjuncture we explore, the patterns of the hero's life are traceable therein. 'L'*Esclave enchaîné...* s'épuise toujours en son effort stérile' (p. 473): Barois is a kind of bound Prometheus and the trammels of history are endless.

Notes

[1] 'Son œuvre est ... celle du doute, de la raison déçue et perséverante, de l'ignorance reconnue et du pari sur l'homme sans autre avenir que lui-même', Camus, 'Roger Martin du Gard', in Roger Martin du Gard, *Œuvres complètes* (Paris: Gallimard, 1955), tome I, p. x.

[2] Roger Martin du Gard, *Œuvres complètes* (Paris: Gallimard, 1955), t. I, p. 551. All subsequent references to the text of *Jean Barois* will be to this edition; page references hereafter will appear in the body of the article. The author's name will appear in the notes as RMG.

[3] RMG, *Correspondance générale* (Paris: Gallimard, 1980), t. I, p. 291.

[4] The most detailed account of the family background will be found in Claude Sicard, *RMG. Les Années d'apprentissage littéraire (1881-1910)* (Paris: Honoré Champion, 1976), livre I, pp. 37-52.

[5] Réjean Robidoux, *RMG et la religion* (Paris: Aubier, 1964).

[6] Cf. Robidoux, op. cit., p. 105 *et seq.*; see also Tidavar Gorilovics, *Recherches sur les origines et les sources de la pensée de RMG* (Budapest: Tankönyvkiado, 1962).

[7] RMG, *Corr. gén.,* t. I, p. 173.

[8] ibid., t. II, p. 150.

[9] ibid., t. I, p. 167 (à Marcel Hébert; 30 juin 1910).

[10] ibid., t. I, p. 333 (à Albert Foucault; Novembre 1913).

[11] op. cit., p. 23.

[12] ibid., p. 85.

[13] ibid., p. 113.

[14] The remark figures in the concluding paragraph of Jean Delay's introduction to the *Correspondance Gide-Martin du Gard* (Paris: Gallimard, 1968), t. I, p. 118.

[15] André Gide, *Romans. Récits et soties. Œuvres lyriques* (Paris: Gallimard, 1958), p. 140.

[16] RMG, *Œuvres complètes,* t. I, p. lvi.

[17] RMG, *Corr. gén.,* t. I, p. 163.

[18] ibid., t. I, p. 171.

[19] ibid., t. I, p. 190.

[20] ibid., t. I, p. 203.

[21] ibid., t. I, p. 217.

[22] ibid., t. I, pp. 292-93.

[23] André Gide, *Romans, etc.,* p. 114.

[24] Camus, op. cit., p. xviii.

[25] ibid., p. xvii.

[26] op. cit., p. 111.

[27] ibid., p. 112.

[28] Charles Moeller, *Littérature du vingtième siècle et christianisme* (Paris: Casterman, 1964), t. II, ch. 3, *passim.*

[29] op. cit., p. 113.

[30] Owen Chadwick, *The Secularization of the European Mind in the Nineteenth Century* (Cambridge University Press, 1975), p. 23.

[31] ibid., p. 26.

[32] Ernest Renan, *Souvenirs d'enfance et de jeunesse,* in Renan, *Œuvres complètes* (Paris: Calmann-Lévy, 1948), t. II, p. 713.

[33] F. Brunetière, *La Science et la religion* (Paris: Perrin, 1913), *passim* and p. 28. The text first appeared in the *Revue des deux-mondes,* with the title 'Après une visite au Vatican', in January 1895.

[34] Moeller, op. cit., p. 223.

[35] Chadwick, op. cit., p. 15.

[36] Moeller, op. cit., p. 248.

[37] The reader who disagrees can appeal to RMG for support. In a letter to Félix Le Dantec, at the time of publication of *Jean Barois,* RMG wrote: 'Oui, c'est Luce qui est mon homme. Luce, c'est un peu *vous,* si vous me permettez de vous dire toute ma pensée. Je suis heureux que vous ayez bien vu ce que je pensais' (RMG, *Corr. gén.,* t. I, p. 338). It would be possible to gloss the remark in ways which reduce its force, but the only real issue is whether or not my account of the text is persuasive. *Ai-je bien vu ce qu'il pensait?*

Le Diable amoureux and the pure Fantastic

Roger Cardinal : University of Kent

WITHIN the canon of the literary Fantastic, there is no denying the high standing of Jacques Cazotte's tale of diabolical possession, *Le Diable amoureux*.[1] Critics like Irène Bessière, Max Milner and Pierre-Georges Castex have explicitly nominated the work as the first true example of the Fantastic.[2] So it is hardly surprising that Tzvetan Todorov, the master theorist of the Fantastic as genre, should select it as his initial exhibit in *Introduction à la littérature fantastique,* extracting from Cazotte's text one striking feature as the keystone for his model of the Fantastic – the notion of hesitation. For Alvare, the hero of the story, lives with a woman called Biondetta who may or may not be the Devil in disguise; Alvare is unable to decide whether or not to give credence to the supernatural phenomena he encounters. 'Le fantastique, c'est l'hésitation éprouvée par un être qui ne connaît que les lois naturelles, face à un événement en apparence surnaturel', proposes Todorov.[3]

What is odd about Todorov's position is that, having taken his cue from the hesitant Alvare, he should so soon jettison Cazotte's work as being of limited relevance to his thesis: *'Le Diable amoureux* offre une matière trop pauvre pour une analyse plus poussée: l'hésitation, le doute ne nous y préoccupent qu'un instant'.[4] This is odd because, I want to argue, Alvare's doubts about Biondetta's identity are in fact sustained *throughout* the sweep of the narrative, and are backed by a scheme of thematic and indeed grammatical equivocation of a high order of density and tension. Moreover, the tale may also be shown to meet the three criteria which Todorov will go on to establish as limiting conditions for the Fantastic, namely:

1. that the reader should hesitate between a natural and a supernatural explanation.
2. that such hesitation should be experienced by a character within the text (in this case, Alvare).
3. that the reader should reject a facile allegorical reading.

My guess is that Todorov's disparagement of *Le Diable amoureux* may have been prompted by the popular assumption that it is basically a light-weight exercise in the devil-tale tradition, from which Cazotte admittedly took much of his material. Certainly it is the case that many of Cazotte's contemporaries felt the piece to be non-disquieting and rather flimsy: 'Cette brochure ressemble à ces nuages légers, transparens, argentés qui se promènent dans le vague des airs' wrote one reviewer in 1772.[5] But my submission is that, far from being a careless flight across fashionably demonological territory,[6] *Le Diable amoureux* should be recognized as a pioneering contribution to the genre of the Fantastic, and indeed as a work of considerable literary subtlety and occasionally alarming intensity.

Cazotte's story cleverly exploits two versions of the concept of *possession*. On the one hand, Alvare finds Biondetta sexually alluring and is thus tempted to possess her physically. On the other, the Devil, in female guise, is out to capture Alvare's soul, to possess him in a metaphysical sense. To possess or to be possessed: the active and passive moods run in close conjunction, albeit without absolute coincidence (by the end of the story, Alvare has made love to Biondetta, but seemingly does not forfeit his soul). Suspense derives from the implied struggle for mastery: is Alvare in control of events, or is he the passive victim of Biondetta's manipulations? From the outset, the first-person narrator Alvare gives repeated assurance of his self-confidence: even if he feels qualms about Biondetta's credentials, he is able to make light of them, claiming that whenever he chooses to dismiss her, he can always do so.

Alvare's bravado colours what we might call the manifest narrative, whereas the alert reader will be sensitive to the unspoken or latent narrative which is the Devil's perception of the same events. Indeed an important part of the reader's pleasure must derive from the sense that Cazotte intends such dual interpretation. A good example is the passage where Alvare first summons up the Devil in the ruins at Portici. Alvare has boasted that he has no fear of the Devil and will prove it by tweaking his ears. The cabalist Soberano draws a magic circle on the ground and tells Alvare the verbal formula with which to invoke the Devil. When Alvare calls, the Devil appears as a monstrous camel's head, but Alvare recovers his composure and peremptorily tells him to turn into a spaniel. Once the camel has spat out a small dog, Alvare's bravado reaches its peak.

> Ma confiance était montée jusqu'à l'audace: je sors du cercle, je tends le pied, le chien le lèche; je fais un mouvement pour lui tirer les oreilles, il se couche sur le dos comme pour me demander grâce; je vis que c'était une petite femelle. (DA, 60)

From Alvare's viewpoint, all is well. He is fully in control: he can leave the safety of the circle with impunity, he can allow the Devil-as-dog to lick his boots, he can idly tweak the animal's ears, it is no more than a playful pet. Yet from the Devil's viewpoint, the trap is sprung and Alvare is caught. Having left the circle, he has exposed himself to the diabolical influence, and the submissiveness of the spaniel is only a ruse. Implicitly, Alvare fails actually to tweak the creature's ears as it rolls over; and what it discloses to his ignorant eye is its sexual parts – those of a bitch. The Devil's tacit joke is that, whereas Alvare finds this disclosure comforting and innocuous, notice is in fact being served that he is about to be challenged by a version of female sexuality which is powerful, purposeful and aggressive. [7]

The episode is followed by a sequence of startling metamorphoses in which the dog turns into a page-boy, then into a female opera-singer and back into a page-boy. But Alvare is hardly nonplussed. The surprises can only enhance his demonstration to his friends that he can consort with demons and get away with it. He is enjoying himself so much that he happily sets aside the issue of whether or not things are real: what is important is that they are dependent on his will.

But as the narrative evolves, Alvare's image of Biondetta alters from that of 'un fantôme colorié, un amas de vapeurs brillantes' (DA, 90) to that of an actual flesh-and-blood woman. And correspondingly he shifts from an attitude of bravado to one of progressive infatuation. This infatuation (which, from the Devil's point of view, is but the prelude to actual possession) is elaborately signalled to the reader by a series of skilfully accented allusions to Biondetta's sexual charms. The erotic situation is, I think, twofold, being at once a more or less straightforward case of sexual seduction by a woman who combines virginal naiveté with bolder, more mature allurements, and, concurrently, a more perverse case of erotic and, so to speak, intellectual seduction by a creature of enigmatic gender.

To the extent that Biondetta is, most of the time, represented in the text as a woman, she exhibits two basic aspects. Firstly, she is shown as a tender, virginal creature. She blushes readily: 'Elle rougit, ce qui lui arrivait toujours avant de parler' (DA, 76). She is artless in her expressions of love, and when alone, voices rapture at the mere thought of Alvare calling her by the lover's name Biondetta. Her gracefulness is appraised in purely conventional terms: 'Mille grâces répandues dans la figure, l'action, le son de la voix' (DA, 93) is one hyperbolic flourish.

On the other hand, the magnetism of Biondetta's sexuality becomes increasingly apparent during their enforced proximity as master and servant living in confined quarters. Alvare is in any case prone to voyeurism – there are two or three moments when he secretly observes her, once at least through a keyhole! – and he takes delight in minute details of her physique and clothing. Biondetta has alluring eyes, 'd'un pénétrant, d'une douceur inconcevable' (DA, 64). Her complexion is perfect, her lips well-formed and of lively colour. Her hair constitutes 'une épaisse forêt de cheveux blonds cendrés' (DA, 70). Her figure immediately strikes the eye when she exchanges the clothing of a page-boy for the dress of an opera-singer. Alvare moons over her feathery hat, her crimson hairnet, her sumptuous *déshabillés*. She is seen to possess perfect white arms and thighs. Watching her undress, Alvare falls prey to sexual longings; he sees her naked again when she has to be undressed by a doctor following the stabbing by the jealous Olympia. An atmosphere of exacerbated desire is thus discreetly fostered across the narrative, leading us through a series of comic frustrations when the lovers' union is forestalled by those accidental interruptions or 'secours extraordinaires' (DA, 124) – the breaking of an axle or a wheel, the arrival of a pet dog or a guest for dinner – and on to the ultimate consummation at the Marcos farm.

The penultimate seduction attempt in a thunderstorm is a scene in which Biondetta's erotic purposiveness is strongly emphasized. We are here treated to some fine touches of libertine periphrasis, elegance combining with raciness, as when Biondetta begs Alvare to place his hand to her chest and feel the fearful palpitations of her heart:

> Quoiqu'elle se trompât en me faisant appuyer sur un endroit où le battement ne devait pas être le plus sensible, je démêlai que le mouvement était extraordinaire. (DA, 105)

And when she finally inveigles him into the posture most conducive to his sexual arousal, this stratagem is expressed in almost innocuous terms relating to her girlish fear of the storm (albeit with a thrust of sexual symbolism in the image of the thunderbolt):

> Enfin un coup plus effrayant que tous ceux qui s'étaient fait entendre part: Biondetta s'y dérobe de manière qu'en cas d'accident il ne pût la frapper avant de m'avoir atteint moi-même le premier. (DA, 105)

Intercourse is finally achieved in the cramped bedroom which the couple are obliged to share at the Marcos farm. Here Biondetta throws a scene calculated to knock her partner entirely off balance, combining taunts, appeals, self-abasement and weeping. Alvare sits by her, at his wits' end.

> Les yeux sont à demi fermés, le corps n'obéit qu'à des mouvements convulsifs, une froideur suspecte s'est répandue sur toute la peau, le pouls n'a plus de mouvement sensible, et le corps paraîtrait entièrement inanimé, si les pleurs ne coulaient pas avec la même abondance. (DA, 116)

It is bizarre that at the very moment one might expect her to be most aroused, Biondetta should lose all her body-heat. In a moment or two, the lovers will pass from kissing to the full union of their bodies, signalled in the text by a discreet line of suspension points: can it be accidental that Cazotte should preface this with an evocation of Biondetta as cold and corpse-like?[8] I take the point to be not so much a hint of necrophilia, as a disturbing reminder that Biondetta is not exactly human. Hers is no average pulse-beat because she is, in the final analysis, *other* than a normal woman. Her unnatural coolness and rigidity, belying the 'naturalness' of her tears, can be construed as a deliberate marker of the Fantastic, a reminder to read the tale on the two levels and to entertain doubts alongside surface certainties.

Now, whereas most descriptions of Biondetta and her actions reinforce her primary aspect as a desirable female, the hero, and the reader with him, is intermittently alerted to her secondary sexual aspect. For Biondetta is also Biondetto. At the outset, the equivocation seems harmless enough, in that the narrative premiss of a young woman being disguised as a boy fits into the artistic convention of the *travesti,* well known to Cazotte's first audience. On this level, Biondetta's ambiguous gender is the occasion of mild erotic titillation, as when the boy blushes like a maiden, or is seen combing his fingers through a mass of hair which, as we have seen, is rhetorically coded as being feminine. This much of the ambiguity creates a superficial piquancy, and hardly modifies the obvious theme of a struggle between chasteness and lust within Alvare. But the deeper import of this confusion of gender is that it in turn articulates a more disturbing ambiguity which Alvare is at pains to ignore – the fact is that Biondetta not only vacillates between female and male, but also between human and non-human. Is she mortal, or is she the Devil? Each allusion to her maleness, however straightforward in terms of the *travesti* convention, may, on this reading, be taken to function equally as a covert reminder of a more devastating otherness.

As I see it, Cazotte's whole strategy for sustaining tension in the tale is to dissuade the reader from a spontaneous identification of Biondetta with the amorous devil of the title. To this end, as I have suggested, he spends a lot of time delineating a Biondetta who is unmistakeably corporeal and not the 'être fantastique' (DA, 88) of Alvare's repressed thoughts. At the same time, Cazotte wants to make allowance for hesitation. This he does by retarding the resolution, emphasizing the feminine yet also dropping hints of duality. Among these are some varyingly provocative uses of the pronouns *il* and *elle*.

In the first part of the story, Alvare's use of the names Biondetto or Fiorentina reflects an obvious logic of gender identification in relation to the shifting appearances of page or singer. And once *le page* or *la cantatrice* occur as nouns in the text, the corresponding pronouns are, naturally, masculine or feminine. Such usage is grammatically normal. But something a little strange will ensue. In the passage where Alvare peeps in on his companion's preparations for sleeping, I sense a curious drift from one gender to its opposite.

> A travers la gaze de mon rideau, je vois le prétendu page arranger dans le coin de ma chambre une natte usée qu'il a trouvée dans une garde-robe. Il s'assied dessus, se déshabille entièrement, s'enveloppe d'un de mes manteaux qui était sur un siège, éteint la lumière, et la scène finit là pour le moment; mais elle recommença bientôt dans mon lit, où je ne pouvais trouver le sommeil. (DA, 68-69)

The male appearance of the page-boy is tacitly belied by the disclosure of femaleness, once clothing is removed. There is in fact no 'she' in this paragraph, except by implication. None the less, the reader will be alert to the likelihood of an *elle* occurring, and when, in the last main clause, that pronoun arises, may almost misread *elle* as meaning 'she'. Of course, a strict parsing of the sentence makes it clear that this *elle* refers not to the woman but to the noun *la scène;* all the same, a presentiment of femininity, so to speak, is made vocal.

The text goes on in an interesting way, with practically a full page being devoted to an account of Alvare's sleepless fantasies and yet somehow avoiding any direct reference to a female being. Revolving around the image of Biondetta, the text contrives to cite that name but twice, foregrounding instead such non-committal references as 'cet objet ravissant' or the metonymic allusions 'cette bouche' or 'ce cœur'. Finally the actual Biondetta enters on the scene as Alvare's bed collapses: the comedy of the moment is at once modified by a flicker of eroticism.

> Comme je ne la perdais pas de vue, malgré mon accident, je la vis se lever, accourir; sa chemise était une chemise de page, et au passage, la lumière de la lune, ayant frappé sur sa cuisse, avait paru gagner au reflet. (DA, 69)

The quickening of Alvare's lust seems to derive from the equivocal nature of Biondetta-Biondetto: it's *her* thigh, but *his* night-shirt, and that fetishistic nuance may make the reader open a silent window on to the thought of Alvare being sexually aroused by a young boy's nakedness, enough to lend this passage a whiff of the salacious. The detail, I would contend, is less significant as a sexual comment, counting above all as another signal of the Fantastic, as the concurrent glimmering of the moonlight may confirm.[9]

While I recognize the dangers of reading sexual meaning into gender usages which are simply a function of normal French grammatical practice, I have found at least three occasions in the later development of the story where Cazotte, referring to Biondetta, contrives to use the pronoun *il* in an eye-catching and almost perverse manner. At one point, just after his arrival in Venice, Alvare is entertaining some ungracious thoughts about her, and voices the masculine nouns *lutin* and *créancier*. It is not the nouns in themselves which are disquieting, but the way they allow the masculine pronoun then to be foregrounded.

> Mais que te voulait ce lutin, qui ne t'a pas quitté depuis vingt-quatre heures? Il avait pris une figure bien séduisante; il m'a donné de l'argent, je veux le lui rendre.
> Comme je parlais encore, je vois arriver mon créancier; il m'amenait deux domestiques et deux gondoliers.
> "Il faut, dit-il, que vous soyez servi..."

Thus for a few sentences, Biondetto is in the ascendent in Alvare's mind, and femininity is only restored when he addresses his companion by her female name, with a feminine ending on the ensuing participle: 'Je suis content de votre choix, Biondetta, lui dis-je; vous êtes-vous logée ici?'. (DA, 75)

A few pages later, there is a similar symptomatic veering towards the masculine when Alvare confronts Biondetta and refers to her as 'l'écueil de ma raison', a characterization which becomes the pretext for calling her *il* in the next four clauses (DA, 78). A couple of pages later, she is designated as 'l'être dangereux dont j'avais agréé les services', a circumlocution in the masculine which then gives rise to an extraordinarily evasive statement: 'Je détournais les yeux pour ne pas le voir où il était, et le voyais partout où il n'était pas' (DA, 80). The wilful avoidance of the feminine pronoun (and person) can be taken on one level as meaning that Alvare is seeking to censor the obsession of femininity, but on another as an unconscious acknowledgment of a generalized uncertainty. As such lapses from the naturalness of the feminine usage tend to discredit Biondetta as a plausible lover for Alvare, so they filter the macro-themes of unnaturalness and imposture into the micro-texture of the style.

What we must not forget is that the narrative focalization of *Le Diable amoureux* is governed by an intradiegetic narrator whose subjectivity is inseparably meshed into the seeming objectivity of the events related. A certain degree of modalization is manifested in phrases on the model of 'je crus voir' or 'je crois distinguer' which undermine the credibility of the first-person eye-witness, in what will become a typical device of the Fantastic. [10] More pervasive are the references to the protagonist's emotional and indeed physiological reactions. Allusions to the 'léger frisson' or the 'sueur froide' he feels, to his hair standing on end or his heart speeding up, are so many signposts locating the points of intrusion of the Fantastic. (The code of symptomatic physical reflexes like the icy shudder will, of course, become the stock-in-trade of the Gothic idiom of a few years later.) What is noticeable here is not the use of such details, probably already clichés, but the implicit recognition that such responses are appropriate not only to the experience of confronting the supernatural but also to that of confronting the sexually provocative. That is, Alvare's sexual sensations, evidenced in a constellation of urbane euphemisms – 'un frémissement singulier', 'un désordre inconcevable', 'un trouble extraordinaire' – may be seen as strictly identical to the sensations elicited by the supernatural. The agitations of carnal desire are of the very same order as the *frisson* of the fantasmal. So much so that Cazotte's insistent use of the noun *frayeur* (along with cognates like *effrayant* and *effrayer*) seems to invest it with the special meaning of a disturbance at once terrifying and pleasurable. Indeed *frayeur* may be said to be the paradigmatic concept which regulates the text, its negative and positive connotations ambiguously blending the hero's sensations of risk and delight, and in turn mirroring the paradoxical thrills offered to the reader of such fiction.

How then does Alvare see his situation? I can see three basic options as regards interpreting his attitude to his companion.

1. he knows all along that she is the Devil.
2. he forgets, or does his best to forget, that she is the Devil.
3. he cannot make up his mind, and this uncertainty is never decisively dispelled.

Tempting though it might be to correlate the first reading with Baudelaire's notion of 'la volupté dans le mal' or with Georges Bataille's assimilation of sexual arousal with the idea of violating a taboo,[11] I would contend that there are insufficient pointers in the text to support the view that Alvare is always aware of, or is perversely excited by, the Devil's presence.

The second reading seems more defensible.[12] It leaves us with the image of a naive hero who vainly pursues an illusory happiness by ignoring unpleasant facts, and is brought back to reality with a bump. Such a reading takes us in the direction of seeing the tale as an allegory, bearing the obvious moral that 'one should never trifle with the Devil'. Of course, if we choose to stick to such a reading, we shall automatically disqualify the work from the canon of the Fantastic, since it falls foul of Todorov's prohibition on an allegorical reading, mentioned earlier.[13]

My own inclination is to favour the third reading, less clearcut yet more intriguing, for it leads us truly to the heart of the Fantastic. According to this reading, the sexual dynamics of the narrative are associated with postures of doubt and hesitation. Indeed I would submit that the whole point of *Le Diable amoureux* is that it seeks to equate sexual enthralment and metaphysical bewilderment. On this view, Alvare falls for Biondetta not because she is the Devil, nor because she can (with an effort) be thought of as a woman, but because she is so thrillingly enigmatic. What more alluring, more desirable, than a partner whose animated and impetuous behaviour so vehemently suggests, without ever conclusively disclosing, a mysterious supranormal potency? When the couple are paired at the wedding feast, Biondetta puts on a dazzling performance.

> Biondetta paraissant tour à tour livrée à la passion ou au dépit, la bouche armée des grâces fières du dédain, ou embellie par le sourire, m'agaçait, me boudait, me pinçait jusqu'au sang, et finissait par me marcher doucement sur les pieds. En un mot, c'était en un moment une faveur, un reproche, un châtiment, une caresse: de sorte que livré à cette vicissitude de sensations, j'étais dans un désordre inconcevable. (DA, 114)

Sulky and cajoling, bitchy and charming, Biondetta here incarnates the cultural archetype of the demonic enchantress, the *femme fatale* (and exhibits a certain resemblance to Manon Lescaut, as Milner has noted (DA, 17)). My point is that a specifically Cazottian edge to the cliché of female duplicity is given by the fundamental, one might even say over-determined nature of her ambiguousness.

For if Biondetta is both woman and devil, beautiful and repellent, amorous and cynical, she is also, at once and indistinguishably, *real and illusory.* Let us consider this last paradox.

Cazotte's narrative ends with a final twist after Alvare has emerged firstly from the stupor attendant on his seduction and then from the terror of a momentary diabolical vision. By the time he reaches his home in Maravillas, he has recovered enough of his old sang-froid, and is sufficiently encouraged by his mother's tender reception, to be able to look back over the whole adventure and declare it to have been a dream – 'le songe affreux que je viens de faire' (DA, 122).[14]

Various items of evidence are adduced to back up this declaration. Firstly Alvare has himself noticed that the hair net which Biondetta placed around his dishevelled hair after their lovemaking, in a gesture at once humble and triumphant, had completely vanished by morning. Secondly, his mother points out that there is no such farm in the region as the one he describes; that the servant Berthe, whom the lovers supposedly met near the farm, had been bedridden in Maravillas all the while; and that the squire who allegedly brought money to Alvare in Venice had at the time been several months in his grave. At this stage, Cazotte seems to be nudging us towards a clear resolution after all. If it is the case that 'it was only a dream', if the entire adventure with Biondetta has been no more than an extended hallucination, we find ourselves with a typical case of a marvellous episode susceptible of a rational explanation, dream narratives being, almost by generic convention, tolerable deviations from the natural frame of waking life. In Todorovian terms, we are at this point sliding from the Marvellous to the Uncanny, assigning the tale to the sub-genre of *le fantastique-étrange.* This is indeed how Todorov finally, though I think negligently, situates *Le Diable amoureux,* as a fantastic tale 'excused' (or defused) by its rational conclusion. [15]

Notwithstanding, even at this late stage, I must insist that, despite the best efforts of Alvare's mother and her tame theologian Don Quebracuernos, who is engaged *in extremis* to draw the tale to a safe moral conclusion, [16] there still persists considerable uncertainty as to the status of the events in question. The alert reader must surely sense the inadequacies of the dream hypothesis. If we are to believe that Alvare's liaison with Biondetta took place only in his mind, to what point should we trace back the duration of that delusion? The most telling corroborations of the dream hypothesis relate only to recent events at the Marcos farm, aside from the mystery of the money brought to Venice. If we are to understand Alvare's qualification of the complete adventure as a 'songe affreux' in the literal sense, [17] then we shall want to date the onset of the nightmare at least back to the apparition of the camel's head at Portici, near the beginning of the text. But what then of Alvare's companions at the lavish banquet who, for instance, salute Fiorentina the opera-singer, 'saisis par la vérité de la scène au point de se frotter les yeux' (DA, 63-64)? Is their testimony simply to be dismissed by the ruling that they too – as characters appearing *after* the camel – are also figments of Alvare's oneiric imagination? And what of the earliest example in the tale of a supernatural event, the lighting of Soberano's pipe by an alleged spirit (DA, 56)? If we say that this too forms part of the global dream, we are well on the way to dating the onset of Alvare's delusion back to the opening pages of the book. At which point we begin to doubt whether he was ever stationed in Naples in the first place! To my mind, it would be highly unsatisfactory to bracket off practically the entire text as *unreal* and to point to the last few pages as being solidly *real* in contrast. [18] This would mean lumping together as uniformly preposterous all those subtle threads of plausibility and implausibility which make up the finely crafted pattern of Cazotte's textual performance at large.

Turning again to the closing pages, we find that there is a witness we have overlooked, the mule-driver who brings Alvare home from the Marcos farm. It seems that in a village on the road, both he and Alvare had been informed by several people that Alvare's female companion had driven through, though without stopping. Must this testimony as to Biondetta's existence also be rejected as mere hearsay? Should we suspect the mule-driver of being the Devil's accomplice, engaged to help cover up the matter, – that is: to leave things diabolically unsettled? Unfortunately for Alvare's mother, and for the reader anxious for a solution, Cazotte allows no opportunity for interrogating the man, who, on arrival at Maravillas, had at once left, not even waiting to be paid. We are not actually assured that anyone other than Alvare spoke to him, and there is no way of establishing whether or not he could have borne out Alvare's recollections.

How then *did* Alvare get home from Italy? Did he perhaps travel alone and in a delirium, recovering his senses only in his mother's presence? Was he ever in Venice anyway, and did he ever live with a woman called Biondetta? If she existed, was she the Devil in disguise, and did Alvare get seduced by that creature? Did the Devil fall in love? To all these questions, Cazotte's text answers, absurdly, yes. Neither the dream hypothesis nor a blanket acceptance of the supernatural can be finally satisfying in isolation: we need to hold both alternatives in mind, and to honour the symbiotic economy of the narrative whereby each informs and enhances the other. Once granted that the terms of reference of *Le Diable amoureux* are, if I may say so, *firmly equivocal,* the story can indeed be counted as an authentic specimen of the Fantastic. Simultaneously the account of an illusion and of a literal encounter with unnatural beings, it both denies and confirms the existence of the supernatural, thereby contributing to what Bessière calls 'un discours conflictuel sur le réel'.[19] At the end, the reader remains in a state of perfect bewilderment, and this lingering sensation of being left without any handholds, clutching at a 'sens flottant', in Milner's phrase (DA, 24), is, I believe, absolutely congruent with Todorov's criteria for *le fantastique pur.* As Alvare once asks, 'Où est le possible? . . . Où est l'impossible?' (DA, 94). For character and reader alike, the despair at forfeiting certainty may equally be experienced as a rare poetic pleasure, a hesitation between contraries, a hovering, irresolute yet wonderfully intent, at the vibrant heart of the Fantastic.

Notes

[1] I refer to the 1788 version of Cazotte's text in Max Milner's pocket edition (Garnier-Flammarion No. 361, Paris 1980), page-references to this being signalled by the abbreviation DA.

[2] See I. Bessière, *Le Récit fantastique,* Paris, Larousse, 1974, p. 93; M. Milner, 'Introduction' in DA, 24; and P.-G. Castex, *Anthologie du conte fantastique français,* Paris, Corti, 1963, p. 9.

[3] T. Todorov, *Introduction à la littérature fantastique,* Paris, Seuil, Coll. Points, 1976, p. 29.

[4] ibid., p. 31.

[5] Fréron, quoted by M. Milner in *Le Diable dans la littérature française*, Paris, Corti, 1971, vol. I, p. 83. Much the same view is voiced by Jorge Luis Borges in his introduction to the tale: 'Le style, délibérément frivole, (. . .) ne se propose jamais de nous alarmer' (in J. Cazotte, *Le Diable amoureux*, Retz-Franco Maria Ricci, 1978, p. 10). For his part, Jacques Finné passes over Cazotte as being too theologically serious a writer to be capable of what he sees as the essential playfulness of the Fantastic mode! (*La Littérature fantastique*, Editions de l'Université de Bruxelles, 1980, pp. 14-15).

[6] I have deliberately avoided assessing Cazotte's real-life involvement in the Occult. The thesis that *Le Diable amoureux* may reflect its author's passage from a mocking disbelief to a pre-initiatory credulity is sketched by Nadia Minerva in 'Des Lumières à l'Illuminisme: Cazotte et son monde', *Studies on Voltaire and the 18th Century*, No. 191, 1980, pp. 1018-19.

[7] Kathryn Hoffmann points out the neat reversal of initiative here, the apparent master in fact becoming the servant's prey ('La Ruse du diable: Jacques Cazotte, *Le Diable amoureux*', *Neophilologus*, LXV No. 3, July 1981, p. 377).

[8] Théophile Gautier will elaborate the disturbing equation of demonic seductress and icy corpse in his tale *La Morte amoureuse* (1836).

[9] In a celebrated passage of the 'Custom House' introduction to *The Scarlet Letter* (1850), Nathaniel Hawthorne draws attention to the power of moonlight to create a territory 'where the Actual and the Imaginary may meet', i.e. it is a privileged medium for the Fantastic (quoted in Peter B. Messent, *Literature of the Occult*, Englewood Cliffs, N.J., Prentice-Hall, 1981, p. 7).

[10] Cf. Georges Décote, *L'Itinéraire de Jacques Cazotte (1719-1792)*, Geneva, Droz, 1984, pp. 236-37 and Todorov's discussion of modalization in Nerval's *Aurélia*, in op. cit., pp. 42-45.

[11] Cf. G. Bataille, *L'Érotisme*, Paris, Editions de Minuit, 1957, pp. 118-19.

[12] See Décote (op. cit., p. 220) and Bessière (op. cit., p. 91) for discussions of the premiss that Alvare suppresses his conviction that Biondetta is the Devil.

[13] Cf. Todorov: '(Le fantastique) est tué par l'allégorie' (op. cit., p. 73).

[14] It should be noted that the dream hypothesis, balanced by material suggestive of a decisive orientation to the Fantastic, was only interpolated in the 1776 edition, after Cazotte's readers complained that the 1772 version ended too abruptly. An outline of Cazotte's revisions can be found in Milner's introduction, DA, 24-26.

[15] Cf. Todorov, op. cit., p. 50.

[16] The only literary merit of the concluding sermon is that its longwinded and muddled logic mirrors the ambiguities of the tale: the learned Don Quebracuernos both assures Alvare that his adventure *was* only a dream *and* insists that he is jolly lucky to have escaped the Devil's clutches!

[17] Décote suggests that the reference may be metaphoric, hence that Alvare *doesn't* think Biondetta was an illusion: after all, it is Alvare who appeals to the mule-driver for corroboration (see Décote, op. cit., p. 239).

[18] We may be well advised to look askance at the name 'Maravillas': there is no guarantee that this apparently secure location for waking certainties is immune from the contagion of the Marvellous!

[19] Bessière, op. cit., p. 93.

Quelques réflexions sur le *réalisme* et sur Marivaux

Henri Coulet : University of Provence (Aix)

EXISTE-T-IL un système interprétatif en littérature que ne démente sur quelque détail ou sur l'essentiel votre lecture des textes, ou qui ne vous blesse au plus profond de votre plaisir à les lire? En existe-t-il, en revanche, qui ne vous apprenne à mieux lire une ligne, une page, voire un livre tout entier? ou, pourquoi ne pas l'avouer, dont ne vous reste incompréhensible quelque ligne, quelque page, voire le développement entier? Qu'on me pardonne ces propos décousus. De quelque savoir qu'ils se barbouillent, ils ont leur origine dans mes impressions.

> ... coiffée le plus souvent en mauvais battant-l'œil, elle ne dédaignait plus d'aller affronter la poudre qui s'élevait des tas de blé remués ... c'était une charrette conduite par un petit garçon, qui pour éviter le chemin creux avait fait monter son cheval sur un terrain semé d'orge ... quand [les batteurs] étaient fatigués, ils se reposaient sur un tas de blé; et étendant un coin de leur habit, ils tiraient d'un panier une collation composée de fromage, et d'un pain nourrissant et noir. Un pot ébréché plein de vin mêlé avec l'eau leur fournissait à boire ... Regardez-le, le beau garçon! il a son habit des dimanches; il se carre: il est aussi fier dans sa peau qu'un coq sur un fumier ... on voyait des cavales ou juments, madame, c'est la même chose, suivies de leurs petits poulains fringants comme un papillon ... il enfonce son chapeau jusqu'aux oreilles, met ses quatre brins de cheveux dessous, retrousse la manche de son habit et raccommode sa jarretière ... il gelait, nous avions tous au nez la roupie, et nous soufflions comme des chevaux; chacun avait les mains dans ses pochettes ... je vis des étangs gelés; des maisons bâties de terre, et d'autres de paille; des puits au milieu du bourg, et force tisserands ... à la fin, le cheval se fatigua; on eût dit, à le voir, que c'était comme une lampe qui s'éteignait; il ne sautait plus que brins par brins; et je descendis comme un César de dessus ... Brideron et Oménée regardaient par la petite fenêtre, et tâchaient par les gestes de Phocion de deviner ses

discours ... j'aperçus dans ma cabane un jeune gars, qui avait des bottines à ses jambes, et une cocarde à son chapeau; il était assez joli garçon, s'il n'avait pas eu le nez court ... j'ai encore sa pipe; ce garçon attendait qu'elle fût entièrement noire, pour la piler et la mettre en poussière; il disait que cela purgeait.

Progrès: l'art de la Perse antique est passé du non-figuratif au figuratif, en quelques siècles. En quelques siècles le roman français a appris (avait appris), en tâtonnant, à respecter la vraisemblance matérielle et morale, la cohérence temporelle, et à tenir compte du monde extérieur. Dans les premières décennies du XVIIe siècle, les objets réels composent un décor minutieusement décrit; à l'époque classique, le réel est saisi dans des instantanés significatifs d'un état d'âme; Marivaux sait très bien montrer le détail révélateur, mais chez lui la réalité est déjà, comme atmosphère plus que comme complexe de choses visibles, analogique des personnages, occasion pour eux de souffrance, de plaisir ou de curiosité – curiosité qu'il prête au lecteur lui-même. Elle n'est pas encore, comme elle le sera au XIXe siècle, l'ensemble des conditions qui déterminent le mode d'existence des personnages et leurs rapports, la gangue dans laquelle se matérialisent et s'aliènent l'identité, la liberté et la valeur des individus.

Où et quand Marivaux a-t-il appris à voir une cour de ferme, un chemin creux, les battages, la campagne en hiver, une cuisine dans un château de province, un paysan maîtrisant un jeune cheval? A-t-il couru les champs dans sa jeunesse à Riom et bavardé avec les paysans et les artisans des villages? La Limagne était encore marécageuse: il a pu contempler lui-même ce paysage d'étangs gelés et de chaumières que Brideron aperçoit de sa fenêtre, dans le bourg dont Pymion est seigneur. M. Gilot, G. Bonaccorso ont réuni quantité de détails sur la Monnaie de Riom, sur la gestion de Nicolas Carlet, sur l'appartement qu'il habitait, sur le collège des Oratoriens et sur les maîtres qui y enseignaient quand le jeune Pierre Carlet pouvait être leur élève; mais aucune preuve, aucun document ne nous assure que Pierre Carlet a suivi les cours de ce collège, rien de ce qui nous renseigne sur le père et sur le milieu riomois ne nous parle nommément du fils et de la façon dont il a vécu son enfance et son adolescence. Et quand nous le saurions, en quoi cette connaissance nous ferait-elle mieux comprendre ses écrits? La question est vieille maintenant de près d'un siècle et la réponse, depuis Proust au moins, est si accablante pour la curiosité biographique que l'on n'ose plus établir une relation entre un homme et une œuvre, sauf à la faire passer par toutes sortes de médiations qu'il n'est pas aisé de définir et dont il est encore plus malaisé de démonter le jeu d'actions réciproques.

Jean Giraudoux a fait remarquer que La Fontaine n'avait jamais pu observer de dragon à plusieurs têtes ou à plusieurs queues. Mais il avait tort d'en inférer qu'il n'avait sans doute pas mieux observé l'agneau, le bœuf, la colombe ou l'enterrement d'une fourmi. D'abord, la fable des dragons n'est pas ce que le fabuliste a écrit de plus vivement imaginé. Ensuite, il n'est pas besoin d'avoir beaucoup vu pour beaucoup faire voir, pas plus qu'il n'est besoin de beaucoup dire pour faire beaucoup entendre; mais il faut avoir vu assez pour que l'imagination (Marivaux eût dit: l'instinct) restitue dans toute sa force ce que d'autres ont eu devant les yeux sans l'apercevoir, et le leur révèle.

S'il n'avait pas lu Horace, Charles Sorel, Scarron, Boileau et quelques autres, Marivaux n'aurait pas décrit la réalité comme il la décrit. Il n'aurait pas eu l'idée de la décrire, il ne l'aurait même pas vue, bien qu'il l'ait eue devant les yeux à douze, à quinze ou à dix-huit ans. Puis il a fait de la littérature, et il faut admirer qu'il s'en soit débarrassé si vite, pour voir et faire voir sérieusement le réel dans le livre le plus plaisant qu'il ait écrit.

Le réalisme du *Télémaque travesti* emprunta trois voies. La vision: le narrateur dit ce qu'il a vu, ou ce que l'*on* voyait; la réalité se découpe ainsi en petites scènes expressives, en tableaux que parcourt le regard; ce sont parfois effectivement des tableaux, peints au-dessus d'une cheminée ou sur le bouclier de Brideron; les comparaisons: elles sont tirées du même domaine que la chose comparée, ou bien elles sont proverbiales; l'univers du *Télémaque travesti* se sert à lui-même de référence; la parole: l'auteur décrit parfois lui-même ('l'*on* voyait'), mais le plus souvent c'est un personnage qui parle, et l'univers du *Télémaque travesti* est ainsi saisi par le regard et rendu par les mots de ceux-mêmes qui l'habitent. Bel exemple d'autonomie du texte, dira-t-on, et d'illusion de vérité produite par la seule cohérence textuelle.

Flaubert était peut-être Emma Bovary, mais Marivaux n'est certainement pas Marianne. Aussi peut-il, au contraire de Flaubert, laisser le personnage parler à la première personne et donner à voir par l'élaboration de son discours personnel les difficultés et les ambiguïtés de la connaissance de soi, d'autrui, du monde social, connaissance qui passe inévitablement par le langage. Ce personnage qui parle est sans naissance, sans référence, et c'est une femme. G. Benrekassa a écrit là-dessus des pages pénétrantes (*Fables de la personne*); il discerne dans certains propos de Marianne sur la féminité quelque masculinité, mais subvertie. Après tout, dans une société où l'homme domine, la femme ne peut se penser elle-même qu'à partir de l'image que l'homme en a dessinée. Mais le mimétisme langagier est généralisée dans ce roman: Mme Dutour, Climal, le père Saint-Vincent, M. Villot, la prieure, l'abbesse parlent chacun leur langage, et le tout est enveloppé dans le langage extrêmement caractérisé de Marianne. Dans tous ces cas, le style suffit à faire entendre ce que l'analyse développe, quand Marivaux juge bon de le développer. Lui qui a fait la théorie du langage exact n'a pas fait celle du style imitatif. Il l'a supérieurement pratiqué dans *Le Télémaque travesti.*

Un écrivain qui condamne l'inexactitude du langage parce qu'elle est inexactitude de pensée peut-il être décrypté comme si ses mots ne livraient qu'un sens incomplet et obscurci, comme s'il parlait par allusions et sous-entendus, comme s'il ne savait pas ce qu'il dit ou ne disait pas ce qu'il sait?

'Lecteur, je ne veux pas vous tromper.' De cent façons différentes, Marivaux a fait si souvent répéter cette déclaration par ses porte-parole qu'autant vaudrait voir dans son œuvre un assemblage incohérent de formes graphiques que de ne pas croire à sa conviction. On l'a accusé de 'courir après l'esprit'. Il répond que son style particulier n'est pas une fantaisie de jongleur cherchant des unions bizarres de mots et des images incongrues; il est l'expression même de son esprit 'abandonné à son geste naturel': sa pensée serait trahie s'il la formulait autrement. Le langage est pour Marivaux un instrument si infaillible que le problème de l'expression semble ne pas se poser pour lui, et qu'il est fort irrité d'être attaqué sur son style. De la pensée aux mots, il n'y a pas d'intervalle; mal écrire, c'est mal penser, les mots disant toujours exactement ce que l'on veut dire; ils sont exactement au niveau de l'esprit comme le liquide est nécessairement au même niveau dans deux vases communicants: 'Un homme qui sait bien sa langue, qui sait tous les mots, tous les signes qui les composent, et la valeur précise de ces mots conjugués ou non, peut penser mal, mais exprimera toujours bien ses pensées'. Marivaux répond encore que penser, ce n'est pas arranger habilement des syllogismes, c'est appréhender la vérité telle qu'elle est. Vérité difficile à apercevoir, car il faut une intuition aiguë pour pénétrer dans les replis du cœur humain; mais vérité universelle.

La réalité psychologique que Marivaux veut formuler est si peu connue (d'abord) du commun des hommes, qu'il n'y a pas de mots usuels pour la désigner. Elle est réelle pourtant, il la sent, et tous les hommes peuvent la sentir à des degrés divers, pourvu qu'on la leur dénote. 'Nous n'avons des nouvelles un peu sûres de nous que par le sentiment', dit Marianne.

Le lecteur *innocent* est celui qui croit à la vérité littérale de ce qu'il lit. Mais le lecteur qui cherche aux mots un sens caché sous leur sens obvie et qui déduit du texte avoué un texte inavoué ou inavouable n'est pas un lecteur vicieux. C'est l'innocence qui fait ici la culpabilité. Elle donne l'illusion que les personnages d'un roman, leurs actions, leurs pensées, leurs émotions, le monde où ils figurent seraient l'image directement reflétée des gens que vous et moi connaissons ou que l'auteur a connus, de leurs actions, de leurs pensées, de leurs émotions et de leur monde. Il ne sait pas que ces personnages sont des êtres de papier; que tout ce que nous pouvons dire d'eux est dans les phrases du texte ou dans les implications de sa structure; que la critique, quelque subtilité qu'elle déploie, et elle ne s'en fait pas faute, ne peut que décrire le texte, sous peine de tomber dans la paraphrase narrative ou dans le psychologisme et le sociologisme *vulgaires.* Les écrivains aussi tombent dans cette illusion; nos romanciers récents ont appris à l'éviter et tiennent à cet égard leurs lecteurs dans une sécurité (ou une insécurité) parfaite. Mais l'illusion réaliste a été celles des romanciers du XIXᵉ siècle, de Balzac à Zola, de leurs grands prédécesseurs du XVIIIᵉ siècle et de quelques précurseurs *comiques* du XVIIᵉ. Elle est née le jour où un romancier a prétendu offrir à ses lecteurs ce que l'un d'eux a appelé *la vérité, l'âpre vérité.*

Cette prétention n'est pas *innocente:* naïve confiance dans la transparence du langage, croyance irraisonnée que la littérature serait un limpide miroir des êtres et des choses. Un lecteur qui n'est pas *innocent* a vite fait de démêler la mauvaise foi de cette candeur et d'énoncer en clair les préjugés et les conformismes auxquels le texte est asservi. Mais les illogismes du texte, les contradictions entre la proclamation *réaliste* d'une préface et l'irréalisme d'une fiction ne sont pas *innocents* non plus, et c'est une vive jouissance pour un lecteur non *innocent* que de faire sonner ces dissonances et d'entrer en complicité avec un auteur aussi peu *innocent* que lui.

La vérité du cœur humain occupe plus de place que celle du monde extérieur dans *Les Effets surprenants de la sympathie,* où l'on ne trouve pourtant encore qu'une promesse de la pénétrante finesse propre aux comédies et à *La Vie de Marianne.* Avec *Pharsamon* apparaissent les ambiguïtés de la conscience, la complexité des rapports de sentiment entre les personnages, d'une part, et de l'autre les réalités familières. Dans *Le Télémaque travesti* enfin la vigueur, le mouvement, le bariolage, les mille cocasseries du monde *réel*: Marivaux n'aura jamais une plus grande précision dans le regard ni un bonheur plus grand dans le langage. L'histoire de Marianne et celle de Jacob sont bien ancrées dans la société de l'époque et dans son cadre matériel, mais le romanesque y est presque tout intérieur. Le *moi* est une réalité encore, dont les métamorphoses, si elles peuvent être classées selon une grille de concepts de plus en plus affinés, ne sont finalement exprimées, comme événements singuliers, que

par des notations très concrètes que Marivaux refuse d'appeler métaphores.

L'éblouissement, l'ivresse, la stupeur, le pétillement, qu'ils viennent du
soleil ou de l'émotion amoureuse, du vin ou de la vanité, d'un coup de
massue ou du désespoir, de la chair rôtie au feu ou de l'allégresse, sont des
réalités senties, qu'on ne peut pas nommer autrement que par leur nom
propre, à moins de croire que la vie intérieure n'est qu'une métaphore des
sensations. Mais Marivaux n'écrit pas en géomètre. L'exactitude du
langage, qui est l'exactitude de l'idée, n'est pas donnée d'emblée ou n'est
pas d'emblée intelligible. Il faut y préparer par la surprise, le pathétique,
le rythme des phrases, les enchaînements hardis, les interpellations au
lecteur. Chez Marivaux, le langage poétique de la suggestion n'est pas le
dépassement du langage précis de la dénotation, la marche est inverse: les
formules de l'exactitude la plus directe et la plus serrée naissent de
l'abandon apparent à l'élan verbal.

'Marianne n'est point un auteur, c'est une femme qui pense.' Elle écrit
comme si elle conversait. Les longues lettres où elle raconte une partie de
sa vie à son amie ont été trouvées au fond d'une armoire, dans une maison
qui venait d'être vendue. L'éditeur n'a rien changé au manuscrit que le
nom de deux personnes et 'quelques endroits trop confus et trop négligés'.
Marivaux n'est ni le premier ni le dernier romancier qui ait présenté une
fiction comme une histoire authentique. Philip R. Stewart a inventorié ces
procédés. Mais on ne peut guère admettre que le lecteur en ait été dupe, et
le romancier ne cherchait pas à le duper. Vivienne Mylne, qui a étudié les
techniques de l'illusion, leur efficacité et leurs limites chez Marivaux, a
signalé la persistance des poncifs romanesques et les invraisemblances de
La Vie de Marianne et du *Paysan parvenu.* Les traits *réalistes,* par l'écart
même qui les sépare de ces conventions, ressortent plus hardis et plus
frappants. Toutes les affirmations d'authenticité, toutes les circonstances
alléguées pour expliquer la découverte d'un manuscrit, toutes les protesta-
tions de fidélité littérale ne sont que des signaux indiquant au lecteur qu'il
entre dans le pays de Romancie. Mais le pays de Romancie n'est pas plus
le pays du mensonge que l'invraisemblance n'est le contraire de la vérité.
La réalité n'entre dans les mots qu'à certaines conditions de forme et de
style. Sur ce point non plus, Marivaux ne veut pas tromper son lecteur.

'La bonne vieille histoire littéraire', disait R. Jakobson cité par J. P.
Faye (*Le Récit hunique*), 'ressemble à cette police qui, se proposant
d'arrêter quelqu'un, aurait saisi à tout hasard tout ce qu'elle aurait trouvé
dans la chambre, et même les gens qui passaient dans la rue'. Comparaison
n'est pas raison, et il n'y a pas lieu de réfuter une image dont R. Jakobson

et J. P. Faye savent combien le pouvoir d'explication est relatif. Mais, comme l'enseigne le Cliton de *Pharsamon,* 'quand on conte quelque chose, il faut y mettre la paille et le blé, et dire tout'. Voici donc la fin de l'histoire: la police ayant saisi choses et gens (disons que c'était à Paris), l'investigation des uns et l'interrogatoire des autres confirmèrent l'identité du criminel et firent comprendre les raisons et les circonstances de son acte; car il ne suffit pas de mettre en prison, il faut juger. Le même jour, sur une frontière du pays, un individu à qui l'on demandait ses papiers se crut découvert et avoua qu'il était le coupable; sur sa seule déclaration on l'arrêta, sans hésiter, et sans avoir encore la moindre information de l'enquête menée à Paris. Le même jour encore, bien loin de là, un misérable se livra à la police et s'accusa du crime, qu'il décrivit dans le plus menu détail. On dut le relâcher le lendemain, c'etait un fabulateur.

Mes amis, mes proches, les étrangers, n'importe quel humain qui vit ou qui a vécu, je ne les connais pas autrement que des personnages de fables. A partir d'indices limités, gestes ou paroles, mon imagination et mon expérience me les donnent à comprendre, et je déborde sans cesse leurs signes pour me faire d'eux une image intelligible, même dans ses contradictions, ses énigmes et son incomplétude. – Mais ils peuvent répondre à vos questions, réagir à vos actes? – Pas tous, pas toujours. Et qu'est-ce que cela change?

Le romancier décante, ordonne les données de l'expérience; il les fait entrer dans un ensemble imaginaire, clairement lisible ou difficile à interpréter. C'est sa façon d'être *réaliste*. Le sens qui résulte de son travail est complexe, libéré plus ou moins des contraintes idéologiques, au mieux s'appuyant sur elles pour les enfreindre. Mais tout ne fait pas sens dans un roman. Roland Barthes assignait un *effet de réel* aux détails concrets qui ne servent ni à l'intrigue, ni à l'explication des personnages: détails *insignifiants,* qui ne représentent qu'eux-mêmes, ou plutôt qui renvoient au monde réel, qui créent l'illusion d'une réalité extérieure, résistante, dont le roman tirerait sa légitimité. Il y a de ces détails chez Marivaux, mention rapide de personnages qu'on ne reverra plus (le chanoine de Sens, la dame qui accompagnait Climal chez Valville), scènes sans lien avec l'intrigue et sans conséquences (les deux dames en visite chez Mme de Miran). Mais au contraire des affirmations d'authenticité, qui sont des marques d'artifice et qui ne font pas illusion, ces détails font illusion parce qu'ils sont identiques à ceux dont nous composons l'image usuelle du monde où nous vivons effectivement. Nous ne parlerons pas comme R. Barthes d'*illusion référentielle,* mais de référence exacte et sérieuse. On peut penser avec Georges Benrekassa que ces *épisodes complètement allogènes* déséquilibrent l'affabulation et disloquent sa cohérence. Dans un autre contexte et par d'autres moyens, *Pharsamon* et *La Voiture embourbée, Le Télémaque travesti* lui-même, qui semblent continuer Scarron et Furetière, annoncent la manière critique dont Diderot inscrira la réalité dans le roman. On peut ajouter que les deux romans les plus importants de Marivaux sont inachevés, ce qui frappe d'ambiguïté l'*insignifiance* même des détails inutiles. Qui sait si nous n'aurions pas revu le chanoine de Sens, ou le 'cavalier de bonne mine, quoiqu'un peu âgé' qui donne la main à Mme de Miran lors d'une cérémonie au couvent (ce cavalier n'est pas l'officier 'd'un certain âge' qui proposera à Marianne de l'épouser, dans la VIIIe partie)? Certes, nous ne les aurions pas revus, puisque, comme j'ai essayé de le montrer ailleurs, l'inachèvement est un des traits les plus nécessaires de la structure de ces romans. Mais ce que Marivaux a voulu, c'est précisément que nous ne sachions pas si ...

L'inachèvement démontre avec la plus grande force qu'on peut dire beaucoup en ne disant rien. On ne peut le réduire à un sens simple, il en a plusieurs, tous justes: comme la musique instrumentale ou l'esquisse d'un tableau pour Diderot.

'Là où la vie entre dans la littérature, elle devient littérature elle-même', dit encore J. P. Faye, faisant une autre citation. C'est vrai sans doute, mais je dirais quant à moi ceci, qui me paraît vrai également: quand la vie entre dans la littérature, la littérature devient elle-même vie.

The Sieur de Villette's love-letters to Louise d'Aubigné*

Robert Dawson : University of Texas at Austin

A s Bernard Bray has so brilliantly shown,[1] there is a direct correlation between model love-letters, the 'secrétaires' of the sixteenth and seventeenth centuries in which they were published, and the birth of fiction in epistolary form. In a volume largely devoted to French fiction, it would perhaps not be inappropriate to present fact versus fiction in the form of a small collection of eight letters written by Benjamin de [or Le] Valois, sieur [also known as the marquis or seigneur] de Villette[2] to Louise-Artémise d'Aubigné, daughter of one of the most important and influential poets of the age. Aside from the historical interest of the letters, they possess a distinct literary value. Not the least of their attractions is that, in spite of their literary style, they are far from being the abstractions, of varying quality, found in the 'secrétaires' of the time, for they were actually sent.

Some historical background is in order. Théodore Agrippa d'Aubigné (1552-1630) and his first wife, Suzanne Lezay were married 6 June 1583. Part of her dowry comprised the domains of Surimeau and Mursay (sometimes written Murçai or Mursai) in Poitou. Five children were born of their union, two dying in infancy. The survivors were Marie, Louise-Artémise and the notorious Constant, later baron de Surimeau. Marie was married off to Josué de Caumont, sieur d'Ade (or d'Adou), and Constant, from his second wife, Jeanne de Cardilhac, had two children, Charles and Françoise. The latter was later to become Mme Scarron, then mistress to the King of France and Mme de Maintenon.

* I would like to thank the University Research Institute of the University of Texas and the National Endowment for the Humanities for support without which this study could not have been completed. I am also grateful to Annie Angrémy for her kindness in replying with considerable detail to my queries concerning manuscripts in the Bibliothèque Nationale and to Marie-Hélène Tesnière for introducing me to the fermesse.

Of his three children, Agrippa seems to have preferred Louise, developing a special relationship with her and her husband, Benjamin. D'Aubigné tenderly addressed his daughter as 'ma fillette', signed his letters as 'votre bon père' and inserted such loving messages as 'je serais bien aise de voir vostre doux maytre et vous, pour vous faire gouster la douceur que Dieu donne à ma vieillesse'.[3] It was Louise and Benjamin who were to take in Charles and Françoise, their nephew and niece. (As the reader might recollect, the future marquise de Maintenon was born in prison.) Raised by her aunt and uncle, she would forever retain the warmest memories of the couple she considered her parents.

As for the author of the letters in question, Benjamin de Villette was an excellent husband and father, a man who was to distinguish himself in the service of his father-in-law and even that of the King of France, as numerous epistles attest. (See, for example, Agrippa d'Aubigné's letters to the King, *Œuvres complètes,* II.689, 695-96.) The sieur de Villette died 3 August 1661, aged 79, in the dawn of the personal reign of the Sun-King (information derived from A. Briquet, 'Commentaire sur une pièce autographe et signée de Mme de Maintenon' in *Bulletin du bibliophile et du bibliothécaire,* 1860, pp. [1501]-1519).

Most of the letters that have survived by de Villette concern business or politics. Those interested in pursuing this avenue of research might begin with the Clairambault collection in the Bibliothèque Nationale (e.g. Clair. 1166, ff. 11-18, 23, 24, 27-28, 60-61, etc., dated for the most part from 1616 to 1620). That part of his correspondence has above all an historical value. The letters presented here show a very different side of the coin. They reflect a tranquil love-story, one beset by no discernible difficulties. The two lovers eventually obtained the consent of their relatives, married, and lived happily ever after, one assumes as harmoniously as circumstances warranted! The marriage contract was signed 22 October 1610 in the presence of Constant and Marie (Garnier, III.29).

As can be seen by the addressee's name and quality, the letters which follow were written before the happy event and can thus be dated before the autumn of 1610, and probably to within *c.* 1607 and 1610. Now, how is it possible to put forth such an assertion when none of the letters bears a year? The beginning date is partly based on the fact that one of the letters, 'Chère mignonne, Je ne te parlerai point de notre séparation...' (No. VIII), was written on a sheet of paper manufactured in London which, thanks to the watermark, can be dated to 1607.[4] It would appear doubtful, too, that our lovers would have been in correspondence for much more than three or four years before their wedding. And, as mentioned, all the letters predate that event.

The literary value of these eight letters resides in the harmonious elegance of their baroque style in which it is not difficult to perceive that the writer, in spite of his effusions, is completely in control, master of word and situation. In each of the missives, the epistolarian develops one or two images in a sort of 'précieux' style, but one that is far from aping the insipidness and ridiculous exaggeration of letters inserted in, for example, Jean Puget de La Serre's *Secrétaire à la mode, ou méthode facile d'escrire selon le temps diverses lettres de compliment, amoureuses et morales* (1641) or Claude Jaunin's *Compliments de la langve françoise. Œuvre très-utile et nécessaire à ceux qui sont à la Cour des grands, et qui font profession de hanter les compagnies* (1630; title from the 1645 edition).

In love with the favourite daughter of one of the greatest literary geniuses of the time, it is hardly surprising that Benjamin de Villette would have taken considerable pains over his correspondence. It is also evident that he was a solidly educated man, and might well have read and appreciated Girolamo Parabosco's *Lettere amorose;*[5] Etienne Pasquier's *Lettres amoureuses* (1555); Nathanaël Adam's *Secrétaire français* (1585); the anonymous *Lettres douces* (1589),[6] or any one of several other collections of the time, in French or Italian, containing model love-letters. My goal here is not to ascribe possible sources to this packet of personal letters which have lain hidden away for nearly four hundred years. However, after having read through about a dozen of those 'secrétaires', I was above all struck by the elegance and beauty of de Villette's letters, an individuality and sensibility so foreign to the formulae and clichés found in ordinary 'modèles de lettres d'amour'.

In Benjamin Le Valois's love-letters, there is an impassioned enthusiasm of style without the epistolarian's ever falling into the errors of confusion or pedantic exaggeration. We have here a set of letters which, although they burn with the flames of love, are also meant to speak to the addressee's mind. A dialectics of love is expressed: the lover is a logician and seems to think that the object of his passion is, too. It is true that Agrippa d'Aubigné's daughters received an education well beyond that accorded most women of the age. Witness d'Aubigné's memoirs addressed to all three of his children, male and female alike. The beginning is revelatory: 'Mes enfans, vous avez de l'antiquité de quoy puiser les vies des Empereurs [in Latin] et des Grands exemples et enseignements . . .' (*Sa vie à ses enfants* in *Œuvres complètes,* I.[3]; see too Garnier, II.162-68).

Thus it is likely that Louise was appreciative of her lover's efforts. It is regrettable that none of her replies have come down to us.

A brief discussion of the seventh letter in the series, a particularly interesting one, can serve for the rest. Addressed to his 'chère mymy', Benjamin implores Louise's favour while developing a series of Petrarchan metaphors: night is opposed to day, and the obscurity of the falling evening parallels the distance separating our two lovers. As his mistress grows ever distant, the lover finds himself surrounded by the ever-thickening shadows of darkness until they totally obscure his vision. Louise carries with her all-benevolent light; the now blind lover has lost 'l'horison de ses plaisirs'. The disappearance of his diurnal star (Louise) has plunged him into the horrors of an emotional night.

The meaning of the entire letter is simple enough: de Villette is asking for a reply, for some reassurance from his mistress. It is the way the request is worded that is remarkable. Since the light has disappeared with Louise, her lover is tormented by a newly inflicted cecity. She retains the power of piercing the shadows of darkness by her 'conseil familier'. A letter would function as a guide; her very words would constitute the flaming torches of hope. Just as the firmament consoles the world with stars after the sun has set, so would a letter from his beloved return at least a portion of his sight: 'Imite donc le soleil', he begs. Benjamin might find some solace from words metamorphosed into the sparkling suns of night. The letter gallantly ends with her lover assuring Louise that a letter might shed light on his dark world, but could not rekindle the flames of his passion, for those would only cease with his life.

Although there are few concrete details given in the letters, for we are travelling in an ethereal realm of love, every now and then there is an echo of the outside world. By No. III we learn Constant d'Aubigné himself was to deliver the missive, but the way that fact is expressed virtually renders it an abstraction: 'Monsieur Constant, favorisant ma constance, veut bien en conduire vers vous quelque témoignage'. That is all we hear of Louise's brother. In the next letter, de Villette indicates the messanger is an old man who remains the only link with the outside world, exception made of the realm of letter-writing and passion, that is: 'Je cherche entre les mouvements plus réglés de ma passion de quoi charger les pas tardifs de ce vieillard qui s'en va vers vous, mais je n'y trouve point de commission à donner à une allure si lente'. In the fifth letter, the epistolarian indicates that Louise's travels will carry her through 'le péril des eaux et les incomodités de la terre'. Nonetheless he retains his personal courier and intends himself to reach the object of his affections in a few days, leaving the interesting possibility that Benjamin delivered his own letter! The last missive finds de Villette wandering through some 'pays où tu eusses pu craindre' with no indication of where, or really what it is.

The world of cities and towns, of carriages, daily preoccupations and external, interpersonal relationships is replaced by that of the heart and mind. There are no details concerning any possible physical manifestations of the marquis de Villette's love for Louise. Yet in a clear and precise fashion, his love-letters translate into prose what the metaphysical and 'precious' baroque poets of the age expressed in their verse, what Herbert Grierson has termed that 'peculiar blend of passion and thought, feeling and ratiocination which is their greatest achievement' (*Metaphysical lyrics and poems of the seventeenth century, Donne to Butler, selected and edited with an essay,* Oxford, Oxford U.P., 1958, p. xvi).

In commenting on Grierson's interpretation, Odette de Mourgues re-emphasizes that the poetical and stylistic fusion of passion and intellect, heart and mind is scarcely due to chance: it is 'a perfect poise between the play of intellect and the depth of passion' (*Metaphysical, baroque and précieux poetry,* Oxford: The Clarendon Press, 1953, p. 7). Such is also the case with our epistolarian, metaphysical prose-writer, impassioned poet by his subtle marriage of hyperbole and control, by the submersion of the heart to the dialectics of love.

The Letters

The eight epistles form a small packet of damp-stained sheets, pierced hither and thither by holes due to the ravages of time. Some have been folded and refolded so many times that they are about to fall apart. Perhaps Louise was the guilty party; at least it would be romantic to think so. But the letters, like a woman who retains her beauty in the autumn of life, have lost none of their appeal. Most have gilt edges, and the wax seals still retain traces of the silk ribbons which tied the finished products. Flourishes have been used to justify the margins, and the handwriting is of a clarity and elegance truly pleasing to the eye. (The marks de Villette used to justify the lines are given here as two dashes.)

Benjamin took the trouble to beautify the presentation of his texts with decorations at the beginning, in the text, and sometimes after the salutation, or embracing his signature. This is a special kind of symbol, called an 'S-barré' or 'fermesse' (masculine or feminine) in French, forming a large s-shaped character pierced through the middle from top to bottom with an arrow, in this case pointing down. (I am adopting the term 'fermesse' into the English language.) Originally it was associated with love. Hobson gives three, generalized possible interpretations: 'Sanctus, Spiritu'; 'Souverain'; 'Souveigné vous de moi'. These are associated with fidelity: 'c'est surtout dans la seconde moitié du xvie siècle que l'*S* fermé comme symbole de fidélité semble avoir connu une certaine faveur chez nous au sein d'un milieu aristocratique et cultivé' (p. 68). It was used within this context by, for example, Henri IV and Louis XIII. And the design-source would be the gothic 'S'.[7] In an article published in the *Intermédiaire des chercheurs* ('La Reliure à l'S barré', 1888, XXI.297-99), Léon Gruel disagrees with G. de Chanciot in *Le Livre* that the fermesse was a decoration so frequently used it came to lose any special significance. He sees it as an 'S' cut into two, forming two identical halves joined by a line, a symbol of 'l'union éternelle'. The fermesse is often found on old prayer and mourning book-covers, and Gruel provides a most interesting example.

Bypassing a few other articles in the same periodical, we come to a note by one 'C. P. V.' who remarks that sixteenth-century letter seals often had the initials struck through with a line like that used in the 'S-barré', any sort of letter, 'ce fait que je constate chaque jour au dépouillement d'une correspondance commerciale de ce temps' (1888, XXI.335; for further information yet, see J. Adrien Blanchet, 'La Reliure à l'S barré', *Intermédiaire,* 1888, XXI.496-97).

Within the context of his love-letters, de Villette seems quite obviously to associate the symbol with his passion which would logically have included the concept of fidelity, union – and much more! But, after having read other holograph letters by our correspondent, I can only conclude that he used the fermesse in various ways: in a special way for Louise, and in a more rhetorical fashion later on, when writing, for example, to Pontchartrain. However, considering the close relationship between the two men, it was surely a symbol associated with friendship, as he ends: 'Vostre tres humble & affectioné / Serviteur [space] de Villette .$. [with another fermesse below]' (letter dated 3 April 1616, BN ms Clair.1166, f. 11-12). There are many other such examples, and examples, too, of letters with no fermesses.

Finally it might be noted that the same kind of ornament is to be found in the manuscript containing Pontus de Tyard's *Modèles de lettres d'amour* (Lapp ed., op. cit., facsimile reproduction p. [36], fig. 4; at the end of the penultimate letter). The fermesses are transcribed in this text as a dollar-sign, which they vaguely resemble in the original.

That Benjamin took considerable trouble to compose his letters to Louise d'Aubigné is borne witness by the occasional inserted word, indicating he probably carefully copied out the letters, but occasionally made a mistake. As further proof, in one case he inadvertently copied two words twice: 'Vous ne vous ne vous / ennuirez point . . .' (No. II). In another case, he employed a deliberate stratagem. The letter in which he states: 'Je vous donne cette page brouillée pour la carte blanche de ma vie . . .' (No. IV) is indeed 'brouillée', without a doubt on purpose.

His signature, where it consists of an initial, forms two capital 'V's entwined (transcribed here as double capital Vs), which are also to be found in other letters, for example, in a letter to Pontchartrain (BN ms Clair.1166, f. 18). The 'double-V' or 'deux-V' is a sort of visual anagram, or logogram if you will: the marquis most often signed himself 'de Villette' and the homonym formed by 'deux-V' and 'de V' in French requires no explanation.

The letters have been placed in what I believe is the most probable, chronological order. Since none of them bears a year indicator, the only evidence is circumstantial, based on the texts themselves. There is a progression in the lovers' affair marked not only by the move from the 'vous' to the 'tu' but by the evolution of a man who is somewhat uncertain about the feelings of his beloved to one who eventually evinces no doubt.

As far as the text is concerned, all the vagaries of the spelling and punctuation have been carefully transcribed. Sometimes it has been necessary to opt for an upper- or lower-case letter, for the epistolarian is very casual about differentiating between the two. Little attention was also paid to punctuation, and I have interpreted as a full stop the frequent use made of 'swash-periods' resembling commas. In one case, I have transcribed a punctuation mark as a comma although de Villette might have intended a period, for the precise meaning is dependent on how the mark is interpreted: 'Je pense avoir passé le pays où tu eusses pu craindre pour moi. Je n'y ai trouvé de difficulté . . .' or 'Je pense avoir passé le pays où tu eusses pu craindre[.] Pour moi, je n'y ai trouvé de difficulté . . .' (No. VIII). Those interested in spelling styles of the period, aside from some specialized studies, would do well to consult Charles Beaulieux's basic work, *Histoire de l'orthographe française* (2 vols, Paris: Champion, 1927). For the language, see Ferdinand Brunot (compiled by Charles Bruneau), *Histoire de la langue française des origines à nos jours*, II: *Le XVIᵉ siècle*, bibliography and additional notes by Hélène Naïs (Paris: Λ. Colin, 1967); III: *La Formation de la langue classique, 1600-1660*, bibliography by Roger Lathuillère (Paris, 1966).

Each letter is followed by a brief physical description: size, watermarks, seals, and so on. Lineation is also given to help the reader capture the flavour of the originals.

Brackets indicate that something is missing, for sometimes a letter or two has been obliterated.

No. I

\$ \$

Sy cest a ma perte ou a mon salut que Vous / consentez par vr̃e silence, Je n'en puis Juger / q̃ par vr̃e Jugement \$ Ma Chere Maitresse. / vous estes trop sage pour perdre ce quy / est a vous & trop Juste pour ne sauver / pas ce quy vous adore auec tant de devotion / pourveu que vr̃e main ne me soit chiche / que par bienseance Je souffriray auec patience / La necessité de voz faueurs, car J'ayme beaucoup / mieux ṽre gloire q̃ mon contentement permetez / moy d'imputer a La seuerité des Loix de vr̃e / sexe ce que vous ne respondez [point: added above the line with a caret indicator] a mes suplications / en ce faizant J'honoreray tout ensemble vr̃e / sagesse & vr̃e bon naturel, La ou au contraire / J'offencerois L'un & L'autre en L'attribuant au / mespris. Croyez \$ ma belle \$ q̃ je n'interpreteray / Jamais rien a mon auantage quy ne soit / premierement au vr̃e & que sy je tasche de / tirer ma vie de vostre douceur & de La / conseruer par vr̃e grace Cest pour vous La / rendre toute entiere en deuoirs, & services / tres humbles cõe

Vr̃e seruiteur

Ce 17 Auril

devillette.

The address: 'A Mademoiselle / Mademoiselle de Murçay [\$?]'.
Description: 1 p. in-8vo; two seals of black wax with silk strands; the watermark, only partially present, is indecipherable; 21.875 × 16.1 cm; gilt edges.

No. II

\$ \$

Chere \$ Maitresse \$

La passion m'arrache encor cecy En me / persuadant qu'on ne peut trop souuent prier / ce qu'on doit adorer vous ne vous ne vous [sic] / ennuyrez point de me[z] veux sy vous estes aussy / encline au bien que Capable de le faire. \$ / Belle M'amour quand vous verrez toutes / ces lignes nayez esgard qu'a l'intention, Encore / quelles soyent trop frequentes Elles ne doyuent / pas estre Jmportunes. La main Les tire du / cœur quy Les donne en Crainte & ne les a / Laysse presque aller qu'afin q̃ Cette crainte / ne vous soit point chachee. passez Les yeux / sur

L'importunite arrestez Les sur sa cauze / mais non, voyez bien tout & vous / aymerez tout de

> Vostre serviteur

Ce 24 Auril

> De villette

The address: 'A Mademoiselle / Mademoiselle de Murçay'.
Description: 1 p. in-4to; two seals of black wax with silk strands; the watermark consists of a bunch of grapes in nine rows, with a stalk and initials [IR?] at the bottom (not in Briquet or Heawood); 28.125 × 22.2 cm; gilt edges.

No. III

$ $

Ma Chere Maitresse $

 monsieur Constant favorizant ma constance / veut bien en conduyre vers vous quelque tesmoingnage / Je rends celuy cy comme tesmoin en ma propre / cauze, mais cest en Vous faizant Juge en La – / vr̃e & vous reconnoissant souueraine sur Le tout / de vous & de moy $ Jugez donc Justement / Ma Belle $ & soyez certaine que Je ne – / m'attribueray Jamais rien q̃ pour vous dessirer / dauantage. Ce Veu nouueau en La parolle / & Vieil dedans mon Cœur, me permet de Vous / dire & vous enjoint de croyre, quil n'y peut / rien avoir au monde plus parfait q̃ Mon amour. / Je mets a part Vr̃e merite. Mon amour le / respecte comme son pere & comme enfant bien / apris ne fait point de comparaizon auec Luy, Jl / tasche seulement de sy rendre comparable & – / Jncomparable a tout autre. Sil a quel- que – / familiarite c'est auec sa mere quy est mon / Jnclination au Sein de Laquelle Jl verse souuent / des Larmes pour vr̃e eslongnement En luy reprochant / qu'elle ne La mis au monde que pour souffrir. Elle / pour L'appaizer Le met entre Les bras de L'Esperance / quy Luy promet d'heureux changements, Luy cependant / Jure de ne changer Jamais & veut que ma main / vous en donne encore ce gage en Vous asseurant / que Je seray toute ma Vie

> Vostre seruiteur

Ma chere Maitresse $

> De Villette

The address: 'A Mademoiselle / Mademoiselle de Murçay'.
Description: 1 p. in-folio; two seals of black wax with silk strands; the watermark seems to be the same for letter No. II; 33.2 × 22.2 cm; gilt edges.

No. IV

Ma belle Maitresse

Je cherche entre Les mouuements plus reglez de ma / passion de quoy charger les pas tardifs de ce vieillard / quy s'en va vers vous mais Je n'y trouue point de – / comission a donner a vne allure sy lente. toutefois / par ce q̃ La bonté le conduit tousiours Jay creu qu'enfin / Jl aura ce bonheur de voir la beauté & n'ay pas voulu / q̃ ce fust sans luy porter quelque offrande de ma – / part, receuez La Ma chere m'amour, cõe La plus belle / du monde du plus fidelle quy viue Cest moy quy – / vous L'adresse par cette main Caduque voizine du / trespas pour vous monstrer q̃ dans le trespas mesme / Je chercherois les moyens de vous honorer, Encor que / vous ne voÿiez icy que du papier & de L'ancre ne Le / negligez point, cest La plus digne conception de mon ame / & La derniere & plus forte resolution q̃ Je prendray / Jamais, dont vous pourrez uzer souuerainement & / tout ainsy quil vous playra Car Je vous donne / cette page brouillee pour La Carte blanche de ma / vie mettez y telles loix & telles conditions que – / vous voudrez vous y trouuerez tousiours mon nom / au dessous pour vous asseurer q̃ Je suis & veux / estre obligé d'Estre entierement a vous & pour Jamais

DE VILLETTE $

Ce 26ᵉ Auril

The address: 'A Mademoiselle / Mademoiselle de Murçay'.
Description: 1 p. in-folio; no watermark; two seals of red wax; 33.2 × 22.5 cm; gilt edges.

No. V

$

Ma chere Maitresse $

depuis La triste matinée que Je vous Laissay, le plus / dezolé homme du monde, Je n'ay point eu de bien / & n'en auray point que Je ne scache L'yssue de vr̃e / veage. Jay tousiours eu deuant les yeux Le peril / des eaux & Les Jncomoditez de La terre que vous / aurez a passer. J'ay prié dieu de tout mon cœur / pour vr̃e conseruation. Jl est vray que vous ne m'en / scaurez point de gré, La mienne estant attachée a / la vr̃e. J'estois prest de faire partir hõe expres / quy me tirasse de peyne a son retour en me raportant / de voz bonnes nouuelles. toutefois cette occazion – / s'estant présentée, Jay retenu mon messager – / particulier, pour quelques Jours encor, afin d'en / auoir deux foix pour vne, en attendant que J'aille / moy mesme en apprendre sur Le Lieu. Jugez sy cette / heure me doit tarder, $ mon tout $ car vr̃e seule / veuë est ma seule Vie. Jl ma esté ordonne Jcy vn / certain temps quy me dure fort. Jay peur quil / m'eschapera de L'abreger Je L'eusse desia fait mais / Je craingnois de n'en estre pas sy bien venu. Jl / faut desplaire le moins qv'on peut a ceux a quy on / veut obeir, en ce sejour que Je fay a cette heure / Jcy mon deuoir & mon amour ont desia fort combatu / L'amour

cest tousjours trouué Le Vainqueur mais / Jl fait courtaizie a Lautre en me
Laissant entre ses / mains Jusques a ce que j'en parle par sa permission / ce q̃
Jespere bien tost, car ces deux quy ailleurs / sont com̃unement ennemis s'accorde-
ront ayzement / en ce fait. Jls ne sont plus en debat que du temps / & veulent
absolument que Je vous ayme & vous / serue de tout mon Cœur, ce que Je feray
toute ma / vie brefue ou Longue. Adieu donc \$ ma chere maitresse \$ / souuenez
vous de

Vr̃e petit seruiteur tres
humble & tres fidelle DE Villette

ce 23 Januier.

The address: 'A Mademoiselle / Mademoiselle de Murçay'.
Description: 1 p. in-folio; no watermark; two seals of red wax with silk strands; 32.85 ×
22.3 cm; traces of gilt on the edges.

No. VI

\$ \$

Ma chere Maitresse

Sy Je ne vous escry a toutes les heures que Je Le dezire / cest a toutes Les
occaisons que Je Le puis, sy vous vous / souueniez aussy souuent de mes affections
q̃ moy de / voz perfections Jl ny a point de moment quy ne nous fust / vne
obligation reciproque car bien que tout vous soit deu – / on ne peut faire ce que Je
fay sans meriter que dy-ce fair[e] / cest souffrir seuelement, mais auec telle
constance & tel zele / quil ny a point d'action sy vertueuse quy esgale cette vertu
/ La principale gloire des beautez est d'estre parfaitement aymees / sy vous en estes
aussy dezireuse que digne ouvrez Les yeux / pour voir La verité que Jescry Jcy
estant a La gehenne de / vr̃e absence, sy vous m'objettez que je vous en ay dit
[autant: added above the line with a caret] autrefois / sans question. sachez que ce
n'estoit pas sans contrainte / puisque Je voyois que ce discours ne vous estoit pas
agreable / comme Jl le devoit estre & que J'eusse voulu souuent – / estoufer ma
parole & ma vie mesme pour ne vous point / Jmportuner sil n'y eust eu que de
mon Jnterest, mais / Le vr̃e m'estant plus cher sans comparaizon me faisoit passer
/ vr̃e gré pour sacrificr a voz graces plus belles que bonnes / Jusques Jcy pour moy.
sy elles ne se peuuent rendre / propices par Veux & par Larmes elles courent
fortune / destre souillees de sang ou pour Le moins accuzees de / celuy que Je leur
espandray par quelque accident – / fauorable a vn malheureux quy peut estre en
changeant / d'estre & de nom Leur donnera pour Jamais Celuy / d'ingratitudes,
Emportant dans le tombeau L'Estre & layssant dessus, pour reproche Eternelle ã
vous & pour / Jnscription glorieuse a Luy, Le nom de

VOSTRE SERUITEUR
\$ VV \$

The address: 'A Mademoiselle / Mademoiselle de Murçaiz'.

Description: 1 p. in-folio; the watermark seems to be the same as for No. II; two seals of black wax with silk strands; 38.15 × 22.35 cm; gilt edges.

No. VII

$ $

Chere Mymy

Je suis assez eslongne pour me plaindre / puisque Je Le suis assez pour souffrir & / puisque J'ay perdu Lorizon de mes plaisirs / non seulement en Cessant de te voir mais / des aussy tost q̃ tu eus destourné tes yeux / de dessus moy. ayes donc pitié de moy / cõe d'vn aueugle non point faute / d'yeux mais faute de Lumiere, & / fay qu'en cette nuit J'aye pour guyde / ton conseil familier, puisque La Veuë – / m'est Jnutile toutefoys tu La rapeleras / a quelque partie de son office sy en / cette obscurité tu me fais promptem̃ / & souuent paroistre tes paroles q̃ je / prendray pour flambeaux nocturnes / Ainsy q̃ Les Astres au deffaut du / Soleil, Jmite donc Le Soleil aussy / [bien: added in margin] en ta faueur qu'en ton naturel quy / esclayre eschaufe & atire & quoy q̃ mon / deuoir face violence a cette derniere – / Vertu n'en desdaignes le soin de ma / vie mais remarque Cõe Jl ne se cache / Jamais a noz yeux qu'il ne nous / donne d'autre [sic] Luminaires en mesme / temps haste ces estincelles q̃ J'atens / pour rallumer la Clarté & non Les feux / quy brusleront Jusques au tombeau

Ton Serviteur

§ VV $

The address: 'A Mademoiselle / Mademoiselle de Murçay'.
Description: 1 p. & 1/2 in-8vo; no watermark; two seals of red wax; 21.95 × 15.8 cm; gilt edges.

No. VIII

Chere Mignonne $ Je ne te parleray point / de nr̃e separation ny des tristesses quelle me cauze / Je croy q̃ ton cœur t'en dit ce q̃ j'en sens. Je pense / auoir passé le pays ou tu eusses peu Craindre – / pour moy, Je n'y ay trouué de difficulte qu'a / combatre Le soin & La courtaizie en autrui & / ton absence en moy. Je suis bien a plaindre / pour le long chemin q̃ Jay affayre en La compaignie / de ce dernier ennemy. car pour toutes les autres / Jncomoditez Je ne Les conte q̃ comme deues a La / fin de mon martire q̃ j'espere a ce coup – / Terminer a ton contentement & au mien quy / ne seront Jamais qu'vn, anonce moy les douceurs / de cette vie deziree en m'escriuant comme tu / scais comme du dois, & q̃ Je trouue a paris des / consolations de ta main & des memoyres de / tout Ce q̃ tu voudras q̃ je face n'ayë soin q̃ de ta / santé & rien en L'esprit q̃ de La Joye afin de / fayre Viure en toy celuy qui meurt en soy / mesme pour estre trop, non selon son merite / mais selon son sentiment

Ton serviteur

$ VV $

The address: 'A Mademoiselle / Mademoiselle de Murçay'.
Description: 1 p. in-folio; watermark according to Heawood for London, 1607 (see the introduction); two seals of red wax; 34.8 × 23.35 cm; edges not gilt.

Notes

[1] *L'art de la lettre amoureuse: des manuels aux romans, 1550-1700* (Paris, La Haye: Mouton, 1967). The interested reader should also consult the introduction and notes to John C. Lapp, *Modèles de phrases, suivi d'un recueil de modèles de lettres d'amour,* both probably by Pontus de Tyard (University of North Carolina Studies in the Romance Languages and Literatures, LXX, Chapel Hill, 1967). Laurent Versini, in *Laclos et la tradition: essai sur les sources et la technique des 'Liaisons dangereuses'* (Paris: Klincksieck, 1968), gives an overview of the epistolary tradition (pp. 231-42 *et passim*).

[2] The letters are in my collection. As for the author, in Louis-Pierre d'Hozier and d'Hozier de Sérigny's *Armorial général, ou registres de la noblesse de France,* we find listed 'Benjamin le Valois Ecuyer, seigneur de Villette' as 'Ecuyer de la Petite Ecurie du Roi, Maître d'Hôtel ordinaire de Sa Majesté' (3 November 1638), later 'Conseiller en son Conseil d'Etat et Privé' (11 January 1643); in the first 'registre', second part (Paris 1788; reprt. Paris 1865). Benjamin was the son of Louis le Valois, 'écuyer', 'seigneur d'Escoville' and of Catherine Bourdin. His parents were married 14 February 1560. Catherine was herself the daughter of 'maître' Jean Bourdin, seigneur de Villette, which is presumably the origin of the title borne by the grandson (Hozier, pp. 598-600). For the record, the Villette family described in a sort of crude geneology in BN, ms Duchesne 6, f. 144, although dealing roughly with the same period which concerns us here, would seem to have nothing to do with Benjamin's. Those interested in the d'Aubigné family will want to consult Armand Garnier's excellent thesis, *Agrippa d'Aubigné et le parti protestant: contribution à l'histoire de la réforme en France,* 3 vols (Paris: Fischbacher, 1928).

[3] *Œuvres complètes,* Eugène Réaume and F. de Caussade eds (Paris: A. Lemerre, 1873-92); I.565, letter to Mme de Villette, 8 March 1622; p. 567, to the sieur de Villette, 21 June 1626; p. 575, to Mme de Villette, 9 August [1627?].

[4] It is the same reproduced in Edward Heawood, *Watermarks mainly of the seventeenth and eighteenth centuries,* vol. I of *Monumenta chartae papyraceae historiam illustrantia, sive / or Collection of works and documents illustrating the history of paper* (E. J. Labarre, general ed., Hilversum: Paper Publications Soc., 1950, pl. 298, p. 112, no. 2131).

[5] This work was several times republished in the sixteenth century; according to my copy of an early seventeenth-century edition, conveniently dated to 1607: *Quattro libri delle lettere amorose ... di nvovo ordinatamente accomodate, ampliate, & ricorrette per Thomaso Porcacchi,* Venetia, Girolamo Polo.

[6] Because of its rarity, further information is in order. (I appear to have the only copy of the first edition and could not find it listed in any source dealing with sixteenth-century French literature.) The collection contains one hundred and thirteen numbered letters and

'billets' which rise above the ordinary by style and content. The full title is: *Lettres. Douces pleines de desirs et imaginations d'Amour.* [extensive engraved device] A Paris, Chez Abel l'Angelier au premier pillier de la grande Salle du Palais. [rule] 1589. Auec Priuilege. 150 numbered ff., in-12. The privilege, to Abel L'Angelier, is dated 9 December 1588 (signed 'Gogier'). My thanks go to Dominique Coq of the Réserve, BN, for being so kind as to check the Philippe Renouard manuscript bibliography; in course of publication.

The book was re-edited in 1593, bearing an imprint for Tours, 'Par Clavde de Montr'œil, & Iean Richer'. The only known copy is in the BL (10909.a.23). The date is given as 'M D LXCIII.' which has led bibliographers and the compilers of the BL catalogue erroneously to suppose a seventeenth-century printing. I hope to edit a critical edition of this work which will contain more information than it is possible to give here.

[7] Geoffrey D. Hobson, *Les Reliures à la fanfare et le problème de l'S fermé,* 2ᵉ éd. aug. par Anthony R. A. Hobson (Amsterdam: G. T. van Heusden, 1970). A more recent, and equally interesting study is Claude Dulong, 'Les Signes cryptiques dans la correspondance d'Anne d'Autriche avec Mazarin: contribution à l'emblématique du XVIIᵉ siècle', in *Bibliothèque de l'Ecole des chartes: revue d'érudition publiée par la Société de l'Ecole des chartes* (1982), CXL. [59]-83; especially pp. 67-83. Further information can be gleaned from various articles published in the nineteenth century in the *Intermédiaire des chercheurs et curieux,* some of which are cited here.

The use and abuse of history:
Victor Hugo and *L'Homme qui rit*

Robert Gibson : University of Kent

W H I L E we would doubtless need some time choosing the *worst* novel in French written by a distinguished author,[1] agreement over what is the most bizarre would be much more readily forthcoming. Both its detractors and its defenders are unanimous that it is Victor Hugo's *L'Homme qui rit*. For George Saintsbury, who was determined to bury and not to praise it, it was 'probably the maddest book in recognized literature; certainly the maddest written by an author of supreme genius without the faintest notion that he was making himself ridiculous'.[2] For Pierre Albouy who, in recent years, has played a leading part in disinterring it and elevating it to a position of unwonted eminence, '*L'Homme qui rit* est sans doute le plus *fou* des romans de Hugo. Histoire d'un monstre, il se devait d'être lui-même tératologique'.[3] Much the same could be said of most of the criticism devoted to the novel over the past hundred years or so: the calibre of the writing has matched the nature of the subject and in the course of this article, I propose to review that writing and to consider some of the issues I think it raises.

The sheer dottiness of *L'Homme qui rit* can most readily be conveyed by a brief outline of the plot. The setting is supposed to be the England of Queen Anne but the most momentous single event of the whole novel has taken place before it begins. James II has already enlisted the services of the *comprachicos,* a cosmopolitan bunch of desperadoes whose stock-in-trade is the abducting and mutilating of children. Their victim on this occasion is the rightful heir of Linnaeus, Earl of Clancharlie (and Baron Hunkerville) whose republican sympathies have kept him defiantly in exile in Switzerland. James II is so incensed at this that he puts the *comprachicos* to work. The victim who is called (presumably by the *comprachicos*?) Gwynplaine is so brutally mutilated that his features remain

locked in a permanent grin (hence the title of the novel). When William of
Orange outlaws the *comprachicos,* they abandon Gwynplaine, now aged
ten, in a snowstorm at Portland Bill. They then put out to sea and are all
drowned, just after they have cast overboard a sealed bottle containing a
full account of their crime. Gwynplaine makes his way through the storm,
encounters first the corpse of a man hanging from a gibbet and then the
corpse of a young mother with a new-born blind baby girl beside her. He
carries the baby on through the blizzard till he is rescued by Ursus, a
quack doctor-cum-strolling player who lives in the Green Box, a caravan
which is drawn round the countryside by a trained wolf called Homo.
Ursus names the little girl Dea and over the next fifteen years, with the
assistance of two female handmaidens Fibi (Phoebé) and Vinos (Vénus),
they become so popular as entertainers touring the provinces that Ursus
decrees they should take their act to London. There they are so pheno-
menally successful that they attract the attention of fashionable society (or,
as Hugo has it, *tout la jeune lordship*). Because Gwynplaine, the star of the
show, is so repellent, he attracts the attention of the decadent Duchess
Josiane, an illegitimate daughter of James II and bitter rival of Queen
Anne. She has one black eye and one blue one (because she isn't *wholly*
evil?). Her infatuation with Gwynplaine arouses the jealousy of Lord
David Dirry-Moir, her fiancé, and the official (though illegitimate) heir to
the Clancharlie earldom and Hunkerville barony. He is an aristocratic
playboy (aged forty-four) who is a leading member of every Hellfire Club
in London, and likes nothing better than donning a sailor-suit and going
round in working-class circles where he is known to one and all as
'Tom-Jim-Jack'. The fast coagulating plot thickens even more when the
villain of the work, one Barkilphedro, confidant of Queen Anne, of
Josiane and of Lord David, but who seeks revenge on all three, is handed a
bottle just fished out of the sea. As Official Receiver of Jetsam and State
Opener of Sealed Bottles at the Admiralty, he has the right to break the
seal and he finds inside the *comprachicos'* long-lost confession which
establishes that it is Gwynplaine and not D. D. Moir who is the true
inheritor of the Clancharlie title. Gwynplaine takes his place in the House
of Lords and delivers a long and impassioned speech on the rights of the
poor which is received with hysterical laughter. Having been rejected by
the Duchess Josiane, for whom he instantly loses all his attractions when
Queen Anne orders them to marry, he returns to his one true love Dea
who, being blind, is the one person able to see his true self. With Ursus
and Homo, they set sail to seek happiness elsewhere. Dea, who had long

since given him up for dead, promptly dies of joy, whereupon Gwyn-plaine, impatient to rejoin her, throws himself into the sea.

Apart from its plot, the novel is full of all manner of other oddities. The names of nearly all the characters are outlandish to a degree. In addition to the principal characters listed above, there are the *comprachicos* Gernardus Geestemunde, the leader and Hardquanonne, the surgical mutilator. Given that these are foreign criminals of no fixed abode, a touch of exoticism is perhaps in order, but the names bestowed on members of the British working classes are not conspicuously homely: the London innkeeper who gives hospitality to Ursus and Co. is called Nicless Plumptre *(sic)*, his potboy is called Govicum, and when a championship boxing match is staged, it is between a Scot, Helmsgail, and an Irishman, Phelem-ghe-madone. The chapter-titles tend to be either portentous or sententious and are sometimes both: 'Quelles raisons peut avoir un quadruple pour venir s'encanailler parmi les gros sous', 'Aucun homme ne passerait brusquement de la Sibérie au Sénégal sans perdre connaissance', 'C'est avec l'excès de grandeur qu'on arrive à l'excès de misère'. Even more noteworthy, however, are the occasions when Hugo's ever-fertile imagination is let off the leash. Prominent amongst these is the figure of the dreaded Wapentake, the law-enforcer, who silently stalks London's streets, dressed entirely in black, carrying his sinister 'iron weapon': once touched with it, you must immediately follow to wherever he leads you. When he marches off with Gwynplaine shortly before the next perfor-mance of their ever-popular playlet, Ursus, who just happens to be a virtuoso ventriloquist and bird-warbler, tries to persuade Dea that all is well by imitating not only the voice of the departed hero but the sounds of an extremely demonstrative audience. And if it is difficult to suspend one's disbelief at this particular episode, it is well-nigh impossible to do so over the premiss on which so much of the novel's action is grounded, namely that Gwynplaine's features are so risible that everybody, of high and low estate, has but to see them to be at once convulsed with cruel and hysterical laughter. At every performance in the market-place, the crowds split their sides. His maiden speech in Parliament has the Lords almost literally rolling in the aisles:

> Les lords riaient, les évêques riaient, les juges riaient. Le banc des vieillards se déridait, le banc des enfants se tordait. L'archevêque de Canterbury poussait du coude l'archevêque d'York. Henry Compton, évêque de Londres, frère du comte de Northampton, se tenait les côtes. Le lord-chancelier baissait les yeux pour cacher son rire probable. Et à la barre, la statue du respect, l'huissier de la verge noire, riait.[4]

As odd as any of this, however, is the fact that while he was writing *L'Homme qui rit* and after it was published, Hugo continued to insist that it was a profoundly serious work and that it had a great deal to do with History.

Writing to his publisher in October 1868, two months after completing the novel he had taken two years to complete, he declared it would be 'à la fois drame et histoire. On verra là une Angleterre inattendue. L'époque est ce moment extraordinaire qui va de 1688 à 1705. C'est la préparation de notre dix-huitième siècle français. C'est le temps de la reine Anne, dont on parle tant et qu'on connaît si peu. Je crois qu'il y aura dans ce livre des révélations, même pour l'Angleterre. Macaulay n'est, après tout, qu'un historien de surface. J'ai tâché de fouiller plus au fond'. [5] In April 1869, he wrote (in French) to the Editor of *The Daily Telegraph* to explain: 'Ce n'est pas un livre anglais: c'est un livre humain. Il est anglais cependant en ce sens qu'un certain côté, presque inconnu, de l'histoire d'Angleterre y est mis à nu et exposée en pleine lumière, ce qui semblera à l'Angleterre brusque peut-être, mais, à coup sûr, instructif'. [6] In October of that same year, he declared in a letter to the London publisher who was bringing out an English translation of *L'Homme qui rit:* 'Mon livre n'est pas, à proprement parler, un roman; il veut instruire en même temps qu'inté- resser, et il mêle l'histoire et la philosophie. Les pages d'histoire et de philosophie sont donc très importantes, puisqu'elles expliquent le but de l'auteur, et je les recommande à votre excellent esprit'. [7]

The hitherto unknown area of English history Hugo claimed to have explored is identified more precisely in drafts for a preface to *L'Homme qui rit* which were, in the event, not utilized: 'Le monstre fait, par caprice royal et de main humaine, est un fait, le plus effrayant peut-être de ceux qui caractérisent le vieux monde. L'histoire l'effleure et l'indique à peine. Il nous a paru utile de mettre ce côté du passé en pleine lumière . . .' [8]

A further fragment develops this further and provides a sketch of Hugo's Grand Design:

> L'histoire amasse lentement le dossier de tout ce vieux crime qu'on appelle la monarchie . . . Un fait terrible du bon plaisir royal a été longtemps laissé dans l'ombre. Un fait de mutilation qui commence chez le pape et ne finit pas chez le sultan. L'auteur a éclairé ce fait. Il est nécessaire que tout ce qui, soit en France, soit en Angleterre, a amené 93, soit approfondi.
> Ce devoir, l'auteur a voulu le remplir. [9]

The preface that was finally published was, for Hugo, remarkably terse, consisting of two short paragraphs only, the second of which emphasizes his historical preoccupations and outlines his literary strategy:

> Le vrai titre de ce livre serait *l'Aristocratie.* Un autre livre, qui suivra, pourra être intitulé *La Monarchie.* Et ces deux livres, s'il est donné à l'auteur d'achever ce travail, en précéderont et en amèneront un autre qui sera intitulé: *Quatrevingt-treize.* [10]

Even although, in the interval between early draft and final version, the emphasis has switched from English king to English aristocracy, the polemical scenario remains substantially the same: the ruling classes begin by oppressing the poor in the most brutal fashion conceivable but, in the end, they in turn are to be brutally destroyed in the Terror of 1793. The fact that it is the English working classes who are oppressed in *L'Homme qui rit* and the French aristocracy which is slaughtered in *Quatrevingt-treize* is all one to Hugo: 'La révolution française est à beaucoup d'égards, la révolution anglaise. 1789 a travaillé en Angleterre presque autant qu'en France'. [11] This eminently debatable proposition, together with the other oracular pronouncements about his literary programme, suggest an attitude to History that was, to say the least, idiosyncratic. Analysis of how that programme was enacted in *L'Homme qui rit* demonstrates that it was positively cavalier.

The principal item in Hugo's bill of indictment against the English monarchy – and, incidentally, the main cog in the machinery of the plot of the novel – is James II's hiring of the *comprachicos* to mutilate the infant son of a political opponent. If Macaulay overlooked this in his five volume *History of England from the Accession of James II* it was not, as Hugo contemptuously alleged, because he was merely 'un historien de surface': it was because the *comprachicos* never existed outside Hugo's own imagination. [12] To be sure, Hugo's 'techniques of illusion' – references to scholarly authorities, footnotes, Latin tags and the rest – are skilful enough to inhibit disbelief but the *comprachicos,* together with their international background and the manual of instructions for their surgical operations, are, like all the principal characters, the Wapentake and many of the legal practices, wholly fictitious. As well as incriminating James II by the Big Lie direct, Hugo tries to make his alleged crime more plausible by what we would now call the 'smear' technique. Roman Catholics in high authority created *castrati* for the Vatican choir, James II was a Roman Catholic in high authority and he had shown how ruthless he could be by ordering

Judge Jeffreys at the 'Bloody Assizes' to pass the death-sentence on hundreds of his enemies imprisoned after Monmouth's abortive rebellion: *ergo* he could have had a child's features mutilated. And if one is as rabidly anti-Royalist as Hugo was, 'could have' and 'must have' were simply synonymous.

Although he professed to admire certain features of English life, Hugo was essentially an Anglophobe. He felt considerable antipathy towards Queen Victoria because of her support for Napoleon III and because of the hostile treatment he received from her ultra-loyal subjects while in exile in Guernsey. He also remained convinced that nowhere on earth were the rich richer or the poor poorer than in England: 'L'Angleterre ... crée admirablement la richesse: elle la répartit mal. Cette solution qui n'est complète que d'un côté la mène fatalement à ces deux extrèmes: opulence monstrueuse, misère monstrueuse'.[13] Allied to the ineradicable French conviction that the English are very, very odd, these beliefs determined the 'historical' authorities Hugo consulted and the use he made of the data they provided. In briefing himself on the historical background to *L'Homme qui rit,* he displayed none of the meticulous care which Flaubert lavished on *Salammbô* or Martin du Gard on *Jean Barois* and *L'Eté 1914.* There are yawning gaps in his reconstruction of the period in which his novel's action is set: he scarcely mentions the 'Glorious' Revolution of 1688 which established the elementary liberties of the British subject against the State; William and Mary do not appear, and there is not the slightest hint that the major events of Queen Anne's reign were the war against the French and the political struggle between the Tories and the Whigs (or, as Hugo once calls them in what may or may not be a significant lapse, 'the Whighs'). He seems to have spent no time studying the memorialists of the period he was evoking as Mérimée did for his *Chronique du règne de Charles IX* or Stendhal for his *Chroniques italiennes.* He cannot have set out with serious intentions to capture the true flavour of Queen Anne's London. The profligate behaviour of London's rich young clubmen was at its most riotous under the reign of Charles II; boxing did not become truly popular with the London upper classes until the reign of George IV: Hugo brings them all anachronistically together in Queen Anne's Lambeth in 1705. Given the choice, he would always prefer *Dichtung* to *Wahrheit* and in this case, it was a choice dictated by ideological as well as dramatic considerations.

He began to write *L'Homme qui rit* with a relatively simple message to impart. The English Royal Court, at the end of the seventeenth century, was, as it had always been, inordinately wealthy, grossly over-privileged and thoroughly decadent. The only documentary sources that interested him were those which confirmed his own prejudices.[14] On the whole, these sources were sufficiently obscure for a critic as sympathetic to Hugo as Péguy to express some scepticism ('Il m'abrutit des références les plus extraordinaires qui ne me laissent aucun doute sur son érudition. Des noms qu'on n'a jamais ni vus ni connus'[15]) but they were genuine enough even if, by modern standards of historiography, they leave a great deal to be desired. Hugo's two principal sources were the French translations of two Baedeker-style English gazetteers: Edward Chamberlayne's *Etat pré-sent de l'Angleterre* (Amsterdam, 1688 edition) and James Beeverell's *Les Délices de la Grande Bretagne* (Leyden, 8 vols, 1707).[15] From Chamber-layne, who concentrated on historical, constitutional and legal data, Hugo borrowed wholesale: precise details of legal procedures, of the dress of Court officials, of the possessions and privileges of the English ruling classes and heraldic paraphernalia of all sorts. From Beeverell, who systematically described the physical and geographical features of the British Isles, region by region, Hugo transcribed no less copiously, paying particular attention to descriptions or illustrations of stately homes and gardens and to such regions as Southwark, Vauxhall, Portland and Chesil (which features in *L'Homme qui rit* as Chess Hill throughout). As well as evidence of the yawning gulf between the rich and poor in England, Hugo was especially attracted by the picturesque, the quaint and the monstrous, and he found ample provision of these in a French reference work, the thirteen volume *Nouveau dictionnaire historique* by C-M. Chaudon and F.-A. Delandine, Lyon, 1804, which gave the same pride of place to scandalous features in the lives of the good and the great as *Private Eye* does today (and with as much or as little accuracy): they would seem to have been the authority for his belief that Anne Boleyn had six fingers on one hand, one breast larger than the other and a conspicuously protruding tooth, that James II's mistresses were particularly repellent and that Queen Anne had various extra-marital adventures.

The standard view of reputable historians is that Queen Anne was eminently respectable, distinctly dowdy and somewhat dull, while most note that she bore her husband sixteen children, all of whom died in infancy. If Hugo failed entirely to mention this fact it is either because of ignorance or, more probably, because it would have run the risk of arousing unwanted human sympathy for a character he was committed to blackening. To achieve this end, if the authorities at his disposal could not provide the necessary evidence, he proceeded to manufacture it. Two examples will suffice. In transcribing a passage from Macaulay (a source

Hugo used relatively sparingly), in which the Duchess of Marlborough was alleged to have no will, no judgement or no conscience that did not derive from the Churchill family, Hugo substituted Queen Anne's name for that of the Duchess and declared simply that she 'n'avait pas de volonté, pas de jugement, pas de conscience'.[16] According to Hugo, Queen Anne 'aimait beaucoup son lord Stewart *[sic]*, William Cavendish, duc de Devonshire, qui était très imbécile. Ce lord, qui avait tous les grades d'Oxford et ne savait pas l'orthographe, fit un beau matin la bêtise de mourir'.[17]

The *Dictionary of National Biography* tells rather a different story: 'In architecture and fine art [Cavendish] was reputed a consummate judge . . . He was a good Latin scholar and especially a student of Horace, acquainted with Homer and Plutarch . . .'[18] Because *L'Homme qui rit* is littered with careless errors or deliberate distortions of this sort, one can readily appreciate why Saintsbury should have dismissed it as 'a torrent of silliness, sciolism and sheer nonsense' and why he likened Hugo to Margites, the Classical archetype of all pretentious ignoramuses 'who knew many things but knew them all badly'.[19]

Even if Hugo had been a great deal more scholarly in his historical documentation, *L'Homme qui rit* would still deserve serious censure for the clumsy fashion in which the data is purveyed. The style is set in the preamble which introduces Ursus and his caravan, the inside walls of which bear two elaborate inscriptions. The first, headed 'seules choses qu'il importe de savoir', is an interminable list (extending over three closely printed pages in the Flammarion edition) of the legal rights and privileges of the English aristocracy. The second, entitled 'Satisfactions qui doivent suffire à ceux qui n'ont rien' is twice as long, and consists of a detailed catalogue of a great many stately homes and gardens. Both lists are transcribed, more or less verbatim, from Chamberlayne, and similar lists, from the same source, regularly recur in the discourse of Ursus and of Hugo's Narrator. Each of these shows a pedantic concern for historical and legalistic minutiae that borders on the manic, each of them is given to pontificating made all the more insufferable by their fondness for heavy-handed humour and homespun moralistic maxims. Typical examples of the Narrator's name-dropping technique is the following parenthesis as the *comprachicos* sail towards their doom:

> A l'ouest, Burhou, Sadteriaux, Anfroque, Niangle, Fond-du-Choc, les Jumelles, la Grosse, la Clanque, les Eguillons, le Vrac, la Fosse-Malière; à l'est, Sauquet, Hommeau, Floreau, la Brinebetais, la Queslingue,

Croquelihou, la Fourche, le Saut, Noire Pute, Coupie, Orbue. Qu'est-ce que tous ces monstres? des hydres? Oui, de l'espèce écueil.[20]

Or this, from the opening of the immensely long and minutely detailed account of the investiture of Gwynplaine in the House of Lords:

Leicester entrait et serrait la main de Lichfield; puis Charles Mordaunt, comte de Peterborough et de Monmouth, l'ami de Locke, sur l'initiative duquel il avait proposé la refonte des monnaies; puis Charles Campbell, comte de Loudoun, prêtant l'oreille à Fulke Greville, lord Brooke; puis Dorme, comte de Caërnarvon; puis Robert Sutton, baron Lexington, fils du Lexington qui avait conseillé à Charles II de chasser Gregorio Leti, historiographe assez mal avisé pour vouloir être historien; puis Thomas Bellasye, vicomte Falconberg, ce beau vieux; et ensemble les trois cousins Howard, comte de Bindon, Bower-Howard, comte de Berkshire, et Stafford-Howard, comte de Stafford; puis John Lovelace, baron Lovelace, dont la pairie éteinte en 1736 permit à Richardson d'introduire Lovelace dans son livre et de créer sous ce nom un type... Le jeune comte d'Annerley abordait le vieux lord Eure, lequel n'avait plus que deux ans à vivre, car il devait mourir en 1707...[21]

This, assuredly, is an object-lesson in how *not* to use local colour. It is applied not so much with a brush as with a trowel and it ends up ostentatiously inert athwart the narrative neither advancing the action nor enhancing the atmosphere.

Occasionally, as a variation on the straightforward catalogue, Hugo introduces a snatch of dialogue in which one character is totally ignorant and the other is quite omniscient. In the following example, Ursus, who worked as a 'philosopher' in the household of a Lord before he became a mountebank, informs Gwynplaine about the sinister significance of the Wapentake:

–Voix-tu ce passant?
–Cet homme en noir?
–Oui.
–Qui a une espèce de masse au poing?
–Oui.
–Eh bien?
–Eh bien, Gwynplaine, cet homme est le wapentake.
–Qu'est-ce que c'est que le wapentake?
–C'est le bailli de la centaine.
–Qu'est-ce que c'est que le bailli de la centaine?
–C'est le *præpositus hundredi.*
–Qu'est-ce que le *præpositus hundredi?*

–C'est un officier terrible.
–Qu'est-ce qu'il a à la main?
–C'est l'iron-weapon.
–Qu'est-ce que l'iron-weapon?
–C'est une chose en fer.
–Qu'est-ce qu'il fait de ça?
–D'abord il jure dessus. Et c'est pour cela qu'on l'appelle le wapentake . . .[22]

This is Ursus at his least characteristic; normally, he is heavily sarcastic and insufferably garrulous like so many of Hugo's characters. There are few exceptions in *L'Homme qui rit.* If Gernardus Geestemunde takes leave of his band of *comprachicos* as does Dea of Gwynplaine with lengthy set-speeches, most readers will doubtless accept this as the conventional Romantic response to the proximity of death: however ill they may be, they always have enough breath for one final aria. There are, however, two other 'performances' which are peculiarly Hugolian. One is Josiane's when, alone – at last! – with Gwynplaine in her bedchamber, she delivers a speech extending over six pages. The other is the very much longer harangue Gwynplaine makes before the Lords which is, at one and the same time, a monumental rebuke to them and a grandiloquent tribute to Ursus's powers as a teacher. Just a few days previously, Gwynplaine couldn't tell his Iron Weapon from his *præpositus hundredi.* Now he ranges far and wide through English social history detailing the aristocratic malpractices which have made him a monster and reduced all England to penury. Hugo provides him with the last of the novel's many catalogues of names and incidents drawn, on this occasion, from Beeverell, and 'edited', in characteristic fashion, by omitting any detail that might nuance the picture, or blatantly turning white into black.[23]

Curiously and significantly, Hugo did not defend this practice, as conceivably he might have done, by claiming that he was writing a Romance and then pleading poetic licence. He continued to insist that only the *characters* in *L'Homme qui rit* were invention; everything else was true:

> Quand je peins l'histoire, jamais je ne fais faire aux personnages historiques que ce qu'ils ont fait, ou pu faire, leur caractère étant donné, et je les mêle le moins possible à l'invention proprement dite. Ma manière est de peindre des choses vraies par des personnages d'invention.[24]

He claimed that the section of the novel in which 'mœurs et histoire' predominated was what he liked the best[25] and when he surveyed the whole work, he declared: 'Je pense, en effet, n'avoir rien fait de mieux que *L'Homme qui rit'*.[26]

With a few notable exceptions, critics have taken a different view of his evaluation of the novel and of the role played within it of the historical element. The earliest French reviewers were prompt to recognize the political message of *L'Homme qui rit.* It was a 'catapulte braquée contre l'édifice social',[27] but though they either endorsed or attacked this strictly from their left or right wing viewpoint, none of them paused to examine the accuracy of Hugo's documentation. The general view seems to have been that he was so towering a genius that he was beyond criticism. 'Je ne viens pas ici juger Victor Hugo', declared Banville, 'sans parler de ce qu'il y aurait d'absurde à ce que Gros-Jean voulût en remontrer à son curé'.[28] 'Il ne faut pas subtiliser ni ergoter avec le génie', wrote another reviewer, 'et lorsqu'il a mis son empreinte quelque part, il faut le reconnaître et s'incliner. C'est ce que je fais'.[29]

When, at almost the same time, the earliest English reviewers approached the translation of *L'Homme qui rit,* they expressed neither respect nor approval. The *Times* correspondent observed 'Being a Frenchman's book upon England, it necessarily contains as many errors as there are subjects of discussion' but he was less concerned by Hugo's historical inaccuracy than by his obscenity. 'French indecent writing is like no other . . . it is simply and utterly bestial'.[30] The *Saturday Review* declared: 'It will do no man good . . . no woman or child aught but unmitigated harm',[31] the *Athenaeum* pronounced it 'horrible, disgusting, untrue and un-Christian',[32] while *The Spectator* labelled it 'unfit for the reading of decent and sensible people'.[33] It would be pleasant to record that these were all reactions to the quality of the English translation which included such collector's items as 'the malicious man blooms hideously', 'a swarm of black blisters struggled in obscurity' and 'You felt that the man had known the foretaste of evil which is the calculation, and the aftertaste which is the zero',[34] but, more predictably, they were all provoked by the programme of seduction undertaken by the libidinous but (so we are asked to believe) entirely virginal Duchesse Josiane. Again predictably (to those who know his critical track-record), the one English critic of distinction to praise *L'Homme qui rit* was Algernon Charles Swinburne. He admired Barkilphedro ('a bastard begotten by Iago upon his sister Madame de Merteuil') and claimed to see in Josiane 'the virgin harlot . . . new-blown and actual as a gathered flower, in warm bloom of blood and breath . . . passionately palpable'.[35] The historical elements, on which Hugo laid such stress, were, in Swinburne's view, relatively unimportant: 'What touches on life or manners we see to be accidental byplay as soon as we see what the book is indeed; the story of the battle of a human spirit, first with Fate, then with the old Three Subordinate enemies: the World, the Flesh and the Devil'.[36] And, like his French contemporaries who pronounced themselves intimidated by the Master's consummate artistry, he advised readers to discard all critical considerations: 'This is a book to be rightly read, not by the lamplight of realism, but by the sunlight of his imagination reflected upon ours. Only so shall we see it as it is, much less understand it. The beauty it has, and the meaning, are ideal; and therefore cannot be impaired by any want of realism . . . I shall leave the dissection of names and the anatomy of probabilities to the things of chatter and chuckle . . . There is never any lack of them, and it will not greatly hurt the master poet of an age that they should shriek and titter, cackle and hoot inaudibly behind his heel'.[37]

Robert Louis Stevenson was equally dismissive of any criticism levelled at *L'Homme qui rit* for its historical inaccuracies. He was by no means as eulogistic (nor as dithyrambic) as Swinburne – indeed, so overwritten did he find Hugo's account of the sinking of the *Matutina* that on each re-reading, he 'could do nothing but cover his face with his hands' – but he found the story 'admirably adapted to the moral' and was much moved by the love between Gwynplaine and Dea: 'it seems to be above the story somehow, and not of it, as the full moon over the night of some foul and feverish city'.[38] He conceded that Hugo's English scholarship left much to be desired but held that this was of no consequence:

> The large family of English blunders . . . are of a sort that is really indifferent in art. If Shakespeare makes his ships cast anchor by some seaport of Bohemia, if Hugo imagines Tom-Jim-Jack to be a likely nickname for an English sailor, or if either Shakespeare or Hugo or Scott, for that matter, be guilty of 'figments enough to confuse the march of a whole history – anachronisms enough to overset all chronology' [prefatory letter to *Peveril of the Peak*], the life of their creations, the artistic truth and accuracy of their work, is not so much as compromised.[39]

As has already been intimated, Stevenson's contemporary, George Saintsbury, took quite the opposite view of Hugo's historical errors: there were just too many of them, they were too gross to ignore and they made a nonsense of the whole enterprise (and he could have added, for good measure, that whereas Shakespeare made no claims to being a geographer, Hugo repeatedly went out of his way to remind his readers that he was teaching them a history lesson). Nevertheless, it is a significant expression of Victorian taste that he shared Stevenson's high regard for the love between Gwyn-plaine and Dea: indeed, he declared that after the 'tedious insanity' of the rest of the novel, their reconciliation in death was 'not far short of the greatest things in literature'. [40]

For all that, after its brief period of notoriety in the 1870s, *L'Homme qui rit* vanished from public view almost as spectacularly as the sealed flagon bearing the *comprachicos'* final confession and it remained unwept, unhonoured and virtually unsung for the best part of a century. Just occasionally, over this period, it became the object of scholarly attention: three major articles devoted to the genesis of the novel appeared in learned journals on the eve of the First World War and these were supplemented in a doctoral thesis which appeared twenty years later, in 1933. [41] In that same year, together with all the rest of his works, it became the basis for the first full-scale psycho-analytical examination of Hugo and was ad-judged to be a particularly rich repository of recurrent themes, images and obsessions. [42] It contains a vengeful Father Figure (James II), a possessive Mother Figure, often likened to a spider or an octopus (Josiane) or to the sea (*mère* and *mer* being convenient homonyms), fratricidal rivalry (Gwynplaine and Dirry-Moir), further evidence of a lifelong preoccupa-tion both with mutilation and monstrosity (Han d'Islande, Quasimodo, Triboulet) and with birth-fantasies expressed in cloacal images of sewers, cells and dungeons. It is positively awash with the antitheses which are so prominent a feature of all Hugo's writings and so effectively express his ambivalent view of himself and the world around him: light and dark, rich and poor, grotesque and sublime, good and evil, heights and depths, an ugly hero with a beautiful soul, the corruption of Josiane and the purity of Dea, and much more besides. The only important antithesis left unconsi-dered was the one highlighted by Stevenson, between literary truth and historical falsehood.

Thirty more years were to elapse before *L'Homme qui rit* re-emerged from obscurity but after doing so, the revival in its fortunes has been quite spectacular. There have been two separate scholarly editions. [43] In France, it has been made a prescribed text for the *agrégation des lettres*. In England and U.S.A., under the title *The Man who Laughs,* it has appeared as Number 71 in the strip-cartoon series 'Classics Illustrated' (published by Strato Publications Ltd). It has been presented at the *Théâtre National Populaire,* in a production devised by François Bourgeat, starring Gérard Guillaumat. It has been the subject of studies by some of the outstanding French and American scholar-critics of the day and was recently accorded a volume of fourteen essays, all to itself, by la Société des études romanti-

ques. [44] It should be instructive to inquire why quite so many good scholars
should have been attracted to so bad a novel. A possible explanation is
that, like the massive challenge Everest permanently offers to mountain-
eers, *L'Homme qui rit,* with all its rebarbative bulk and daunting angulari-
ties, was simply *there.* Given that Hugo is one of France's very greatest
writers (with or without Gide's snide *hélas*), some formula should surely
be devisable to excuse if not explain so monstrous an aberration as his
last-but-one novel – it being fairly generally accepted that the last one of
all, *Quatre-vingt-treize* (1873), is much less eccentric. One formula has
been to link *L'Homme qui rit* to a mode in which oddities are not only
acceptable but almost *de rigueur.* So it has been characterized as *oni-
rique* [45] (which means, I take it, that anything goes) or as *baroque,* [46] the
principal themes of which have been identified as 'ceux de la métamor-
phose, de la tentation, de l'inversion, du pêle-mêle, du monstre, du
spectacle, de l'illusion, du rêve et du masque'. [47] For Victor Brombert, on
the other hand, Hugo is the father of the polycentric novel, 'the creator of
a liberating but always problematic counter-code', and *L'Homme qui rit* is
both a *roman-poème,* partaking of romance and myth within a particularly close-knit linguistic and metaphoric structure, [48] and a Quest Novel.

Another explanation is that to some modern scholars, the concepts of
'goodness' and 'badness' in literary criticism are outmoded: what is of
much greater importance are the intricacy and coherence of the novel's
structures or the 'relevance' to our times of its ideological message. Thus,
R.B. Grant can frankly observe that: '*L'Homme qui rit* is an extremely bad
piece of writing, so bad in fact that few critics have bothered to take it
seriously on the grounds, no doubt, that it was not worth the effort . . .
Even so, this work, remarkably bad as it is, is a work that rewards the
serious critic for his effort'. [49] The rewards he finds are the striking
apocalyptic images expressing archetypes of Hell (corrupt Society) and of
Heaven (two young people in their Green Box), as the hero descends into
Hell then escapes in the end to achieve wholeness: 'the vision transcends
the personal mythic quest to become a commentary on aristocratic society
of the prerevolutionary period'.

While one might take issue with Grant over his historical judgement
– Hugo's representation of English aristocracy in 1705 is unmitigated drivel
and it is situated *after* England's revolution rather than before it – at least
he concedes that Hugo's faults are serious. French critics, from the outset,
have been curiously reluctant to do so. The one who has come closest to
doing so has been Pierre Albouy. He accepts that 'les "défauts" de Hugo
sont portés au comble: exagération et fausseté dans le tableau de l'aristo-

cratie anglaise sous la reine Anne, invraisemblance des caractères et de l'action, délire verbal et érudition en folie dans les tirades du bateleur philosophe Ursus',[50] but the very fact that he puts the word 'défauts' inside inverted commas is a clear indication that he considers them of little account; indeed, he at once proceeds to argue that those who attach importance to such 'défauts' 'n'auront pas su *lire* ce roman comme il demande à être lu . . .'

Albouy, Grant and Brombert all see *L'Homme qui rit* as a *roman initiatique* and, in so doing, express a debt of gratitude to Léon Cellier who did more than anyone else, in recent times, to promote this particular reading. While it is, in essence, little more than a variation on the theme first orchestrated by Swinburne a century earlier of Gwynplaine's being engaged in a desperate struggle with Fate, the World, the Flesh and the Devil, Cellier develops some colourful notions of his own. The most noteworthy of these is that *Chaos vaincu,* the entertainment devised by Ursus which wins fame and fortune for Gwynplaine, is of capital importance. Ursus, dressed in a bearskin and Homo (representing *les forces féroces de la Nature*) struggle wordlessly on a darkened stage with Gwynplaine (representing Mankind) and are just about to overcome him when he calls for help. Thereupon, the white-clad form of Dea (representing the Spirit) emerges from the wings and, singing *in Spanish,*[51] invites the beasts to depart and Gwynplaine to love. At this moment, a shaft of light illuminates his face and, at the sight of his twisted grin, the audience invariably dissolves in helpless laughter. Later critics have reacted somewhat differently. J.-P. Weber has roundly condemned the whole thing as ludicrous, stating that it is 'd'une indigence et d'une sottise navrantes'.[52] Cellier, who argues that it is emblematic of the whole novel, would seem to rate it as highly as the author himself ('Ursus ne haïssait point cette œuvre, longtemps couvée par lui. "C'est dans le genre d'un nommé Shakespeare", disait-il avec modestie').[53] Cellier, disregarding the adverbial irony, has no hesitation in linking *L'Homme qui rit* with some very big names indeed. It is Hugo's bid to vie with Dante 'avec cette étonnante variante toutefois que le héros descend aux enfers sous la conduite, non de Virgile, mais de Shakespeare. Le Shakespeare de *L'Homme qui rit,* c'est Ursus, auteur de *Chaos vaincu*'.[54] As for Gwynplaine, with the mystery surrounding his birth, an adolescence spent in obscurity and the humiliations heaped upon him when he reaches manhood, there is only one conceivable comparison: 'il lui reste à connaître – et l'identification au Christ s'impose de plus en plus – l'Agonie au Jardin des Oliviers'.[55]

These are not the only critical pronouncements made on *L'Homme qui rit* in recent years which might prompt thoughtful readers to view each other with a wild surmise. J.-P. Weber thinks that Gwynplaine symbolizes the unmarried mother (yet another of Hugo's fixations) and that, as such, 'il [or elle?] porte son sexe sur son visage'.[56] Michel Granet takes a rather different approach. After identifying twelve incontrovertible references within the novel to the twelve trump cards in the Tarot pack, he says of Hugo:

> Avec Michelet et mieux que Marx, il montre dans *L'Homme qui rit* l'homme symbole du symptôme, plus, du stigmate de l'exploitation qui ne consiste pas uniquement dans la confiscation de la plus-value mercantile, mais dans celle de la plus-value que permet l'enrichissement théorique de la force du travail: la parole de l'Homme qui dit. L'aliénation de la parole du symbolique, c'est la capture par l'imaginaire, c'est la regression possible vers le sur-moi archaïque, féroce et obscène du corps morcelé, sevré, vers le moi-idéal maternel de toute puissance séparatiste, la délinquance et le terrorisme.[57]

On the other hand, for Suzanne Nash:

> With the internalization of the dialogue and a structuring principle of his own discourse and the multiplication of himself into the world's body, Gwynplaine as the man who laughs or mankind laughing takes on a symbolic plenitude he never possessed... The figure of disfiguration becomes a prophetic agent.[58]

This array of critical comments prompts a number of questions – apart from the obvious one 'What do some of them actually *mean*?' Can one readily bring to mind a novel by a major author which has elicited quite so many irreconcilable reactions? The love between Gwynplaine and Dea which, for Stevenson was 'above the story somehow, and not of it', is, for Albouy, absolutely central, and when they are united in their Romantic *Liebestod* it is 'le commencement de leur véritable vie et de l'accomplissement de leur amour'.[59] For somewhat different reasons, Suzanne Nash declares 'This is indeed a novel of hope ... and the man who laughs is an enunciating subject who constitutes himself as the powerfully determining symbolic subject of his own discourse'.[60] J.-B. Barrère will have none of this: *L'Homme qui rit* is 'le roman d'une tentation morale et d'un échec social qui aboutissent au suicide du héros et à la mort de sa compagne. C'est probablement l'œuvre la plus pessimiste de Victor Hugo'.[61]

The disparities here and, for that matter, throughout the long life of *L'Homme qui rit,* are too wide to be altogether accountable by differences in temperament, taste or background on the part of the critics; they are, in fact, so wide that one is bound to ask whether they have all been studying the *whole* of Hugo's text. However much they may differ, most of the critics of *L'Homme qui rit,* from first to last, have one important element in common: they have either entirely ignored – or, at most, taken only the briefest of glances at – the historical accuracy of the novel. This is what we are all bound to do when we know next to nothing about the real historical background of any work, as is the case with *Macbeth* or *King Lear,* but should we be quite so uncritical when we know as much about the period as we do about the Age of Queen Anne? The question is that much more pertinent when the author said, not once but repeatedly, as Hugo did, that to set down the history of that age was one of his prime intentions and that, in his considered opinion, he had done his work well. Has the time come, I wonder, to reopen the debate on the 'Intentional Fallacy', in which W.K. Wimsatt argued persuasively that 'the design or intention of the author is neither available nor desirable as a standard for judging the success of a work of literary art'?[62] While, to all intents and purposes, most nineteenth and twentieth century critics of *L'Homme qui rit* seem to have accepted Wimsatt's line as axiomatic, what Hugo would have thought about it all is matter for conjecture. As a connoisseur of antitheses and paradoxes, he may have appreciated the spectacle of admirers snatching victory from defeat by ignoring what he considered of supreme importance and making central what he rated as secondary, but confronted by critics claiming to know more about *L'Homme qui rit* than he did himself, one suspects that this supreme egotist would have found it no laughing matter.

Notes

[1] See J.G. Weightman, 'Critical judgement and eighteenth century literature', A.U.M.L.A., No. 18, November 1962, a splendidly provocative paper, in which academics are enjoined to spend as much time evaluating texts as on uncovering their sources and *La Nouvelle Héloïse* is described as 'one of the greatest bad books ever written'.

[2] George Saintsbury, *A History of the French Novel,* Macmillan, London, 1919, p. 122. Expanded version of book first published in 1882.

[3] Pierre Albouy, *Mythographies,* Corti, Paris, 1976, p. 221.

[4] *L'Homme qui rit,* edited by M. Eigeldinger & G. Schaeffer, Flammarion, 2 volume edition, 1982. Vol. 2, p. 295. (Reference hereafter *H.Q.R.*)

[5] Letter to Armand Lacroix, 6 October 1868, *H.Q.R.,* Vol. 2, p. 404.

⁶ Letter to Editor of *The Daily Telegraph,* 26 April 1869, ibid., p. 407.

⁷ Letter to Joseph Hatton, first published in *The Gentleman's Magazine,* Vol. 4, 1869, p. 711 and reprinted in K.W. Hooker, *The Fortunes of Victor Hugo in England,* Columbia University Press, New York, 1938, p. 176.

⁸ *Projets de préface, H.Q.R.,* Vol. 2, p. 400.

⁹ ibid., p. 401.

¹⁰ *H.Q.R.,* Vol. 1, p. 43.

¹¹ *Projets de préface, H.Q.R.,* Vol. 2, p. 401.

¹² The most authoritative examination of the genesis of Hugo's *comprachicos* still remains Paul Berret: 'Les comprachicos et la mutilation de Gwynplaine dans *L'Homme qui rit*' in R.H.L.F., XXI (1914), pp. 503-18. They are shown to be an amalgam of Hugo's own memories of bandits he saw on a visit to Spain in 1843 and old folk-legends associating gypsies with child-stealing. Subsequently, a number of other scholars have suggested a likely literary source of inspiration in Le Sage's *Don Guzman d'Alfarache* in which a Genoese beggar, one Pantalon Castelleto, deliberately cripples his own infant son in the hope of gaining more pity and more money.

¹³ *Les Misérables,* Flammarion ed., Vol. 3, p. 24.

¹⁴ The quality of Hugo's erudition in *L'Homme qui rit* has remained a subject of critical controversy to this day and antagonists have divided – no doubt significantly – along national lines. For Saintsbury, Hugo in *L'Homme qui rit* was 'dealing with a subject of which he knew practically nothing and about which he was prepared to believe, or even practise, anything', Saintsbury, op. cit., p. 127. Professor J. Heywood Thomas is equally scathing in his doctoral thesis *L'Angleterre dans l'œuvre de Victor Hugo,* Bibliothèque de la Fondation Victor Hugo, Paris, 1933. On the other hand, Jules Janin, a critic normally very hard to please, declared: 'A chaque page de *L'Homme qui rit,* on démontrerait facilement la science et l'autorité de M. Victor Hugo', quoted in the 1907, Ollendorff edition of the novel (p. 594), and reprinted in the most recent French article defending Hugo's *modus operandi,* Jean Gaudon's 'Les vicissitudes du Savoir' in *'L'Homme qui rit' ou la parole-monstre de Victor Hugo,* S.E.D.E.S., Paris, 1985, pp. 26-34. (Reference hereafter S.E.D.E.S.)

¹⁵ The most detailed analyses of Hugo's borrowings from these two sources remain the articles contributed by Christina MacLean to the M.L.R. in 1913: 'Victor Hugo's use of *Les Délices de la Grande Bretagne* in *L'Homme qui rit*', April, pp. 173-84, and 'Victor Hugo's use of Chamberlayne's *L'Etat présent de l'Angleterre* in *L'Homme qui rit*', October, pp. 496-510. These articles are supplemented and, in some particulars, corrected in Heywood Thomas, op. cit., pp. 158-222.

¹⁶ Quoted in Thomas, op. cit., p. 165.

¹⁷ *H.Q.R.,* Vol. 1, p. 307.

¹⁸ Thomas, op. cit., p. 180.

¹⁹ Saintsbury, op. cit., pp. 122-23.

²⁰ *H.Q.R.,* Vol. 1, p. 178.

²¹ *H.Q.R.,* Vol. 2, pp. 267-68.

²² *H.Q.R.,* Vol. 2, p. 30.

²³ Heywood Thomas provides some striking instances of this process: *Gwynplaine:* 'A Ailesbury, ville dont l'un de vous est lord, la disette est en permanence' (*H.Q.R.,* Vol. 2, p. 288), cp. *Beeverell* 'Ailesbury est un beau bourg, à 44 milles de Londres, placé dans une belle et fertile vallée . . . Il est grand, bien peuplé, et dans une situation fort agréable au milieu de belles et vastes campagnes . . .' (Bk. II, p. 157); *Gwynplaine:* 'A Strafford, on ne peut dessécher le marais, faute d'argent' (*H.Q.R.,* Vol. 2, p. 288), cp. *Beeverell:* 'Autrefois Stafford étoit bordée d'un marais au Nord-Est: mais les habitants ayant eu l'industrie de le dessécher, on y voit aujourd'hui une belle et agréable campagne, moitié champs, moitié prairies' (Bk. II, pp. 349-50). Quoted in Thomas, op. cit., pp. 198-99.

²⁴ Letter to Lacroix, December 1868, *H.Q.R.,* Vol. 2, pp. 4-5.

[25] Letter to Lacroix, 10 January 1869, ibid., p. 406.

[26] Letter to Vacquerie, 27 January 1869, ibid., p. 406.

[27] Pierre Douhaire, review in *Le Correspondant*, LXXIX (July 1869), pp. 160-61, quoted in Max Bach: 'Critique littéraire ou critique politique? Les derniers romans de Hugo vus par les contemporains', *French Review*, XXVIII, 1954, p. 29.

[28] Review in *Le National*, 15 June 1869, quoted in Bach, loc. cit., p. 29.

[29] Review in *Le Siècle*, 17 May 1869, quoted in Bach, loc. cit., pp. 29-30.

[30] Review in *The Times*, October 14 1869, p. 4. Quoted in Hooker, op. cit., pp. 179-80.

[31] *Saturday Review*, Vol. 28, 9 October 1869, p. 487, ibid., p. 178.

[32] *Athenaeum*, No. 2166, 1 May 1869, p. 604, ibid.

[33] *The Spectator*, Vol. 43, 5 November 1870, p. 1326, ibid.

[34] ibid., p. 177.

[35] A.C. Swinburne, review of *L'Homme qui rit* in *Essays and Studies*, Chatto and Windus, 1888, p. 6, first published in *The Fortnightly Review*, 1 July 1869.

[36] ibid., pp. 3-4.

[37] ibid., p. 3.

[38] 'Victor Hugo's Romances' in *Familiar Studies of Men and Books*, Chatto and Windus, 1909, p. 18. The essay appeared earlier as Introduction to the English translation, *The Man Who Laughs*, Vol. 6 of *The Works of Victor Hugo*, The Nottingham Society. The storm-tossed seascapes which Stevenson found so over-written were, to Paul Claudel, an example of Hugo at his best: 'On peut dire sans exagération que le sentiment le plus habituel à Victor Hugo, celui où il a trouvé ses inspirations les plus pathétiques, celui auquel il n'a jamais recours en vain et qui lui fournit un répertoire inépuisable de formes et de mouvements, sa chambre intérieure de torture et de création, c'est *l'Epouvante*, une espèce de contemplation panique'. The most memorable expression of this feeling was 'cet album de lithographies épiques et paniques qui à mon avis est le chef d'œuvre du grand poète, *L'Homme qui rit* (de quel rire, accentuant celui de Voltaire!)': Claudel, *Œuvres en prose*, Pléiade ed., Gallimard, 1965, pp. 22-24 ff.

[39] Stevenson, op. cit., p. 19.

[40] Saintsbury, op. cit., p. 125.

[41] *v.* note 15.

[42] Charles Baudoin, *Psychanalyse de Victor Hugo*, Editions du Mont-Blanc, Geneva, 1933. Because he also found *L'Homme qui rit* so full of Hugo's characteristic themes and images, Albouy later claimed: 'Ce roman est un de ses chefs-d'œuvre les plus significatifs: il est, au cœur de l'univers hugolien, une œuvre-clé', Albouy, op. cit., p. 195.

[43] Volume 14 of the *Œuvres complètes, édition chronologique sous la direction de J. Massin*, Le Club français du livre, 1967-70 and the two volume edition of Marc Eigeldinger and Gérald Schaeffer, Flammarion, 1982.

[44] *v.* end of note 14.

[45] J.B. Barrère, *La Fantaisie de Victor Hugo*, Paris, Klincksieck, 1972, Vol. 2, pp. 412-14.

[46] *v.* Marcel Raymond, 'Hugo le Mage' in *Génies de la France*, La Baconnière, 1942, and Michel Collot, 'L'Esthétique baroque dans *L'Homme qui rit*' in S.E.D.E.S. volume, pp. 99-121.

[47] Collot, art. cit., p. 121.

[48] Victor Brombert, *Victor Hugo and the Visionary Novel*, Harvard U.P., 1984, p. 7 and pp. 169-204.

[49] R.B. Grant, *The Perilous Quest. Image, Myth and Prophecy in the Narrations of Victor Hugo*. Duke University Press, Durham, N.C., 1968, p. 202.

[50] Albouy, op. cit., p. 194.

[51] The fact that English audiences listened with equanimity to Dea's Spanish song is readily explained by Hugo: 'l'espagnol était alors une langue-courante, et les marins anglais parlaient castillan de même que les soldats romains parlaient carthaginois' (*H.Q.R.*, Vol. 1, p.

92). Be that as it may, the crowd flocking to see *Chaos vaincu* seems to number few sailors in its ranks: in the countryside, it consists wholly of peasants, in London, principally of 'estafiers, ruffians et . . . blackguards' (*H.Q.R.,* Vol. 2, p. 20).

[52] J.-P. Weber, *La Genèse de l'œuvre poétique,* Paris, 1960, p. 159.

[53] *H.Q.R.,* Vol. 1, p. 378.

[54] Léon Cellier, '*Chaos vaincu,* Victor Hugo et le roman initiatique' in *Parcours initiatiques,* A la Baconnière, Grenoble, 1977, pp. 165-66.

[55] ibid., p. 170.

[56] Weber, op. cit., pp. 157-61.

[57] Michel Granet, 'La mise en abyme de l'aventure et de l'écriture dans *L'Homme qui rit*' in S.E.D.E.S., p. 53.

[58] Suzanne Nash, 'Transfiguring Disfiguration in *L'Homme qui rit.* A Study of Hugo's Use of the Grotesque' in *Pre-text, text, context. Essays on Nineteenth Century French Literature* (ed. R.L. Mitchell), Ohio State University, 1980, p. 12.

[59] Albouy, op. cit., p. 219.

[60] Nash, art. cit., p. 8.

[61] J.B. Barrère, *Hugo, l'homme et l'œuvre,* Boivin, Paris, 1952, p. 220.

[62] W.K. Wimsatt, 'The Intentional Fallacy' in *The Verbal Icon,* The Noonday Press, New York, 1954, p. 3.

Maupassant's *Bel-Ami* and the art of illusion

Robert Lethbridge : Fitzwilliam College, Cambridge

R E A D E R S of *Bel-Ami* have seldom been in any doubt about the novel's significance. For it is seen as Maupassant's last *roman de mœurs,* assuring him of a place in the Balzacian tradition which brings fictional heroes and authorial ambitions to the Parisian stage. The fact that its central protagonist makes his career in journalism inevitably invites comparison with *Illusions perdues.* But Rastignac remains the most pertinent model simply because, in Vial's words, 'Duroy, comme Rastignac, réussit'.[1] *Bel-Ami* can thus be contrasted with the biography of private failure in *Une Vie,* giving the 1885 text the status of an authentic record of the apotheosis of bourgeois capitalism under the Third Republic. So rigorously, indeed, has Maupassant adhered to the imperatives of the *vraisemblable* that *Bel-Ami* is considered to be an indiscrete transposition of the fortunes of one of the régime's most prodigiously successful representatives, whose anonymity scholars have felt bound to respect.[2] 'Rarement', wrote Brunetière of the novel as a whole, 'on a de plus près imité le réel',[3] and later critics have accordingly focused on those 'techniques of illusion' which serve to erode the dividing-line between its imaginary world and the reality outside *Bel-Ami* to which the latter effectively refers.[4] Maupassant virtually encourages such an approach in his oft-cited remark that 'les Réalistes de talent devraient s'appeler plutôt des Illusionnistes'.[5] He also stresses, however, that, behind the resulting 'apparence si simple', such techniques themselves disguise 'le sens définitif de l'œuvre'. The aim of the present essay is to explore the implications of that art of superimposed illusion for our reading of *Bel-Ami.*

It is not difficult to understand why *Bel-Ami* should be seen as 'a novel of ascent'.[6] This can be qualified, of course, by the recognition that the success of a mediocre individual is simultaneously an indictment of the society which has allowed him to flourish. 'Voulant analyser une crapule', Maupassant wrote, 'je l'ai développée dans un milieu digne d'elle afin de donner plus de relief à ce personnage'.[7] Sartre goes so far as to refer to Duroy as 'un ludion dont la montée témoigne seulement de l'effondrement d'une société'.[8] The illusion of upward movement nevertheless remains a powerful one. Those vertical diagrams elaborated by the novel's commentators[9] merely confirm that Duroy's apparent rise is minutely charted. The distance between the opening and closing pages of *Bel-Ami* seems self-evident: the unknown provincial eking out a living on the margins of society has a personal and material triumph consecrated in the fashionable heart of the capital; a Georges Duroy too poor to buy a drink has become the baron Du Roy de Cantel, his sights now set on the political arena which seems to beckon the conquering hero. There is a properly euphoric tone to the final chapter of *Bel-Ami,* so that Duroy's confidence is complemented both by the admiration of the assembled onlookers at his feet and the complicity of Maupassant's readers undeniably inscribed within this double point of view.

At one level, therefore, it is unsurprising to find *Bel-Ami* inserted in a literary tradition almost ritually extended back to *Le Paysan parvenu.* Yet in inviting the perceptive reader to discover 'tous les fils si minces, si secrets, presque invisibles, employés par certains artistes modernes à la place de la ficelle unique qui avait nom: l'Intrigue',[10] Maupassant alerts us to the potentially deceptive qualities of the latter. To base one's interpretation on the shape of a conventional plot merely reveals how completely we have forfeited our critical detachment. And it is all the more ironic that we should subscribe to the illusions of *Bel-Ami* at the same time as being afforded a privileged view of the construction of linguistic fictions. For one of the book's explicit preoccupations is, precisely, the language of duplicity. Its mastery is seen as the prerequisite of social integration and amorous advancement. Forestier's Vautrin-like advice to Duroy is couched in instructive terms: 'on colle les autres au moyen d'un dictionnaire' (p. 38).[11] Much of the novel demonstrates the efficacy of such a strategy, as the manipulation of words becomes synonymous with the manipulation of others, whether for speculative or seductive ends. What is true of sexual dalliance, marked by 'le moment des sous-entendus adroits, des voiles levés par des mots, comme on lève des jupes, le moment des ruses de langage' (p. 114), is equally true of the journalist's profession, where 'il faut, par des sous-entendus, laisser deviner ce qu'on veut' (p. 155). Above all, in both the private and public domain, language is seen as a substitute for reality rather than a reflection of it. The practices of *La*

Vie Française speak of an utter contempt for readers unable to discriminate between fact and fiction. The paper's very existence is inseparable from the fascination exerted by its frontage's 'trois mots éclatants' (p. 38). And, in the same way, Duroy's own identity literally depends on the self-assurance provided by seeing his name in print, perceived by others in the article he signs (pp. 86-87) or the visiting-card he needs in order to confirm his new persona (p. 90). Conversely, self-doubt is equated with a blank where his name should be (p. 99), and an attempt to write is the immediate reaction to compensate for such a loss of outline (p. 190).

The significance of this preoccupation is considerably enlarged, indeed, by the fact that Duroy's gradual assimilation of social eloquence (p. 58) is reflected in an apprenticeship which takes him from creative impotence (p. 66) to the acknowledgement of his status as a writer (p. 410). Here the obviously autobiographical dimension of *Bel-Ami* is extended to a demystificatory gaze (p. 173) and those secretive verbal procedures (p. 219) which Maupassant insists elsewhere are the most prominent features of his own art. And this by no means precludes the irony of lucid self-appraisal. Duroy's lessons in grammar and style (pp. 74-78) point to Flaubert's former pupil as surely as 'cette vanité et cet orgueil ombrageux d'écrivain' (p. 260) wounded by declarations that his texts are barely distinguishable from those of his mentor; so too does the detail that 'il avait toujours le début difficile' (p. 256), and the reference to Duroy's habit of reworking earlier material (p. 305). Potentially more problematic, however, is the way in which, once again, imaginative elaboration is seen to be divorced from experience, Duroy 'ne pouvant joindre le geste aux paroles' (p. 297) and being incapable of expressing on paper what he feels (p. 190). The novelistic 'histoire attendrissante' (p. 135) is a form of deceit, his 'récit dramatique' (p. 197) of the duel a blatant fabrication, and his *Souvenirs d'un chasseur d'Afrique* a self-conscious exercise in metaphor and rhetoric.

Much of this, it need hardly be said, is thematically consistent with the duplicity which informs the entire novel. Its emphasis on *le paraître* embraces the facial expressions characters adopt, the clothes Duroy hires, and the decorations he uses to hide the prosaic ugliness of his room. What lies behind the mask is mercilessly exposed. For *Bel-Ami* is no exception to Maupassant's familiar exploration of the theatrical. 'La mise en scène' is the overriding concern of both the offices of *La Vie Française* (p. 80) and the Walter residence (p. 150); and within the latter's sumptuous décor we are treated to 'une comédie mondaine et convenable, répétée bien souvent' (p. 151). Those privy to scandal fall into the category of 'acteur, confident ou simplement témoin' (pp. 111-12). Love-affairs are similarly defined: Mme Walter surrenders 'avec une petite comédie de pudeur enfantine' (p. 316), avowing her bliss 'comme l'aurait fait une ingénue, au théâtre' (p. 317); and Mme de Marelle, faced with her husband's importunate return, announces to her lover: 'Nous aurons donc relâche huit jours' (p. 126). M. Walter 'avait toujours manœuvré sous un masque souriant de brave homme' (p. 154). Duroy himself 's'étudia comme font les acteurs pour apprendre leurs rôles' (p. 50), and becomes a consummate performer: 'il parlait maintenant avec des intonations d'acteur, avec un jeu plaisant de figure' (p. 239).

As Duroy's 'images transparentes' (p. 121), however, also reflect his state of mind, so too, it can be suggested, *Bel-Ami* offers us more than a transparent screen through which the world's hypocrisy is laid bare. For in the same way as a preoccupation with writing is potentially self-reflexive, the text intermittently mirrors its own design. The paintings which decorate the novel's interiors, for example, have not been innocently invented. [12] Mme de Marelle's 'quatre pauvres tableaux, représentant une barque sur un fleuve, un navire sur la mer, un moulin dans une plaine et un bûcheron dans un bois' (p. 104) all refer us back to Duroy's impoverished isolation at the time; at his parents' home, by contrast, 'deux images coloriées représentant Paul et Virginie sous un palmier bleu et Napoléon Ier sur un cheval jaune' (p. 247) reflect the context of a triumphant honeymoon, as well as being subsequently, and ironically, echoed in the Virginie (Walter) he seduces, whose husband conceives 'une idée à la Bonaparte' (p. 348). The latter's own series of pictures are significant in a rather different way, elaborated to the point where they constitute a veritable *mise-en-abyme* of the novel's thematic concerns: apprenticeship in *La Leçon,* the struggle in *L'Obstacle* and, above all, vertical perspective in *Le haut et le bas.* As these are described as the works of 'les fantaisistes' (p. 161), so when Duroy, the author of 'une petite série fantaisiste sur l'Algérie' (p. 58), wonders of the Marelles 'quel fantaisiste a bien pu préparer l'accouplement de ce vieux et de cette écervelée' (p. 199), the answer is, of course, that it is Maupassant himself.

It is a critical commonplace to point out that, throughout his career, the most prevalent of Maupassant's motifs is that of the mirror – both literally and as metaphor – which dramatizes the tension between self as identity and self as other. In *Bel-Ami* this is repeatedly used as a means of presenting the protagonist's introspection within the constraints of aesthetic objectivity. But Duroy's alienating self-spectacle is also emblematic. For the text too bears witness to what Maupassant calls in *Sur l'eau* 'une sorte de dédoublement de l'esprit' transforming the writer into both 'acteur et spectateur de lui-même et des autres'. [13] This sense of watching himself 'dans le miroir de ma pensée' in the very act of observing reality may well account for the ambivalence of the self-portrait located in Duroy. Yet that ambivalence is thereby extended to the novel itself, lodged between the realities it records and the imaginative construction it must necessarily be if it is to articulate a distinctive vision. In a society in which art is a commercial proposition and occupies a decorative space, *Bel-Ami* thus provides alternative images of itself: on the one hand, as has been suggested, there are Duroy's empty journalistic inventions; on the other there is the Marcowitch painting, explicitly self-referential ('il vous ressemble, Bel-Ami' (p. 367)) and described as 'l'œuvre puissante et inattendue d'un maître, une de ces œuvres qui bouleversent la pensée et vous laissent du rêve pour des années' (p. 356); but, as we are reminded, 'il fallait bien regarder pour comprendre'.

Maupassant's novel ultimately makes the same demands on us. For we are constantly made aware of Duroy's illusions and yet subscribe to his point of view. As the 'Echos' of *La Vie Française* lose none of their impact by being echoed in others, the reflections in Duroy's mirror tend to be confirmed rather than exploded by our perception of the mirroring process. Even the name 'Bel-Ami', the frivolous product of childish adoration (p. 121), is finally the one through which the eponymous hero's story is authoritatively told. At his 'coronation' in the Rue Royale, when Du Roy 'se croyait un roi' (p. 412), we may well overlook the self-deluding focus underlined by the word-play of the apparently invisible narrator. To do so is to be equally blind to the fact that this 'novel of ascent' is organized in patterns of stasis, circularity and regression.

In so far as they end with 'son œuvre de conquête commencée' (p. 64), the opening chapters of *Bel-Ami* are exemplary in this respect. [14] They appear to set in motion the dynamics of differentiation and future triumph, while simultaneously establishing a paradigm of subversive ironies. The scene at the Folies-Bergère thus functions as yet another mirror in which Duroy, with his own 'raie au milieu du crâne' (p. 32), fails to recognize himself in the figure of the trapeze-artist:

> On voyait, sous le maillot, se dessiner les muscles des bras et des jambes; il gonflait sa poitrine pour dissimuler son estomac trop saillant; et sa figure semblait celle d'un garçon coiffeur, car une raie soignée ouvrait sa chevelure en deux parties égales, juste au milieu du crâne. Il atteignait le trapèze d'un bond gracieux, et, pendu par les mains, tournait autour

> comme une roue lancée; ou bien, les bras roides, le corps droit, il se
> tenait immobile, couché horizontalement dans le vide, attaché seulement
> à la barre fixe par la force des poignets. (p. 44)

Duroy too, 'se dandinant avec grâce' (p. 34), is repeatedly admired for
his strength; that immobility, however, punctuates his perambulations
(pp. 31, 33, 35, 39, 64) and his fearful contemplation of the duel (p. 188),
and anticipates the novel's close when he is transfixed on the steps of the
Madeleine (p. 413). That, of course, was his initial destination (p. 35), so
that via another Madeleine (Forestier), he has come full circle. Asked
where he is going, Duroy replies: 'nulle part, je fais un tour avant de
rentrer' (p. 36), taking him to a symbolic Arc de Triomphe (p. 95) and
back.

   In a sense, the novel as a whole simply repeats Duroy's earlier
experience, as we are told of his 'succès de garnison, des bonnes fortunes
faciles et même des aventures dans un monde plus élevé, ayant séduit la
fille d'un percepteur qui voulait tout quitter pour le suivre, et la femme
d'un avoué qui avait tenté de se noyer par désespoir d'être délaissée'
(p. 69), thereby prefiguring a sexual destiny which takes him from Rachel
to Mme Walter and her daughter. The underlying structure of *Bel-Ami* is
itself essentially reduplicative, with its repeated scenes of self-contem-
plation, its staircases and dinner-parties, and its complementary views of
Paris and Rouen. Such symmetries serve to erode the illusion both of
movement and difference. As the reporters at *La Vie Française* are
differentiated only by their hats, 'comme si cette forme les eût distingués
du reste des hommes' (p. 40), so the presence of prostitutes at all levels in
the rising tiers of seats at the Folies-Bergère undermines the semblance of
social hierarchy (p. 46); and, in the same way, Duroy's 'rapports continus'
with categories as apparently distinct as cabinet-ministers and cab-drivers
leave him 'les confondant dans son estime' (p. 101). Between the dinners
at the Forestiers, the Café Riche and the family tavern, equally characterized by smut, there is only the superficial difference of décor. Parallels
between the text's female figures have an analogous function, in the
pairing, for example, of Laurine and Suzanne and their respective
mothers. The two prostitutes at the Folies-Bergère are recalled in Mme
Forestier and Mme de Marelle (p. 52), and the sequence of early-morning
visits to the latter align them as surely as the process of substitution is
confirmed by Duroy's subsequent return to Rachel when his society
mistresses are not available. The hesitant seduction of the experienced
Madeleine finds its inverted image in Mme Walter's virginal timidity,

divested of its emotional particularity in Duroy's 'ce qui m'est bien égal' (p. 309) and in his using the same 'paroles d'amour' (p. 328) irrespective of the object of desire.

As far as Duroy himself is concerned, a text which ends with the declaration that he is 'au-dessus des autres' (p. 410) in fact reveals that differentiation to be illusory. Others are judged by him as hypocritical and corrupt; he is only vaguely aware, however, that 'il y avait quelque chose de commun entre eux, un lien de nature, qu'ils étaient de même race, de même âme, et que son succès aurait des procédés audacieux de même ordre' (p. 174). He and Mme de Marelle are fellow-members of the same 'race aventureuse des vagabonds' (p. 319). His colleague Thomas also has an adopted name: 'c'est au journal qu'on m'a surnommé Saint-Potin' (p. 94). Duroy's status as 'un des maîtres de la terre' (p. 411) simply echoes the description of M. Walter as 'un des maîtres du monde' (p. 347). Another Duroy is the contemptible Laroche-Mathieu, with his 'machiavé-lisme du village [qui] le faisait passer pour fort' (p. 259); as the former does in the Marelle household, he takes over in the 'maison Du Roy' the role of 'second maître' (p. 350) vacated by the Vaudrec who had preceded Georges in Madeleine's extra-marital affections. And we are told of her, in epilogue-like fashion, that Duroy's successor is a Jean Le Dol, 'un jeune homme, beau garçon, intelligent, de la même race que notre ami Georges' (p. 406). The most explicit surrogacy remains, of course, the pairing of Duroy and Forestier, with their double-act reflected in that of the two trapeze-artists. From the moment he dogs his footsteps on the pavement when they renew their association, Duroy's illusions of individuality are subverted by the husband he eventually replaces. As his literary apprenticeship repeats Forestier's own, he appropriates his domestic chair and professional responsibilities, his newspaper column and his pen, his salary and decoration, his bilboquet set and home, to the point where 'on ne l'appelait plus que Forestier' (p. 259). Waiting for Mme Walter in the church, he spots a stranger engaged on an identical mission, only to imagine in this provincial reflection of himself, 'qu'il ressemblait à Forestier' (p. 302). And, in his deteriorating relationship with Madeleine, his retrospective jealousy foregrounds an obsession with difference which Forestier's posthumous presence consistently denies.

What this network of parallels underlines is that though he may seem self-assertive, 'poussant les gens pour ne point se déranger de sa route' (p. 32), Duroy is ultimately, as this first glimpse of him already suggests, subordinate to the collective 'courant des promeneurs' (p. 46). Apparent conquest, in other words, is merely surrender to material and social determinants. In a fictional world elaborated in structures of causality which make of individuals impotent victims of such fatalities, Duroy's power is relativized by his passivity. If his motivation is explained in terms of economic circumstances, he is equally subject to his chemistry and appetites. As he is unable to resist quenching his thirst (p. 33), so his perception of triumph is figuratively intoxicating (p. 59). Moving up towards the Champs-Elysées, he goes down the significantly-entitled rue Notre-Dame de Lorette, his progress checked by sexual desire (p. 33) and his aspirations for elegant love-affairs interpolated by the temptations of the base; and his 'succès' (p. 45) with the 'grosse brune' is ironized by the bestiality which attracts him to her. An unrefined violence lies only just below the surface of the control he sometimes barely maintains (p. 262). And Maupassant's metaphorical assimilation of his superficially different conquests is particularly revealing: for as Laurine is 'apprivoisée' (p. 64) by Duroy's charm, he jumps on his new wife 'comme un épervier sur une proie' (p. 237) with the same savagery he displays in his treatment of Mme Walter; that she too is seized 'comme une proie' (p. 309) further reminds us of his fantasy of wringing the necks of the rich as he had the chickens of the Arabs, themselves 'la proie naturelle du soldat' (p. 34). As *Le haut et le bas* points to carnality, the novel's animal imagery is reflected in the painting of the *Sauvetage* and its feline contemplation of a drowning fly (p. 162). Because it dramatizes such a struggle for life, *Bel-Ami* exemplified, for contemporary reviewers, 'le Darwinisme littéraire'. But the survival even of the fittest is framed by the biological destiny voiced by Norbert de Varenne: 'Vivre enfin, c'est mourir!' (p. 169).

The implications of the Duroy-Forestier substitution are inescapable. The advice that 'tout dépend de l'aplomb' (p. 37) is offered by a character whose substantial appearance only masks his inner disintegration. The warship the two ex-soldiers see off Cannes is appropriately called the *Dévastation* (p. 210), and when Duroy climbs up to the Villa Jolie to begin his wooing of Madeleine, the spectacle of Forestier's death brings him face to face with a vision of his own. He is haunted throughout the novel by this *alter ego;* Forestier's imminent physical disappearance accordingly gives him the illusion of freedom and a new-found independence, 'un sentiment de délivrance, d'espace qui s'ouvrait devant lui' (p. 202). Yet that space is ultimately the same as the 'néant illimité' he will perceive (p. 216), the 'abîme profond' (p. 65) below his Rastignac-like view of Paris, the 'immense tranchée' of the station and the tunnels in which surrogate trains are buried (p. 66), and the 'creux' left by his body on the bed (p. 67), as Laroche-Mathieu's shape in his wife's is that of a corpse (p. 378). For the sub-text of this 'novel of ascent' is the emptiness at its centre, the nothingness of human toil represented in another group of paintings (p. 161) and articulated by Norbert de Varenne. Here, Maupassant's ferocious pessimism receives expression in an almost embarrassingly transparent commentary. Norbert's discourse, however awkwardly inserted in the fiction, nevertheless illuminates the true significance of *Bel-Ami's* vertical structures: 'la vie est une côte. Tant qu'on monte, on regarde le sommet, et on se sent heureux; mais, lorsqu'on arrive en haut, on aperçoit tout d'un coup la descente, et la fin, qui est la mort' (p. 167). This encroaching mortality, he tells us, 'm'a défiguré si complètement que je ne me reconnais pas' (p. 168). In the same way, Duroy can barely recognize the dying Forestier (p. 203), and nowhere is that characteristic alienation in the mirror more uncompromisingly explored than on the night before the duel when 'il se reconnut à peine' (p. 189) in the contemplation of his own death. Norbert's speech opens up a 'trou plein d'ossements, un trou inévitable où il lui faudrait tomber un jour' (p. 172), prefigured in Duroy's 'sensation de tomber dans un trou' (p. 110) at the Café Riche and recalled in 'ce petit trou noir et profond du canon dont allait sortir une balle' (p. 191). As his social persona is no more than the reverberation of 'son nom dans un appartement vide' (p. 150), so he and Madeleine's self-admiring 'rire de triomphe' is undercut by their spectral reflections in the glass, 'prêts à s'évanouir dans la nuit' (p. 346).

The force of these thematic patterns and remorseless symmetries is to equate all human activity with an illusion of the ego which seeks to assert its own reality in an unacknowledged void. The repeated church scenes thus erode the apparent differences between an illicit liaison, a wedding and a funeral. Like that of the trapeze-artists, such behaviour is essentially a performance in 'le vide'. For the trivial games that people play, whether bilboquet or cards, are indistinguishable from their overtly serious concerns. In the 'cercles', described as 'la grande ressource' (p. 173), these are inscribed in an appropriate circularity. Colonial rapacity is 'une escapade' (p. 34) embracing the hunting metaphors of Duroy's later exploits. 'Moi, je joue toute la journée', he tells Laurine (p. 107), and then engages in a game with her which exactly anticipates his chasing Mme Walter round her chairs (p. 289). Sophisticated conversations about elections to the Académie are reduced to a 'jeu de la mort et des quarante vieillards' (p. 153). Related to its theatrical conception of experience, major episodes in *Bel-Ami* constitute a miming of action and a substitute for it. Complementing the visit to the Folies-Bergère, the 'gymnastique effrénée' (p. 281) of the 'salle-d'armes' chapter also goes beyond the anecdotal. It is hardly by chance that the combat enacted by its 'marionnettes vivantes' (p. 280) refers back to the duel Duroy had imagined as real – in spite of its absurd pretext and the overwhelming backcloth of an indifferent nature (as in the landscape paintings (p. 161)) which invalidates its significance. Duroy's stabbing his rival's visiting-card with a pair of scissors (p. 188), his shooting at the 'carton blanc' in practice (p. 280) and shadow-boxing against the wall (p. 234) are all seen in a similarly ironic perspective. Where this is again more problematic, in respect of *Bel-Ami's* own mimetic status, is Maupassant's extension of an oblique self-portrait to include Duroy's 'jeu' of observing his society at play (p. 173) and the 'jeu vague qui ne prenait point sa pensée' (p. 77) of filling in 'le carré blanc' of the unwritten page.

Abstracted from it in this way, Maupassant's novel may well seem as contrived as the geometry of its paintings or the contents of Walter's hothouse with their 'air de plantes factices, invraisemblables, trop belles pour être vraies' (pp. 60-61). The fact that we take the 'Illusionniste' 's artifice at face-value – at the level of *paraître* in spite of its thematic subversion – is nevertheless revealing. Duroy's progress does indeed seem uninterrupted in so far as we can discount his *return* to his origins or to his first article, and are barely conscious, at its climax, that the final image of him is going *down* yet another set of stairs, subject once again to the animal sensuality of Mme de Marelle. Even the text's internal rhythm sustains a forward momentum hardly checked by its narrative interludes or the prosaic 'Georges Duroy avait retrouvé toutes ses habitudes ancien-nes' (p. 225) at the opening of Part II, which takes us back to the beginning. And Norbert's gloomy truths introduce a merely temporary anxiety, not only on account of their incongruous design, but above all because they are displaced by the confidence of Duroy's alternative focus. Authorial self-effacement leaves his as the privileged point of view within which the reader shares an illusion of mastering the world of people and events. For that reason too, Duroy is not an unattractive figure: as Delaisement writes, 'pourquoi nier certaine sympathie pour un héros que la réussite comble toujours quand, la chance aidant, il s'impose à plus vil et plus machiavélique que lui'.[15]

To acknowledge that that sneaking sympathy is not Maupassant's alone is to admit our enjoyment of both Duroy's demystificatory stance and the vicarious experience of domination and control. The text provocatively establishes the challenges to be overcome. Madeleine's declaration that she will never ever be his mistress (p. 147) is an invitation to read on as surely as Mme Walter's reputation as being 'inattaquable' (p. 272) merely whets Duroy's appetite: 'la Patronne l'excitait par la difficulté de la conquête' (p. 291). In that respect she is not unlike Mme Tourvel, the présidente of *Les Liaisons dangeureuses,* whose virtue becomes a legitimate target in the same insidious way.[16] Henry James, it must be said, was outraged by the Mme Walter episode.[17] One is left wondering how many other readers of *Bel-Ami* can retain the same admirable moral rectitude, faced with the choice between cynical intelligence and the blindness of piety. And in the comic scene in which Laroche-Mathieu is discovered *en flagrant délit,* the reader long held in suspense about the basis of the rumours surrounding the awesome Madeleine is likely to identify with Duroy's machinations and the disappointed satisfaction of knowing the truth. The conventions of dramatic irony ensure that we do not take the side of the gullible; witnessing Duroy's financial trickery or his plans for the abduction of Suzanne, his stature is enhanced. He emerges in the reader's mind as somehow superior to those he dupes, so that when an individual as obviously successful as M. Walter marvels at Duroy's cunning, his 'il est fort tout de même' (p. 395) secures our assent and reinforces the character's subjective view of his own abilities. As we follow the underdog up the stairs of social values or the recurrent hills which afford an overview of the novel's topography, that subjectivity is itself validated. The self-deception we may not notice is, in any case, relativized by the delusion of others. As Norbert puts it, 'dans le royaume des aveugles les borgnes sont rois' (p. 167). In all these ways, it can be suggested, the rascal's illusion of ascent and superiority becomes a reality as difficult to resist as his charm.

The supreme irony of this modulation of our sympathies is that we thereby become as gullible as Mme Walter, as effectively stripped of her moral scruples as her respectable clothes. She is seen prostrate and suspending her disbelief before the Marcowitch painting, unable to distinguish between reality and artistic representation, confusing the 'Homme-Dieu' invoked in church (p. 411) and the 'Homme-Dieu' located in the frame (p. 356). As she is taken in by Duroy's 'banale musique d'amour' (p. 292), so, by analogy, we may justifiably ask to what extent this corresponds to the reader's confrontation with *Bel-Ami* itself, so often considered an exemplary Naturalist text in its detailed and utterly prosaic recording of 'la vie française' epitomized by its fictional newspaper.

Whether such a definition is adequate is open to debate. For by involving us directly in the overlaid paradox that this construction of the 'Illusionniste' both demystifies and confirms the illusions of experience, Maupassant certainly seems to enlarge the critical questions posed by his

novel. And its moments of self-questioning tell us much about the nature
of his achievement. Of Duroy we are told, for example, that 'comme il
éprouvait une peine infinie à découvrir des idées, il prit la spécialité des
déclamations sur la décadence des mœurs, sur l'abaissement des caractères,
l'affaissement du patriotisme et l'anémie de l'honneur français' (p. 200).
As well as caricaturing a certain kind of journalism, here Maupassant
alerts us to the fact that his own writing is not just that sort of facile
polemic, and yet runs the risk of being no more than that in its similar
castigations. Duroy's satirical pleasure is his own: 'ce jeu l'amusait
beaucoup, comme s'il eût constaté, sous les sévères apparences, l'éternelle
et profonde infamie de l'homme, et que cela l'eût réjoui, excité, consolé'
(p. 173). Alongside the recognition of hypocritical self-indulgence, however, there is Norbert de Varenne's 'derrière tout ce qu'on regarde, c'est la
mort qu'on aperçoit' (p. 168). In the 'miroir de ma pensée' mentioned
earlier, Maupassant is uneasily situated between the authority of the
eccentric poet and the partial self-portrait offered by Duroy. That unease
will receive its fullest examination in *L'Inutile Beauté* (1890), in which art
is conceived as both the free-play of the imagination momentarily transcending deterministic forces, and yet ultimately as insubstantial as other
human activities. Such an ambivalence towards his own writing, alter-
nately asserted as a *raison-d'être* and cynically dismissed as a way of
earning a living, is undoubtedly registered in *Bel-Ami*. Norbert's lines are
more instructive than they might seem:

> Et je cherche le mot de cet obscur problème
> Dans le ciel noir et vide où flotte un astre blême.
> (p. 171)

They suggest the extent to which Maupassant is himself looking for a form
in which to express the poet's intuitions: 'Oh! vous ne comprenez même
pas ce mot-là, vous, la mort' (p. 168). And Norbert's presence in the text
may testify to the uncertainty of Maupassant's achievement, to a fundamental lack of confidence, on his own part, that 'le sens définitif de
l'œuvre' will be understood by readers whose illusions will simply be
confirmed in the mirror of Duroy's triumphant progress.

This essay has tried to show that the distinctive quality of Maupassant's vision lies in the way *Bel-Ami*'s mirrors simultaneously effect
a process of estrangement. For, as his self-appraisal is not synonymous
with an undifferentiated self-reflection, that vision is the measure of the
originality of the novelist's recognizably realist text which is not simply a

copy of the particular reality it seems to transcribe. Duroy is himself disorientated by optical illusions: 'il se trompa d'abord de direction, le miroir ayant égaré son œil' (p. 150); and he misjudges heights: 'il se laissa tomber, l'ayant cru beaucoup plus haut' (p. 151); but there is no mistaking 'le léger trouble moral que produit un changement à vue' (p. 161) and the significance of Mme Walter looking in the mirror 'pour voir si rien n'était changé en elle' (p. 393). In the same way, it can be argued, the reader finds in *Bel-Ami* an alienated version of himself, inviting him, as Norbert puts it, to see 'l'existence d'une autre façon' (p. 170).

The Marcowitch painting too is deceptive. Beneath the 'apparence si simple' of its traditional subject, however, its composition brings together many of the significant details which underlie the novel's own. Thus, for example, the metaphorical infrastructure of *Bel-Ami*'s final chapter, with its 'bruit d'une mer lointaine' (p. 407) of the crowd and the waves of sound filling the church, is anticipated in the pictorial representation of *Jésus marchant sur les flots;* what distinguishes it is the darkness surrounding the central figure and the vastness of the firmament, both integral to Norbert's poetic formulation of the insignificance of human activities and Maupassant's pervasive relativization of fame and fortune. The fictional painting itself 'semblait un trou noir sur un lointain fantastique et saisissant' (p. 356), thematically consistent, as we have seen, with the recurrent focus on such emptiness; and the Folies-Bergère scene, with its performer 'immobile [. . .] dans le vide' (p. 44), is recalled in the 'homme immobile, debout sur la mer' (p. 356). Above all, the impact of the painting derives from its theatrical lighting and the admiring gaze of the apostles, their faces 'convulsées par la surprise' (p. 356). For Mme Walter, 'il ressemblait tellement à Bel-Ami, à la clarté tremblante de cette lumière l'éclairant à peine et d'en bas, que ce n'était plus Dieu, c'était son amant qui la regardait' (p. 398). And her illusions, as has been suggested, are potentially our own.

Her unthinking involvement can be contrasted with Maupassant's nostalgic evocation, in an essay exactly contemporary to the preparation of *Bel-Ami,* of an 18th-century public appreciative of a writer's secretive procedures: 'Il cherchait les dessous, les dedans des mots, pénétrait les raisons secrètes de l'auteur, lisait lentement, sans rien passer, cherchait, après avoir compris la phrase, s'il ne restait rien à pénétrer'.[18] The cautionary 'Il fallait bien regarder pour comprendre', as far as the Marcowitch painting is concerned, has to be read in this wider context. For, as Maupassant repeatedly stresses, the novelist's aim 'n'est point de nous raconter une histoire, de nous amuser ou de attendrir, mais de nous forcer à penser, à comprendre le sens profond et caché des événements'.[19] And this necessitates both involvement in, and abstraction from, a recognizable fictional reality, neither exclusively symbolic, nor simply anecdotal, like Duroy's journalistic constructions which also cater for the gullible. Mme Walter's suspension of disbelief leaves her, literally, unconscious. But there are more perceptive responses to the internal ambiguities of the great work of art she confuses with life: 'Comme ils en ont peur et comme ils l'aiment, ces hommes! Regardez donc sa tête, ses yeux, comme il est simple et surnaturel en même temps!' (p. 367). As adoring identification and fearful estrangement may be elicited in the complicitous mirrors held up by its hero, so, applied to the novel as a whole, that 'simple et surnaturel en même temps' encourages the reader to see illustrated in *Bel-Ami* what is considered the most succinct statement of Maupassant's aesthetic: 'Une œuvre d'art n'est supérieure que si elle est en même temps un symbole et l'expression exacte d'une réalité'.[20]

It is far from certain that this ideal is fulfilled, or that the novel ranks as 'une de ces œuvres qui bouleversent la pensée et vous laissent du rêve pour des années'. Maupassant will not be alone in the doubts about his achievement. Alongside the self-deprecating irony directed at Duroy's verbal facility and Norbert's intrusive discourse aimed at those readers of *Bel-Ami* unable to discern its 'sens caché' as well as believe in its 'événements', unequivocal assessment of that achievement is not entirely pre-empted by the caricaturally philistine reactions of those who fail to understand the painting at its centre, 'et ne parlaient qu'ensuite de la valeur de la peinture' in monetary terms (p. 356). It could be argued, indeed, that Maupassant's worst fears have been realized in critical assimilation of *Bel-Ami* and the Balzacian tradition it is deemed to continue. Vial writes that the novel 'se rattache directement à Balzac',[21] and Delaisement cites the author of *Illusions perdues* as 'le modèle incontesté'.[22] Such remarks implicitly minimize the distinctive qualities of the work and overlook the fact that the model *is* contested, specifically in the denial of the Balzacian point of reference in the curious mention of Duroy that he 'n'avait pas lu Balzac' (p. 93), but also, and more generally, in the text's demystification of the heroic ethos it seems to propose. Not the least intriguing aspect of *Bel-Ami,* and this is perhaps where its originality lies, is that in a composition as stylized as that of the 'fantaisiste', Maupassant's art of illusion generates a fiction not about the loss of illusions – that clichéd 19th-century theme – but about their construction and their reality.

Notes

[1] André Vial, *Guy de Maupassant et l'art du roman* (Paris, Nizet, 1954), p. 358.

[2] See Vial, op. cit., pp. 299-301.

[3] 'Le Pessimisme dans le roman', *Revue des Deux Mondes,* 70 (1885), 215.

[4] See J. R. Duggan, *Illusion and Reality. A Study of Descriptive Techniques in the Works of Guy de Maupassant* (The Hague, Mouton, 1973).

[5] In 'Le Roman'; *Pierre et Jean* (Paris, Gallimard, 1982), p. 52.

[6] Edward D. Sullivan, *Maupassant the Novelist* (New Jersey, Princeton University Press, 1954), p. 74.

[7] 'Aux critiques de *Bel-Ami:* une réponse', *Gil Blas,* 7 June 1885; in Guy de Maupassant, *Chroniques,* ed. Hubert Juin, 3 vols. (Paris, Union Générale d'Editions, 1980), III, pp. 166-67.

[8] *Situations II* (Paris, Gallimard, 1948), p. 173.

[9] See Gérard Delaisement, *Maupassant. 'Bel-Ami'* (Paris, Hatier, 1972), pp. 25-26, 37, 45.

[10] 'Le Roman' (loc. cit.), pp. 50-51.

[11] *Bel-Ami,* ed. Jean-Louis Bory (Paris, Gallimard, 1973); all interpolated page references are to this 'Folio' edition of the novel.

[12] That they have been invented is confirmed by Bory in his annotation for the 'Folio' ed.; see pp. 427-29.

[13] *Sur l'eau* (Paris, Marpon et Flammarion, 1888), p. 117.

[14] See R. B. Grant, 'The Function of the First Chapter of Maupassant's *Bel-Ami'*, *Modern Language Notes,* 76 (1961), 748-52.

[15] op. cit., p. 45.

[16] See Valerie Minogue's suggestive *'Les Liaisons dangereuses:* a Practical Lesson in the Art of Seduction', *Modern Language Review,* 67 (1972), 775-86.

[17] *Partial Portraits* (London, Macmillan, 1888), p. 278.

[18] See his 1884 essay on Flaubert, *Chroniques,* III, p. 109.

[19] 'Le Roman' (loc. cit.), p. 49.

[20] *La Vie errante* (1890); cited by Vial, op. cit., p. 75.

[21] Vial, op. cit., p. 358.

[22] Delaisement, op. cit., p. 46.

Le Lieutenant-Colonel de Maumort: a posthumous life

Roisin Mallaghan : Pembroke College, Oxford

Dᴜʀɪɴɢ his lifetime, Roger Martin du Gard enjoyed considerable public recognition for his literary works. He followed his well-received early novel, *Jean Barois,* with the widely acclaimed series, *Les Thibault,* for the final volumes of which he was awarded the Nobel Prize for literature in 1937. And in 1955 these achievements were crowned with the glory of publication in the Bibliothèque de la Pléiade collection – a tribute only rarely accorded to living writers either then or now. Yet this final accolade was something of a dubious privilege. If early elevation into the literary firmament was undeniably an honour, the title chosen for the two-volume edition, *Œuvres complètes,* in a sense served to consign him early to the grave by seemingly signalling that his literary career was at an end, and that his final fictional work, *Le Lieutenant-Colonel de Maumort,* would never see the light of day.[1] Yet *Maumort* has at last appeared, albeit in an unfinished form, and this essay will be principally concerned with some of the issues raised by this final work. Before considering these, however, it is useful to set the scene by describing the circumstances in which Martin du Gard found himself, in the years leading up to the Pléiade publication of 1955 which was to mark his demise.

Preparations for his funeral service could in fact be said to have begun some years earlier, the death knell having been rung in 1950 by the critic Claude-Edmonde Magny in her work *Histoire du roman français depuis 1918.*[2] In her essay on Martin du Gard, Magny proposed as an epitaph for him words taken from the diary of Antoine with which *Les Thibault* concludes: 'Suis condamné à mourir sans avoir compris grand-chose à moi-même, ni au monde . . .'.[3] And to these she added her own damning version: 'Ainsi apparaît-il d'ores et déjà comme un naturaliste attardé dans l'après guerre, représentatif de toute une génération de romanciers médiocres, que ne viennent sauver ni ses dons ni son extrême honnêteté intellectuelle'. [4] Julien Green's revelation that Martin du Gard had the 'quasi-inhumain' ability to leave the telephone ringing while at his work was given emblematic significance by Magny, as if such a practice irrefutably demonstrated a basic inability to communicate with or relate to the world in which and about which he wrote.

Of Magny's condemnatory essay, Martin du Gard wrote to Gide:

> C'est un bel éloge funèbre qui suit une exécution capitale... Me voilà prévenu: je comparaîtrai les mains vides, en somme, au tribunal de la postérité. [5]

These sentiments were echoed in the self-critical 'pensée testamentaire' which he composed at the end of the following year:

> Je ne suis qu'un aboutissement. Je n'ai rien apporté de neuf. *Je n'ai rien fait d'autre que de cultiver avec soin, avec goût, avec probité, des terres que les romanciers français, russes et anglais avaient défrichées au XIXe siècle.* [6]

It is true that well before Magny's essay, Martin du Gard had described himself as out of touch with the 'modern' world. In his diary he noted in December of 1945:

> C'est le passé seul dont je suis contemporain: ce que je puis penser, ce que maintenant je pourrais dire, ne répond à aucune des interrogations que se posent aujourd'hui, que se poseront demain, les hommes jeunes qui survivront aux désastres actuels. (OCI, p. cxxi) [7]

Earlier still he had written to Gide of his work in progress, saying that he was convinced that it would be 'du posthume' (OCI, p. cxiv). But these very fears and self-doubts also had the more positive effect of convincing him of his own sincerity and clarity of insight:

> Le fait que la révélation de mon juste poids d'écrivain ne m'est pas venue de l'extérieur, qu'elle est née de mon propre examen, de ma propre clairvoyance sur moi-même, cela allège ma déception, m'épargne le désespoir, et me permet encore une relative sérénité. (OCI, pp. cxxii-iii)

It would thus appear that his personal anxieties about his own ability were at most occasional, surmountable, obstacles. Certainly, they did not prevent him from setting out to write the novel which was to be his literary testament, *Maumort:* 'Je crois pouvoir faire de Maumort une belle figure . . . Une figure *exemplaire,* qui serait comme mon testament' (OCI, p. civ). That the post-war would be radically different from the world in which he had lived until then was something which he frequently acknowledged. Recommending *Les Temps Modernes* to Gide, in the summer of 1947, he wrote:

> Bonne occasion pour mesurer combien, et comprendre en quoi, les points de vue de la génération Sartre diffèrent totalement des nôtres. Ce sont des produits d'un autre climat; mais non des produits dégénérés. Bien instructif pour nous.[8]

Such differences were not, however, interpreted by him as precluding the possibility of further literary activity on his own part. *Maumort* was to be not just a personal testament, but 'le testament d'une génération à la veille d'une scission complète entre deux âges de l'humanité' (OCI, p. cix). Martin du Gard still saw himself as a potential spokesman for the older generation to which he felt he belonged.

Magny's accusations, however, put an end to all that, as she alleged that throughout his active life he had been out of step with his times: 'On dirait que sa montre s'est arrêtée au moment où meurt son héros, Antoine, et qu'il n'a plus progressé spirituellement à partir de 1918, qu'il a cessé de vouloir accompagner le monde dans son évolution'.[9] By the time the Pléiade edition of his works appeared, he was therefore in no position to contend that they were not in fact 'complete'. In his introduction to the *Journal de Maumort,* contained within the first volume of that edition, he himself observed: 'Force m'est d'accepter aujourd'hui l'éventualité d'un renoncement qui risque d'être définitif!' (OCI, p. c). Albeit in cautious terms, and in the present tense, he thus tacitly confirmed that if *Maumort* was not yet laid to rest, it was almost definitely destined to lead only a posthumous life.

That posthumous life began in 1983, with the publication by Gallimard of this final, unfinished work, in a third Pléiade volume providing a 1300 page supplement to the *Œuvres complètes.* The volume, edited by André Daspre, includes a description by Daspre of the 'genèse du roman', and a discussion of the editorial decisions involved in presenting the text. These are followed by Martin du Gard's version of the life of Lieutenant-Colonel Maumort in the form of memoirs ostensibly written by Maumort himself at the age of seventy, by the remains of a later attempt to write the novel in the form of letters addressed by the septuagenarian Maumort to a medical friend, Gévresin, and by a selection of notes relating to the work, taken from Martin du Gard's 'dossiers de la boîte noire', now deposited at the Bibliothèque Nationale. [10]

Martin du Gard worked on this novel for nearly two decades, and it saw numerous changes of direction during that time. The task of editing the work was thus an enormous one, and it is hardly surprising that as many years were needed to produce a publishable edition from the unfinished manuscript as had been necessary to produce that manuscript itself. How satisfactorily Daspre has carried out the task will only be clear when the material from which he selected is made available for general consultation by the Bibliothèque Nationale. Even without this information, however, and although the text as it survives provides a detailed version only of Maumort's first twenty-five years, this posthumously published work nevertheless casts a new and intriguing light on Martin du Gard and his *œuvre* as a whole.

As one might expect, there are numerous similarities between *Maumort* and Martin du Gard's other works. The presentation of characters situated in a recognisable milieu, minutely described; the interest in the impact of major historical events upon individuals' lives; the concern to follow the course of these lives across a considerable period of time: these are all features which *Maumort* has in common with *Jean Barois* and *Les Thibault*. Moreover, according to the plan for *Maumort,* the three decisive moments of Maumort's life were to be his realisation that he did not believe in God, his discovery of the truth about the Dreyfus affair, and his learning that the 1914-18 war had begun. Not only are these three moments described by Dr Philip in *Les Thibault* as the decisive moments of his life (OCII, p. 597), but they are also the events with which the earlier works are principally concerned. So, as far as its historical details are concerned, *Maumort* appears to retread well-trodden ground. There are also many parallels between the observations and opinions of Maumort himself and the views expressed by the other two 'elders' of Martin du Gard's writings, Luce in *Jean Barois* and Dr Philip in *Les Thibault*. In addition, the young Maumort appears to have much in common with Bernard Grosdidier, with the young Jean Barois, and with both Jacques and Antoine Thibault. He seems in fact to be an amalgam of the positive qualities of all these earlier men; or, to take a metaphor from biology, he emerges as a perfectly adapted specimen of a species whose evolution has been traced in the course of the earlier works. The appearance of *Maumort* thus seems to prove the validity of a prediction made by Martin du Gard in a letter to Marcel de Coppet in 1915: 'Je vais d'étape en étape vers quelque chose que je ne distingue pas encore, mais qui, de mon premier à mon dernier livre sera présent, sous-jacent, et immuablement un'.[11]

More interesting, however, than the features in *Maumort* which assure a degree of unity to Martin du Gard's work as a whole, are the aspects of it which constitute a new departure for him. For the first time, the reader is presented not with pairs of principal characters, but with a single central figure. Instead of the procedure characteristic of his earlier novels, whereby conflicts and tensions are presented dramatically through dialogues between central figures about the different options open to them, in *Maumort* the focus shifts to a single figure, and to conflicts and tensions within him – dramatised through the debates he has with himself, and through his comments about the different roles he had opted to play in the past. Moreover, whereas the principal characters of the other works often appear to be dwarfed by and inferior to those who surround them, Maumort emerges as an exceptional figure who, in spite of his modest estimation of his own worth, is seemingly superior to the majority of men in that he is able to stand apart from the differences which divide them. He is indeed a remarkable man since he is portrayed as having enjoyed the privilege of meeting most of the major intellectuals of his time before the age of 25, and these (improbable) experiences endow him with the maturity and authority to plead on behalf of all the major achievements of what he sees as his generation.

A precursor for Maumort can, in some respects, be seen in the figure of Antoine as he is presented in the *Epilogue* volume of *Les Thibault.* Alone and dying, in the closing days of the 1914-18 war, Antoine re-examines his life and reflects upon the differences between himself and the other individuals he has known. The *modus vivendi* he goes on to outline appears to be an attempt to transcend, or at least reconcile, the contradictions and oppositions which have torn his generation apart. However, it is too late for Antoine to demonstrate the practical value of this new code of conduct as he is about to die. Maumort, on the other hand, acquires this wisdom at a much earlier stage in his life and thus can be seen to constitute Martin du Gard's first truly exemplary protagonist.

But perhaps the most striking manner in which *Maumort* differs from Martin du Gard's other works is that it is written wholly in first person form. Maumort not only plays an exclusive role within the work but is in addition the ostensible author of the text. A precedent for this too can in fact be found in the *Epilogue* volume of *Les Thibault,* since it concludes with the diary ostensibly written by Antoine. His diary affords insights into only the last months of his life, however, and is just one of a number of techniques used to characterise him. Maumort's memoirs or letters are, in contrast, the sole means by which he is portrayed. They are, moreover, documents which are meant to provide information about the whole of his life, a period of some seventy years. Martin du Gard appears to have encountered considerable difficulty in trying to write his novel in this way, since at an early stage he considered the possibility of transforming the memoirs into a series of 'nouvelles', and towards the end of his life he switched to an epistolary form. Yet it is clear from the notes and manuscripts which survive that he definitely favoured the use of some form of first person narrative for the work, whatever difficulties this entailed. Given the central and exemplary role Maumort was expected to play, it was obviously necessary for Martin du Gard to find a way of introducing details not only about his character's public but also his private life, and the use of some form of first person narrative was perhaps an obvious means of meeting this requirement. At the same time it is significant that he eschewed the variety of other means he could have employed to the same end, when these included techniques which he had successfully used in the past. His decision to depart from his previous novelistic practice and use a new form thus warrants further explanation, particularly as it posed so many problems for him: 'Crise de grande perplexité. Crise latente depuis un mois. La forme que j'ai choisie pour la biographie de Maumort se trouve remise en question' (OCI, p. cxvi).

This was not the first form-induced crisis of Martin du Gard's literary career. He had experienced similar periods of anxiety during the course of writing *Les Thibault.* Nonetheless, he had always been particularly un-enthusiastic about the use of first person narrative, feeling that he tended to mishandle 'tout ce qui n'est pas scène, dialogue directe: à plus forte raison, ce qui serait commentaire'.[12] In the early stages of work on *Maumort,* he remarked that he enjoyed the freedom of a form 'qui s'accommode (et même bénéficie) du tout-venant' (OCI, p. cxiv), and he later observed that he considered it the easiest form a writer could choose to employ:

> Je me souviens d'avoir écrit vite les *Papiers posthumes* du Père Thibault; et le *Journal* d'Antoine. (. . .) Ce genre de travail va beaucoup plus vite que la mise en scène d'un épisode. Ah, les faiseurs de récits à la première personne ne connaissent pas leur chance! (OCI, p. cxxiv)

He came to the conclusion, however, that it was not the easiest form for him:

> Pourquoi ai-je choisi cette forme de 'mémoires', de récit à la première
> personne? (. . .) La seule chose que je sache faire à peu près, c'est de
> mettre le lecteur en prise directe avec la scène que je lui décris. (. . .) Dès
> que je suis contraint à commenter un caractère, à analyser un sentiment,
> j'éprouve de l'embarras, et m'en tire avec gaucherie. (. . .) Or la forme du
> journal me condamne à l'explication, à l'analyse. (. . .) Me suis-je engagé
> dans une mauvaise voie? (OCI, pp. cxvi-vii)

It was at this stage that he entertained the possibility of writing a series
of 'nouvelles', concerned with different aspects of Maumort's character
and different aspects of his life (OCI, pp. cxvii-xx). Indeed this would
appear to have been the more logical course for him to take, given that he
wanted to present Maumort as a man of action as well as a man of
reflection. But the reasons he put forward to explain his original decision
also help to explain why he persevered with it.

Firstly, he noted that a work in the form of memoirs or letters could be
concluded at any point, the abrupt ending being explained as a consequence
of the old man's death (OCI, p. cx). And he actually wrote such an ending
describing the circumstances of the death of Maumort (OCIII, p. 804).
Even so, this argument appears somewhat disingenuous, as the way in
which Martin du Gard proceeded in the writing of *Maumort* meant that
the work, as he did leave it, is far from taking the form of a piece of
continuous prose to which such an ending could satisfactorily be attached.
He even appears to have foreseen the likelihood of such a situation, since
seven years into his project, he commented with respect to his method:
'C'est la première fois que je compose ainsi, à la façon d'un mosaïste.
L'inconvénient de ce mode de travail pour un type de mon âge, c'est que si
je venais à claquer – par inadvertance – il n'y aurait rien à tirer de ces
petits morceaux de pierre destinés à s'encastrer dans un ensemble' (OCI,
pp. cxxxii-iii). Moreover, for it to have been viable to end the narrative
convincingly in such a way, the specific details of the different episodes of
Maumort's life would have had to be of only minor importance within the
work, and this was not the case:

> La vie que je construis actuellement n'est d'ailleurs pas arbitraire: tous
> les événements s'enchaînent, se tiennent, peuvent se justifier. (. . .) Que
> j'aie le temps de déterminer mon œuvre, et tout se trouvera remis à sa
> place, en ses justes proportions. (OCI, p. cxiii)

But the pretence that the work could be satisfactorily concluded by
means of such a strategy allowed him to continue to work on a novel

which he knew might be brought abruptly to an end by his own death. This alone was perhaps sufficient to recommend the use of a first person form to him.

Secondly, he argued that the writing of a novel in the form of personal papers, ostensibly intended for private consumption, legitimised the presence of details to which the more fastidious reader might otherwise object. It thus gave him a licence to examine issues he had previously felt unable or unwilling to address (OCI, p. cxxix). And finally, he observed that telling Maumort's story by means of memoirs or letters, ostensibly written in the post-war period, allowed him the opportunity to include comments about contemporary events and their repercussions, where and when he felt it appropriate to do so. This enabled him to create the impression that, in spite of his protagonist's predilection for past times, the work itself concerned the modern world.

It would seem, therefore, that even for Martin du Gard, the advantages of first person narrative in fact far out-weighed any potential disadvantages, as such a form left him free to move back and forward in time at will, and to intersperse political commentary amongst material of a more intimate nature. But another, less artistic, reason would also appear to have influenced his decision, and encouraged him to abide by it. For personal reascns, he felt it necessary to stress the importance of personal papers as a source of information about people's lives, and presenting Maumort's story in the form of memoirs or letters was an obvious means of doing so. Why Martin du Gard felt compelled to persuade others of the importance of such documents will be considered later. It is first necessary to examine how he set about presenting his case.

The strategy Martin du Gard intended to employ in the event of publication of the final work, was to preface Maumort's papers with an introductory passage, purporting to explain how they had come into his possession, and why he had decided to publish them in spite of a testamentary instruction: 'A brûler sans lire' (OCIII, p. 1065). In the notes presented by Daspre at the end of the volume, alongside a variety of possible titles in which Martin du Gard's role is represented as that of editor of the text, we find a projected version of the proposed preface:

> Maumort pourrait m'avoir légué ce manuscrit pour que je le détruise. Mais je pourrais ne pas avoir voulu le faire, en pensant qu'un tel témoignage d'une ère révolue a une valeur documentaire qu'il faut sauver, fût-ce au prix d'une trahison posthume. (OCIII, pp. 1065-66)

And in the case of the novel in letter form, he envisaged a similar solution – a preface was to explain how the letters had been passed on to him, and his reasons for deciding to publish them:

> Il nous a paru, en fin de compte, que, malgré ses multiples défauts, cette correspondance offrait aux lecteurs qui auront la persévérance nécessaire, un ensemble assez exceptionnel de documents, non seulement pour la petite histoire des classes moyennes en France entre 1870 et 1950, mais, comme toute confidence authentique, pour l'étude de l'homme en général. (OCIII, p. 1245)

In either case, therefore, the text was to begin with an introduction which served as a defence of public interest in personal papers. It was to be argued that their publication was justified because of the secrets they revealed, the memories they revived, and the survival they ensure for their author:

> Si j'ai voulu assurer une forme moins périssable à cette correspondance manuscrite, c'est (. . .) en prévision d'un temps où peut-être (. . .) certains lecteurs (. . .) s'intéresseraient soudain à cet honnête témoignage d'une expérience humaine, s'étonneraient d'y trouver malgré tout matière à réflechir, à réviser certains jugements, et – qui sait? – se découvriraient avec le vieux solitaire du Saillant quelque tardive parenté spirituelle. (OCIII, pp. 1245-46)

Leaving the prefaces for the pages which they were intended to introduce, we find that the motive Maumort gives for writing them is the loss of a previous record he had kept of his life, a diary which had allegedly been stolen, burnt or otherwise destroyed. He repeatedly emphasises the importance he attached to these lost papers. In the first letter to Gévresin, for example, he says of them:

> Les souvenirs ne sont rien; des dessins sur le sable, comparés à ce qu'était ce *Journal,* ce monument que le temps avait construit, et qui avait une existence à lui, indépendante de la mienne. Privé de ces carnets, j'ai l'impression d'être dépossédé de moi-même, comme si ma personnalité s'était liquéfiée en même temps qu'eux, et comme si je n'étais plus maintenant qu'une coque vide. (OCIII, p. 812)

The lost papers are thus described by Maumort as the veritable substance of his life, the one firm trace of the man he was. A similar observation is made in the 'Mémoires' version of the text: 'Ils étaient ma raison d'être, la preuve que j'avais existé; ils étaient la substance même et l'œuvre de ma vie. Comment me consolerais-je, aujourd'hui, d'en être irrémédiablement dépossédé?' (OCIII, p. 803). In both cases, Maumort in effect asserts that the most authentic image of him was contained within his diary pages, which have been destroyed, suggesting even that his existence has somehow been threatened as a result of their loss. And it is this lack of substance, or material proof of his existence that he seeks to compensate for by consigning details of his life to paper again, this renewed activity being presented as an attempt to conserve some image of himself which might survive after his death (OCI, p. civ). Though he claims he is writing for himself alone, he appears to have his eyes fixed on some future reader as he writes:

> Demain, j'emporterai dans ma tombe la dernière trace des Maumort sur cette terre où depuis quatre siècles au moins on peut suivre leur cheminement, j'emporterai avec moi tout ce que je sais des miens, tout ce que je sais de moi, tous mes souvenirs, toutes mes expériences. Il ne restera rien des Maumort.
> Ce journal? . . . (OCIII, pp. 642-43)

So, like the projected prefaces, Maumort's comments within the main body of the text help to create the impression that personal papers are valuable by representing them as documents which both reveal the essence of a man, and promise him the possibility of some form of posthumous life. This point is then further stressed by Maumort's discussion of personal papers belonging to two other characters who had played an important part in his life.

The first set of papers we are invited to consider belong to Xavier de Balcourt, a figure who, according to the plan for the work, was intended to play a crucial role, providing a foil against which certain aspects of Maumort's character could be set in relief. Exactly how Xavier's papers were to be introduced into the text, Martin du Gard was unable to decide. He wanted to present at least one of the documents not through Maumort's words but as if expressed by Xavier himself, and this posed a number of problems for him. If Maumort was writing his memoirs because his diary and other papers had been destroyed, how could Xavier's papers have survived? And if these papers had somehow survived, what plausible reason could be found to explain Maumort's decision to copy them out again?

These questions were not in fact answered by Martin du Gard, but one possibility he considered as a way round the problem was to make passing reference in the text to the events which Xavier's papers were supposed to explain, while leaving the mystery intact – and then to leave Xavier's 'fictional' documents among his own papers, for researchers to find at a later date. This strategy provides further proof of Martin du Gard's fascination with personal papers, representing what amounts to an attempt to ensure simultaneously for his own and his character's papers some form of posthumous life, by creating confusion between the two. In the memoir version of the text, however, Daspre has included accounts of all of Xavier's papers, some in Maumort's words and the rest as if in Xavier's own. Whether this would have been Martin du Gard's final solution remains a question for speculation, but we can usefully examine the fictional version of the problem, looking at Maumort's discussion of Xavier and of the papers the latter supposedly left.

Maumort's first encounter with Xavier occurs when Xavier arrives as resident tutor at the Maumort family home, Le Saillant. The two then meet again in Paris, ten years later, and a firm friendship then develops between them which is to last until Xavier's death. In spite of this friendship, however, Xavier remains for Maumort an enigmatic figure throughout, torn by inner conflicts, the true nature of which he is reluctant to reveal, even to his most intimate friends. While we are informed that he is a socially successful character, particularly with women, the impression is nonetheless created that he is never quite at ease, or open about himself.

This is first suggested in Maumort's account of Xavier at Le Saillant:

> La présence de Xavier de Balcourt m'a fait faire, dans cette voie, un pas de plus, et fort important. J'ai eu soudain notion de la place que tient le mensonge dans la vie sociale; j'ai eu la révélation de sa nécessite évidente, et, jusqu'à un certain point, de sa parfaite légitimité. (OCIII, pp. 143-44)

So in Xavier's behaviour, the young Maumort begins to perceive 'cette extraordinaire faculté de dédoublement qui est en nous' (OCIII, p. 144), and from this the idea begins to emerge that there exists some other, secret, Xavier, about whom knowledge is necessary before it is possible fully to understand him. This impression that Xavier is concealing certain aspects of his life and thought is then further reinforced in Maumort's account of their second encounter, when he notes an observation made by his friend:

> Tout homme a deux vies bien distinctes, et souvent contradictoires: sa vie sociale, c'est-à-dire sa vie devant les autres, en famille, dans le monde; et puis sa vie secrète, disons tout net: sa vie sexuelle, dont presque personne autour de lui n'a, en général, la moindre notion; une vie complètement

> cachée et camouflée, où chacun de nous vit son vrai personnage. (. . .) Eh
> bien, rappelez-vous ceci: on ne connaît quelqu'un que lorsqu'on a pu
> pénétrer dans ce labyrinthe secret. Et c'est fort rare. (OCIII, pp. 402-3)

Xavier, thus echoes Maumort's childhood observation, prompting the
latter to remark moreover:

> que tous les hommes ont des bas-fonds qu'ils dissimulent soigneusement
> à tous, et que, derrière leur façade connue, ils recèlent des oubliettes
> jalousement gardées, où se passent des choses cachées, clandestines, des
> chambres de Barbe-Bleue, où ne pénètrent que de rares complices. (OCIII,
> p. 403)

These passages lead us to surmise that Xavier lives a secret life about
which we have not been told, and it is to his personal papers that we are
encouraged to turn for further elucidation.

There are three documents left by Xavier to which specific reference is
made within the text: a short story 'détournement de majeur', the draft
versions of some poetry, and a diary he had kept in the days leading up to
his death. And even before we are told of their contents, their importance
is repeatedly stressed:

> Je n'ai vraiment connu le fin mot de cette histoire, qu'après le suicide de
> Balcourt, lorsque j'ai eu à dépouiller les carnets intimes, les notes, les
> manuscrits trouvés dans ses tiroirs. (OCIII, p. 163)

> Bien d'autres expériences de sa vie passionnelle m'ont été ainsi devoilées
> par le dépouillement de ses notes. (ibid.)

> Je ne l'ai découvert qu'après la mort de Xavier, en trouvant dans ses
> paperasses un brouillon de cette brochure. (OCIII, p. 422)

> Les deux 'nouvelles', inachevées, laissées à l'état de notes, que j'ai
> retrouvées dans ses tiroirs (. . .) m'ont aidé à lever un coin du voile sous
> lequel il cachait orgueilleusement et douloureusement le secret trouble de
> sa vie privée. (OCIII, p. 411)

These references function on one level merely as a means to excite the
reader's interest in the text by building up suspense. But the regularity
with which they occur, and the similarities between them and Martin du
Gard's statements in the pseudo-prefaces to the work, point to the
importance Martin du Gard attached to personal papers in general. This
importance is further underscored when the actual details of Xavier's
papers are disclosed.

The draft versions of Xavier's poetry reveal that what Maumort had believed to be poems about and dedicated to women were in reality addressed to and concerned with a number of men. The unfinished short story similarly casts light upon its author's sexual life. It offers an account of a liaison between a tutor and a student in his charge; the affair eventually being discovered by the authorities with the result that the tutor either is incarcerated or takes his own life. In this outline, Maumort recognises a transposed version of events which had actually occurred at Le Saillant, where Xavier had been infatuated with Maumort's cousin, Guy. So this second document reveals the decisive nature of a passion Maumort had only vaguely perceived and had failed to understand fully before then, reviving in him memories of Xavier at the time of the original events.

The third document is presented in the section entitled 'L'Histoire de Xavier'. It too casts light upon Xavier's sexual life, but more particularly, it helps to illuminate his suicide, the reasons for which Maumort had been unable to discover elsewhere. Written in the form of a diary completed partly day by day and partly retrospectively, it provides an account of yet another passion in Xavier's life, this time for a young boy he had met while on military manœuvres in a rural area of France. The opening section tells of the lengths he went to, first to lodge in the same household as the boy, and then to arrange a meeting alone with him. The second discloses the tragic end to the episode – the boy drowning before Xavier's eyes as he tries to swim across a river to the rendezvous spot – and records the ensuing investigation in which Xavier's part in the affair escapes detection, but continues to torment him. It is shortly after this incident that he commits suicide, unable to live with himself.

The three documents combine to clarify our picture of Xavier, helping to explain the nature of his sexuality and the reasons for his death, and providing us with a picture of him which contrasts strikingly with the impression we have been given of the figure he cut in public life. The inclusion of these documents and, more especially, Maumort's discussion of them, thus serve to demonstrate on a more general level the potential value of access to an individual's personal papers. Were this the only set of papers discussed within the text, however, one might conclude that they are shown to be significant only in the case of characters such as Xavier who are enigmatic by nature, and not as a general rule. But such a conclusion is undermined by the introduction of another personal document, again posthumously discovered by Maumort, this time belonging to his sister, Henriette.

If Xavier is presented as a mysterious character, so that the discovery of his 'secret life' comes as little surprise, Maumort's sister, Henriette, could be said to represent the opposite extreme. She is presented as someone whose every act Maumort believes he intuitively understands. It is to her that he declares himself to have been most attached, and he contrasts their close ties with all the other relationships of his life:

> Je voudrais préciser un peu les sentiments si forts, si exceptionnels, qui nous unissaient. Ils prenaient leur source dans une communion foncière que la fraternité seule peut expliquer. L'affection, ni la solidarité de vie, n'aurait suffi à faire naître et à maintenir aussi durablement cette parfaite harmonie entre deux êtres (. . .).
>
> Je pense à ma femme, aux quelques amis intimes que j'ai eus. Aucune analogie. Ni l'amour, ni l'amitié ne parviennent jamais à supprimer la singularité essentielle et étanche qui différencie deux êtres. (. . .) Entre ma sœur et moi cette dualité, ce parallélisme de nature n'existaient pour ainsi dire pas. (OC III, p. 644)

Thus, in a world where friendships are represented as inevitably strained, Maumort claims a special place for his relationship with his sister, presenting her not just as the only individual he has fully understood but as the only individual who had understood him.

She appears, therefore, as a kind of counterpart to Xavier, in that no obvious barriers exist between her and Maumort. Even actions of which Maumort disapproves in her life – such as the attitude she adopts over the Dreyfus affair, or her religious practices – fail to impair their relationship. Indeed, her very marriage, of which Maumort disapproves to the point of delighting in the news of her husband's death, serves not to sever but to strengthen their bonds. Of the changes in her which matrimony had produced, Maumort remarks:

> J'avais quitté une jeune fille, je retrouvais une femme. J'avais quitté les fraîcheurs du printemps, ses verdeurs hésitantes, ses confuses promesses. Je retrouvais la stable chaleur de l'été et son rayonnement, chargé de fruits. Notre entente, qui m'avait paru, au temps de notre jeunesse, une chose rare et accomplie, ne devint véritablement parfaite, je l'ai compris depuis, qu'après mon retour au Saillant, après la rencontre qu'Henriette avait fait de l'amour. (OCIII, p. 661)

Given the fact that they have attained such a perfect level of mutual comprehension, it might be expected that Henriette's life would hold no further secrets or surprises for her brother, Maumort, but this is not to be so. A document, which he discovers later, discloses the existence of another, less appealing Henriette.

In fact, there are other indications of a possible secret side to her. Maumort was to remark that 'on a souvent l'impression d'une eau dormante dont les dessous cachent une floraison enchevêtrée de lianes aquatiques, invisibles, impossibles à soupçonner, et dangereuses, inquiétantes' (OCIII, p. 1211), implying that even this most limpid of creatures might have hidden depths. And further illustration of this possibility was to be provided by a passage in which Maumort recalled an occasion when they had stood together before a drained lake. Of the sight they found before their eyes, Maumort observes:

> Ce n'était plus qu'une immense cuvette (. . .) dont le fond révélait une végétation touffue, où palpitaient des poissons argentés, noyés dans la vase et l'odeur (. . .) était suffocante. Nous étions stupéfaits de découvrir cette nauséabonde pourriture à la place de cette surface limpide qu'était pour nous l'étang de notre enfance. (OCIII, p. 1211)

He then recalls his sister's response, faced with this monstrous sight: 'Je pense que sous les caractères les plus propres, les plus rassurants, il y a de ces bas-fonds invisibles, insoupçonnables, où fermentent des horreurs' (OCIII, p. 1211). So in similar terms to those used by Xavier, Henriette implies that there might be a second, more sinister side to her nature, by suggesting that this is often the case with seemingly admirable individuals. Then in 'L'Histoire d'Emma', Maumort relates the discovery and contents of a document which supports this general hypothesis, by proving that it is certainly applicable to the case of Henriette.

Maumort introduces the episode with the words: 'Une autre histoire, bien étrange, ct dont je n'ai jamais bien compris les dessous dans la vie d'Henriette' (OCIII, p. 663) – words that serve to prepare us for a revelation which, rather than explaining Henriette, will instead demonstrate the existence of the inexplicable within her. The story Maumort proceeds to tell is of his sister's adoption, against his will, of a child called Emma, and of the strange attitude she adopts towards this child. Emma, when Maumort first meets her, installed in the family home, is cossetted and treated as an adored object by Henriette, a devotion which Maumort considers somewhat unnatural. On his later visits, he observes a gradual change in his sister's attitude, whereby the child is little by little reduced to the position of an unpaid servant in the house, a situation which also alarms him. Nonetheless, he seeks a logical explanation of this 'reversal of fortunes', viewing it in terms either of faults in the child, or changes in his sister's religious beliefs: however inexplicable his sister's behaviour appears, he assumes that there is some rational cause.

After Henriette's death, however, he finds evidence which completely undermines all his former attempts to proffer a rational explanation for the course of events he had observed. While sorting out her personal papers, he chances upon a note-book in which she had recorded every detail of the cost of the child's upkeep, from the very day of her entry into the house. And on its opening page, he finds the startling instruction: 'A remettre à Emma après ma mort' (OCIII, p. 695). The very fact that Henriette had kept such a record strikes Maumort as strange and slightly sinister; the presence of the malicious request on its opening page, written 'd'une main volontaire' (OCIII, p. 695), compels him (and the reader) to conclude that Henriette's past actions towards the child had also been carried out with deliberate malice in mind. It is thus confirmed that an unrecognisable, unfathomable Henriette lay concealed beneath the angelic exterior that Maumort had always admired:

> Cet acte inélégant ressemble si peu à Henriette . . . Pour avoir cédé à cette tentation sordide, pour avoir eu cette pensée posthume, diabolique, il faut qu'elle ait nourri contre Emma des sentiments cachés que je préfère ne pas chercher à tirer trop au clair. (OCIII, p. 695)

Once again then, it is suggested that individuals invariably lead double lives, presenting one face in public, and another more honest if not necessarily more attractive face to themselves. Yet again, moreover, it is stressed that personal documents provide access to, or at least some insight into these secret, and oftimes sombre, private worlds. If Henriette's note-book is a far cry from Maumort's memoirs, or Xavier's diary, it nonetheless provides both Maumort and the reader with a startling revelation about its author's internal state of mind. Thus even the slightest of documents is shown to have considerable potential significance.

From this evidence it can be seen that Martin du Gard went to considerable lengths to convince the reader that personal papers were valuable.[13] The text contains what amounts to a running commentary on the subject, its message being that personal papers generally afford a privileged perspective upon individuals and events, and thus are both interesting and illuminating to read. In the pseudo-prefaces, the 'editor' directly states that Maumort's papers are likely to be of interest to the public at large. Then, in the main body of the text, Maumort's own remarks about his lost diaries and his efforts to replace them reveal that he at least places considerable store by them, while his comments about the documents left by Xavier and Henriette serve to suggest that personal papers are intriguing and illuminating not just on rare occasions but as a general rule. Although far from identical, the various extracts and episodes we have examined can clearly be seen to make the same general point: that personal papers are a valuable source of information about a character's life, and should not be ignored. Why Martin du Gard was so concerned to make this point remains to be explained, however, and will be considered in conclusion here.

It could obviously be argued that he simply wanted to convince the reader that the story told by Maumort was an interesting one; that, having decided to write his novel in the form of personal papers of some kind, he needed to ensure that the reader did not dismiss these documents as being of no account. The different statements about the value of personal papers certainly perform this role, as they interact like a system of mirrors strategically placed so that they focus the reader's attention on the papers which constitute the main body of the text, making him curious about them and encouraging him even to believe that he is likely to profit from reading them. And no doubt this was one of Martin du Gard's reasons for making the point as forcefully as he did: he obviously wanted the reader to be interested in Maumort. But he had another, more personal reason for drawing attention to this issue so often, and with such insistence. He was in fact concerned about the fate of his own personal papers at the time, and it seems that he saw the possibility of using *Maumort* to generate an interest in them.

Generally, Martin du Gard avoided making public statements of any sort, refusing either to confirm that he shared the views of his various protagonists, or to reveal what his own views in fact were. Readers who enquired as to his opinions were invariably rebuked: 'Comme si c'était là la question! Qu'est-ce que ça peut leur foutre, ce que je pense, moi?'[14] And people who called upon him to comment publicly about other writers, or to make statements about the course of national or world events, were even more cursorily dismissed. He was determined to be neither pedagogue nor prophet, insisting that his works could and should speak for themselves, and that he had nothing further to add. In short, more so than most writers, he protected his privacy and refused to talk publicly about himself, his work, or anything else.

However, this reticent, unassuming public persona masked a much more vocal and opinionated private man. And not only was he not lacking in opinions or ideas, but he in fact kept a detailed written record of them. In his diaries, in his thousands of letters to close friends, and in his mountainous files of notes, he recorded his reactions to current events and trends, his thoughts about his own life and actions, as well as details of numerous secrets others had confided to him. He thus managed to accumulate a substantial collection of personal papers, constituting what he considered to be a comprehensive and detailed account of his life and times. And while, in the early stages of his career he kept these documents exclusively for his own purposes, imagining them to be of interest only to himself (OCI, pp. lxxxvi-vii), he later decided that after his death he wanted other people to have access to them, intending, posthumously, to reveal the man behind the mask. Believing that he had in fact created a false impression of the man he actually was, he decided that it was essential to set the record straight, and provide a more faithful portrait for people to judge him by, or perhaps even learn from.

Consistent with this plan, towards the end of his life he sorted out all his personal papers, and deposited most of them at the Bibliothèque Nationale. The remainder, constituting the 'dossiers de la boîte noire', now kept at the Bibliothèque Nationale as well, he left to his grandson, Daniel de Coppet, in the hope that the latter 'trouve profit à lire ce recueil de réflexions, de notations accumulées au cours de toute une vie' (OCIII, p. 1253). In addition, he made known the fact that this collection of papers existed, stressing the importance he attached to it, and informing people even that it was pointless to try to understand or evaluate him without reading his papers first. This point is made abundantly clear in a letter he wrote to Jacques Brenner, in 1957:

> Je me suis aperçu que j'avais accumulé, depuis un demi-siècle, un ensemble impressionnant de documents intimes, constitué non seulement par mon *Journal,* mais par d'importantes *correspondances,* de multiples *notes,* etc . . ., et que s'il est possible de porter un jugement sur mes livres (. . .) il faut attendre, pour porter sur moi un jugement renseigné, d'avoir pris connaissance de toutes les paperasses, assez révélatrices, que je laisserai derrière moi. (. . .) Depuis que je sais quel *exact* portrait on pourra faire de moi en utilisant tous les éléments que je laisse, je repugne à autoriser un ami à ébaucher une esquisse qui serait fatalement infidèle. [15]

As this letter amply demonstrates, he was convinced that his papers were of considerable value, believing them to provide a fascinating picture of his own 'bas-fonds'. [16] He was convinced, moreover, that others would recognise their importance too, and that a future for them was therefore assured. This was important because it meant that he himself was guaranteed a form of posthumous life.[17]

During the years he spent working on *Maumort,* however, his previously confident view of his prospects suddenly became clouded; he began to fear that his posthumous life was far from being assured. In a letter to Gide, in 1945 he announced that he and his generation were outmoded, and no longer had any real role to play: 'nous sommes des survivants, des "anachronismes". Encombrés de vieux concepts; pareils à des gardiens de musée dans leurs antiquailles' (OCI, p. cxxvi). And although he described his situation in humorous terms, he was alarmed by the actual state of affairs he foresaw: 'J'avais rêvé une autre vieillesse; moins inexorablement solitaire, et moins déracinée . . .' (OCI, p. cxxvi). He had good reason to be distressed. If the postwar world was as different as he predicted, future generations were unlikely to find much of interest in his works as, inevitably, they too were 'encombrés' by his 'vieux concepts'. And if this was so, there was little chance that people would seek access to the collection of papers he intended to leave. His 'oubliettes jalousement gardées' seemed destined to remain permanently locked, their treasured contents abandoned to 'l'oubli qui nivelle tout'.[18]

However, Martin du Gard did not resign himself to this fate. In spite of all his anxieties about *Maumort,* he continued to work on it until the end of his life, and always with a view to publication, with an audience in mind. The various alternative versions he proposed and produced may well have reduced the work's chances of completion, but they testify nonetheless to his continued concern with its finished form. Faced with the prospect of being forgotten, he looked to *Maumort* as a means of escape, believing that by stressing the importance of personal papers in the novel he could encourage his readers to take an interest in his own papers, as well as in those of Maumort. The posthumous publication of *Maumort,* an event which Martin du Gard not only looked forward to but in fact requested, was meant to ensure a posthumous life for its author, one in which he could reveal his true face.

The shape of *Maumort,* as it was left by Martin du Gard at his death, testifies to his efforts in this direction. Little information is provided, other than in note form, about Maumort's active life; his military training and active service in the company of Lyautey, in particular, are scarcely mentioned in the text. Instead, it is composed almost entirely of accounts of Maumort's more personal and sentimental experiences – his private life – and of passages singing the praises of his present occupation, busily absorbed recording a version of his past experiences for posterity. As has been shown, this last issue in particular is given considerable emphasis, the intriguing and illuminating nature of personal papers being repeatedly stressed. Thus in place of the exemplary tale, which the novel was originally designed to be, we find a work more closely resembling an apologia for the writing and reading of documents of a personal kind. In effect, it presents us with a preface or introduction to the personal papers of Martin du Gard.

This is not, of course, the only noteworthy feature of *Maumort*. The protagonist's story is interesting in its own right, and not just for what it tells us about Martin du Gard. It is an important issue, nonetheless, as it reveals a rather different Martin du Gard from the distant, detached figure of the past who had claimed that he wanted his protagonists to be 'assez vivants pour que le spectacle qu'ils donnent fût le seul, le véritable intérêt du livre'.[19] In a letter to Roger Froment, written in 1927, Martin du Gard confessed that there was a glaring contradiction between '(sa) vie, (ses) mœurs, et bien des paroles même, et (sa) pensée secrète', but warned the young man to stay clear: 'N'essayez pas trop de pénétrer au fond de ma pensée. L'air n'y est guère respirable'.[20] *Maumort* appears to contain a counter-command, inviting the reader to descend beneath the 'surface limpide', to discover 'des bas-fonds invisibles, insoupçonnables, où fermentent des horreurs' (OCIII, p. 1211). It seems appropriate that an essay which can only hope to provide an introduction to *Maumort* should focus upon this new development, showing how, in addition to revealing the 'bas-fonds' of the protagonist, the work also provides an introduction to the more intimate writings of its real author, documents which supposedly record a faithful portrait of his own 'pensée secrète'. It is to be hoped that the publication of these papers will follow shortly, completing the picture of Martin du Gard, further illuminating his works, and ensuring a long life for both.

Notes

[1] *Le Lieutenant-Colonel de Maumort*, Paris, Bibliothèque de la Pléiade, 1983. In subsequent references to the work, the title will be given as *Maumort*, and page references will use the abbreviation OCIII.

[2] 'Roger Martin du Gard ou Les Limites d'un monde sans envers', in *Histoire du roman français depuis 1918*, Paris, Editions du Seuil, 1950, pp. 305-50.

[3] ibid., p. 350.

[4] ibid.

[5] June 9, 1950, André Gide / Roger Martin du Gard, *Correspondance,* Paris, Gallimard, 1968, vol. II, p. 487.

[6] 'Roger Martin du Gard: pensée testamentaire', in *La Quinzaine Littéraire,* Paris, July 16-31, 1970, p. 5.

[7] Page references are to Martin du Gard's *Œuvres complètes,* Paris, Bibliothèque de la Pléiade, 1955, and will use the abbreviations OCI and OCII.

[8] August 10, 1947, A.G./ R.M.G. *Corr.,* vol. II, p. 376.

[9] op. cit., pp. 349-50.

[10] The 'dossiers de la boîte noire' are made up of a collection of notes used by Martin du Gard in the course of work on *Maumort.* Some of the notes contained in the files, however, date back to the years before he wrote *Jean Barois.* These 'dossiers' were left by Martin du Gard to his grandson, Daniel de Coppet, and have since been deposited at the B.N. They are not yet catalogued. For further information, see Daspre's introduction to *Maumort* (OCIII, p. L), and his comments in the notes at the end of the volume (OCIII, pp. 1253-56).

[11] April 22, 1915, letter to Marcel de Coppet, in Jacques Copeau / Roger Martin du Gard, *Correspondance,* Paris, Gallimard, 1972, vol. I, p. 172.

[12] March 1, 1923, A.G./ R.M.G. *Corr.,* vol. I, p. 213.

[13] That personal papers are valuable is also suggested in Martin du Gard's earlier works. See Abbe Lévys's diary (OCI, pp. 537-44), and Jean Barois's testament (OCI, pp. 557-58) in *Jean Barois;* Jacques's 'cahier gris' (OCI, pp. 619-27) and short story (OCI, pp. 1171-93), M. Thibault's posthumous papers (OCI, pp. 1325-45), and Antoine's diary (OCII, pp. 928-1011), in *Les Thibault.* In particular, Antoine's comments about his father's papers (OCI, pp. 1343-44), and about his reasons for writing his own diary (OCII, pp. 932-33), anticipate many of the remarks made by the 'editor' and Maumort.

[14] Letter to Ferdinand Verdier, Sept. 13, 1918, Roger Martin du Gard, *Correspondance générale,* Paris, Gallimard, 1980, vol. II, p. 245.

[15] 'Le Boeuf sur la langue', in *Bulletin des Amis d'André Gide,* Lyon (14e année), vol. IX, n.º 52, Oct. 1981, pp. 481-82.

[16] In 1928, he made a similar point to Gide, insisting upon the importance of his letters to Marcel de Coppet, and his diary: 'Je ne pense pas que j'en sorte agrandi, au contraire, mais cela ne peut pas ne pas être un document humain curieux', *Les Cahiers de la Petite Dame,* n.º 4 of *Cahiers André Gide,* Paris, Gallimard, 1973, p. 387.

[17] Claude Sicard, who is editing Martin du Gard's diary for publication, sees the desire for survival as one of Martin du Gard's principal reasons for recording an account of his life: 's'il a décidé de tenir registre de sa propre vie, c'est aussi, n'en doutons pas, pour faire échec à l'oubli, au vieillissement, à la néantisation progressive', 'Le *Journal* de Roger Martin du Gard', in *Folio: Roger Martin du Gard Centennial (1881-1981),* Number 13, Oct. 1981, p. 91.

[18] Roger Martin du Gard: *Noizement-Les-Vierges,* Liège, A la Lampe d'Aladdin, 1928, p. 46. This short work by Martin du Gard is a modified version of an extract from his diary, concerned with his childhood at Clermont, and his first encounter with death. The lines with which the work concludes reveal Martin du Gard's concern with survival once again: 'C'est avec émotion que je confie au papier cette ineffable vision d'un passé dont il ne reste d'autre visage. Il me semble le sauver pour quelques années encore, de l'oubli qui nivelle tout'.

[19] Letter to Ferdinand Verdier, Sept. 13, 1918, *Correspondance générale,* vol. II, p. 244.

[20] 'D'André Gide, il m'écrivit . . .', in *Bulletin des Amis d'André Gide,* Oct. 1981, IX, 52, p. 413.

Journalistic fictions and editorial realities: Beffroy de Reigny and the *Cousin Jacques* series (1785-1792)

Angus Martin : Macquarie University

B E F F R O Y de Reigny has attracted little attention among scholars in recent years, although he is known to historians of the Revolution and to specialists in late eighteenth-century theatre. His progress from young provincial *abbé* with literary pretensions, absent-mindedly encouraged by Voltaire, to the precarious existence of impecunious man of letters in the 1780s and 1790s was outlined by Charles Monselet in his *Oubliés et dédaignés* in 1861. And in 1930 Charles Westercamp published at Laon a full-length life-and-works of Beffroy, who was one of that city's more colourful sons and whose contemporary notoriety was won principally under the pseudonym of 'le Cousin Jacques'. [1]

It is as a journalist that Beffroy de Reigny will concern us here. Between 1785 and 1791, he brought out an almost continuous series of periodicals: *Les Lunes du Cousin Jacques* (monthly, January 1785-June 1786; twice monthly, July 1786-May 1787); *Le Courrier des planètes* (weekly, January 1788-December 1788; fortnightly, January 1789-December 1789); *Le Cousin Jacques* (fortnightly, January-September 1790); *Les Nouvelles Lunes du Cousin Jacques* (weekly, January-July 1791). The formula was revived in a somewhat altered form between January and August 1792 with *Le Consolateur ou journal des honnêtes gens* (twice weekly). Beffroy's *nom de plume* not only figures prominently in most of these titles, the convention is largely observed throughout the series that le Cousin Jacques is the author of the periodicals as well as the hero of many of the fanciful and less fanciful fictional narratives that occupy a considerable portion of the editorial content. The references to the moon and planets are part of this 'persona', as le Cousin Jacques is not only an eccentric and facetious jester figure, but also is credited with travels in space and particular connections that explain his 'lunatic' humours. [2]

Overall, the content of the periodicals is extremely varied. The auth-
or's avowed aim is to amuse, to make his readers laugh at his eccentricities, his 'folies', and the style of much of the content is deliberately
familiar and facetious. Dialogues, verse, playlets, songs, guessing games,
readers' letters follow one another in erratic sequence, although during
the Revolutionary years a more serious note is struck in the treatment of
current affairs and political questions. It is Beffroy's very frequent use of
imaginative narratives that first aroused my own interest in his work,
within the context of a survey I had undertaken of short fiction in French
periodicals of the eighteenth century. These are not the fictions, however,
that are referred to in the title of this paper. Here, I should like rather to
examine the imaginary personality of le Cousin Jacques and the ways in
which, through him, Beffroy presents a comic but detailed image of
himself as journalist. The device of the eccentric authorial figure in a
periodical was by no means a new one, of course, by the time Beffroy de
Reigny exploited it. Marivaux's *Indigent Philosophe* (1727) is no doubt
the most illustrious example from the French domain, but he is kept good
company during the century by many a *Babillard,* a *Censeur,* a *Compère,*
a *Discoureur,* a *Diogène,* a *Fantasque,* a *Grapilleur,* a *Misanthrope,* a
Persifleur, a *Radoteur,* not to mention the *Observateurs,* the *Spectateurs*
and other *Philosophes* of every ilk. What seems remarkable, however, in
Beffroy's use of the formula is that he takes it to extreme lengths. On the
one hand the fictional persona is developed beyond its existence in the
pages of the journals and, as Beffroy inhabits the role for his public, he
becomes, in modern terms, a media personality. On the other hand, le
Cousin Jacques serves as a mouthpiece for Beffroy's worries over the
material problems he encounters in producing his periodicals. An inordin-
ate amount of editorial space – especially in the *Lunes* and the *Courrier
des planètes* – is taken up fulfilling this latter function, and, as time passes,
ever-increasing difficulties produce tensions between the comic persona
and the desperate economic circumstances in which Beffroy appears to
find himself.

From the start Beffroy is eager to promote the image of this Cousin
Jacques, about whom – or so he claims in one of the multitude of *Avis* in
which he converses with the public – intrigued readers wanted more
details. At first Beffroy insists on his anonymity, asking his readers to 'se
borner à la plume & laisser-là l'Ecrivain' (L5, 7), and, although the
author's name is gradually revealed (a clear statement of identity is made
in April 1789 (CP59, 68-69)), 'le Cousin Jacques' remains far more in
evidence throughout the series than 'M. de Reigny' ever is. Beffroy invents

an autobiography that sees his hero as the almost centenarian son of Languedoc shoemakers (L8, 5-39) and explains that his sobriquet comes from a simple-minded peasant he once met when taking the waters at Saint-Amand (L33, 9-22). Readers are offered 'audiences' with Jacques both by day (bookings from the bookseller Lesclapart) and at night: 'Toutes les nuits, au clair de la Lune, dans la plaine des Sablons, depuis onze heures du soir jusqu'à une heure après minuit' (L11, 15-16). Provincial visitors are especially invited to attend and it is regretted that the almanachs do not quote le Cousin Jacques as one of the essential sights of Paris (L26, 95-96).

Le Cousin Jacques thus makes strenuous attempts to maintain at least the illusion of a close rapport with his public, although it is far from clear how far he actually acted out his part in contacts with his readers. Yearly excursions in 1786-1788, to Artois and Flandres – Beffroy's home territory – are reported in the *Lunes* and the *Courrier des planètes* in terms of the triumphant – often delirious – reception the Cousin receives. Other ceremonies, such as the transfer of the *Bureau lunatique* when the publisher Lesclapart changes his address (L5, 145; L7, 117-23), a ball organised for readers (L25, 18-32) or celebrations in honour of an expected child (CP66, 8-55) appear to have been purely imaginary. An 'Académie de la Lune' is founded for all faithful subscribers: *brevets* marked with its official seal (L23, 92-93; L30, 3-4) are offered to readers who write in for them (L30, 11-18); lists of its officers and members are published from time to time in the pages of the journal (L21, 62-65; L32, 153); a pair of architects propose a design for a suitable Academy building (L33, 34); questions are set for discussion by members (L25, 44-50; L33, 122-240; CP21, 5-6). There is even a facetious proposal that the Académie found a colony on the moon under the leadership of the Cousin: volunteers are called for (L21, 94-96) and the 'lunar library' to be taken along is discussed (L26, 88-94).

In turn, subscribers are able to express themselves through the pages of the periodicals. Readers' letters of enthusiastic support are regularly published, in spite of accusations that the Cousin writes them himself (L8, 214-15) and is guilty of 'une vanité insupportable' (L14, 54). Various 'passetemps de Société' (L26, 5), such as 'charrades' and the regular *bouts-rimés* (where verses are written to a set of rhyming words), elicit so many responses that only the first to arrive can be published unless the contributor lives more than 200 leagues from Paris (C12, 192). Original pieces sent in by readers (what Beffroy calls 'productions étrangères') eventually become so numerous that it is proposed they be limited to no more than one page of prose, three couplets of a song or half a page of verse and that they normally only be accepted from persons on the official list of subscribers (CP55, 66-67n).

Whilst many of these promotional activities smack somewhat of the *canular,* Beffroy appears to have a quite practical and indeed modern eye for the marketable souvenir. Readers are told they can buy a style of 'bonnets' or 'chapeaux à la Lune' from M. de Sijas, 'au magasin de modes des Arts réunis': 'Bien entendu que les seules personnes, qui s'abonneront, auront permission de porter ce bonnet, & que très-expresses défenses sont faites à toute autre de se le procurer' (L11, 90-95; L26, 7-23). Crystal goblets 'au cousin Jacques' are on offer for fifty *sous* each from 'Andrieu, marchand fayancier' (CP62, ii). An engraved portrait of the Cousin, by 'M. Violet, peintre du Roi' is available from Lesclapart for 36 *sous,* with a smaller version for 24 *sous* (L8, 98; L9, 76-80, 163; L10, 8-9). Later, a new portrait (three quarters rather than profile) is announced at a cost of 36 *sous* for the public and 24 for subscribers: it is drawn by Madame Moitte an engraved by Mademoiselle Moitte her sister-in-law, but these good ladies cannot be hurried and the older version is eventually reissued (CP75, 54; CJ8, 57-58; CJ18, 59; N21, 3-4). For those not satisfied with an engraving, an eighteen-inch plaster cast of a bust sculpted by a certain M. Martin, 'étonnant par la parfaite ressemblance', may be had for 6 *livres,* while the warning is given that the busts sold at the Théâtre des Italiens are poor imitations (L14, 3-5; L17, 3-4; L22, 4; CJ3, 35-37). The Cousin realises belatedly that his price is too low and puts it up to 12 *livres* (CP14, 5): 'chaque plâtre me revient à 6 liv. [mais] il faut que je paye la caisse & l'emballage' (CJ18, 59). A second bust is announced, by 'un des plus habiles élèves de l'académie royale de sculpture de Paris, & retouché par le premier sculpteur du royaume', four times larger than the first one, to be sold likewise for twelve *livres* but the proceeds to go to the young artist (CP75, 53).

Certain other undertakings of the 'Auteur des Lunes' are less clearly connected with the personality of le Cousin Jacques, but show a struggling man of letters apparently attempting to profit from the success of his creation: lessons in literature ('plus cheres que celles de la plupart des Maîtres' (L1, ii; L5, 11-16; L7, 3-4; L9, 166; L15, 42; L21, 3)) and music (L22, 3); the proposed publication – requested, we are told by more than a third of the subscribers to the *Lunes,* but never in fact realised – of a course in rhetoric (L15, 5-40; L27, 4); together with frequent advertisements for Beffroy's other works, such as the collection of songs published under the title of *Les Délassemens du Cousin Jacques* (L25, 36; L27, 4;

CJ18, 66-67). Later in his career, he offers lessons in singing and declamation (in his own home three days a week, in other peoples' houses a further three) or manuscript copies of the latest songs (over 50 of them for a subscription of 6 *livres*); he proposes a book ordering service to those 'qui voudront s'en rapporter à mon choix pour se procurer des livres nouveaux'; he is ready to board and educate up to six children; and he will also undertake to direct amateur theatricals (CP48, 20-24; CP75, 51; CP76, 41). He will write or correct *mémoires* for those involved in legal disputations (CJ6, 34-37), having learned by experience not to undertake any such 'travaux de commande [. . .] sans des sûretés pour le paiement' (CJ16, 4); but he has to turn away those who think, because of his connections with the stars and the planets, that he will be able to tell their fortune! (CJ13, 26-33). An isolated attempt to market cloth sent to him by a subscriber in the Hainault is a financial disaster, leading to losses of 1.000 or 2.000 *francs* (CP76, 3-10).

Apart from all these peripheral items, the principal commodity that Beffroy is attempting to sell by exploiting the persona of le Cousin Jacques, is, of course, the periodicals themselves. Whilst one does find the traditional type of *Avis* baldly setting out the price for Paris (from 18 *livres* for the *Lunes* to 24 for the *Consolateur*) and the provinces (from 24 *livres* to 27), and the bookseller's name and address, more remarkable are the facetious prospectuses (CP45, 5-21; CP53, 3-4; CP75, 40-54; CP76, 41; CJ1, preliminaries and 3-12; CJ18, 61-69; N1, 1-4) together with the constant commentary on the details of the subscription system that occupy a regular place in the Cousin's familiar conversation with his readers. 'Réabonnez-vous, s'il vous plaît, le plutôt [sic] possible, afin qu'on puisse faire les *adresses* plus promptement & plus aisément' (L13, 3). And why not a subscription for a friend leaving for the country or else for the object of one's affections? 'Mais je déclare que toute personne, qui donnera pour bouquet à une Dame un Numéro dépareillé de mes *Lunes,* ne réussira pas dans ses projets amoureux; [. . .] il faut donner une année complette, ou rien donner du tout' (L11, 189-90; L23, 68). Sharing subscriptions with a group of other people (up to fifteen in some cases), we are told, has its disadvantages, firstly for the member of the group advancing the money: 'ce n'est pas tout de s'être coabonné, [. . .] il faut payer sa quotepart à celui qui a payé au Bureau la somme entière, au nom de tous les autres' (L35/36, 11). Secondly, such practices perhaps serve to make the author of the periodical better known, but they rob him of an already meagre profit (CP66, 4). Subscribers are advised against lending their copies to friends or neighbours, who will lose them or spoil them and who ought rather to find

the trifling sum necessary to subscribe themselves: 'Qu'on soit bien
persuadé que ce que j'en dis, n'est que par l'intérêt que je prends aux
bibliothèques de mes Abonnés' (L16, 47).

The description Beffroy gives of the 'correct' way for each issue to
be received in a subscriber's house is clearly fanciful: the postman must
knock or ring three times, stand patiently at the door until it is opened and
ceremoniously present the issue in question with the compliments of the
postal authorities (L11, 38-44). The author's irony is directed precisely at
what appears to have been the lack of care exercised by both postmen and
servants. And when he writes that those readers who buy their copies
individually in the bookshop should 'marcher gravement & entrer chez
Lesclapart avec l'air du monde le plus scientifique' (L43-44), we have to
remember that Beffroy is producing an essentially frivolous work. More
convincing details about practical matters are, however, not lacking. On
the atmosphere in an eighteenth-century bookshop, we read elsewhere for
example that the many candles burning in the evening in madame
Lesclapart's shop smell foul, produce no useful light and are twice as
expensive as necessary (L24, 3-4). When the *Courrier des planètes* is
launched readers are promised that each issue will be 'plié avec soin,
enveloppé d'une double bande, sur laquelle sera l'adresse du Souscripteur,
imprimée & parfaitement détaillée' (announcement following L35/36, 2).
Later, the Cousin explains to his reader the advantages of an un-cut issue:
it is too small otherwise to be sewn without damage, and for binding
purposes he will find that a folded sheet is far preferable. Moreover, 's'il
veut le vendre à l'épicier, on tire un meilleur parti du papier *en feuilles*
que des brochures; enfin, s'il juge à propos de s'en servir *in secretis,* il a
beau jeu, chaque feuillet pouvant se déchirer plus commodément' (CP6, 6).

In the days of the *Lunes* and *Le Courrier des planètes,* Beffroy attempts
both to demonstrate the success of his project and to solicit new custom by
publishing long lists of towns where he already has subscribers. The first
of these summaries (L7, 125-36) – curiously justified as a way to 'diversi-
fier nos tableaux & ne pas dire toujours la même chose' – is the most
jocular in tone. To the names of various towns are added coded commentaries: '*Comme ça* veut dire qu'il y a assez d'abonnements eu égard à
l'étendue de la Ville dont on parle [. . .] *Fort bien,* veut dire que l'Auteur
n'a pas lieu de se plaindre, & qu'il est content de cette ville-là [. . .] *Pas
mal* est un degré au-dessous de *fort bien,* c'est le terme mitoyen entre *fort
bien & comme ça'* (L7, 125-26). A note to a fourth list informs the reader
that the first subscriber in the town of Annonai en Vivarais was M. de

Montgolfier. 'Ce nom figure bien heureusement pour moi dans un Ouvrage, qui s'éleve jusqu'à la Lune' (L11, 172n).

In all, some sixteen of these listings, of varying dimensions, give more than 800 references to over 500 different localities, mostly within France, but including some foreign cities, from Brussels to London, and from Geneva to Stockholm (L7, 125-36; L9, 59-61, 101; L11, 172-73; L15, 86-88; L17, 86-87; L19, 10-11; L23, 64-67; L24, 95; L26, 30; L30, 32; L31, 76; CP24, 19-21; CP46, 5; CP66, 3-8; CP74, 68). On top of this it is claimed, in the first summary, that Paris itself has more than the total of provincial and foreign subscribers. A detailed study of the implications of these perhaps quite unreliable data is not possible here (and the verifications it requires are indeed still under way), but *le Cousin Jacques* appears to be claiming a body of subscribers of at least two thousand (a figure also suggested by an estimate of possible postal costs (CJ4, 56)), and a considerably larger readership in view of the subscriptions taken out by groups of readers: in most provincial towns subscriptions are from 'des chambres de lecture ou sociétés littéraires, par le moyen desquelles le livre est connu de tout ce qui lit dans une ville, dans l'espace d'une semaine' (CP24, 19). If one goes by the information given on those readers whose names are quoted throughout the series, one is struck by their almost exclusively provincial domiciles, and their relatively modest station in life (military men, professional men, with a strong representation of clerics). This impression may well, of course, be false, and these are perhaps merely the categories of reader who were most likely to write in or to contribute material. It is true that in 1792 Beffroy notes that his *Consolateur* is 'fait sur-tout pour la province' (C63, 175), but this statement cannot be taken to apply necessarily to the series as a whole, the Cousin claiming at one stage that 'même à la cour, [. . .] mes numéros ont quelque succès' (CP74, 65).

All evidence suggests that the success of le Cousin Jacques was not merely a provincial one, and that Beffroy and his alter ego enjoyed considerable contemporary notoriety. By 1790, the name of the character becomes the official title of the series, as this is what public usage has imposed (CP75, 43-44); and if one penalty of fame is that he receives anonymous abusive letters (CP52, 1-12; CP70, 69), another is that he must submit to being imitated by lesser talents out to exploit his name (L26, 24-27, 34, 94; L31, 54-78). Not all readers will confess that they enjoy the Cousin's comic style (CP45, 7), but others are honest enough to admit openly that they like to laugh (CP45, 10). Friends, family, neighbours squabble over issues of the journal that are shared by a dozen households or that are stolen from 'les Bureaux littéraires' (L24, 93). In Beffroy's text we find frequent allusions to other journals *(Les Petites Affiches de Paris, Le Mercure de France, Le Journal de Genève, La Gazette des Gazettes, Le Journal de Paris, Le Journal général de France,* among others less well-known (L6, 1-5; L11, 183-84; L35/36, 99)) writing more or less favourably about Beffroy's enterprise (CP59, 5), or at least publishing extracts from his prospectuses (CP45, 21; CP53, 3-4n; CP59, 63-69; CP74, 47-54). Reviews found insulting in *Le Journal de la belle littérature des Deux Ponts* (L11, 98-127; L12, 129-32) and *La Gazette de Compiègne* (L21, 18-20; L22, 15-49) provoke a stream of invective from the Cousin and of supportive letters from readers (L26, 3-4). A *Lettre du Corps de la Librairie Académique de Strasbourg, au Cousin Jacques* of 9 June 1786 (L13, 19-22; L15, 84; L17, 3-4; L26, 3-6) announces a German translation of the *Lunes,* which is subsequently received in Paris and its preface is translated for the *Cousin*'s readers (L18, 115-18; L20, 20-21). In 1791 Beffroy asks his journalist colleagues yet again to publicise his prospectus for the following year (CJ18, 60), but is obliged to reiterate that he will no longer send free copies of his periodical in exchange for those of his colleagues: 'deux cents abonnemens *gratis* me feraient un tort irréparable' (CP57, 41-42; CJ5, 70-71). Reference is also made to the way in which other journalists reproduce items from Beffroy's periodicals – a form of flattery which he sees as being commercially disadvantageous to him (CP57, 42). My own data in the area of short fictional narratives certainly show that le Cousin Jacques was commonly pillaged by his *confrères,* while the fact that the pseudonym was usually retained in titles of such items suggests that the personage was not unknown to readers at large.

The Cousin's largely facetious commentary on the material aspects of periodical publication in his day is not confined to self-advertisement and self-congratulation. Beffroy devotes an alarming proportion of his editorial space over the years to the difficulties he encounters, and feels free, through the Cousin, to expound his concerns more frankly and more obsessively than in any other example I know – and this in an age when journalists quite commonly appended brief explanations of delays in publication and changes in management, format or content. Already in the *Lunes* a growing misunderstanding with his bookseller, Lesclapart, is chronicled, first in jocular fashion and then with growing bitterness as legal proceedings are set in train. As late as January 1791, the Cousin is still sufficiently angry as to berate madame Lesclapart roundly as 'cette harpie, vraie sang-sue des gens de lettres' (N4, 7-8). The *Courrier des planètes* and the later titles are published from Beffroy's domicile (two different apartments rue Phélipeaux), although for *Le Cousin Jacques* and *Les Nouvelles Lunes* there appears to have been a distribution arrangement with Belin, and for *Le Consolateur* with Froullé and Denné.

Rather than pursue these largely biographical complexities, I shall attempt here to examine the more generally relevant of the difficulties of the journalist-cum-publisher that the Cousin so freely evokes. Like many of his contemporaries, Beffroy clearly has difficulty in maintaining a regular publication schedule, and already by the third issue of *Les Lunes* is apologising for delays (L3, ii); but a journalist, he reminds us, has to depend on the many skills of the publishing world: 'le Libraire, le Papetier, l'Imprimeur, le Compositeur, le Prote, l'Elève, le Tireur, le Sécheur & le Brocheur' (L3, 159), not to mention a music printer suffering from gout (L9, 52). Over the New Year period, it is even harder to maintain a regular pattern because of the holidays, but more particularly as a result of the bottleneck caused in the publishing and bookselling business at New Year by the rush to sell 'cent-vingt sortes d'Almanachs, des Etrennes de toute espèce' (L8, 213; L25, 3). During the harsh winter of 1788-1789, 'la rigueur du froid obligeait les ouvriers de suspendre leurs travaux; & les feuilles étaient gelées quand on les pliait' (CP55, 41). Again, like other journalists of the time, in the hope of hitting upon the most comfortable formula, he attempts to juggle the intervals between issues, now monthly, now fortnightly, now twice weekly, whilst explaining to readers that they will not lose out (L14, 63-65) and noting the financial repercussions for him of such rearrangements: with two 'fascicules' in the month, 'les frais de brochage, de couverture, d'étiquettes, d'enveloppes, de port &c. augmenteront du double' (L13, 96).

One of the most constant of the worries that beset Beffroy concerns readers' complaints about issues they claim to have received late, in poor condition or not at all. An early reader of the *Lunes* writes from Bordeaux in January 1785 about delays in arrival of his copies 'dix ou douze jours après celui où il a dû paraître à Paris' (L8, 113). Others express dissatisfaction at receiving issues that are 'coupés, salis & même souvent décachetés' (L10, 67). As far as those that are never received are concerned, le Cousin is at first willing to admit there may have been 'un oubli du Libraire', but strict checks are instituted under Beffroy's personal control (CP24, 22), as subscribers to the *Courrier des planètes,* for example, are informed:

> Il est impossible qu'il s'égare un seul *numéro* chez moi; 1o. toutes les adresses étant imprimées de suite, il est clair qu'il n'en échappe pas une, quand on les colle; 2o. la conformité des adresses à mes registres, quand

on a fait l'appel, prévient toute espece d'erreur à cet égard; 3o. les
registres de la poste font foi; on y marque exactement la somme que j'ai
payée à chaque livraison, & il ne serait pas naturel que je donnasse &
qu'on reçût plus d'argent qu'il n'en est dû; ce qui arriverait s'il manquait
un seul numéro . . . (CP24, 16)

Frequent reference is made to the fact that the names and addresses of
subscribers are printed on sheets to produce the correct number of
address-labels (L35/36, 3-4, 100; CP45, 15-16; CP76, 42; CJ3, 70-71):
'Chaque souscripteur a son adresse imprimée vingt-quatre fois; à chaque
livraison, on détache un vingt-quatrieme de la feuille; & ce qui en reste est
une preuve authentique du nombre des *Numéros* envoyés' (CJ15, 39-40).
Readers are at the same time reminded that the fault in all these losses
may well be theirs and are asked to check up on their servants, especially
during periods of absence (L21, 41). Poor writing can also cause problems:
a misunderstanding over a single letter in an address can mean incorrect
delivery, when so many place names in France are similar (L16, 37-38). In
spite of threats to make subscribers who lose their copies help pay for the
replacement – '10 sols par numéro, vu les frais d'adresse & de poste, & la
collection qu'il faut dépareiller' (CP40, ii; CP55, 43-44: 15 *sous* for Paris,
18 for the provinces) – Beffroy appears to maintain the policy of normally
issuing replacement copies gratis, if only in the interest of customer
satisfaction (CJ7, 32).

Inefficient and unscrupulous provincial booksellers are another of the
journalist's bugbears. From the second issue of the *Lunes* a warning is
given that no subscriptions from 'MM. les Libraires de Province' will be
acted upon until payment has been received (L2, i). There are those, it is
claimed, who, fraudulently, like 'le sieur Melleville' of Laon (L7, 126-27n;
L8, 117-18) omit to send either the money or the subscription (L8, 116),
in spite of the discount of between 1 *livre* 10 *sous* and 3 *livres* they receive
together with a thirteenth copy free of charge (L35/36, 3-4; CP45, 17-18;
CP57, 48-49; CJ7, 32; CJ8, 56). Others are more dilatory than dishonest,
at one extreme putting off forwarding subscriptions in the busy New Year
period (CP33, 9; CP55, 36) or at the other extreme thinking it normal to
keep back payment until the end of the year (CP6, 5). The result is that
Beffroy claims to have to write six or seven letters and wait eighteen
months in order to get in the long run no more than ten of the eighteen
livres owing to him (CJ3, 3-4). Some provincial *libraires* make the mistake
of writing to a colleague who may be their habitual correspondent in Paris;
but this colleague may well make up his packages for dispatch only once a

month (and during the waiting time the copy in question may be borrowed by a clerk and thus mislaid) (L21, 41). More disastrously, the Parisian bookseller may go bankrupt and if a receipt has been issued the publisher must furnish his periodical for no payment at all (CP76, 9-10). As Beffroy's financial situation makes it impossible for him to give credit for any length of time (CP45, 17-18), the recommended procedure for subscribers is to write directly to the publisher, using the postal services to transmit the money (L11, 187-88; CP45, 17; CJ7, 33). In some towns he has personal contacts who will take subscriptions for him (CP45, 17; CP58, 46; CP63, 63), and, curiously enough, these include the Lazarist seminaries in various centres, who will arrange for the money to be paid to Beffroy by the *procureur-général* of the order, M. Daudet, in Paris (CP55, 46).

Beffroy's whole enterprise is dependent upon the postal services, the *Petite Poste* serving Paris and the *Grande Poste* with its monopoly of deliveries to the provinces. Subscribers are informed, for example, that bundles of copies of the *Courrier des planètes* are handed in every Tuesday before eleven o'clock for delivery outside Paris and on Thursday before midday for local distribution (CP24, 15; CP45, 15). Unfortunately, complaints about the subsequent service are endemic. When the *Inspecteur général de la Poste de Paris* checks up on missing deliveries, le Cousin is ready to accept that the fault lies principally with negligent *Suisses* and *Portiers* (CP14, 3). The *Grande Poste,* however, is the major source of dissatisfaction. It is true that some delays in distribution are understandable: it may be necessary to hold back a portion of the copies in a batch in order to stagger the work of the Paris office and the couriers' loads (L8, 116); or addresses given by subscribers may not be sufficiently precise, particularly if the province or the nearest large town is not indicated (L16, 37-38; L31, 76-77). And if the post refuses to transport the Cousin's bust (normally forwarded by 'diligence'), this is comprehensible in view of the 'gêne incroyable' it would cause amongst the packets and letters (CP14, 5-6). Also, some subscribers are excessively impatient and unrealistically demanding: letters dated 2nd January arrive from thirty leagues away complaining of the non-receipt of issues posted only at midday the day before, with no account taken of the severity of the weather and the fact that the postal services are overloaded at New Year (CP55, 35-36). The normal delivery time should be calculated before complaints are made (CP76, 14). However, it is clearly an abuse for the directors of postal offices or their employees (in such centres as Beffroy's home town of Laon) to open copies, to cut the pages and indeed not only to read them but to lend them to their friends, with the result that 'M. le Curé' and 'M. le Bailly' enjoy them before 'M. l'Abonné' (L10, 67; L24, 93; CP76, 13; CJ7, 29-30). Some corrupt provincial officials steal a number here and a number there and finish the year with the whole collection (CP24, 16) – an accusation for which the Cousin apologises shortly afterwards (CP30, 1-3). But he later affirms that he has been the victim of a boycott in certain offices as a result of his accusations of dishonesty: 'j'ai failli, sous le regne des abus, voir mes livraisons suppri-mées, pour n'avoir pas eu la complaisance de prendre sur moi les fautes d'autrui' (CJ15, 37). Why is he the one to suffer such losses, Beffroy laments, while subscribers receive regularly and in good order the *Mercure* and the *Journal de Paris,* which are products of wealthier enterprises much better able to absorb this financial disadvantage (CJ7, 30).

Le Cousin Jacques normally aims to maintain good relations with the administrators of the Paris offices of both postal organisations (speaking of the 'zèle obligeant qu'ils m'ont toujours témoigné') and assures his provin-cial subscribers these gentlemen will promptly investigate disappearances on receipt of a certificate from the local office attesting that a given issue had never been received (CP55, 43-44). Parisian readers should complain to the journal office within a week and le Cousin Jacques will transmit these claims to 'son *cousin* l'inspecteur général de la poste de Paris' (CP58, 68). In 1790, le Cousin Jacques appeals for help, in the face of increasing losses in the mails, to one of the *administrateurs généraux,* a certain M. Richard (CJ7, 28), who arranges the reimbursement of 136 *livres* in compensation for copies not delivered (CJ15, 38), but whose efforts overall prove fruitless in the face of some 300 lost periodicals (CJ18, 53-54). Perhaps as a result the Cousin is at least able to publish a letter from the *Inspecteur-Général du Bureau du départ, à la grande poste* (signed Gouin) attesting that the copies are the most carefully prepared and presented of all periodicals received at the office, where investigations have revealed no irregularities (CJ13, 44-45).

One of le Cousin Jacques's more obsessive concerns is the cost to him of mail received: most letters at the time were sent *en port dû* as insurance against their delivery. This was a source of common annoyance to public figures and to the proprietors of journals in particular, whom the postal regulations made liable for any mail received unless they published a public notice to the contrary. From the start, the Cousin announces that 'il oubliera de lire les Lettres qu'on aura oublié d'affranchir', and the statement is tirelessly repeated throughout the series (L16, 18; L35/36, 102; CP7, 20-21; CP55, 37; CJ4, 70; N31, 73). It is claimed that if such a policy were not adopted postal costs would represent twice the costs of printing *Le Courrier des planètes* (CP7, 20-21), as the author receives some twenty letters per day at an estimated cost of eight *sous* each (CP33, 8). Correspondents are warned in passing that their servants may in some cases be pocketing the money given them to pay postage, as letters are received with the words *port payé* written on the envelope but not stamped as such by the post (L16, 18). A major problem for the journalist is, however, that it would in fact be in his interest to accept and to pay for any correspondence concerning subscriptions and payments. Beffroy thus asks booksellers writing to him to put their names and addresses on their letters so that they may be identified, or else to pay postage and deduct it from payments made to the author (CP7, 21). Subscribers are told when sending money to mark the words 'Avec 21 livres' on the envelope of the letter of advice (CP53, ii.; CP55, 37). Contributions from readers, on the contrary, will not be accepted unfranked: even in answers to parlour games like the *bouts rimés,* the Cousin calculates he could be up for 1200 *livres* in a year (CJ12, 61n). If he received only five letters from each reader, that would make a total of some ten thousand letters per year (CJ4, 56).

Purely financial considerations – and especially what turns out to be the underlying unprofitability of the venture – assume a considerable importance quite early in the Cousin Jacques's commentary on his journalistic career. His problems really start after the break with Lesclapart, when Beffroy assumes commercial as well as editorial responsibility. 'Je n'étais qu'auteur jusqu'ici; aujourd'hui me voilà commerçant' (CP1, 5). Although he writes 'l'établissement de mon entreprise m'avait mis à sec', in his first year he cannot even hope to reach the sum of 800 *livres* in profits (CP33, 8-9). Out of a subscription fee of 21 *livres* he begins to calculate that he may be lucky to retain twenty *sous* in profit, with distribution costs taking more than a seventh of the total, booksellers' discounts absorbing a further sixth and general correspondence eating up at least a third of what remains – before paying paper and printing costs. Once a book is printed most of the rest is profit, but a periodical costs twice as much to produce and should cost the consumer twice as much (CP10, 22-24; CP24, 9): 'l'impression & le papier ne font que la moitié de la dépense d'un *journal*' (CP75, 48). With the onset of the Revolution, the price both of paper and of printing rises alarmingly (CJ14, 71), and these items added to the hidden costs – which the Cousin 'n'avait point assez soigneusement calculés' – bring him to a point of crisis (CP75, 44-45). He offers – how seriously it is not clear – to accept subscriptions in kind:

candles, wine, truffles, even minor repairs to his shirts and handkerchiefs! (CP75, 52). In what appears to be a somewhat desperate measure in the last days of the *Courrier des planètes* (having made no profit at all in 1789 (CP76, 15)), the Cousin proposes introducing a supplement that would publish readers' contributions, but at the readers' expense (CP75, 45-48). 'Qu'on calcule [. . .] ce que coûterait séparément l'impression de douze pages de *petit texte* en caractère usité pour l'*in*-8o; on verra que ce qui revient ici à 48 liv., reviendrait tout compris, la distribution, &c. au moins à 150 liv.' (CP75, 49). This expedient, in spite of various changes to the conditions of payment (CJ1, 12-13; CJ2, 49-51; CJ11, 49-50) does not stave off the eventual necessity to reduce the number of pages in each issue. He assumes his readers will not wish him to ruin his family by continuing to offer at the same price a publication that now costs a third more to produce (CJ14, 72). However, he offers any malcontents a reduction equivalent to the booksellers' commission of three *livres* on their next subscription (CJ8, 56; CJ18, 55), when he must 'suspendre un tems le cours de mon ouvrage' (CJ18, 54).

Debts – already a problem in 1788 (CP30, 3) – begin to pile up in 1789 (CJ15, 36). In launching the fifth year of his series, le Cousin Jacques begs his lagging subscribers to pay accounts going back to 1789 and even 1788: 'Il m'est dû sur l'an passé 4195 livres, & sur cette année 1790, plus de 2000 francs'. He claims to be unable to pay the printer, his paper supplier, his postal charges (CJ3, 3). In 1788 and 1789 more than 1800 *livres* are lost in replacing mislaid issues (763 in 1789 alone (CJ4, 56)) and paying postage on them over again (CJ7, 28). As 1790 proceeds, the sums owing rise to 7000 *livres* and Beffroy despairs of ever being paid, in view of the bankruptcies occurring all around him (CJ7, 31; CJ14, 72; CJ18, 51). And at the end of 1791 his expenses again outstrip his receipts, this time by 4762 *livres* (C18, 285-86). To pay his own costs he is forced to borrow: 'L'intérêt de ces emprunts consume tout le fruit de ses travaux' (CJ15, 36). He cannot maintain the lease on his apartment, must sell his furniture and go and live with a friend (CJ18, 52). His printer will only hand over the work in exchange for cash, as otherwise he in turn is unable to pay his workmen (CJ15, 37). Freedom of the press seems a mixed blessing to Beffroy (CP67, 8-10; CP70, 3; CP71, 46; CP76, 41-42), and an alarming picture is painted of conditions in the printing trades. Artisans are hard to find, on the one hand because of the torrent of brochures of all kinds that are being produced (CJ18, 50), and on the other because 'les fêtes continuelles de la fédération ont aussi débauché tous les ouvriers de la capitale' (CJ14, 71). Those artisans who remain willing to work are demanding what Beffroy sees as outrageous wages: 'chacun est maître de demander le prix qu'il veut de son travail, & peut exiger 100 écus dc cc qui vaut 18 francs' (CJ14, 70-72). One result of these chaotic conditions is that a bookseller of his acquaintance has had to pay 75 *livres* per small in-duodecimo sheet that only the previous year would have cost no more than 34 *livres* (CJ18, 51).

The periodical entitled *Le Cousin Jacques* comes to an untimely end in September of 1790, and its successor *Les Nouvelles Lunes du Cousin Jacques* survives only thc first six months of 1791. When Beffroy launches his *Consolateur* the following year, he somewhat belatedly offers subscribers to the preceding series, who received only 29 out of 52 issues, 22 numbers of his new venture, but is touched that some of his readers have refused this offer (C18, 285-86). He proposes another money-making scheme, which consists of publishing free for subscribers 'toutes les annonces, avis, demandes, lettres, réclamations, etc. pourvu qu'elles n'excèdent pas une demi-page', but offering to print two or three hundred extra copies of the relevant issue and charge them only for labour and none of the setting charges (C21, 339). Earlier he had refused the many advertisements looking for work sent him by 'une infinité de personnes sans place', referring them to the *Petites Affiches* and the *Supplément à la Feuille du jour* (C63, 175). Readers' literary contributions on the other hand will now be published free of charge and are actively solicited (C, prospectus, 4), even though Beffroy finds himself apologising for losing at least one manuscript (C63, 175).

The worsening financial situation in the last years of the periodical series often makes it difficult for the Cousin to maintain his resolutely jocular approach (CJ7, 32), and there are references not only to personal quarrels (C3, 33-36; C6, 84-90) and family tragedies (CP29, 2-3; CJ18, 52-53), but also to the impossible workload that Beffroy feels he has taken on. Already in 1789 he laments the ceaseless labour required to support a 'famille sans patrimoine', the strain caused by the illness both of a friend who acted as secretary and of his porter who ran his messages, together with a virulent eye inflammation from which he himself suffered as a result of his strenuous labours (CP55, 41). An absence of two months results in a pile-up of 117 letters, 23 *mémoires* to be read and corrected, the manuscripts of 11 plays and other works to examine and 35 printed works to examine, involving him in ten hours of toil in his office per day (CP74, 53-54). In 1790, there is overwork, illness (CJ8, 58) and again a backlog of correspondence, twenty letters arriving each morning (CJ16, 3-5; CJ18, 57). He complains that his drawing room is full of visitors from seven in the morning until midday and that the only really free time he has for writing is during the night between eleven and three (CJ18, 56, 58). Other periodicals, he points out, not only call upon the talents of a number of writers but draw their subject matter from the news, from books published or advertisements, whereas Beffroy has to produce 'un journal de pure imagination' (CP55, 38-39; CJ7, 30). 'Je me demande s'il est possible qu'un seul homme écrive vingt lettres par jour, fasse, en outre, plusieurs envois, satisfasse aux réclamations, compose de la musique, & invente dix à douze pages de gaîté' (CJ16, 3-5). The journalistic persona increasingly drifts towards that of the impecunious and put-upon man of letters, especially when he complains about the fraudulent use of his pseudonym and of his theatrical works (CJ15, 41-46; CJ18, 67-72; N17, 15-16). 'Mille & mille pardons, mes lecteurs, si je coupe le fil de mes folies pour vous parler d'affaires; mais j'y suis contraint' (CJ15, 35-41; CJ18, 49-72). This mixture of tones, of the tragic and the comic, is not, of course, without its 'pre-romantic' implications. Laughter is seen as a necessity to make the burdens of existence bearable. In public terms, at least, Beffroy justifies the continuation of his facetious periodicals into the Revolutionary period with the argument that merriment is all the more necessary now that everyday living has become so traumatic and uncertain (CP75, 42). Nevertheless, the period where the personality of the Cousin Jacques served as an essential presentational device is over. The 'author' of the *Consolateur,* in his prospectus, insists on his anonymity, and although this rule is soon bent (C, prospectus, 3-4) or broken (C3, 36; C6, 159) and indeed a portrait (by M. Bureau after Violet) is once again offered to readers in colour for 3 *livres* or *au bistre* for 40 *sous* (C11, 171-72), the overwhelming exuberance of the Cousin's presence is missing.

Thus we have what seems an appeal to past notoriety (with references for example to 'un Journal du même Auteur, qui a joui long-temps du plus brillant succès' (C, prospectus, 3)) rather than a new development of those earlier formulae – formulae through which, as this paper has attempted to demonstrate, Beffroy had made a spectacularly original use of the device of the eccentric narrator, exploiting it to describe in unusual detail the everyday problems of running a periodical. Whereas a 'serious' journalist speaking in his own name would certainly have felt constrained to maintain a far greater degree of classical decorum, Beffroy as le Cousin Jacques is free of inhibitions concerning the propriety of overwhelming a reader with such practical and material information: 'Je n'ai ni le titre, ni la qualité, ni les talens d'homme de lettres; mon genre est à moi' (CP48, 28). In a sense paradoxically, the comic mask, the fictional persona, appears to allow him to deal with a form of reality that would otherwise have been beneath the attention of a more conventional literary aesthetic. What we have been examining is clearly no artless and unmediated testimony. Prudence here as always is necessary in attempting to interpret a fictional discourse as a historical document, especially if one remembers that the gloomy picture found in the periodicals from late 1790 is contemporaneous with Beffroy's greatest theatrical success, *Nicodème dans la lune*. The formal, personal and conventional distortions in the picture le Cousin Jacques draws of the life of an eighteenth-century journalist need to be taken into account in future work on this material, as an attempt is made to measure it against more directly documentary evidence.

Notes

[1] Charles Monselet, *Les Oubliés et les dédaignés,* Paris, Charpentier, 1876, 149-214. Charles Westercamp, *Beffroy de Reigny, dit le Cousin Jacques [...],* Laon, Editions des Tablettes de l'Aisne, 1930. The most recent publication concerning Beffroy is a critical edition of his play *Nicodème dans la lune* edited by Michèle Sajous (Biblioteca della ricerca. Testi stranieri, 3, Fasanio di Puglia, Schena, Paris, Nizet, 1983), which is an essential reference for this author's theatrical career and for the general biographical and bibliographical information it provides.

[2] J. Sgard *et al., Dictionnaire des journalistes (1600-1789),* Presses universitaires de Grenoble, 1976, pp. 311-12, gives a summary of Beffroy's journalistic career. See also Sajous, op. cit., pp. 213-15. I have not taken into account in this article either *Le Lendemain,* 1790-1791, or *Le Défenseur du peuple,* 1791, as these are outside the *Cousin Jacques* series. Because of constraints of space it has been possible to give only a selection of references to Beffroy's text, and they should not be taken to be exhaustive. The abbreviations used are L, CP, CJ, N, C, followed by issue number and pagination (i-ii refer to recto and verso of front cover). The numbers of the issues of L become confused between 13 and 18, and 73 and 74 are used twice in CP, but I have quoted those Beffroy finally assigns to them. CJ starts technically at 113, but I have used rather the number of the 'quinzaine'.

Contradiction and irony in Voltaire's fiction

Haydn Mason : University of Bristol

T H E pure inconsequentiality of things in the world troubled Voltaire greatly. As early as 1742, we find him stressing the point with typical clarity: 'Plus on voit ce monde, et plus on le voit plein de contradictions et d'inconséquences'.[1] There follows a long list of the absurd illogicalities of human behaviour; indeed, adds Voltaire, inconsistency is at the very heart of man's conduct: 'Si je voulais continuer à examiner les contrariétés qu'on trouve dans l'empire des lettres, il faudrait écrire l'histoire de tous les savants et de tous les beaux-esprits; de même que si je voulais détailler les contrariétés dans la société, il faudrait écrire l'histoire du genre humain'.[2] This conviction was to remain with him throughout the rest of his life. Three decades later, he expresses it thus: 'Où est le peuple dont les lois et les usages ne se contredisent pas?'[3] He goes on: 'Si quelque société littéraire veut entreprendre le dictionnaire des contradictions, je souscris pour vingt volumes *in-folio*'.[4] (One wonders whether he might have fulfilled that promise a century later when appeared Flaubert's post-humous onslaught on 'la bêtise humaine', the *Dictionnaire des idées reçues*.)

As is clear from these quotations, Voltaire is speaking here only of human contrariness. But an awareness of disorder in the physical world at large is equally strong in him from at least 1740, as emerges clearly from a little-known passage in the *Eléments de Newton,* missing from the Moland edition of the *Œuvres complètes,* which René Pomeau has done us the great service of rescuing from its obscurity.[5] Voltaire, seeking to convey how one can become an atheist, composes a mini-*conte.* A number of intelligent people find themselves living for a fortnight in a northern island subject to every kind of climatic upset: ice and fog in late May, followed by a heatwave; a storm that brings down trees and an invasion of voracious insects; a brilliant moon, followed by a solar eclipse and afterwards the disappearance of the stars; an earthquake, with immediate casualties, and subsequent deaths from hunger, disease, ravaging beasts. How, in the face of all that, argues Voltaire, will these reasonable spectators of so much chaos believe willingly 'les Arguments Métaphysiques qui prouvent un Etre souverainement sage et bienfaisant?'[6]

Voltaire goes on to counter this by his usual deist argument of design, indicating by contrast our own climates and their benevolent, ordered arrangements, which conduce to a belief in the Creator of such a world. Even so, the hypothesis has been entertained, and in years to come the freezing weather and earthquakes will reappear, not in some far-off northern land, but in Western Europe as seen in *Candide*.

But one does not have to wait for *Candide* to see the natural absurdities of our own world set forth in considerable detail. The brief *conte Songe de Platon* provides an extensive dossier. The *génie* Démogorgon who has created Earth (in this Platonic dream, God is thereby spared from direct accusation) has blundered in many ways:

> Vraiment, vous avez bien opéré: vous avez séparé votre monde en deux, et vous avez mis un grand espace d'eau entre les deux hémisphères, afin qu'il n'y eût point de communication de l'un à l'autre. On gèlera de froid sous vos deux pôles, on mourra de chaud sous votre ligne équinoxiale. Vous avez prudemment établi de grands déserts de sable, pour que les passants y mourussent de faim et de soif. Je suis assez content de vos moutons, de vos vaches et de vos poules; mais, franchement, je ne le suis pas trop de vos serpents et de vos araignées. Vos oignons et vos artichauts sont de très bonnes choses; mais je ne vois pas quelle a été votre idée en couvrant la terre de tant de plantes venimeuses, à moins que vous n'ayez eu le dessein d'empoisonner ses habitants. Il me paraît d'ailleurs que vous avez formé une trentaine d'espèces de singes, beaucoup plus d'espèces de chiens, et seulement quatre ou cinq espèces d'hommes: il est vrai que vous avez donné à ce dernier animal ce que vous appelez *la raison;* mais, en conscience, cette raison-là est trop ridicule, et approche trop de la folie. Il me paraît d'ailleurs que vous ne faites pas grand cas de cet animal à deux pieds, puisque vous lui avez donné tant d'ennemis, et si peu de défense; tant de passions, et si peu de sagesse. Vous ne voulez pas apparemment qu'il reste beaucoup de ces animaux-là sur terre: car, sans compter les dangers auxquels vous les exposez, vous avez si bien fait votre compte qu'un jour la petite vérole emportera tous les ans régulièrement la dixième partie de cette espèce, et que la sœur de cette petite vérole empoisonnera la source de la vie dans les neuf parties qui resteront; et, comme si ce n'était pas encore assez, vous avez tellement disposé les choses que la moitié des survivants sera occupée à plaider, et l'autre à se tuer; ils vous auront sans doute beaucoup d'obligation; et vous avez fait là un beau chef-d'œuvre.[7]

It is a formidable indictment, embracing, as Démogorgon quickly realises, 'du mal moral et du mal physique': in the physical world, isolated continents, extremes of climate, useless vast deserts, noxious fauna and flora; in the human domain, a creature of little wisdom, highly vulnerable to enemies and disease, and given to massacre of its own species. One would like to believe, with M. Van den Heuvel, that this brief tale dates from 1737-38[8] for it would indicate that Voltaire's fully explicit awareness of *la force des choses* was formed earlier than has hitherto been supposed. But that thesis has recently been challenged, on cogent grounds, by Renato Galliani, who puts the period of composition back to its more traditional date of the early 1750s (it was first published in 1756);[9] and one has to confess that this fits in better with other evidence of the evolution in Voltaire's concern with the problem of evil.

However, the sense of latent disorder, present throughout such *contes* as *Le Monde comme il va, Zadig, Scarmentado, Candide,* finds many an explicit expression over the years. The wise old Mambrès in *Le Taureau blanc* (1774) comes to perceive it: 'Tout bien pesé, je commence à soupçonner que ce monde-ci subsiste de contradictions [. . .]'.[10] He is echoed by the equally sensible Sidrac of *Les Oreilles du comte de Chesterfield* (1775): 'De quelque côté que je ne me tourne, je ne trouve qu'obscurité, contradiction, impossibilité, ridicule, rêveries, impertinence, chimère, absurdité, bêtise, charlatanerie'.[11]

It is of course one-sided simply to present in isolation these intimations by Voltaire of the anarchy in the universe. The *philosophe,* in fact, scarcely ever lets such contradictions stand without some counter-argument or other. In *Songe de Platon,* for instance, Démogorgon is allowed the right of reply. He points out the incongruity of giving man liberty and then expecting him never to abuse it, as too the impossibility of creating an entirely harmonious, harmless world from the individual elements that go to make it up. These assertions, often repeated in Voltaire's work, receive perhaps their crowning statement in the *Histoire de Jenni* (1775), where a formal debate is arranged between the atheist Birton and the deist Freind.[12] Birton's arguments revert in large part to those of the *Songe de Platon*: in a largely hostile environment, man lives a derisory existence full of suffering and inflicted atrocities. The argument is rehearsed with force, and at some length. But Freind always has the last word. There is indeed, he replies, much evil on the earth; nevertheless, one should not exaggerate. Basically, the cosmic machine works with order and benevolence. God's existence is certain; how then could He possibly be evil? Perfection necessarily implies goodness. The stars at night reveal His majesty; the voice of conscience displays His justice in our hearts. At the end, Birton falls silent, and believes.

This struggle to see the underlying order beneath the appearance of chaos manifestly runs through Voltaire's fiction. Whether discussing the comparative amounts of good and evil in Parisian life *(Le Monde comme il va)* or the ridiculous but no less firm desire ('une furieuse contradiction')[13] of every civilised being to put reason above happiness in the priorities of existence *(Histoire d'un bon bramin),* this preoccupation is ever present. But the final judgment enunciated by Freind in the *Histoire de Jenni* is necessarily, whatever the cogency of its demonstration, an apologetic statement. More to our purpose, how does Voltaire perceive the *nature* of this universe, whatever the degree of order at its heart? What is the significance of a world, for example, where everything eats everything else?

The author brings such a world trenchantly to life in the brief tale *Aventure indienne* (1766). Pythagoras, who knows the languages of animals and plants, overhears the grass bewailing its fate; it is constantly being eaten by 'un monstre dévorant, un animal horrible', whose mouth is 'armée d'une rangée de faux tranchantes avec laquelle il me coupe, me déchire et m'engloutit'.[14] This appalling creature turns out to be a sheep. Pythagoras comes upon an oyster, which he is about to eat when the oyster expresses its own lament; it is even worse off than grass because, once eaten by man, it will never be reborn. Brought to awareness of his impending crime, Pythagoras pays closer attention to what is going on:

> [. . .] il vit des araignées qui mangeaient des mouches, des hirondelles qui mangeaient des araignées, des éperviers qui mangeaient des hirondelles. 'Tous ces gens-là, dit-il, ne sont pas philosophes.'[15]

Exceptionally, no attempt is made here by Voltaire to respond to this universal predicament, other than through Pythagoras's rueful remark. The scene abruptly switches to specifically human injustice, where Pythagoras is able to bring at least a little reason to bear on a mad world. But the end is sombre. Tolerant himself, he dies (like Jacques in *Candide)* trying to save others from catastrophe. Voltaire's final words echo darkly: *'Sauve qui peut'.*[16]

But although, in the *Aventure indienne,* there is no resolution of the problem of universal slaughter, Voltaire had attempted an answer as early as the *Métaphysique de Newton* (1740). After evoking the spectacle of wolves devouring sheep and spiders swallowing flies, Voltaire turns the argument upside down: 'Ne voyez-vous pas, au contraire, que ces généra-tions continuelles, toujours dévorées et toujours reproduites, entrent dans le plan de l'univers?'[17] The cosmic design, in short, involves constant destruction and constant regeneration. Voltaire draws the same lesson from the fabulous phoenix in *La Princesse de Babylone* (1768) who, having himself just been reborn, goes on to tell Princess Formosante:

> La résurrection, madame... est la chose du monde la plus simple. Il n'est pas plus surprenant de naître deux fois qu'une. Tout est résurrection dans ce monde; les chenilles ressuscitent en papillons, un noyau mis en terre ressuscite en arbre; tous les animaux ensevelis dans la terre ressusci-tent en herbes, en plantes, et nourrissent d'autres animaux dont ils font bientôt une partie de la substance: toutes les particules qui composaient les corps sont changées en différents êtres.[18]

This vision is integrated into Freind's definitive world-view. Countering Birton's argument that all created beings perish, 'depuis l'insecte dévoré par l'hirondelle jusqu'à l'éléphant mangé des vers', Freind replies:

> Non, rien ne périt, tout change; les germes impalpables des animaux et des végétaux subsistent, se développent et perpétuent les espèces. Pourquoi ne voudriez-vous pas que Dieu conservât le principe qui vous fait agir et penser, de quelque nature qu'il puisse être? Dieu me garde de faire un système; mais certainement il y a dans nous quelque chose qui pense et qui veut [...][19]

One might say, then, that Voltaire's investigation of the possible incoherence in first causes follows his own advice in the *Lettres philo-sophiques* à propos of Newton's explorations: *'Procedes huc, & non ibis amplius'.*[20] Beyond a certain point, fundamental order reigns, whatever the final truth on discrete phenomenal disparities and ambiguities.

It is this approach, bearing with it its own element of unease in certain areas, which underlines the particular quality of Voltaire's irony. In the eighteenth century, the meaning of 'irony' was generally agreed, as one may see from consulting the various dictionaries of the period. As a typical instance, the article 'Ironie' in the *Encyclopédie,* composed by the well-known grammarian Beauzée, defines it as 'une figure par laquelle on veut faire entendre le contraire de ce qu'on dit'; 'ironie' is equated with 'moquerie', 'plaisanterie'. Voltaire's explicit comments on irony testify that he evidently shared this general view. But within it, there is an evolution during his career. In the *Conseils à un journaliste* (1737) he recommends his interlocutor, when exposing someone else's opinions, to avoid the use of insulting words: 'Point d'animosité, point d'ironie'.[21] As time goes by, however, this equivalence is modified and eventually reversed. In a letter to d'Argental of 1772, Voltaire establishes a contrast between invective and irony: 'Point d'injure; beaucoup d'ironie et de guaité. Les injures révoltent: l'ironie fait rentrer les gens en eux-mêmes, la guaité désarme'.[22] While recognising that 'La figure de l'ironie tient presque toujours du comique' and that therefore it should be used in the most sparing way in tragedy,[23] he had come to see the value of ironic modes, especially in the philosophic crusade against obscurantism. Although the word 'irony' is nowhere mentioned, a full list of such techniques is provided in a *Lettre sur l'esprit* of 1744:

> Ce qu'on appelle esprit est tantôt une comparaison nouvelle, tantôt une allusion fine: ici l'abus d'un mot qu'on présente dans un sens, et qu'on laisse entendre dans un autre; là un rapport délicat entre deux idées peu communes; c'est une métaphore singulière; c'est une recherche de ce qu'un objet ne présente pas d'abord, mais de ce qui est en effet dans lui; c'est l'art ou de réunir deux choses éloignées, ou de diviser deux choses qui paraissent se joindre, ou de les opposer l'une à l'autre; *c'est celui de ne dire qu'à moitié sa pensée pour la laisser deviner.*[24]

Voltaire comes to realise that 'la meilleure manière de tomber sur l'infâme est de paraître n'avoir nulle envie de l'attaquer [. . .] de laisser le lecteur tirer lui-même les conséquences [. . .]'[25] Repeatedly, he stresses that his use of apparent mockery conceals the most serious intentions, discoverable by all enlightened readers who take the trouble to penetrate beneath the surface. Irony, so far as Voltaire is concerned, is an activist strategy.[26] As he puts it in a letter to d'Alembert: 'prêchez et écrivez, combattez, convertissez, rendez les fanatiques si odieux et si méprisables que le gouvernement soit honteux de les soutenir [. . .] Le ridicule vient à bout de tout, c'est la plus forte des armes [. . .]'[27]

Little purpose is served, in the space of a brief article, by adumbrating once again actual instances of irony in Voltaire's *contes* and thereby merely reproducing much useful critical work that has been done in this field.[28] René Pomeau sums up the author's approach: 'Sa manière d'écrire est ludique [. . .] Son tour de style recherche la surprise du choc, du raccourci, des courts-circuits qui déconcertent [. . .] Ce style de jeu apparaît dans toute sa pureté dans les contes voltairiens, conçus à l'origine, on le sait, comme des jeux mondains.'[29] M. Pomeau finds a *joie de vivre* in this style; M. Sareil agrees, in discovering gaiety and 'sérénité de ton' in *Candide;*[30] Roland Barthes, albeit with different ideological inferences, shares this view in describing Voltaire as 'le dernier des écrivains heur-eux'.[31] Such irony is, as Barthes says, 'la mise en évidence d'une *dispro-portion*'.[32]

This irony, moreover, has its chosen field of operation. To return to our initial observations, Voltaire rarely mocks at the physical world. It is the human scene of follies and horrors which rather attracts his attention. In this respect, the *Aventure indienne* is exemplary. Starting with the spectacle of all-voracious nature, to which he appears to have no easy response, Voltaire switches to the domain of man's cruelty to his fellow-man, where the author's ironic stance seems more at home. In the whole corpus of the *contes* there are remarkably few examples of natural disasters. The earthquake in *Candide* is striking because of its exception-ality, and even there Voltaire is much more concerned with the greed evinced by the sailor or the awfulness of the auto-da-fé than by the tragic loss of a good man through an 'act of God'. His sense of evil, manifestly, shines through his *contes* at one with his search for justice in an unjust world. But the injustice upon which he directs his attention is the evil that men do to one another. Natural catastrophes, he seems to decide, are a necessary part of the overall functioning, bits of grit in the cosmic machine, and in no way comprehensible beyond that. Whereas human wrong-doing and absurdity, although equally mysterious in their way, can better inspire his wit and raillery because, at bottom, he can bring his pragmatic consciousness to bear upon them.

This may in part explain the superiority of *Candide* over all the other *contes*. It is possible that some of the briefer narrative sketches could have led, had they been developed, to equally impressive masterpieces; the *Histoire d'un bon bramin*, for instance, contains the seed of a most fruitful paradox. But, apart from *Candide*, the extended *contes* tend to stick to safe ground. In *Zadig*, many men and women are evil; but Zadig is not, an order is glimpsed and success attained. *L'Ingénu* attacks social injustices, *Le Taureau blanc* pokes fun at the Old Testament; and so on. These are misfortunes about which man may do something.

By contrast, *Candide* considers the whole human condition in an existential sense, most notably through La Vieille. She it is who has suffered most and reflected most on the implications. It is she who, at the end, wonders whether the insidious quality of *ennui* is not more terrible than every kind of conceivable suffering. (No other Voltaire *conte* plumbs the depths of *ennui*, which is experienced by Pococuranté as well as by 'la petite société' of the final chapter.) More strikingly still, it is given to her to muse on the absurd folly of the human race in wanting to hang on to life at any price:

> Cette faiblesse ridicule est peut-être un de nos penchants les plus funestes: car y a-t-il rien de plus sot que de vouloir porter continuellement un fardeau qu'on veut toujours jeter par terre? d'avoir son être en horreur, et de tenir à son être? enfin de caresser le serpent qui nous dévore, jusqu'à ce qu'il nous ait mangé le cœur?[33]

This philosophical view of survival promotes Voltaire's irony on to a higher plane in *Candide.* We have left far behind that limited area where irony equates only with witticism and have begun to approach the sense of cosmic irony which such Romantic writers as Friedrich Schlegel were to demonstrate: an attitude springing from the very ambiguities within our nature, relating to the sense of a basic contradiction, unfathomable by reason, in the universe.[34]

But this is Voltaire's farthest limit, metaphysically speaking. Irony represents for him, as we have seen, an essentially comic vision, based on a brilliant intuition of incongruities. It is also founded on an inherent duality, as Jean Starobinski has demonstrated in a remarkable study of *L'Ingénu,* where he finds 'un battement entre le pathétique de certains éléments, et la plaisanterie qui les enveloppe et les allège'.[35] This leads the critic on to discover, behind that procedure, a binary vision of the world:

> Il n'y a pas de bien sans mal, ni de mal sans bien, et cela dans des proportions inégales [. . .] La logique n'y trouve pas son compte. Il est vrai que les hommes ne sont pas souvent heureux. Il est non moins vrai que les hommes peuvent être heureux [. . .] Dans le rythme binaire de ce monde qui cloche et où la parfaite cohérence est à jamais impossible, ce n'est ni le premier ni le second temps qui représente la vérité définitive; l'ironie philosophique constate que l'un ne va jamais sans l'autre, et que si le monde ne clochait pas son mouvement s'arrêterait. De ce mouvement incessant, le conte voltairien nous propose l'image accélérée et caricaturale, oscillant de la nature à la culture, du vice à la vertu, du rire aux larmes, du pessimisme à l'optimisme.[36]

Here we come close to the essential recipe of Voltaire's irony: the contradiction between the ridiculousness of hope and the occasional totally unexpected manifestations of goodness. La Vieille trusts the poor Italian who, like her, has suffered in the massacre; and he whisks her off into slavery. But also, against all expectations, Cacambo does not desert Candide now that the former is rich but loyally keeps the rendez-vous in

Venice. Through it all pulsates an irrepressible life-force. People survive, as long as an ounce of energy remains. But even if they die, or are killed or eaten, they too 'entrent dans le plan de l'univers';[37] for 'la résurrection ... est la chose du monde la plus simple'.[38] Yet, as Starobinski puts it, 'le monde cloche' and will continue to do so.

These comments may summon up thoughts of that other great French ironist of the eighteenth century, Diderot, who has himself been rightly called a 'poète de l'énergie'.[39] The same critic, Jacques Chouillet, elsewhere comments on the incoherences of Diderot's *Jacques le fataliste,* stressing how fundamental they are:

> Non seulement *Jacques le fataliste* est un roman écrit contre les romans [...] mais encore l'idée même de *sens* y est constamment mise en question: refus de répondre au lecteur, dénouements différés [...] récits déviant de leur sens initial [...] complexités de structures rendant la situation du lecteur incertaine [...] pluralité de dénouements [...] et surtout, absence de conclusion.[40]

This succinct account of the indeterminacy reflected in Diderot's novel may serve as a basis for comparison with Voltaire's ironies. *Jacques le fataliste* imitates the disconcerting universe it portrays, in which the nature of things is always unclear, nothing is known for certain, no one is ever in complete control of anything. This onslaught upon the construction of satisfying meanings is begun with the very first words of the novel:

> Comment s'étaient-ils rencontrés? Par hasard, comme tout le monde. Comment s'appelaient-ils? Que vous importe? D'où venaient-ils? Du lieu le plus prochain. Où allaient-ils? Est-ce que l'on sait où l'on va? Que disaient-ils? le maître ne disait rien, et Jacques disait que son capitaine disait que tout ce qui nous arrive de bien et de mal ici-bas était écrit là-haut.[41]

It is possible to find a rough parallel to this passage from within Voltaire's fiction. In the *Histoire d'un bon bramin* (1761), the eponymous hero expresses his distress at the inaccessibility of final truths:

> [...] tout augmente le sentiment douloureux que j'éprouve. Je suis prêt quelquefois de tomber dans le désespoir, quand je songe qu'après toutes mes recherches, je ne sais d'où je viens, ni ce que je suis, ni où j'irai, ni ce que je deviendrai.[42]

The same formulation had occurr ed a few years earlier as part of the anguished interrogation in the *Poème sur le désastre de Lisbonne* (1756):

> Que peut donc de l'esprit la plus vaste étendue?
> Rien: le livre du sort se ferme à notre vue.
> L'homme, étranger à soi, de l'homme est ignoré.
> Que suis-je, où suis-je, où vais-je, et d'où suis-je tiré?[43]

But these intense questions are at a far remove from Diderot's, posed passionately to oneself, whereas the opening paragraph of *Jacques le fataliste* throws them provocatively back at the reader. True, the narrative tone in *Candide* is much more ironic than in the two other contemporary works by Voltaire we have just mentioned; but the essential difference of approach from that of Diderot remains. In René Pomeau's words: 'De la première à la dernière page de *Candide* [...] les éléments sont constamment sollicités de porter sens'.[44] Whereas *Jacques le fataliste* imitates disorder, *Candide* comments upon it. A logic is imposed on this chaotic world, through the insistently sardonic commentary of the narrator. Everything seems susceptible of rational demonstration. But this logic is constantly breaking down, betraying the reader, just as, in a parallel way, Candide is himself being betrayed in his hopeful expectations by Vanderdendur, or Parisian socialites or, for that matter, Pangloss.

Even so, the very intelligence of the narration is based upon a notional order. The Eldoradans recognise it and give thanks to God for it. Even the sceptical dervish accepts that although 'Sa Hautesse' who sends a ship to Egypt is indifferent to the mice in the hold, the existence of 'Sa Hautesse' is not in question. Whereas Diderot's *Rêve de d'Alembert* discusses the generation of the species in terms of a universal flux ('Tout change. Tout passe. Il n'y a que le Tout qui reste'),[45] Voltaire insists rather upon the fixity underlying the reproductive process:

> Le grand, le beau miracle continuel, est qu'un garçon et une fille fassent un enfant ensemble, qu'un rossignol fasse un rossignolet à sa rossignole, et non pas à une fauvette. Il faudrait passer la moitié de sa vie à les imiter, et l'autre moitié à bénir celui qui inventa cette méthode. Il y a dans la génération mille secrets tout à fait curieux.[46]

Movement, for Voltaire, is ultimately inscribed within a predetermined order, not a phenomenon whose sole *raison d'être* is itself.

In brief, Voltaire's ironic procedures are more dissimilar to Diderot's than they are alike. His irony is of the 'stable' kind, whose point of departure is that a covert fixed meaning is possible and decipherable.[47] It knows how to discriminate between what is true and what is false: 'in saying the opposite to what he means, he [the ironist] knows what he means [. . .]'[48] The narrator is uppermost throughout, making clear the absurdities so as to 'laisser le lecteur tirer lui-même les conséquences'.[49] By contrast, Diderot's narrator in *Jacques le fataliste* belongs to a world obeying the principle of total randomness and uncertainty. In keeping with it, he is himself not to be trusted or treated as guide and authority, as the opening lines make clear. His capricious persona images the caprice of fate itself, whatever the 'grand rouleau' may or may not have written upon it. If one agrees with M. Pomeau that Voltaire and Diderot 'se rencontrent dans une [. . .] vision de l'homme se débattant vaille que vaille au milieu d'un univers régi par le hasard et la nécessité',[50] it has to be added that *le hasard* is more freakishly enigmatic in Diderot, *la nécessité* more subject to moral law in Voltaire. Diderot's irony is more problematically 'open', anticipating in certain respects the Romantic ironists.[51] Voltaire's irony, on the other hand, remains brilliantly classical, an intelligence playing upon the endless ambiguities of men and events, proposing in *contes* like *Micromégas, Zadig, Candide, L'Ingénu* a continuous array of false causalities to be held up to the mocking light of true reason – but on the ultimate assumption that beneath all these fallacies there rules a true Cause whose nature is intelligence and justice.

Notes

[1] Voltaire, *Œuvres complètes,* ed. L. Moland, Paris, 1877-85, 52 vols [hereafter Mol.], XVIII, p. 251.

[2] ibid., pp. 254-55.

[3] ibid., p. 256.

[4] ibid., p. 258.

[5] *La Religion de Voltaire,* Paris, Nizet, 1974, p. 202.

[6] ibid.

[7] Voltaire, *Romans et contes,* eds F. Deloffre et Jacques Van den Heuvel, Paris, Gallimard, Pléiade, 1979 [hereafter *Romans et contes*], p. 16.

[8] ibid., pp. 687-91.

[9] 'La date de composition du *Songe de Platon* par Voltaire', *Studies on Voltaire,* 219 (1983), pp. 37-57.

[10] *Romans et contes,* p. 547.

[11] ibid., p. 584.

[12] ibid., pp. 635 ff.

[13] ibid., p 237.

[14] ibid., p. 281.

[15] ibid., p. 282.

[16] ibid., p. 283.

[17] Mol. XXII, p. 407.

[18] *Romans et contes,* p. 373.

[19] ibid., p. 651.

[20] *Lettres philosophiques,* XV, ed. G. Lanson, rev. A. M. Rousseau, Paris, Didier, 1964, 2 vols, II, p. 29.

[21] Mol. XXII, p. 243.

[22] Voltaire, Correspondence, ed. T. Besterman, *The Complete Works of Voltaire,* Geneva, Banbury and Oxford, 1968-   , Vols 85-135 [hereafter Best. D and no. of letter], Best. D 17747.

[23] *Commentaires sur Corneille* (1764), ed. D. Williams, *The Complete Works of Voltaire,* Vol. 54, pp. 24-25.

[24] Mol. IX, p. 3: my italics.

[25] Letter to Damilaville, 9 July 1764, Best. D 11978.

[26] For a fuller account, see my 'L'Ironie voltairienne', *Cahiers de l'Association des Etudes Françaises,* 38 (to appear).

[27] 26 June [1766], Best. D 13374.

[28] Cf., e.g., *Romans et contes,* op. cit.; J. Sareil, *Essai sur Candide* (Geneva, Droz, 1967); S. S. B. Taylor, 'Voltaire's humour', *Studies on Voltaire,* 179 (1979), pp. 101-16; C. Mervaud, 'Sur l'activité ludique de Voltaire conteur: le problème de *L'Ingénu', L'Information littéraire,* 35 (1983), pp. 13-17; V. Mylne, 'Literary techniques and methods in Voltaire's *contes philosophiques', Studies on Voltaire,* 57 (1967), pp. 1055-80; J. Starobinski, 'Le Fusil à deux coups de Voltaire', *Revue de métaphysique et de morale,* 71 (1966), pp. 277-91; my *Voltaire* (London, Hutchinson, 1975), Ch. III.

[29] 'Le Jeu de Voltaire écrivain', *Le Jeu au XVIIIe siècle,* Aix-en-Provence, Edisud, 1976, p. 176.

[30] op. cit., p. 100.

[31] *Essais critiques,* Paris, Seuil, 1964, pp. 94-100.

[32] ibid., p. 95: italicised in text.

[33] *Romans et contes,* p. 172: cf. my *Voltaire,* op. cit., pp. 58-60.

[34] For a brief history of irony, cf. D. C. Muecke, *Irony,* London, Methuen, 1970, which includes a useful bibliography of studies on the subject.

[35] art. cit., p. 282.

[36] ibid., pp. 290-91.

[37] cf. *supra,* n. 17.

[38] cf. *supra,* n. 18.

[39] J. Chouillet, *Diderot: poète de l'énergie,* Paris, PUF, 1984.

[40] *Diderot,* Paris, SEDES, 1977, p. 245: italicised in text.

[41] eds J. and A.-M. Chouillet, Paris, Livre de Poche, 1983, p. 13.

[42] *Romans et contes,* p. 236.

[43] Mol. IX, p. 477.

[44] 'De *Candide* à *Jacques le fataliste', Enlightenment studies in honour of Lester G. Crocker,* eds A. J. Bingham and V. W. Topazio, Oxford, Voltaire Foundation, 1979, p. 247.

[45] *Le Rêve de d'Alembert,* eds J. and A.-M. Chouillet, Paris, Livre de Poche, 1984, p. 40.

[46] *Les Oreilles du comte de Chesterfield* (1775), *Romans et contes,* p. 579.

[47] cf. W. C. Booth, *A Rhetoric of Irony,* University of Chicago Press, 1974, pp. 3-6.

[48] L. R. Furst, *Fictions of Romantic Irony,* Cambridge, Mass., Harvard University Press, 1984, p. 227.

[49] cf. *supra,* n. 25.

[50] 'De *Candide* à *Jacques le fataliste',* p. 251.

[51] S. Werner, 'Diderot: les derniers écrits', *Diderot: les dernières années,* eds P. France and A. Strugnell, Edinburgh University Press, 1985, pp. 171-79.

D'où vient le tapis magique?
Fantaisie et érudition dans
Les Mille et une nuits de Galland

Georges May : Yale University

D E toutes les images qui ont leur origine dans *Les Mille et une nuits,* celle du tapis magique est sans doute une des plus séduisantes pour l'imagination, et, de ce fait aussi, une des plus célèbres. Source d'inspiration de tant d'illustrations, de films et de rêves, elle est entrée si profondément dans notre culture que ceux qui sont le plus familiers avec elle sont aussi ceux qui se soucient le moins de savoir d'où elle nous est venue. Dans lequel des contes de Scheherazade le merveilleux tapis apparaît-il? D'où vient-il? Quel rôle joue-t-il? Autant de questions dont l'intérêt pâlit auprès de l'intensité poétique se dégageant des simples mots 'tapis magique' ou 'tapis volant' et de l'image qu'ils font naître.

Si ce phénomène est en lui-même normal et explicable, en revanche, les circonstances dans lesquelles le conte en question est parvenu jusqu'à nous sont, elles, assez extraordinaires, comme on va le rappeler, pour en faire un récit digne du répertoire fabuleux de Scheherazade. Mais il y a plus surprenant encore: et c'est que ces circonstances, connues déjà depuis longtemps des érudits, soient en général aussi profondément ignorées de l'immense public des *Nuits.* Tout se passe comme si le fameux tapis était le fait d'une création anonyme, présente depuis toujours dans notre culture, échappant donc aux contingences historiques et sur l'origine de laquelle il n'y aurait pas davantage lieu de se poser de question que sur celle, par exemple, de la Toison d'or, de la Table ronde, des Bottes de sept lieues ou du chat de la mère Michel. Tel n'est pourtant pas le cas, comme on va pouvoir en juger.

Le tapis en question apparaît dans un des épisodes de la première partie de l''Histoire du prince Ahmed et de la fée Pari-Banou'. Cette histoire fut publiée pour la première fois en 1717, dans le douzième et dernier volume du recueil composé par Antoine Galland et qui constitue

l'édition princeps des *Mille et une nuits.* Le mot princeps doit être entendu
ici dans toute la force du terme. Cette édition, dont les premiers volumes
datent de 1704, devance, en effet, de très loin toutes celles qui devaient
diffuser par la suite les contes de Scheherazade dans les diverses langues du
monde; à telle enseigne que ce ne sera qu'un siècle plus tard que ceux-ci
paraîtront enfin dans leur langue d'origine, l'arabe. Il y a donc à peine
trois cents ans que l' 'Histoire du prince Ahmed', comme toutes les autres
qui sortirent de la plume de Galland, fit son entrée dans la littérature.
1717: l'année du premier séjour de Voltaire à la Bastille, de la visite en
France du tsar Pierre Ier, de la première Entente cordiale avec l'Angleterre,
de l'achat du diamant baptisé alors 'le Régent' ... et de la révélation du
plus prodigieux moyen de transport jamais connu: 'en s'asseyant sur ce
tapis, aussitôt on est transporté avec le tapis où l'on souhaite d'aller, et
l'on s'y trouve presque dans le moment sans que l'on soit arrêté par aucun
obstacle'. [1]

A la différence, toutefois, de la plupart des autres contes figurant dans
le recueil de Galland, celui où apparaît le tapis n'était pas venu à sa
connaissance par le truchement d'un manuscrit arabe, point d'aboutisse-
ment lui-même d'une longue tradition orale. Aussi surprenant que cela
puisse paraître, le conte en question semble, en effet, n'avoir jamais eu
d'existence écrite dans aucune langue avant l'intervention de l'écrivain
français. [2] En tout cas, c'est uniquement sous sa forme orale que Galland
en prit connaissance. Il note lui-même le fait dans son *Journal,* à la date
du 22 mai 1709. C'est alors qu'un maronite d'Alep nommé Hanna,
rencontré à Paris par l'intermédiaire d'un ami commun, lui raconte cette
histoire, dont il note sur-le-champ les données principales en une sorte de
sommaire occupant près de huit pages de ce *Journal.* Trois ans plus tard,
exactement le 1er juin 1712, toujours selon le témoignage du *Journal,*
Galland se met à rédiger, à partir de ce sommaire, la version du conte
destinée à prendre place dans le douzième volume des *Mille et une nuits.*

Outre que cette version a donc bien pour source unique le récit oral du
conteur alepin, elle se distingue encore de quelques-unes des autres
histoires que celui-ci raconta alors à Galland – par exemple, celle du
'Cheval enchanté' – en ce qu'aucune autre version en aucune langue de
l' 'Histoire du prince Ahmed' n'a été retrouvée depuis. La connaissance
que nous avons aujourd'hui de ce récit, comme de l'épisode du tapis
magique qui en fait partie, repose donc entièrement et exclusivement sur
le texte de Galland. A cette observation, déjà assez frappante en soi pour
qu'on s'y arrête, s'ajoute le fait que, grâce au *Journal* de l'écrivain, nous
connaissons un premier état, pour ainsi dire embryonnaire, de ce texte, et

que nous disposons donc d'une documentation exceptionnelle pour en suivre la gestation.

Il suffit, par exemple, de comparer le résumé de 1709 avec le texte définitif de 1717 pour observer que la rédaction du premier fut aussi hâtive que celle du dernier fut soignée. Galland note, en effet, que ce fut 'l'après-dînée', ou, comme nous dirions aujourd'hui, l'après-midi du 22 mai, que Hanna vint le voir pour lui raconter cette histoire, et que ce fut le jour même qu'il en écrivit le sommaire. Cette remarque suffit à expliquer que, pressé par le temps et soucieux de consigner par écrit les principaux linéaments d'un récit long et complexe, fait de deux parties distinctes et comportant de multiples personnages, alors que le souvenir en était encore frais dans sa mémoire, Galland ait éprouvé la nécessité de laisser courir sa plume. Son écriture est de ce fait sensiblement moins lisible que d'ordinaire et il dut de plus recourir à diverses abréviations – en particulier à *etc.,* dont il use ici à seize reprises – et laisser passer un certain nombre de lapsus tout à fait inhabituels de la part d'un homme mettant en général un soin scrupuleux à tout ce qu'il faisait. En revanche, la rédaction du texte définitif fut conforme, elle, à la méticulosité caractéristique du vieux savant qui en nota, presque au jour le jour, les étapes successives dans son *Journal.* Commencé donc le 1er juin 1712, le premier jet, ou 'brouillon' comme il l'appelle parfois, est terminé le 30 août. Fin novembre, l'écrivain procède à 'la révision et correction' de cette rédaction initiale. Enfin 'la copie au net' de la version définitive n'a lieu qu'au mois de mai suivant. Toute une année s'est donc écoulée. Bien entendu, celle-ci n'a pas été occupée uniquement par la gestation de cette seule histoire. Travailleur infatigable, ayant toujours plusieurs ouvrages différents en chantier au même moment et donnant l'impression de ne se délasser de l'un qu'en se plongeant dans un autre, Galland, quoique âgé alors de plus de soixante-six ans, s'adonnait au cours de cette même année à bien d'autres tâches plus directement en rapport avec ses fonctions de membre de l'Académie des inscriptions et de lecteur d'arabe au Collège royal. Nous en verrons un exemple un peu plus loin. Reste que le passage du temps eut sans doute alors pour effet normal d'estomper, d'une part, le souvenir précis des paroles du conteur d'Alep, et de laisser donc le champ libre, de l'autre, au génie créateur de l'écrivain, tel qu'il se manifeste dans l'amplification qui lui permit d'étoffer le canevas de 1709 et d'aboutir à un texte définitif plus de douze fois plus volumineux.

Certains des changements résultant de ces deux phénomènes sont immédiatement apparents et permettent de mesurer jusqu'à un certain point l'importance des apports personnels de l'écrivain français. Ceux-ci, soit dit en passant, permettent d'opposer un démenti formel à l'idée reçue réduisant le rôle de Galland à celui de simple traducteur, voire de traducteur infidèle.[3] Et puisque c'est avant tout du tapis magique qu'il s'agit ici, les remarques qui suivent porteront d'abord sur ceux de ces changements affectant la connaissance que nous avons de cet objet. Afin d'en faciliter l'appréciation, il convient de rappeler ici les données du conte nécessaires à leur compréhension. Le résumé qui suit est presque entièrement emprunté à celui qui figure dans le *Journal* de Galland:

> Un sultan des Indes avait trois fils, Hussein, Ali et Ahmed et une nièce nommée Lumière du jour, qu'il avait retirée dans son palais, après la mort du prince son frère. Le sultan ne cherchait que l'occasion de la marier quand il apprit que les trois princes en étaient amoureux également. Dans l'embarras où il se trouva afin de ne pas marquer plus de partialité pour l'un que pour l'autre, il leur proposa de les envoyer voyager par le monde, avec promesse de donner leur cousine en mari à celui des trois qui aurait rapporté la rareté la plus précieuse et la plus particulière, et en même temps de leur donner à chacun la même somme d'argent, pour les frais du voyage et pour l'achat qu'ils auraient à faire. Les princes acceptèrent la proposition. [. . .]
>
> Le prince Hussein après avoir passé par plusieurs villes, et par plusieurs provinces, il arriva à une des principales villes des Indes des Indes [*sic*] où il prit logement dans le khan le plus magnifique et le plus beau. Le lendemain il alla où les marchands les plus riches avaient leurs boutiques en un même lieu, et le lieu était spacieux, et bâti solidement, avec plusieurs portes de fer, etc. Comme il se fut assis sur la boutique d'un marchand qui lui en fit la civilité, il vit venir un crieur qui criait un tapis d'environ six pieds en carré dont le prix était à trente bourses. Le prince trouva la somme exorbitante pour un tapis de si peu d'étendue. Il appela le crieur, et lui demanda ce que le tapis avait de si particulier. Le crieur lui dit qu'il n'y avait qu'à s'asseoir dessus, et qu'aussitôt l'on était porté au lieu qu'on souhaitait. Il ajouta que le tapis n'était pas encore où il devait monter parce qu'il avait ordre de ne le livrer à moins de quarante bourses. Le prince n'attendit pas la hausse il compta les 40 b. à condition néanmoins d'en faire l'expérience en allant chez lui où était ses valises en s'assoyant sur le tapis avec le crieur, etc. Le prince qui eut si tôt employé son argent et qui vit bien qu'il ne pouvait faire un meilleur avec espoir ou plutôt avec certitude que ses frères, etc., se mit sur le tapis souhaita d'arriver au lieu où il devait attendre; et il s'y trouva à l'instant, il plia le tapis présentement, il prit logement, et il attendit, etc. Il avait laissé son écuyer avec ordre de revenir à petites journées et d'amener son cheval.

Le frère puîné, Ali se dirige, quant à lui, vers 'une autre grande ville des Indes du côté de l'Océan', où il achète pour la même somme 'un tuyau d'ébène' ayant pour propriété magique 'qu'en regardant par un des bouts, l'on voyait ce que l'on souhaitait de voir, et que l'on y voyait cc qu'il y avait, à quelque distance que ce fût'.

Pour ce qui est du frère cadet, Ahmed, c'est à Samarkand qu'il se procure, toujours pour quarante bourses, 'une pomme artificielle', qui, 'en la faisant sentir même à un moribond, lui rendait la santé parfaitement sur-le-champ'.[4]

Le texte définitif du conte reste en général fidèle à toutes ces données. Les noms des trois frères n'ont pas changé, sinon que celui de l'aîné est orthographié Houssain; le nom de leur cousine non plus, à ceci près que Galland lui restitue sa forme originelle de Nourounnihar qui, selon la note qu'il ajoute au bas de la page, veut dire en arabe *lumière du jour*. Enfin il s'agit toujours des trois mêmes objets merveilleux: le tuyau, le tapis et la pomme. On observe, en revanche, que, si c'est encore bien à Samarkand que le prince Ahmed se procure la pomme miraculeuse, la destination de ses deux frères a changé: c'est à Chiraz, en Perse, et non plus dans une ville anonyme des Indes, 'du côté de l'Océan', que le prince Ali achète le tuyau merveilleux, lequel, soit dit en passant, n'est plus en ébène, mais en ivoire. Enfin et surtout, la 'ville principale des Indes' où le frère aîné découvre le tapis magique porte dans la rédaction définitive le nom de Bisnagar.

Si personne n'ignore où se trouvent Samarkand et Chiraz, en revanche, on chercherait aujourd'hui en vain Bisnagar sur une carte des Indes. Et pourtant ce nom n'a pas plus été forgé par Galland que les autres. Il y a à ce petit mystère plusieurs raisons. La première tient à la graphie: une translitération plus exacte du nom sanscrit original serait, en effet, non pas Bisnagar, mais Vijayanagar (Ville de la Victoire). La seconde est que ce nom désignait d'abord la dynastie des souverains hindous régnant autrefois sur cette région, puis, par extension, le royaume lui-même. Cette dérivation n'était pas, du reste, tout à fait ignorée de Galland, quoiqu'il la présente en sens inverse dans le texte du conte: 'Bisnagar, ville qui donne le nom à tout le royaume dont elle est la capitale, et qui est la demeure ordinaire de ses rois' (III, p. 329). Quant à la troisième raison, elle est que la ville en question, fondée au XIVe siècle sur la rive droite du Tungabhadra, par 15°18′ de latitude nord et 76°30′ de longitude est, et dont le nom est aujourd'hui Hampi (ou Humpi), fut envahie et détruite au XVIe siècle par les conquérants musulmans ct qu'il n'en subsiste plus que des ruines.[5]

Puisque c'est donc bien Galland qui prit l'initiative de désigner Bisnagar comme le lieu d'origine du tapis magique, reste à s'interroger sur la raison de ce choix. Grâce aux travaux de Mohamed Abdel-Halim, celle-ci nous est en grande partie connue. Elle résulte de la simple coïncidence que voici. Peu après avoir mis au net la rédaction finale de l''Histoire du prince Ahmed', Galland, qui, comme on l'a rappelé, avait toujours plusieurs travaux différents en train au même moment, se mit à réviser sa propre traduction d'un ouvrage persan riche en renseignements sur le royaume de Bisnagar au XVᵉ siècle. L'auteur en est 'Abd al-Razzâq, envoyé en mission aux Indes en 1442-1444 par le souverain de Transoxiane Shah Rokh, fils de Tamerlan. Une partie importante de la relation qu'il fit de son voyage est consacrée à son séjour à la cour du roi de Bisnagar et contient de nombreux détails, souvent fort pittoresques, sur les coutumes et les principales curiosités de ce royaume.[6] Les exemples cités par M. Abdel-Halim des emprunts parfois littéraux que fit Galland à ce récit de voyage dans les pages de l''Histoire du prince Ahmed' ayant trait à l'achat du tapis magique ne laissent aucun doute sur leur origine. Même si, çà et là, les renseignements présents dans le conte ne cadrent pas exactement avec ceux donnés par le voyageur persan – celui-ci dit, par exemple, que la ville est entourée de sept enceintes, alors qu'elle n'en a plus que trois dans le texte de Galland – il n'y a pas lieu de douter que ce soit bien à cette source qu'il faille faire remonter le choix que fit Galland de Bisnagar pour y situer l'épisode de l'achat du tapis magique.

Selon le témoignage de son *Journal,* ce fut entre juin et août 1713 qu'il révisa sa traduction du texte de 'Abd al-Razzâq. Or il avait noté, à la date du 8 juin de la même année, avoir achevé alors la mise au net du douzième volume des *Mille et une nuits,* lequel contient l''Histoire du prince Ahmed'. On est donc en droit de supposer que la désignation de Bisnagar fut choisie après coup par Galland, et que les pages dans lesquelles il évoque les curiosités et les mœurs de ce pays furent alors interpolées dans un manuscrit par ailleurs achevé.

Il s'agit, en effet, d'un développement assez important, comprenant, d'une part, une description de la ville, du palais royal et des quartiers commerciaux, y compris celui où le tapis est mis en vente (III, pp. 329-31), et, de l'autre, celle du temple, des environs de la ville, des cérémonies et de la grande fête annuelle qui a pour vedettes les éléphants savants du roi (ibid., pp. 333-35). Malgré son intérêt et ses qualités littéraires, cette partie pour ainsi dire touristique de l''Histoire du prince Ahmed' brise le rythme narratif de manière tout à fait inaccoutumée pour Galland et fait incontestablement figure de hors-d'œuvre. Sans être strictement unique dans *Les Mille et une nuits* – on en évoquera plus loin une autre, insérée dans l''Histoire d'Ali Cogia, marchand de Bagdad' – la digression de Bisnagar, qui occupe environ quatre grandes pages de l'édition Garnier-Flammarion, est de loin la plus longue de toutes et doit donc être jugée de ce point de vue exceptionnelle.

Elle est même si démesurée que Galland éprouva le besoin de lui trouver l'excuse que voici. Lorsqu'au début du conte les trois frères se séparent pour aller à la recherche de l'objet rare destiné à leur assurer la main de Nourounnihar, ils s'accordent un délai d'une année avant de se retrouver au même endroit pour rentrer ensemble à la cour du roi, leur père. Or il fallut 'une marche d'environ trois mois' (III, p. 329) au prince Houssain pour parvenir jusqu'au royaume de Bisnagar. Et comme l'achat du tapis magique, qu'il y fit dès son arrivée, lui assurait la possibilité d'un retour instantané, rien ne l'empêchait dès lors de se livrer tout à loisir aux délices du tourisme culturel: 'Sans faire un plus long séjour à Bisnagar, il pouvait, en s'asseyant sur le tapis, se rendre le même jour au rendez-vous dont il était convenu avec eux [ses frères]; mais il eût été obligé de les attendre trop longtemps: cela fit que, curieux de voir le roi de Bisnagar et sa cour, et de prendre connaissance des forces, des lois, des coutumes, de la religion et de l'état de tout le royaume, il résolut d'employer quelques mois à satisfaire sa curiosité' (ibid., p. 332). On est tenté d'ajouter qu'en même temps que Houssain satisfait sa propre curiosité, en même temps il fournit à Galland l'occasion de satisfaire celle qu'il présume (peut-être à tort!) chez son lecteur pour les observations piquantes et pittoresques présentes dans l'ouvrage du voyageur persan. Du coup, il change les données figurant dans le résumé cité plus haut du récit raconté par Hanna, dans lequel le prince se sert du tapis magique dès l'achat qu'il en a fait, afin de rallier sans délai le lieu du rendez-vous et d'y attendre ses deux frères, alors que son écuyer s'y rend avec son cheval 'à petites journées'. Ayant cédé à son goût de savant en rédigeant la digression consacrée aux curiosités de Bisnagar, Galland était donc, par ailleurs, trop bon écrivain pour n'être pas sensible au danger de déséquilibre que présentait cette interpolation et pour ne pas se prémunir contre les reproches que celle-ci risquait de lui attirer. C'est ce qui ne manqua pas, du reste, d'arriver; car tout indique que ce sont à ces pages, ajoutées par Galland aux données qu'il tenait du récit de Hanna, que songe une des meilleures spécialistes de l'art littéraire des *Mille et une nuits,* Mia I. Gerhardt, quand elle qualifie d''un peu verbeuse'[7] la version que donna Galland de ce conte.

En revanche, une autre critique formulée par la même érudite paraît à la réflexion moins méritée. Elle fait remarquer, en effet, que l''Histoire du prince Ahmed' manque d'unité: la première partie, racontant l'histoire des trois fils du sultan et de la princesse dont ils sont amoureux, est, en effet, un peu lâchement raccordée à la seconde, qui a pour sujet les amours du prince Ahmed et de la fée Pari-Banou et qui est environ deux fois plus longue que la première.[8] Cette observation est parfaitement juste; mais, si l'on examine le résumé fait par Galland de l'histoire, telle que la lui raconta Hanna, on remarque que la responsabilité de ce défaut incombe tout entière au conteur, et non pas à l'écrivain, qui essaya au contraire de le corriger. Voici, en effet, le texte du résumé, qui suit le moment où le sultan renonce à choisir parmi les trois objets rapportés de leur voyage par ses fils lequel est le plus merveilleux:

> Le sultan dans son incertitude a recours à un autre moyen de décision, de prendre chacun un arc, et de voir qui tirerait le plus loin. Le prince Ali tire plus loin que le prince Hussein, et la flèche du prince Ahmed ne se trouve pas. Le prince Ali épouse sa cousine.
> Le prince Ahmed cherche sa flèche, et il la trouve à trois ou quatre lieues, près de certains rochers stériles. Comme il ne pou pas croire que naturellement sa flèche eût pu venir si loin, il s'imagina qu'il y avait du mystère, et que ce mystère regardait son bonheur. Il cherche alentour dans les broussailles, et au travers des buissons une porte de fer en forme de trappe, il ouvre, et après tomba de quelques degrés, il aperçut un palais d'une grande magnificence.[9]

La rupture du fil narratif marquée ici par le passage d'un paragraphe au suivant n'est pas un phénomène unique dans *Les Mille et une nuits*. D'autres histoires présentent des solutions de continuité analogues et donnent parfois l'impression d'être faites de pièces et de morceaux plus ou moins habilement raccordés ensemble. C'est ainsi, par exemple, que celle du 'Dormeur éveillé' comporte, elle aussi, deux parties distinctes remontant sans doute originellement, comme dans le cas du 'Prince Ahmed', à deux contes différents: d'une part, le récit de la mystification perpétrée par le calife Haroun-al-Raschid sur Abou Hassan (II, pp. 425-76); et, de l'autre, celui des facéties d'Abou Hassan et de sa nouvelle épouse Nouzha-toul-Aouadat à la cour du calife et de Zobéide (ibid., pp. 477-503).

Loin d'être aveugle au défaut d'unité présent dans l' 'Histoire du prince Ahmed', telle qu'il en avait entendu le récit de la bouche de Hanna, Galland fit en réalité de son mieux, comme on va le voir maintenant, pour y remédier et pour donner à l'ensemble du conte une forme visant à faire oublier la nature sans doute composite de son origine. Lorsque, au début de la deuxième partie de l'histoire, telle que la raconte Galland, le héros arrive au palais caché de la fée, la moindre de ses surprises n'est pas d'entendre celle-ci le saluer par son nom: 'Prince Ahmed, dit-elle, approchez, vous êtes le bienvenu' (III, p. 348). Et voici l'explication qu'elle lui donne alors de ce petit mystère:

'[...] vous êtes surpris, dites-vous, de ce que je vous connais sans que vous me connaissiez; votre surprise cessera quand vous saurez qui je suis. Vous n'ignorez pas, sans doute, une chose que votre religion vous enseigne, qui est que le monde est habité par des génies aussi bien que par des hommes. Je suis fille d'un de ces génies, des plus puissants et des plus distingués parmi eux, et mon nom est Pari-Banou. Ainsi vous devez cesser d'être surpris que je vous connaisse, vous, le sultan votre père, les princes vos frères et la princesse Nourounnihar. Je suis informée de même de votre amour et de votre voyage, dont je pourrais vous dire toutes les circonstances, puisque c'est moi qui ai fait mettre en vente à Samarcande la pomme artificielle que vous y avez achetée; à Bisnagar, le tapis que le prince Houssain y a trouvé, et à Schiraz le tuyau d'ivoire que le prince Ali en a rapporté. Cela doit suffire pour vous faire comprendre que je n'ignore rien de ce qui vous touche'. (ibid., p. 349)

Un simple coup d'œil au passage correspondant du sommaire de 1709 suffit à montrer que tout ce discours résulte de l'invention de Galland et ajoute au conte un élément capital qui manquait dans le récit du conteur d'Alep. Que lisons-nous, en effet, dans le résumé du *Journal,* à la suite du passage cité à la page précédente? '... il aperçut un palais d'une grande magnificence. Aussitôt il vit une superbement et magnifiquement habillée qui s'avança au-devant de lui. La pervise lui demande qui il est. Le prince lui fait la même demande et elle répond que son nom est Pari Banou etc.; et elle lui fait la proposition de mariage. Ils se marièrent'.[9]

Les modifications apportées ici par Galland à ses sources sont d'une subtilité et d'une habileté telles qu'elles méritent qu'on s'y arrête un moment. Dans le récit raconté par Hanna, Pari-Banou ignore l'identité de son visiteur, dont l'arrivée est purement adventice, résultat d'un événement lui-même inexplicable et fortuit: la portée d'une flèche qui, sans qu'on sache pourquoi, franchit une distance invraisemblable pour parvenir jusqu'à la retraite cachée de la fée. En substituant à ce mécanisme d'un hasard gratuit l'accomplissement soigneusement calculé de la volonté toute-puissante de cette fée, Galland réussit du même coup à relier logiquement l'une à l'autre les deux parties du conte de Hanna, et à donner à la rencontre des deux protagonistes de la deuxième partie une cause vraisemblable et de nature à attirer la sympathie du lecteur: l'amour tenu longtemps secret de Pari-Banou pour Ahmed. Voici, en effet, la fin du discours de la fée, dont le début a été déjà cité, suivie du commentaire du narrateur:

'La seule chose que j'ajoute, c'est que vous m'avez paru digne d'un sort plus heureux que celui de posséder la princesse Nourounnihar, et

que, pour vous y faire acheminer, comme je me trouvais présente dans le
temps que vous tirâtes la flèche que je vois que vous tenez, et que je
prévis qu'elle ne passerait pas même au-delà de celle du prince Houssain,
je la pris en l'air, et lui donnai le mouvement nécessaire pour venir
frapper les rochers près desquels vous venez de la trouver. Il ne tiendra
qu'à vous de profiter de l'occasion qu'elle vous présente de devenir plus
heureux.'

    Comme la fée Pari-Banou prononça ces dernières paroles d'un ton
différent, en regardant même le prince Ahmed d'un air tendre, et en
baissant aussitôt les yeux par modestie, avec une rougeur qui lui monta
au visage, le prince n'eut pas de peine à comprendre de quel bonheur elle
entendait parler. (III, pp. 349-50)

Laissons de côté pour le moment l'impression que nous fait ici
Pari-Banou de penser, de parler et de se comporter comme une héroïne de
roman français du siècle de Louis XIV, plutôt que comme une magicienne
venue de l'Orient médiéval; et remarquons que ce coup de pouce décisif
de l'écrivain français a pour effet de faire des deux parties du récit un
ensemble doté d'une forte unité thématique. Le point de départ du conte
était l'amour de trois princes pour leur cousine; la seconde partie, fondée
désormais, elle aussi, sur l'amour, celui d'une fée pour un prince, paraît
plus solidement et plus harmonieusement liée à la première que dans le
sommaire du récit de Hanna, dans lequel les deux aventures n'ont pour
tout lien que la présence fortuite dans la seconde d'un des personnages de
la première.

    Notons toutefois que, si Galland a bien fait d'éliminer un détail inutile
présent dans son résumé, comme celui des 'portes de fer' du marché où est
mis en vente le tapis magique, il a peut-être eu tort de ne pas en faire
autant du marchandage du crieur 'qui avait ordre de ne le livrer à moins
de quarante bourses', indication qui cadre mal avec le rôle secret qu'il fait
jouer dans cette affaire à Pari-Banou. Reste qu'une petite imperfection
comme celle-ci ne nuit guère aux améliorations substantielles résultant du
génie créateur de Galland.

    Il y a, en effet, plus encore à en dire. Au-delà du thème unificateur de
la passion amoureuse, il est un autre thème, présent dès le récit de Hanna,
dans les deux parties de l'histoire, qui va prendre, grâce aux innovations
de Galland, un relief bien plus marqué, et qui va surtout se combiner
d'une manière riche de sens avec celui de l'amour: c'est celui de la magie.
Trois objets magiques dans la première partie: le tapis, le tuyau, la
pomme. Une fée dans la seconde, dont les pouvoirs surnaturels se
manifestent par divers prodiges. Entre les deux, une flèche, qui disparaît
mystérieusement pour reparaître à une distance extravagante du point

d'où elle a été tirée. Comment ne pas saluer l'heureuse inspiration qui donna à Galland l'idée de faire remonter tous ces objets et événements merveilleux à la seule Pari-Banou, donnant ainsi toute son unité à un ensemble jusqu'alors disparate, et faisant d'un personnage de magicienne de pure convention une de ces grandes et admirables héroïnes dont il semble se plaire, ici comme ailleurs, à montrer la supériorité sur les personnages masculins un peu falots qui les entourent? D'un bout à l'autre de l''Histoire du prince Ahmed', c'est elle désormais qui mène le jeu, tirant les fils si discrètement d'abord que son existence n'est pas même soupçonnée, puis révélant, dès son entrée en scène, ce rôle jusqu'alors caché et accomplissant dorénavant en plein jour ses sortilèges bénéfiques. Dans un cas comme dans l'autre ses actions sont déterminées par le même mobile amoureux. Et voilà du même coup ces deux thèmes unificateurs, celui de l'amour et celui de la magie, comme fondus l'un dans l'autre. Mieux encore: voilà les trois objets magiques de la première partie enrichis d'une signification symbolique à laquelle ne sauraient prétendre leurs homologues technologiques modernes, hélicoptère, télévision et antibiotiques. Prodiges inspirés par la passion amoureuse, le tapis, le tuyau et la pomme ne témoignent-ils pas, en effet, de la puissance de l'amour, qui, lorsqu'il est assez fort, triomphe de tous les obstacles, abolit toutes les distances et apporte remède à tous les maux?

Même si elle ne perd donc sous la plume de Galland aucun de ses attributs féériques, Pari-Banou est dès lors profondément humanisée, modernisée, et, si l'on ose dire, occidentalisée par la grâce de son amour. Même lorsqu'il lui arrive d'exposer à Ahmed les différences qui existent entre les fées et les femmes, elle s'exprime beaucoup moins en fille d'un génie 'des plus puissants et des plus distingués' qu'en fière héroïne de roman et en grande amoureuse: 'il n'en est pas de même chez les fées que chez les dames envers les hommes, lesquelles n'ont pas coutume de faire de telles avances, et tiendraient à grand déshonneur d'en user ainsi. Pour nous, nous les faisons, et nous tenons qu'on doit nous en avoir obligation' (ibid., p. 350).

Comme on le voit donc par cet exemple, ce qui fait l'originalité et la qualité des *Mille et une nuits* de Galland tient dans une large mesure aux libertés qu'il a prises et qu'on lui a trop souvent reprochées au nom d'une notion de la traduction qui n'était pas la sienne. Les marques de ces libertés sont bien entendu particulièrement en évidence dans les histoires qui, reposant sur le simple souvenir des récits racontés de vive voix par Hanna, laissaient à l'écrivain la plus grande marge d'autonomie. L'épisode de Bisnagar est sans doute, de ce fait, celui où Galland a ajouté le plus à sa première source; mais, afin de montrer qu'il n'est pas exceptionnel pour autant, jetons un coup d'œil rapide avant de conclure à deux autres exemples qui permettront de confirmer et de préciser l'impression créée par celui-ci.

Dans l''Histoire du cheval enchanté', les innovations de Galland sont à la fois beaucoup plus rares et plus discrètes. Elles se bornent surtout à ancrer l'enchantement dans une géographie réelle. Que l'on compare le récit de Galland au résumé qu'il fit de celui de Hanna ou aux autres versions de cette histoire qui ont été découvertes depuis, on s'aperçoit, par exemple, que c'est l'écrivain français qui prit l'initiative de situer à Chiraz le début de l'aventure, et d'en placer l'épisode principal dans le palais de la princesse de Bengale. Démarche analogue donc à celle situant à Bisnagar l'achat du tapis magique.

Dans un autre conte de même provenance, connu exclusivement aujourd'hui, comme l''Histoire du prince Ahmed', par la version qu'en donna Galland, laquelle ne repose elle-même que sur un récit raconté par Hanna et résumé dans le *Journal* de l'écrivain, il s'agit encore une fois d'un voyage. 'Ali Cogia, marchand de Bagdad' part en pélerinage pour la Mecque, ce qui ne l'empêche pas, une fois ses devoirs religieux accomplis, de se livrer, en bon marchand qu'il est, à des opérations commerciales prolongeant considérablement son voyage. Voici d'abord le texte du sommaire consigné par Galland dans son *Journal* à la date du 30 mai 1709: 'Ali Cogia part avec une caravane. Il fait quelque négoce à la Mecque il trouve occasion de passer en Égypte, d'Égypte à Damas, de Damas en Perse, dans les Indes. [. . .] Ali Cogia revient des Indes par la Perse et de la Perse il arrive à Bagdad'. [10] Ici encore les apports personnels de Galland vont consister à faire appel à ses propres connaissances de l'Orient pour amplifier les données géographiques de sa source. Dans le cas de la digression de Bisnagar, le résultat était de faire de quelques pages des *Mille et une nuits* une sorte de pastiche des relations de voyage de l'époque, bien connues de Galland, comme celles, par exemple, de Chardin ou de Thévenot. Ici, comme on va pouvoir en juger, le résultat donne plutôt comme un avant-goût de Baedeker ou de Joanne:

> Le jour du départ de la caravane de Bagdad arrivé, Ali Cogia, avec un chameau chargé des marchandises dont il avait fait choix et qui lui servit de monture dans le chemin, s'y joignit, et il arriva heureusement à la Mecque. Il y visita, avec tous les autres pèlerins, le temple si célèbre et si fréquenté chaque année par toutes les nations musulmanes qui y abordent de tous les endroits de la terre où elles sont répandues, en observant très religieusement les cérémonies qui leur sont prescrites. Quand il se fut

acquitté des devoirs de son pèlerinage, il exposa les marchandises qu'il avait apportées, pour les vendre ou pour les échanger.

Deux marchands qui passaient et qui virent les marchandises d'Ali Cogia les trouvèrent si belles qu'ils s'arrêtèrent pour les considérer, quoiqu'ils n'en eussent pas besoin. Quand ils eurent satisfait leur curiosité, l'un dit à l'autre en se retirant: 'Si ce marchand savait le gain qu'il ferait au Caire sur ses marchandises, il les y porterait plutôt que de les vendre ici, où elles sont à bon marché.'

Ali Cogia entendit ces paroles; et, comme il avait entendu parler mille fois des beautés de l'Égypte, il résolut sur-le-champ de profiter de l'occasion et d'en faire le voyage. Ainsi, après avoir rempaqueté et remballé ses marchandises, au lieu de retourner à Bagdad, il prit le chemin de l'Égypte en se joignant à la caravane du Caire. Quand il fut arrivé au Caire, il n'eut pas lieu de se repentir du parti qu'il avait pris: il y trouva si bien son compte qu'en très peu de jours il eut achevé de vendre toutes ses marchandises avec un avantage beaucoup plus grand qu'il n'avait espéré. Il en acheta d'autres dans le dessein de passer à Damas; et, en attendant la commodité d'une caravane qui devait partir dans six semaines, il ne se contenta pas de voir tout ce qui était digne de sa curiosité dans le Caire, il alla aussi admirer les pyramides; il remonta le Nil jusqu'à une certaine distance, et il vit les villes les plus célèbres situées sur l'un et l'autre bord.

Dans le voyage de Damas, comme le chemin de la caravane était de passer par Jérusalem, notre marchand de Bagdad profita de l'occasion de visiter le temple, regardé par tous les musulmans comme le plus saint, après celui de la Mecque, d'où cette ville prend le titre de noble sainteté.

Ali Cogia trouva la ville de Damas un lieu si délicieux par l'abondance de ses eaux, par ses prairies et par ses jardins enchantés, que tout ce qu'il avait lu de ses agréments dans nos histoires lui parut beaucoup au-dessous de la vérité, et qu'il y fit un long séjour. Comme néanmoins il n'oubliait pas qu'il était de Bagdad, il en partit enfin; il arriva à Alep, où il fit encore quelque séjour; et de là, après avoir passé l'Euphrate, il prit le chemin de Mossoul, dans l'intention d'abréger son retour en descendant le Tigre.

Mais, quand Ali Cogia fut arrivé à Mossoul, des marchands de Perse avec lesquels il était venu d'Alep, et avec qui il avait contracté une grande amitié, avaient pris un si grand ascendant sur son esprit, par leurs honnêtetés et par leurs entretiens agréables, qu'ils n'eurent pas de peine à lui persuader de ne pas abandonner leur compagnie jusqu'à Schiraz, d'où il lui serait aisé de retourner à Bagdad avec un gain considérable. Ils le menèrent par les villes de Sultanie, de Reï, de Coam, de Cachan, d'Ispahan, et de là à Schiraz, d'où il eut encore la complaisance de les accompagner aux Indes et de revenir à Schiraz avec eux. (III, pp. 278-79)

Aucune source livresque du genre du *Matla-assaadeïn* de 'Abd al-Razzâq n'a besoin d'être invoquée ici, ni pour rendre compte des références aux monuments religieux de la Mecque et de Jérusalem, aux pyramides, à la vallée du Nil et aux jardins de Damas, ni pour suivre sur une carte, malgré les variations de graphie des noms de lieux, l'itinéraire du marchand de Bagdad et pour remarquer les crochets que lui fit subir Galland afin de lui permettre de faire un pèlerinage à la mosquée de Jérusalem et un séjour dans la ville même dont Hanna était originaire, deux grands sites bien connus de l'écrivain qui les avait visités lui-même en 1674 avec l'entourage du marquis de Nointel, ambassadeur de Louis XIV auprès de la Sublime Porte. [11]

*   *   *

Presque tout le travail de repérage des ajouts apportés par Galland à ses sources au cours de la douzaine d'années que dura la rédaction des *Mille et une nuits* reste encore à faire. Même s'il semble raisonnable de présumer que ceux-ci sont particulièrement nombreux et importants dans les histoires reposant exclusivement sur les récits oraux du conteur d'Alep, comme celles du 'Prince Ahmed' et d''Ali Cogia', [12] on sait qu'il en existe aussi dans les autres, et l'on soupçonne que les sources pourraient parfois en être retrouvées. Quoique ce genre de recherche ait perdu aujourd'hui un peu du prestige dont il jouissait autrefois, on peut espérer que les caprices de la mode ne suffiront pas pour en détourner les esprits curieux de mieux mesurer l'originalité du chef-d'œuvre de Galland et désireux de mieux savourer leur plaisir de lecteurs des *Mille et une nuits.* L'un des secrets du charme des contes de Galland tient en effet, comme on vient de le voir à propos du tapis magique et de la fée Pari-Banou, au contrepoint savant qu'il a eu l'art de mettre en jeu entre l'imaginaire et le réel, entre le merveilleux et le naturel, entre la fable et l'histoire. Le succès que connurent immédiatement les *Nuits,* et qui ne s'est jamais démenti depuis, résulte en partie du hasard heureux qui voulut que l'homme qui fut le premier à donner une forme littéraire à ces contes et à les publier, fût aussi l'un des plus grands savants de son temps dans le domaine même des cultures qui leur avaient donné naissance, de leur histoire, de leurs langues, de leurs folklores. L'originalité et la qualité de sa version des *Mille et une nuits* tiennent, en effet, autant aux libertés qu'il prit en les composant, qu'à ce que ses connaissances de spécialiste lui ont permis d'ajouter, afin de mieux équilibrer le fantastique par le rationnel, la fantaisie par l'érudition.

S'il existe une formule capable de rendre compte d'une réussite aussi brillante, celle-ci a pour composantes, outre la forme et le style avec lesquels Galland a su présenter les matériaux qui étaient en sa possession, ce qu'on pourrait appeler le ton narratif qu'il adopte, en accord avec le goût du public de son temps pour ce qu'on appelait alors le vraisemblable. Comment faire accepter, en effet, à ce public cultivé, raffiné et dédaigneux un univers encombré de talismans, de sortilèges et d'objets ensorcelés, et peuplé de génies, de magiciennes et d'enchanteurs, sinon en plaçant ceux-ci dans un cadre historique et géographique plausible? C'est là ce qu'on l'a vu faire de Pari-Banou et de la boutique de Bisnagar où elle fait mettre en vente le tapis magique.

Il ne s'agit évidemment pas d'amener le lecteur à croire à l'authenticité de ce qu'il lit, mais à en accepter l'illusion. Les procédés littéraires mis en œuvre afin d'atteindre ce but appartiennent donc bien à ces *Techniques of Illusion* dont Vivienne Mylne faisait à juste titre l'image de marque de la tradition romanesque française qui naît à l'époque même où paraissent *Les Mille et une nuits,* c'est-à-dire à l'aube du XVIIIe siècle. Dans les premières pages du livre qui porte cette formule en sous-titre, elle cite la phrase suivante, extraite de la préface que Georges de Scudéry écrivit pour le roman de sa sœur qui a pour titre *Ibrahim, ou l'Illustre Bassa* (1641): 'Comment serai-je touché des infortunes de la reine de Guindaye, et du roi d'Astrobacie, puisque je sais que leurs royaumes mêmes ne sont point en la carte universelle, ou, pour mieux dire, en l'être des choses.'[13] On ne saurait mieux dire.

Qu'on ne juge pas déplacée cette citation tirée d'un livre qui parut cinq ans avant la naissance de Galland et dont la nature est certes moins austère que celle des lectures habituelles du grand savant qu'il fut. Non pas seulement parce que Madeleine de Scudéry eut l'honneur d'être, avec *Ibrahim,* l'auteur d'une des premières en date des grandes 'turqueries' de son temps; mais parce que le goût et l'esthétique des cercles mondains et précieux du milieu du siècle ne succombèrent pas du jour au lendemain aux brocards de Molière, de Boileau et de La Bruyère. Même un homme comme Galland continua à en être affecté. En veut-on un témoignage? En voici un de sa propre main. Alors qu'il était à Constantinople, auprès de l'ambassadeur de Nointel, en 1672, il rédige dans son *Journal,* à la date du 7 mai, une minutieuse description, qui s'étend sur plusieurs pages, du défilé de la garde et de l'entourage du Grand Seigneur, lors d'une sortie 'hors de sa ville d'Andrinople pour l'entreprise d'une expédition contre la Pologne'. Ce long morceau de bravoure, qui dut coûter de vaillants efforts au jeune Galland (il avait alors tout juste passé son vingt-sixième anniversaire), est préfacé par les remarques que voici: 'Si mademoiselle de Scudéry avait pu se forger dans l'imagination quelque chose de semblable, et qu'après l'y avoir représenté avec le crayon de son élégante plume, elle lui eût donné place dans quelque endroit de ses ouvrages, tous ceux qui y prennent plaisir à cause du vraisemblable qu'elle a toujours tâché d'y observer, n'en feraient plus la même estime après avoir lu ce morceau, qui bien loin de leur paraître vraisemblable à l'ordinaire, leur paraîtrait encore au-dessus des extravagances des paladins et de nos Amadis de Gaule.'[14]

Pour en revenir maintenant aux termes dès lors justifiés de la préface d'*Ibrahim,* observons en manière de conclusion que, grâce aux modifications apportées par Galland à l'histoire que lui avait racontée Hanna, le tapis magique vient bien dorénavant d'un royaume existant 'en la carte universelle' et Pari-Banou, toute fée qu'elle demeure, appartient désormais à 'l'être des choses'.

Notes

[1] *Les Mille et une nuits, contes arabes,* ed. Jean Gaulmier, Garnier-Flammarion, 3 vols, 1965, t. III, p. 331. Nous renverrons désormais à cette édition en indiquant, entre parenthèses dans le texte, la tomaison en chiffres romains et la pagination en chiffres arabes.

[2] En dehors de l'"Histoire du prince Ahmed', laquelle, répétons-le, ne nous est connue que par le texte de Galland, il existe certes des objets analogues au tapis volant dans divers contes appartenant au folklore, tant oriental qu'occidental. Voir, par exemple, à ce sujet la note de Richard Burton à sa traduction en anglais de l'"Histoire du prince Ahmed', in *Supplemental Nights to the Book of the Thousand Nights and a Night,* édition originale, t. III, p. 425; édition de Bénarès, t. IV, p. 425.

[3] Sur la question de l'originalité de la version de Galland, voir les chapitres IV et V de notre ouvrage: *Les Mille et une nuits d'Antoine Galland, ou le Chef-d'œuvre invisible,* Paris, Presses Universitaires de France, 1986.

[4] Cité d'après la transcription qu'en donne Mohamed Abdel-Halim, en appendice à son précieux ouvrage, *Antoine Galland, sa vie et son œuvre,* Paris, Nizet, 1964, pp. 438-40. Ici comme plus loin nous avons modernisé l'orthographe, l'accentuation et l'usage des majuscules; mais nous avons laissé tels quels la ponctuation, les abréviations et les lapsus. Le manuscrit holographe du *Journal* de Galland pour les années 1708-1715 est conservé au Département des manuscrits de la Bibliothèque Nationale, sous la cote: Mss. fr. 15277-15280. Selon le *Journal d'Antoine Galland pendant son séjour à Constantinople (1672-1673),* ed. Charles Schefer, Paris, Leroux, 2 vols, 1881, t. I, p. 46, la valeur de la *bourse* était de 500 écus de son époque.

[5] Sur Vijayanagar, on pourra consulter *The Cyclopaedia of India,* Londres, 3 vols, 1885, t. III, pp. 1014-15, ainsi que la note de Richard Burton (op. cit., p. 422), laquelle renvoie à diverses autres sources. Burton semble être le premier à avoir identifié Bisnagar et à l'avoir replacé dans son contexte géographique authentique. On remarque, en effet, par exemple, que, dans son 'Analyse géographique des voyages de Sind-Bad le marin' (*Nouvelles annales des voyages et des sciences géographiques,* t. LIII (1832), p. 15), le baron C. A. Walckenaer identifie le pays du roi Mirhage (destination accidentelle du premier voyage de Sindbad) comme étant 'Bijenagar (Bejinagur)', mais sans faire le rapprochement qui s'imposait avec le nom de la ville de Bisnagar, où le prince Houssain achète le tapis magique. Il est vrai que

Walckenaer fondait son étude sur une édition des *Voyages de Sindbad* autre que celle de Galland.

[6] Sur l'histoire des traductions que firent de ce texte Galland et quelques-uns de ses successeurs, voir M. Abdel Halim, op. cit., pp. 234-38. Les passages de cette relation de voyage concernant Bisnagar, dans la traduction française d'Étienne Marc Quatremère, se trouvent dans sa 'Notice de l'ouvrage persan qui a pour titre *Matla-assaadeïn ou-madjma-albahreïn',* in *Notices et extraits des manuscrits de la bibliothèque du Roi et autres bibliothèques,* XIV (1843), pp. 445-66.

[7] Mia I. Gerhardt, *The Art of Story-Telling: a Literary Study of The Thousand and One Nights,* Leyde, Brill, 1963, p. 300.

[8] ibid.

[9] Cité dans M. Abdel Halim, op. cit., p. 440. Le sens du mot *pervise* (si c'est bien la bonne leçon) n'est pas clair. On trouve l'adjectif *pervis* avec le sens de 'prudent' dans le *Dictionnaire de l'ancienne langue française* de Godefroy, et avec le sens de 'avisé' dans le *Provenzalisches Supplement-Wörterbuch* d'Emil Levy. Or Galland remarque dans son *Journal* (17 mars 1709) que Hanna parlait non seulement l'arabe, mais le turc, le provençal et le français.

[10] Cité dans M. Abdel Halim, op. cit., pp. 461-62.

[11] Voir ibid., pp. 43-50 pour l'itinéraire détaillé de ce voyage.

[12] Voir ibid., pp. 276-87 pour d'excellentes remarques sur quelques-uns des changements apportés par Galland aux sommaires de contes de Hanna.

[13] Vivienne Mylne, *The Eighteenth-Century French Novel: Techniques of Illusion,* Manchester University Press, 1965, p. 7. On trouvera de plus longs extraits de cette célèbre préface dans l'anthologie de Henri Coulet: *Le Roman jusqu'à la Révolution,* Paris, Armand Colin, t. II, 1968, pp. 44-49.

[14] Édition citée (voir note 4), t. I, pp. 122-23.

Nathalie Sarraute's *Enfance:* from experience of language to the language of experience

Valerie Minogue : University College, Swansea

> 'Voilà, je me libère [. . .] j'enfonce . . .'
>
> (*Enfance*, p. 14)

I N a recent comparative study of the 'Childhood' as a subspecies within the genre of autobiography, Richard Coe claims that 'the unique feature – the dominating myth – which characterizes the French, as opposed to any other Childhood is the obsession with language . . . It is as though, for the French child, the relationship between the self and the outside world were rarely direct, but had to pass through the intermediate stage of language, consciously learned and used, before it became a reality'.[1] *Enfance,*[2] in its almost obsessive concern with language, would seem to support such a view.[3] Language in these pages is largely experienced as treacherous, and it creates not only a barrier between the self and the outside world but an obstructive opacity between the self and the immediacy of experience. Verbal packages thus have to be unwrapped, the shell of certain phrases has to be cracked, words, along with their accompanying tone and gesture, have to be squeezed to press out their charge of meaning.

The difficulty is not one that concerns the child alone: the mature narrator of the childhood shows a similar distrust of words from the first paragraph of the book. Sarraute uses, throughout this text, a dialogic form in which one narrative voice constantly sifts and questions what the other presents – a device which undercuts any simple narratorial authority and maintains the writer's characteristic hesitancy. The text opens by expressing suspicion of the notion of 'childhood-recollections', thus casting doubt on the authenticity of the enterprise, and stimulating the reader to a heightened awareness of its inherent dangers. One narrative voice addresses the other: 'Alors, tu vas vraiment faire ça? "Evoquer tes souvenirs d'enfance" . . . Comme ces mots te gênent . . .' (p. 9). The words create embarrassment precisely because they suggest a possible capitulation to narrative, a sacrifice of the reality of experience to *words*. In the pages that

follow, words, whether 'mots' or 'paroles', are a constant source of
concern. Even in the first few pages, for instance, we meet: 'les voici de
nouveau, ces *paroles'* (p. 12), 'dans ces *mots* un flot épais' (p. 14), 'les
paroles m'entourent, m'enserrent, me ligotent' (p. 14), 'Tu connaissais
déjà ces *mots'* (p. 15), 'ces *mots* vaguement terrifiants' (p. 16), 'les *mots*
prononcés par un docteur de Paris' (p. 16), 'C'était ressenti, comme
toujours, hors des *mots,* globalement . . . Mais ces *mots* et ces images sont
ce qui permet de saisir tant bien que mal, de retenir ces sensations' (p. 18),
'des *paroles* devenues sacrées' (p. 19) (my italics throughout): and throughout the whole text, child and narrator alike strive at different levels to
pierce the deceptive 'carapaces' of available language.

While concern with language is natural enough in the childhood
experience of a writer, *Enfance,* I would argue, is no mere recapturing of
fragments of childhood but is also an indirect account of the 'enfantement'
of Sarraute's own language, her passage through 'langue' to 'parole'.
Enfance unfolds the drama of an encounter *with* language *in* a language
that reflects the intensity of that experience and the long meditation it has
provoked. I stress 'enfantement' because the metaphor of gestation and
birth is one that aptly suggests the inwardness of the child's relations with
language and the creative processes by which she moves towards affirmation of her own identity and language.[4] The story of the child's collision
with a pre-existent language prefigures in many respects the efforts of the
mature narrator (and the writer herself) to reject established linguistic
modes and to forge an individual language that will allow communication
of barely accessible 'pre-linguistic' experience.

This is a text which begins with transgression, to reveal the *inside,* and
ends with a reiteration of its attachment to 'quelques mouvements qui me
semblent encore intacts' which had to be released from 'cette couche
protectrice qui les conserve' (p. 257). Reaching out to this inwardness,
Nathalie Sarraute is in the paradoxical situation of one trying to reach
beyond language, by means of language.

Consciously and deliberately, *Enfance* offers only fragments of childhood experience. Moments that were too clear, too embedded in the world
of fact and dates, are rejected.[5] The writer's attention is directed to what
lies hidden, to moments of experience that can only with difficulty be
resuscitated and relived. In avoiding dates and a precise temporal framework, Nathalie Sarraute leaves herself free to assemble her fragments to
suit her purposes. There are one or two references to the year and
occasional mentions of her age – 'Huit ans et demi exactement, c'était en
février 1909. Et le 18 juillet, j'ai eu onze ans' (p. 232) – and brief allusions

indicate that we are in Paris, Meudon, Czarist Russia or elsewhere, but social and political events make little or no impression on the child's daily life. Political events and the Okrhana (the Russian Secret Police) are briefly mentioned (for instance in the reminiscences of the Russian émigrés of her father's acquaintance in Paris), but history and politics remain largely marginal, for the purpose of this novel of childhood is the capturing of inward lived experience.

The emphasis on interiority is evident from the beginning of the text. It introduces a pattern of prohibition, defiance, and rupture of smooth surfaces, and creates a *motif* for all that follows. It is a double opening. The first phase is a dialogue between the two narrative voices. One sets out to 'évoquer des souvenirs d'enfance'. The other bars the way in critical disapproval. This endeavour, says the critical voice, is likely to lead to facility, and to take the writer out of her element into a realm where everything is pre-prepared, '"tout cuit" donné d'avance...' The other voice maintains this is not so: 'c'est encore tout vacillant, aucun mot écrit, aucune parole ne l'ont encore touché, il me semble que ça palpite faiblement... hors des mots...' (p. 11). The 'tout cuit' which is to be rejected is that which has been formulated and packaged in available language, while the fact of being 'untouched by language' is an indicator of authenticity and life. The text takes shape under the aegis of this refusal of the 'tout cuit' and the effort towards seizing a pre-linguistic substance, felt but not formulated. Indeed the text will end when faced by the clearer contours of adolescent experience, for this later period has not remained impervious to the touch of language and the incursions of narrative, unlike the earlier moments still intact under their 'couche protectrice'.

The second phase of the opening comes when, exasperated by the 'objurgations' and 'mises en garde' of the other voice, the narrative takes a defiant plunge into recollection. The first scene recollected repeats the pattern of prohibition and rebellion initiated by the conflicting narrative voices. A very young Natacha ('Je devais avoir 5 ou 6 ans') takes the scissors of the young German woman who is looking after her in a Swiss hotel and threatens to plunge the blades into the back of a sofa. The young woman forbids. Natacha insists. The young woman forbids again, but Natacha plunges the scissors into the blue silky sofa and 'quelque chose de mou, de grisâtre s'échappe par la fente' (p. 14).

One interesting aspect (there are many) of this scene is that it is not merely a pattern of prohibition and defiance, in terms of a physical act, but very strikingly a linguistic event. It is enacted in German, and the author herself expresses surprise: 'En allemand... Comment avais-tu pu

si bien l'apprendre? – Oui, je me le demande.' Words here are stressed in
all their physical weight:

> 'Nein, das tust du nicht.' 'Non tu ne feras pas ça', les voici de nouveau,
> ces paroles ... [...] ... elles pèsent de toute leur puissance, de tout leur
> énorme poids ... et sous leur pression quelque chose en moi ... [...]
> ... se dégage, se soulève, s'élève ... les paroles qui sortent de ma bouche
> le portent, l'enfoncent là-bas ... 'Doch, Ich werde es tun'. 'Si je le ferai.'
> (p. 12)

The words, their sounds and syllables, dominate the scene: '"Ich werde es
zerreissen" ... "Je vais le déchirer" ... le mot "zerreissen" rend un son
sifflant, féroce ...' (p. 13). The child seems to push the words to the limit
but perhaps, she thinks, the young woman will shrug her shoulders and
turn her eyes back to her sewing ... 'et mes paroles vont voleter'. But the
young woman sternly repeats the prohibition: 'elle me dit en appuyant très
fort sur chaque syllabe: "Nein, das tust du nicht" ... "Non tu ne feras pas
ça" ... [...] ... les paroles m'entourent, m'enserrent, me ligotent, je me
débats ... "Si, je le ferai" ...' The words that follow would make an
appropriate epigraph for the whole work: 'Voilà, je me libère [...] j'enfon-
ce ...' (p. 14). The scissors Natacha plunges into the sofa pierce not only
the silky surface of the sofa but the firm surface of the words of
prohibition, just as the narrative itself defies the warning voice of the
opening.[6] Similarly, the narrator, throughout the text, characteristically
pierces the smooth surface of sentences and phrases to expose that 'matière
anonyme comme la lymphe comme le sang'[7] which is Sarraute's central
concern in all her work.

   No doubt the sensitivity of the child to the sound of words was
intensified by her growing up in a polyglot society, and, as is evident in
this scene with its hissing sybillants, the sound and the physical weight of
words play an important part in the child's encounter with the world of
language. The young German woman uses a tone which the narrator
recognises retrospectively as that of a hypnotist or animal-trainer, and the
child shows a powerful resistance to such linguistic compulsion. She will
show, many years later, a similar resistance and a similar aural sensitivity
to the blanket-phrase ('Parce que ça ne se fait pas') by which Véra
'explains' her prohibitions: 'les consonnes cognées les unes contre les
autres s'abattent, un jet dur et dru qui lapide ce qui en moi remue, veut se
soulever ...' (p. 177).

   To the young child, the language of the surrounding world seems
fraught with dangerous powers. When Natacha, again on a visit to her

father, and in another hotel, obstinately chews and chews and chews before she swallows, she hears mothers warning their children not to follow her example: 'c'est un enfant insupportable, c'est un enfant fou, un enfant maniaque . . .' (p. 15). The 'other' narrative voice asks whether she really already knew such words – and gets the answer: 'Ah ça oui . . . je les avais assez entendus . . . [. . .] . . . ces mots vaguement terrifiants, dégradants . . .' (pp. 15-16). The child's dedicated chewing is itself another instance of the power of words, for it is the result of the recommendation of a certain Dr Kervilly that she must chew her food till it is 'aussi liquide qu'une soupe'. This edict had been reinforced by Maman's insistence that it be fully observed while Natacha was away, visiting her father. The almost hypnotic power which the phrase acquires as the 'flag' of Maman planted in the enemy camp is only an early example of many utterances which make landmarks in the world of the child.

Words, however, are not invariably hostile elements: learning the days of the week with her father is a great joy and she delights in her father's endearments – his abbreviation of her name to Tachok, and Tachotchek, and his use of the nickname, 'Pigalitza'. She notices when he ceases to call her 'Tachok' (p. 145), and she observes his avoidance of her mother's name, when he substitutes for it the place where she lives: '"Tu as une lettre de Pétersbourg": les mots "ta mère" qu'il employait autrefois, maintenant, je ne sais pourquoi, ne peuvent plus lui passer les lèvres' (p. 124). Natacha is always sharply observant of tone, gesture and variations of pronunciation, from the grave tone of her mother's reading-voice, from which 'les mots sortent drus et nets' (p. 39), to her father's addiction to the phrase 'Ne t'en fais pas' (p. 113) and his inability to pronounce the French 'r', or again, Véra's clipped speech which crushes the vowels out of existence, and reduces 'Natacha' to 'N't'che' (p. 111). She appreciates Babouchka's excellent, accentless French, and notes her occasional archaisms (p. 212): Mlle de T., the school-teacher, is admired for her clear and precise articulation (p. 225). The child's acute sensitivity to varieties of speech and mannerisms is also shown in her fondness for imitations – she holds mock-classes, playing the teacher, and mimicking her classmates' responses (p. 207), and delights her friend Micha with her imitations of Pierre Laran (p. 134). Her early command of French, Russian and German sufficiently indicates her capacity for and interest in language, and she later learns English with passionate enthusiasm. She is not a child who simply takes language for granted, and her encounter with language is a complex one, involving different languages and different environments as well as conflicting emotional attachments.

An interesting instance of her linguistic awareness occurs during a train
journey early in 1909. Her mother was just going off to join her husband
Kolia in Budapest, and was taking the child as far as Berlin, from where
Natacha was to go on to join her father for two months in Paris (she was
in fact never to return to live with Maman). In her misery, Natacha
transforms the sunlit plains she views from the train-window into two
words, two sets of sounds, the Russian and the French words for 'sun', and
she repeats them endlessly to the rhythm of the train-wheels, noting the
different positions of the tongue in each case: 'Et de nouveau sol-ntze. Et
de nouveau so-leil. Un jeu abrutissant que je ne peux pas arrêter' (p. 104).
It is as if the two strands of her life, divided between Russia and France,
are twisted together into the incantation with which she fights her tears.

It is the figure, and above all, the voice of Maman that dominate the
first part of the text. Maman's words define the child's world, and within
it, mother, child and their respective roles. Many of the most striking
episodes cluster around Maman's 'dictons' which distribute precise roles
and demand particular lines of conduct. When Maman overhears Natacha
talking to her bear and telling him they are both going to see Papa in Paris,
where there will be 'une autre maman', she declares with petrifying
emphasis: 'Tu n'as au monde qu'une seule maman' (p. 104). This will
recur later, when Natacha asks her mother for permission to call her
step-mother Véra 'maman-Véra', and receives a bitter and wounded letter
which makes it clear that 'Je n'avais sur terre qu'une seule mère . . . et elle
n'était pas encore morte' (p. 205). 'Femme et mari sont un même parti'
(p. 72) says Maman when, during a friendly scuffle between Maman and
her husband Kolia, Natacha tries to join in on Maman's side. The words
effectively expel the child intruder, and form part of a sustained pattern of
exclusion and rejection.

The intensity of the child's first trembling adventures into the independent use of language verges on the neurasthenic. The formulation of
independent thoughts is a very hazardous affair. Passing a hairdresser's
shop one day, Natacha sees a doll in the window, and quite unbidden, the
words 'elle est plus belle que maman' (p. 92) float into her head. Maman
has always been beyond any possibility of comparison – 'au-delà': this
thought therefore seems a violation. Overcome with anxiety and fear,
Natacha brings out her 'idée' for Maman to look at, rather, she explains,
as she would have offered up a bruised knee to be blown on and soothed.
Maman however replies with one of the many all-encompassing formulae
that govern so many episodes of this childhood: 'Un enfant qui aime sa
mère trouve que personne n'est plus beau qu'elle' (p. 93). The child

unwraps this package ... 'Un enfant. Un. Un. Oui, un enfant parmi tous les autres, un enfant comme tous les autres enfants. Un vrai enfant empli des sentiments qu'ont tous les vrais enfants' (p. 94). The conclusion is obvious: she is a monster – 'un enfant qui n'aime pas sa mère' (p. 95). These first formulations of thoughts in which Maman is no longer absolute and 'au-delà' are bewildering: she dare not express them, and when asked what is troubling her, she replies 'J'ai mes idées' (p. 98) as one might say 'J'ai mes douleurs. J'ai ma migraine', but with the difference that her 'idées' are 'un mal honteux' (p. 98) that cannot be discussed. On her treatment of this early transgression in *Enfance,* Sarraute has remarked: 'J'ai voulu décrire comment naît la souffrance qui accompagne le sentiment du sacrilège.'[8] From these early violations of 'acceptability' comes a great deal of suffering. But that early suffering leads, in the mature writer, to a conscious rejection of false coinage, a refusal of the lying clichés that distort the truth of experience, and a resolute exploration of the underside of the 'acceptable' surface of language.

It is at school finally that she realises that her 'idées' in their original and disturbing form have gone: 'mes idées' have become 'des idées' (p. 130) and 'Je peux sans crainte penser n'importe quoi' (p. 131). She even carefully formulates the sentence 'Papa a mauvais caractère' to test it out, and it turns out to be quite innocuous: 'Je l'ai pensé et cela n'appartient qu'à moi. Je n'ai à en rendre compte à personne' (p. 131). She is no longer caught in the earlier marasma of guilt: she seems to have acquired 'une complète et définitive indépendance' (p. 131).

That independence is hard-won and much needed, for Maman is not alone in her capacity to wield words like steam-hammers. It is Natacha's step-mother, Véra, who, when asked if they are soon going back 'à la maison', answers with a crushing 'Ce n'est pas ta maison'. It is Véra, too, who chooses to use Russian to tell Natacha that her mother is not going to take her back: 'Tiebia podbrossili' she declares, and 'les mots russes ont jailli durs et drus comme ils sortaient toujours de sa bouche ... "podbrossili" un verbe qui littéralement signifie "jeter", mais qui a de plus un préfixe irremplaçable qui veut dire "sous", "par en dessous" et cet ensemble, ce verbe et son préfixe, évoque un fardeau dont subrepticement on s'est débarrassé sur quelqu'un d'autre ...' (p. 173).

It is scarcely surprising that Natacha regards words with deep distrust when the adults around her so often use them to subdue, exclude, prohibit or deceive. Maman's promise of a visit from Grandmother turns out to be the prelude to a minor throat operation: strawberry jam is a disguise for a dose of calomel. It is again at school that Natacha finds a protective haven from the 'remuements obscurs, inquiétants' of home life, and a shelter from the disturbing ambivalence of the absent Maman: 'il ne pénètre rien jusqu'ici de cet amour, "notre amour", comme Maman l'appelle dans ses lettres . . . qui fait lever en moi quelque chose qui me fait mal, que je devrais malgré la douleur cultiver, entretenir et qu'ignoblement j'essaie d'étouffer . . .' (p. 160). 'Notre amour' – as Maman calls it – takes its place alongside other dubious elements of language dangerous in their power to disturb or distort. Words are objects of suspicion at both the narrative and the experiential level.

When tempted to describe the beautiful image that remains in her mind of Ivanovo, where she was born, the narrator's distrust of words makes her hesitate: 'j'ai envie de la palper, de la parcourir avec des mots, mais pas trop fort, j'ai si peur de l'abîmer . . .' (p. 42). By its very fixity, language threatens the essential mobility of lived experience. Recalling a special moment that happened one day in the Luxembourg gardens, the narrator writes of trees in bloom, and grass covered with daisies ('le ciel, bien sûr était bleu') and shows an acute sense of the gap between language and experience: 'et à ce moment-là, c'est venu . . . quelque chose d'unique, qui ne reviendra jamais de cette façon, une sensation d'une telle violence qu'encore maintenant, après tant de temps écoulé, quand, amoindrie, en partie effacée elle me revient, j'éprouve . . . mais quoi? quel mot peut s'en saisir? pas le mot à tout dire: "bonheur", qui se présente le premier, non, pas lui . . . "félicité", "exaltation" sont trop laids, qu'ils n'y touchent pas . . . et "extase" . . . comme devant ce mot ce qui est là se rétracte . . . "Joie", oui, peut-être . . . ce petit mot modeste, tout simple, peut effleurer sans grand danger . . . mais il n'est pas capable de recueillir ce qui m'emplit, me déborde . . .' Suggestions, alternatives and corrections lead to an expression of a pure intensity of life, a sort of sinking into the elements of the day: 'je suis en eux sans rien de plus, rien qui ne soit à eux, rien à moi' (p. 65).

There is a similar movement to avoid linguistic categorisation when a maid utters to Natacha the no doubt sympathetically-intended reflection: 'Quel malheur quand même de ne pas avoir de mère.' Natacha, in the light of this global definition, examines her situation to see if she is really in a state of 'malheur', recognising that for the maid she clearly *is*: 'elle voit le malheur sur moi' (p. 117). Then she revolts against it: 'Je ne resterai pas dans ça, où cette femme m'a enfermée . . .' (p. 118). The questioning voice asks at this point: 'C'était la première fois que tu avais été prise ainsi, dans un mot?' The other voice replies that she cannot remember any earlier occasion, but 'combien de fois depuis ne me suis-je pas évadée terrifiée hors des mots qui s'abattent sur vous et vous enferment' (p. 118). There is a high sensitivity to the implications and traps of language, especially its capacity for 'adjectivisation', for casting persons or experience into a single fixed mould. Natacha notices even in her father, if he doesn't like someone, a tendency to make of that person 'un personnage' (p. 186). The narrator adopts the caution already observable in the child. Véra, who could so easily become a classic 'wicked stepmother' is never thus categorised by the child. The two voices of the narrative comment on this: '... aucun mot ne vient s'appliquer sur elle ... – Quand on y pense tu ne lui en as jamais appliqué aucun. Même "méchante" ... – C'est curieux, quand il m'est arrivé d'entendre d'autres enfants dire que ma belle-mère était méchante, cela me surprenait ... aussitôt surgissaient des images qui ne trouvaient pas de place dans "méchante" ...' (p. 180). The narrator offers a complex and varying image of Véra, impossible to reduce to a single specific 'character'.[9]

Adjectives and abstract nouns are inevitably reductive but their simplicity and fixity are countered in this narrative by proliferation and hesitation. Such proliferations or repetitions are part of the method Sarraute employs to make language fight against its own tendencies towards fixity. As early as 1963 Maurice Blanchot commented on Sarraute's 'repetitions': 'Répétition répétant non pour envoûter, mais pour désensorceler la parole de la parole même et plutôt pour l'estomper que pour l'enfoncer.'[10] The various alternatives suggested do not work towards specificity and precise definition, but remain possible alternatives, circling around an inward reality – 'le ressenti' – which they evoke rather than describe. The changing attitude to her mother that Natacha observes in her father, for instance, is first noticed not in his words but in his facial muscles: 'dans le froncement de ses sourcils, dans le plissement de ses lèvres qui s'avancent, dans les fentes étroites de ses paupières qui se rapprochent ... quelque chose que je ne veux pas voir ...' The other, more confident narrative voice now takes up where the other has paused, to give a specific meaning to the 'quelque chose': 'De la rancune, de la réprobation ... osons le dire ... du mépris' (p. 123). This categorisation is, however, promptly undermined by a return to the initial refusal of definition: 'Mais je n'appelle pas cela ainsi. Je ne donne à cela aucun nom, je sens confusément que c'est là, en lui, enfoui, comprimé ...' (p. 123). The 'quelque chose' observed in the father's face is to be replaced not by 'mépris' but by 'cela'. The doubling of the narrative voice effectively intensifies the sense of groping towards an undefined but 'felt' fragment of experience. The experiencer and narrator, approaching the matter dialogically, are no more fixed and immutable than the experience itself.

Sensitivity to tone, gesture and the nuances of language is often a source of pain to the child, but it is also a very positive resource. The early development of Natacha's sense of the traps and pitfalls of words is well shown in the episode where she asks her father: 'tu m'aimes, papa?' (p. 56) with a careful control of her tone to avoid any seriousness or anxiety, knowing that 'il déteste trop ce genre de mots, et dans la bouche d'un enfant . . .' One voice asks the other: 'Tu le sentais déjà à cet âge?' (p. 56) and receives the reply: 'Oui, aussi fort, peut-être plus fort que je ne l'aurais senti maintenant . . . ce sont des choses que les enfants perçoivent mieux encore que les adultes.' Once having obtained the needed token – 'Mais oui, mon petit bêta, je t'aime' – she lets him off the emotional hook, saying 'Eh bien, puisque tu m'aimes, tu vas me donner . . .' and the episode ends with Natacha carrying, floating from her wrist, a new blue balloon – a more solid token, for all its fragility, than the equivocal 'notre amour' of Maman's letters.

A similar sensitivity allows the child to perceive in her father's use of 'ma fille', 'comme l'affirmation un peu douloureuse d'un lien à part qui nous unit . . . comme l'assurance de son constant soutien, et aussi un peu comme un défi . . .' (p. 251). Here again, the repeated 'comme', and the three variants, hold off petrifaction. The lesson seems clear: what is verbalised is often deformed or debased, and the world clinks with false coinage. The unspoken and unformulated is all the more precious, though difficult of access.

For Sarraute, language must therefore be directed in part against itself, against its own petrifying power, if it is to achieve authentic and living communication.[11] Mere deployment of language, or creation of fine-sounding phrases is an empty achievement, and the child's history, recounted in these pages, makes the point. The capacity of language to assume control and reduce the living person to nothingness is well exemplified in the episode in which the child is persuaded to 'perform' at a wedding, reciting a very silly poem, 'Mon cher petit oreiller'. Language is here experienced as something that can possess and enslave. The child, grotesquely playing the child, suffers an intense sensation of humiliation, of 'abject renoncement à ce qu'on se sent être, à ce qu'on est pour de bon, mes joues brûlent, tandis qu'on me descend de ma chaise, que je fais de mon propre gré une petite révérence de fillette sage et bien élevée et cours me cacher . . .' (pp. 60-61). This travesty makes a striking contrast with the confident Natacha later reciting in class, in command of her language and her tone, delighting in her own professionalism (p. 170). To reach authenticity, it is necessary not merely to abjure the humiliations of self-travesty, but also to learn the rules in order *not to be ruled,* and to achieve mastery of the medium.

Natacha's first effort at writing is the 'novel' she embarks on at the age of 7 or 8. She writes in red ink and the words sometimes look a bit odd. They are often strange words she doesn't really know, and her subject – a consumptive young prince and a Georgian princess – are also rather intimidating. 'Ils s'enfuient sur un coursier . . . "fougueux" . . . je lance sur lui ce mot . . . un mot qui me paraît avoir un drôle d'aspect, un peu inquiétant, mais tant pis . . .' (p. 85). Hard as she tries, she cannot seem to get close to the elusive characters – 'je m'efforce avec mes faibles mots hésitants de m'approcher d'eux plus près, tout près, de les tâter, de les manier . . . Mais ils sont rigides et lisses, glacés . . . [. . .] . . . ils sont comme ensorcelés' (p. 86).

This very early attempt at fiction is described in relation to a scene in which Natacha is persuaded to show her 'novel' to a literary friend of Maman's. He hands it back to her with the cruel comment 'Avant de se mettre à écrire un roman, il faut apprendre l'orthographe' (p. 86). The budding novelist, thoroughly nipped, puts the book away and never looks at it again. The narrator confesses she has recounted this scene before – it was a very handy way ('un magnifique traumatisme d'enfance') of explaining why she actually began writing so late in her life. But looking back at the episode, she understands it in a new way. She was, she tells us, 'ensorcelée', just like the characters in her story: 'A moi aussi un sort a été jeté, je suis envoûtée, je suis enfermée ici avec eux, dans ce roman, il m'est impossible d'en sortir . . .' (p. 86). The cruel words about the necessities of spelling in fact release her: '. . . ces paroles magiques . . . rompent le charme et me délivrent' (p. 86). The paradox of seeking through language to escape the petrifaction of language is here echoed in the magic words that operate a release from the magic spell of a false and petrified fiction. The cruel blow is redefined as the healing knife.

Her next significant literary effort is a school composition on the subject of 'Votre premier chagrin', and this time, the child who earlier learned that she does not fall into the category of the 'vrai enfant', invents 'un vrai premier chagrin de vrai enfant', where 'vrai' means 'acceptable'. The essay is an affirmation of skill in the manipulation of language, quite free of anything private or personal. She realises that this is not the place for a chagrin 'vécu par moi pour de bon . . . et d'ailleurs, qu'est-ce que je pouvais appeler de ce nom?' (p. 195). Again the fixation of the descriptive category is rejected, and this time in favour of a feeling of dignity, and domination. She will not be ruled by the words but will rule them, giving away nothing of herself: 'je ne livre rien de ce qui n'est qu'à moi . . . mais je prépare pour les autres ce que je considère comme étant bon pour eux, je choisis ce qu'ils aiment, ce qu'ils peuvent attendre, un de ces chagrins qui leur conviennent . . .' (p. 195) and in fact she sets about creating 'un modèle de vrai premier chagrin de vrai enfant' (p. 196).

Whereas in her 'novel', the words were unfamiliar and unmanageable, the words in the 'Premier Chagrin' are known and controlled, and their effects carefully calculated. Unlike the first effort at a 'novel' – so cruelly rejected for its poor spelling – this piece of writing has no 'vilaine faute d'orthographe', no 'hideux bouton' to mar its beauty. Regarding her own experience as irrelevant to the 'vrai',[12] Natacha nevertheless demonstrates her capacity to work successfully within the norms it represents. She has acquired competence and skill in the discipline of writing, but it is a writing devoted to effective manipulation of 'acceptable' and superficial clichés, not to explorations of troubling undercurrents.

Writing is subject to the same perils and problems as talking, and indeed more, for it involves not only the physical skill of writing but also the specific demands of spelling, grammar and syntax. Further, written words have no facial expression, tone or gesture to indicate intention or qualify effect. If the practice of school compositions develops Natacha's discipline and facility, it also encourages a self-protective conventionality, and it fosters enjoyment of the orotund phrase. The narrator recalls with wry amusement the feeling that animated a magniloquent school essay devoted to a description of a picture (Detaille's *Le rêve*): 'un sentiment d'exaltation qui se déversait dans des phrases que j'avais prises je ne sais où, déjà ampoulées à souhait, et les gonflait pour qu'elles s'élèvent encore plus haut, jamais assez . . .' (p. 227). Such inflated writing is far removed from Sarraute's characteristic sincerity and diffidence,[13] indeed it is at the opposite pole from the Sarrautean literary stance which is always ready to 'take Eloquence and wring its neck' in the interests of truth of feeling.

Natacha's experience of writing as a means of communication at the personal and intimate level is not a happy one. In the letters that followed her separation from Maman, a special 'code' was agreed between the two. 'Ici je suis *très* heureuse' meant she was happy, while 'Je suis heureuse' would indicate that she was not. In a moment of despair, while missing her mother intensely, and hoping she would come to get her earlier than arranged, she wrote, in her private and privileged code: 'Je suis heureuse'. Maman promptly wrote to Papa, to tell him that Natacha was complaining of being unhappy, and reproaching him for not looking after her better. Natacha was very deeply wounded by this act of treachery: her 'private line' to her mother was irretrievably destroyed. Maman's response was not even addressed to her, and the child was 'atterrée, accablée sous le coup d'une pareille trahison' (p. 112).

As time passed and the separation from Maman continued, Maman's letters and cards became progressively more and more remote – their style seeming directed to a much younger child: 'Elle ne sait pas qui je suis maintenant, elle a même oublié qui j'étais' (p. 122). This unhappy sense of not actually being the target for Maman's discourse was already present when Maman read her own stories for children to Natacha, her words seeming to be addressed elsewhere, leaving the child with 'cette impression que plus qu'à moi c'est à quelqu'un d'autre qu'elle raconte' (p. 21). The failure of communication is again sharply apparent when, after two and a half years of separation, Maman comes to Paris for the month of August. Maman, searching for some words to utter, is compared to an adult casting about with a helpful assistant in a toyshop for an appropriate present: 'C'est pour un enfant de quel âge? Peut-être un jeu de cubes? Non? Il est trop grand . . . Alors un jeu de construction?' (p. 236). Maman's attitude is in fact very like that of the writer of 'Mon premier chagrin', choosing the words she knows to be acceptable and appropriate, with no self-expression, truth-seeking or sincerity to complicate the task.

The gap between mother and child widens even further when Natacha goes to Versailles for the day with Véra just after her mother's arrival in Paris. Maman is so angry that she leaves the next day. She then, with a very firm sense of plot and characterisation, casts Natacha off, writing, again not to her, but to Natacha's father: 'Je vous félicite, vous avez réussi à faire de Natacha un monstre d'égoisme. Je vous la laisse . . .' (p. 240). Sarraute's particular sensitivity to and distrust of the operations of plot and characterisation may well have found some of their impetus from such cruel personal experience.

Alongside the child's progress at school in recitation, dictation and composition, runs a more personal and often painful apprenticeship in language – an apprenticeship which bears fruits perceptible in the narrative we are reading, a narrative always ironically aware of the perils inherent in narrative, and always reaching out to the reader, inviting participation, challenge, verification or dissent. The words of this text are *not* addressed elsewhere: there is no impression that 'c'est à quelqu'un d'autre qu'elle raconte'. There is no empty deployment of words, no rhetorical pirouetting in response to a 'sentiment d'exaltation' such as that which inspired the school essay on Detaille's painting. One of the major lessons that emerges from Natacha's childhood experience of language is the need to avoid verbal narcissism, such as permeates the ill-directed letters of Maman, in which 'à travers ces récits enfantins filtre comme de la gaieté, de la satisfaction' (p. 122).

One episode in particular seems to stand out as an illustration of the way that narcissistic posturing can debase language and travesty communication. It occurs when Maman, furious that Natacha has gone to Versailles with Véra, announces her decision to leave at once. Natacha is 'médusée par l'étonnement. Ecrasée sous le poids de ma faute, assez lourde pour avoir pu amener une pareille réaction' (p. 239). What remains uppermost in her mind from this last meeting before Maman's departure is a scene in which, just as Natacha had earlier played with the French and Russian words for 'sun', Maman plays with two words for 'rage'. With her profile – 'son joli profil doré et rose' – etched against the sunset, she gazes into the distance, then turns to Natacha with the remark:

> C'est étrange, il y a des mots qui sont aussi beaux dans les deux langues . . . écoute comme il est beau en russe, le mot "gniev", et comme en français le mot "courroux" est beau . . . c'est difficile de dire lequel a plus de force, plus de noblesse . . . elle répète avec une sorte de bonheur "Gniev" . . . "Courroux" . . . elle écoute, elle hoche la tête . . . Dieu que c'est beau . . . et je réponds "Oui". (p. 249)

A sophisticated adult here makes a cruel and studied refusal of direct and personal communication with her child, in favour of an apparently impersonal and abstract commentary on the very words whose meaning silently saturates the scene. Their physical quality is appreciated and their overwhelming content ignored. The child is reduced to subjugated contemplation of her mother's self-applauding performance.

This passage exemplifies the way Sarraute at times communicates what is almost incommunicable: I can think of few passages that more tellingly touch the quick of a child's distress, without any sentimentality, without any overt emotionalism – 'sans y toucher', as it were. And it is important for Sarraute Not to Touch – i.e. to allow the experience to flow through, untouched by petrifying adjectives, or the rigidities of descriptive language.

Memory, in this text, seems to have selected significant episodes to make its own patterns. Among them we see a personal and affective drama of rejection and a search for identity, a struggle to find a path to a personal language. That path is full of pitfalls, dramatised in many childhood episodes, while the dangers and difficulties of arriving at 'clean' communication are encountered and acknowledged by the child Natacha and also by the mature narrator and author. The great challenge Sarraute has faced in this text is to reach out to the living inwardness of childhood and communicate it without falling into the rigidities inherent in formulation. She has also, in recounting Natacha's adventures in the world of language, outlined the path along which she moved towards the capacity for facing that challenge.

Enfance offers a privileged insight into the processes by which currently available language is, as it were, internalised, filtered and refined by experience, to emerge ultimately as a controlled, poetic and highly individual means of communication. Language is, in effect, gestated, and out of the sounds and shapes, the deceptions and revelations, is ultimately born a personal idiom. Such processes no doubt characterise most language-learning, but the more verbally sensitive the learner, the more complex the processes, and few have mapped with such subtlety – and humour – their early transactions with language, and the struggle to achieve a precarious union between the fixities of language and the elusively complex currents of lived experience – 'une union à chaque instant menacée, un équilibre si difficile qu'il paraît parfois impossible'. [14]

Notes

[1] Richard N. Coe, in *Proceedings of the Leeds Philosophical and Literary Society, Literary and Historical Section,* Vol. XIX, Part VI, p. 28 (Leeds, December, 1984).

[2] *Enfance,* NRF, Gallimard, 1983. Page references to this edition are given in brackets in the text.

[3] Nathalie Sarraute was born in Ivanovo, in Russia, and her emotionally, linguistically and geographically complex childhood, split between France and Russia, seems to combine the characteristics Richard Coe attributes to the French childhood with what he identifies, in contrast, as the 'positive assimilation of the shape and texture of words as *words*', characteristic of the English and the Russian child (Coe, op. cit., p. 30).

[4] Certain childhood incidents seem to metaphorise the creative impulse. The longing for a baby brother or sister leads the child to offer Maman a spoonful of dust, since it was, Maman had said, as a result of her swallowing some dust that she had produced Natacha (p. 30). A few pages further on, Natacha, in a long white veil and with a daisy-crown on her head, leads a solemn garden-procession to plant a water-melon seed, in the hope that from its burial-place will spring 'une tendre pousse vivante' (p. 35). Elsewhere, the creative impulse takes a more specific form, as when Natacha embarks on a novel, just like her novel-writing mother ('j'en écris un, moi aussi', p. 85), and a good deal of the book is concerned with the pleasures and pains of learning the art of writing.

[5] In conversation with Viviane Forrester, Nathalie Sarraute mentioned some of her omissions: 'Par exemple, la Beauce. Les vacances de Pâques, là-bas. Elles avaient un rôle

pourtant. Mais c'était plat. Des images d'Epinal. Ça m'assommait prodigieusement.' (Viviane Forrester, 'Portrait de Nathalie', *Magazine littéraire,* 196, juin 1983, pp. 18-21, p. 19.)

⁶ Further extensive textual patterning (which I have outlined in an article in *Romance Studies,* 9, Winter, 1986), suggests that there is also a thrust against the silky surface of Maman. If the exposure of the grey stuffing of the sofa reflects the finding of the writer's own artistic substance, the defiant gesture it involves may also be associated with the rejection of the language of Maman.

⁷ *Portrait d'un Inconnu,* Gallimard, 1956, p. 72.

⁸ Forrester, art. cit., p. 20.

⁹ Viviane Forrester comments on Véra: 'Elle est là, elle aussi, une femme jeune et vulnérable... dans l'œuvre de Sarraute, le mot de "marâtre" ne peut, seul, définir une femme.' Forrester, art. cit., p. 21.

¹⁰ Maurice Blanchot, 'A rose is a rose', *Nouvelle nouvelle revue française* (July, 1963), p. 91. 10.

¹¹ Cp. N. Sarraute '... ces efforts pour faire accéder au langage ce qui sans cesse se dérobe ont présenté de grandes difficultés. Ces efforts, en effet, ont rencontré un obstacle redoutable, celui que dressait devant eux le langage lui-même. Un langage partout installé, solidement établi sur des positions qui paraissent inexpugnables tant elles sont universellement respectées.

Là où ce langage étend son pouvoir, se dressent les notions apprises, les dénominations, les définitions, les catégories de la psychologie, de la sociologie, de la morale. Il assèche, durcit, sépare ce qui n'est que fluidité, mouvance, ce qui s'épand à l'infini et sur quoi il ne cesse de gagner.' ('Ce que je cherche à faire', in *Nouveau roman: hier, aujourd'hui,* vol. 2, *Pratiques,* UGE, Coll. 10/18, 1972, pp. 36-37.)

¹² This early exercise is, however, remembered as having given its author 'un sentiment de satisfaction, de bien-être' (p. 200), stronger than any other piece of her writing. It is tempting to suggest that while part of the satisfaction came simply from successful manipulation of the given theme, part may have derived from less patent causes. The 'chagrin' centres on the death of a little white dog – 'la boule blanche... quoi de plus imbibé de pureté enfantine, d'innocence'. First the little white dog makes its way to a pond, but the railway proves more attractive to the young writer, and more dramatic, with its 'énorme, effrayante locomotive'. That choice may well be linked with her own childhood, in which the railway is the very emblem of separation. The model story involves an ideal family, with a loving Papa and Maman, grandparents, brothers and sisters, an ideal house, beautiful garden, and the little white dog which is a birthday present. The 'boule blanche', symbol of childish purity and innocence, is crushed on the railway on the child's fictional birthday. The cliché-ridden story is surprisingly suggestive, after all, of a real 'premier chagrin' in which childish innocence and idyllic family life were alike destroyed. Clichés are perhaps only 'petrifying' when used in earnest, and not when their falsity is fully acknowledged. Clichés and conventional linguistic units are here consciously assembled for their artificiality and effectiveness. It may be the apparent security of the story's impersonal 'acceptability' that allows a certain symbolic truth to filter through. In this intricately patterned work, when the linguistic surfaces are not being pierced to reveal the underside, the underside seeps upward to permeate the ostensibly superficial.

¹³ Though it recalls certain satiric passages of *Les Fruits d'or* – e.g. 'Sous cette chaude lumière, en lui la sève monte, les mots hardiment s'élèvent... "Admirable..." Plus haut... "Une pure œuvre d'art..." Plus haut... "Rien dans nos lettres de comparable..." Plus haut, encore plus haut... "Ce qu'on a écrit de plus beau..." toujours plus haut, les cimes immenses se déploient...' *Les Fruits d'or,* Gallimard, 1963, p. 46.

¹⁴ Sarraute, 'Ce que je cherche à faire', in *Nouveau roman: hier, aujourd'hui,* vol. 2, *Pratiques,* UGE, Coll. 10/18, 1972, p. 33.

L'Education sentimentale: a critic's novel?

Brian Nicholas : University of Sussex

My father, who came to literary criticism late in life, pronounced two judgments on *Madame Bovary:* first, that it was a damned good yarn, and next, that Emma was a nasty bit of work. He placed himself thus in a critical tradition which was to last from Flaubert's own time till the 1950s.

One would not immediately think of Henry James as a partisan of the novel as good yarn. But to go back to his essays on Flaubert is to re-enter something like a world of innocence. His terms of praise for *Madame Bovary* are that it is 'spontaneous and sincere', whereas *L'Education sentimentale* is 'mechanical and inanimate', 'to the finer sense, like masticating ashes and sawdust'.[1] This distinction is in fact modified later, and the same sort of reservations are applied to both novels, though much more severely to *L'Education*.[2] James wonders why Flaubert chose 'as special conduits of the life he proposed to depict such inferior and, in the case of Frédéric, abject characters'. They are 'limited reflectors and registers' for 'so large and so mixed a quantity of life' as Flaubert 'clearly intends' to describe. Flaubert 'takes Frédéric on the threshold of life and conducts him to maturity, without apparently suspecting either our wonder or our protest – "Why, why *him*?"'. The portrayal of Mme Arnoux, his one attempt to 'represent beauty otherwise than for the senses', is vitiated by the fact that Flaubert 'has not been able not so to discredit Frédéric's vision ... that it makes a medium good enough to convey adequately a noble impression'. James feels that, if the purpose is, precisely, to portray mediocrity, 'then the purpose itself shows as inferior'; and he declines to believe that it could make up 'the whole vision of a man of Flaubert's quality', this picture of life seen through the lens of Frédéric.

Here there is no doubt that the novel is primarily a representation of reality, that its main business is the portrayal of significant characters; and that, judged by these criteria, *L'Education* is badly flawed. Irony, that all-atoning quality for some critics, is called by James the 'refuge' of irony, and he wonders whether Flaubert might not have resisted that temptation to flight and 'fought his case out a little more on the spot'.

In his essays, James acknowledges a great debt to Emile Faguet, who calls *L'Education* 'un livre assez ennuyeux', but says that it improves with re-reading. But here lies another problem, that of readability; and Faguet rather quaintly compares the novel to 'ces personnes qui gagnent à être connues, mais qui ont ce malheur, qu'elles n'inspirent pas le désir de les connaître'.[3] In many ways, Faguet and James reflect, while refining it, the hostile reaction to the novel on its first appearance. And the same kind of judgment has been voiced on Flaubert in general many times since. For D. H. Lawrence Flaubert's characters are 'little people' unworthy to express the 'great tragic soul' of Flaubert;[4] while for Mauriac 'Flaubert croit représenter la vie et il l'ampute de tout ce qui n'irrite pas ses nerfs'.[5]

There were, of course, from the start, more favourable judgments – Zola, for instance, praises *L'Education* as a transcription of what James would have called 'middling experience'. But the best starting-point for my present purpose is Proust's essay,[6] in which he says that no-one who has stepped on to 'ce grand trottoir roulant que sont les pages de Flaubert, au défilement continu, monotone morne, indéfini', can fail to realise that he is in the presence of something new in literature. And, rather ominously, he sees the finest thing in the novel as not words but a blank, a silence, the gap between the chapter ending with Frédéric's recognition of Sénécal in his new authoritarian role – 'et Frédéric, béant, reconnut Sénécal' – and the beginning of the next, the penultimate of the book: 'Il voyagea. Il connut la mélancolie des paquebots . . .' Proust, with his reduced emphasis on character and action, provides a foretaste of more recent criticism. The new novelists claim Flaubert as a predecessor: for Robbe-Grillet, Flaubert's ambition, 'bâtir quelque chose à partir de rien' is now 'l'ambition de tout le roman';[7] for Nathalie Sarraute, surely taking Flaubert's aspiration for the deed, his novels are 'about nothing, almost devoid of subject, rid of characters, plots and all the old accessories'.[8] Others find new intellectual and aesthetic pleasures. For Leo Bersani, what Flaubert's novels are 'most interestingly about' is 'the arbitrary, insignificant, inexpressive nature of language', a language which 'refers to nothing beyond its own impersonal and discouraging virtuosity'.[9] Gérard Genette[10] rejects Valéry's criticism that Flaubert errs by concentrating on 'l'accessoire au dépens du principal', and sees the best things in Flaubert as the moments when he abandons a narrative that obviously bores him and suspends the action, when 'le récit se perd et s'oublie dans l'extase'. Flaubert wrote novels 'tout en *refusant* – sans le savoir mais de tout son être – les exigences du discours romanesque', and operated that '*dédramatisation,* on voudrait presque dire *déromanisation* du roman par où commencerait toute la littérature moderne'.

Stylistic appreciation takes a new turn. Proust had already picked out for praise the dying fall of the sentence in *Salammbô:* 'Les Celtes regrettaient trois pierres brutes, sous un ciel pluvieux, au fond d'un golfe plein d'îlots.' Barthes's preference goes to the washing-line in *Bouvard et Pécuchet:* 'Des nappes, des draps, des serviettes, pendaient verticalement, attachés par des fiches de bois à des cordes tendues.' 'Je goûte ici', he says, 'un excès de précision' – and he compares the technique to that of Robbe-Grillet.[11]

During the seventies there was a good deal of work on *L'Education.* Titles like Alan Raitt's article 'La décomposition des personnages dans *L'Education sentimentale'*[12] indicate a general trend. Raitt takes as his starting-point Pommier's very traditional "Essai d'onomastique littéraire' of 1950, which had noted a correlation between Flaubert's decreasing concern with the naming of his characters and a falling-off in 'characterisation', especially of the minor figures. Raitt questions several assumptions in the argument, and suggests that the very vagueness with which Flaubert treats names, addresses and *états civils* (what is Mme Arnoux's real Christian name? why doesn't Rosanette's child have a name at all? where does Regimbart live and what does he do?) is indicative of a new conception of the novel, which will have 'des retentissements incalculables' for Proust, Gide, Robbe-Grillet, Nathalie Sarraute, Claude Simon and Georges Perec. P. M. Wetherill, in 'Flaubert et les incertitudes du texte',[13] situates Flaubert between the nineteenth and twentieth centuries, and sees the distinctive interest of his work in the *va-et-vient* between concern with the world and pure 'littérarité'.

His position is defined in part-reaction to what is perhaps the richest and most interesting statement of the modern position, Jonathan Culler's *Flaubert. The uses of uncertainty.*[14] Flaubert here is seen as inaugurating a novel different in kind from those of Balzac and Stendhal, whose worlds, though complex, are ultimately intelligible, and whose aim is to render them for the readers' comprehension. Flaubert, on the other hand, plays tricks with his reader, inviting him to seek meaning but denying him the satisfaction of finding it. Having tried to connect the text with the world, he is left with the text as the only reality. Description is used in Balzac to explain the personal and social, and there is frequent appeal to the readers' shared knowledge, which the writer will build on and complete ('une de ces maisons parisiennes', 'une de ces femmes qui' is the recurrent formula in this connection). But Flaubert resists this sort of 'recuperation'. It is often impossible to say from whose point of view, or to what end, a description is being made. Culler, surely rightly, rejects (pp. 91-93) those laborious symbolic interpretations of Charles's cap: the detail is gratuitous – there never was such a cap in literature or life, and the 'une de ces coiffures' which introduces the description parodies the Balzac mode.

The notion of Flaubert as 'psychological novelist' is also vigorously attacked. Culler entitles the main section of his book: 'The Perfect Crime: the Novel'; and the textual evidence for this new relationship between author and reader is backed up (pp. 78-79) by Flaubert's expressed intentions: his early ambition to be a 'démoralisateur' and his comment, in a projected preface to the *Dictionnaire des ideés reçues,* that he will dispose his material 'de telle manière que le lecteur ne sache pas si on se fout de lui, oui ou non'.

Not all these recent approaches overtly state a preference for *L'Education,* but the implication is often there, as it already had been in Proust, who saw Flaubert, after *Madame Bovary,* as purging himself of 'tout ce qui n'était pas lui-même'. Culler feels (pp. 146-47) that the 'thematic indeterminacy' of *Madame Bovary* is blemished by the unquestioned assumption that Emma *was* depraved by her reading, and finds no such 'central flaw' in *L'Education.* Roger Sherrington, in many ways a traditional 'recuperator', concerned to establish the relevance of all the material in terms of the characters' 'points of view', seems to see *L'Education* as more sophisticated than *Madame Bovary,* with its straightforward irony and accessibility to the general reader.[15]

The trend is clear. Those things which a James, and in many moods Flaubert himself, thought of as faults, have become available to be treated as virtues: ubiquitous irony, evasiveness, boringness, 'l'accessoire au dépens du principal', the devious relationship with the reader, gaps, unattributable viewpoints, weak reflectors and registers – these are now seen as praiseworthy moves towards the creative advances of the twentieth century.

A number of questions are suggested by these critical approaches. How meaningful, for instance, is it to talk about the relationship between the writer and the reader, as if readers constituted a homogeneous category? Culler's notion of the vindictive novelist and the novel as perfect crime, with the author slipping away unpunished, seems to assume a naïve reader: as he says (pp. 86 ff., 108 ff.), the reader will have to be led on by an appearance of a connection with the world, but the author's intention is to demoralise him, or, in more positive terms, to 'undermine conventional modes of order and raise awareness to a higher plane'. Barthes talks similarly of writing producing a 'malaise salutaire'. But suppose that, to meet the perfect criminal, the reader has been prepared by the perfect detective – Barthes or Culler, as it might be; then the vituperative novelist would be defeated, his strategies transmuted into aesthetic pleasure. How well pleased would he be by that? Culler, especially, seems to me to hover between valuing the text's punitive and consciousness-raising function and publicising its aesthetic possibilities. For him, by attempting thematic and symbolic readings of Flaubert's descriptions, we are depriving ourselves of 'other sources of delight in the text' (p. 91). But, again, what precisely are these delights? In what way is one piece of gratuitous description better than another? Or is the pleasure simply in the fact of catching the artist out at, or the readiness to go along with, his gratuitousness? If so, does not the length of the novel become an important issue? Genette's position reminds us of that problem. If the greatness of Flaubert lies in the suspension of action and the move to ecstatic contemplation, what is the relation of the parts to the whole? Would an anthology of Proust's, Barthes's and Genette's favourite passages do the best justice to Flaubert? Or is it the fact of being embedded in a very long and apparently traditional novel that gives them their value? What about the means by which Barthes excavates and enjoys the bit about the washing-line? How is he feeling by the time he gets there? Genette's approach raises the possibility of our doing the opposite of what the average reader is supposed to be tempted to do – skipping the action and hastening on to the description. But would it work? Or does our pleasure depend on our sharing Flaubert's delayed relief at getting away from the action? Do we have to read for our supper?

I have raised these questions, but not with the intention of confronting them systematically; rather in order to suggest that the approaches mentioned are highly selective, and that they might seem to ignore, or over-simplify, the actual business of starting to read, and going on reading (each of us with different equipment and expectations) a longish novel. This ought to be given close attention; for even the most advanced critics assume as an axiom – *their* only 'certainty' perhaps – that, for whatever reason, moralising, demoralising, patronising or pathological, the author wants us to read his work. He must propel us through its length at least once, though we may pick among its sentences later. Culler's view (p. 80) is that Flaubert gives us just a big enough, and carefully enough meted out, dose of the real, to achieve his aim of undermining the normal conventions of reading without making us 'throw down the books in outraged frustration'. I should like now to look very briefly at what seem to me to be some of the problems and solutions of Flaubert's undertaking in *Madame Bovary,* in relation to the business of propelling the reader through the novel.

One aspect of Flaubert's *gageure,* as he liked to call it, can be defined very briefly. His view of human relations was, in theory if not in practice, nihilistic, and one of his concerns in writing about Emma was to exhibit, and to enforce on the reader, 'l'éternelle monotonie de la passion'. The reader must be brought to share Flaubert's point of view – to share Emma's in any great measure would be to lose the sense of the book. But if the demonstration is too slick, or is premature, he may well give up reading, anticipating that the affairs with Rodolphe and Léon will go the same way as the marriage with Charles. Flaubert must present a closed world in an apparently open way, so that the completion of the demonstration coincides with the end of the novel itself.

The famous scene of the Bovarys' arrival at Yonville seems to me a perfect example of Flaubert's strategies at work. It begins with the devastating satire of Léon's and Emma's artistic conversation, counterpointed by the socio-medical one between Charles and Homais. But then we have the picture of Emma and Léon in the dying firelight – and this sentence:

> C'est ainsi, l'un près de l'autre, pendant que Charles et le pharmacien devisaient, qu'ils entrèrent dans une de ces vagues conversations où le hasard des phrases vous ramène toujours au centre fixe d'une sympathie commune.

Here we have the Balzacian 'une de ces', appealing to the reader's shared experience, and I see no conspicuous irony. The next sentence is perhaps more complex:

> Spectacles de Paris, titres de romans, quadrilles nouveaux, et le monde qu'ils ne connaissaient pas, Tostes où elle avait vécu, Yonville où ils étaient, ils examinèrent tout, parlèrent de tout jusqu'à la fin du dîner.

There is irony here, in the 'titres de romans' that they have not read, and deliberate flatness in 'Tostes où elle avait vécu, Yonville où ils étaient'.

Yet the listing technique works in two ways: it enforces the speakers' intellectual poverty, by suggesting the speed with which they exhaust successive subjects; but by its very length the sentence achieves a certain sweep, a certain lyricism, promotes a certain sympathetic involvement. The end of the chapter makes a similar effect:

> C'était la quatrième fois qu'elle couchait dans un endroit inconnu ... et chacune s'était trouvée faire dans sa vie comme l'inauguration d'une phase nouvelle. Elle ne croyait pas que les choses pussent se représenter les mêmes à des places différentes, et, puisque la portion vécue avait été mauvaise, sans doute ce qui restait à consommer serait meilleur.

We are meant to take the negative implications of '*comme* l'inauguration' and to note the false logic of the conclusion. Yet, again, that very false logic is expressed in a sentence of a certain lyric sweep, and invites us to take the false logician seriously. It is an enticing invitation to *read on*.

Similes and metaphors are traditional means of valuation, and sometimes of epic or tragic enlargement. Some of Flaubert's are so bad, so bizarre, that they might perhaps be taken as parody of the traditional technique. One thinks of Emma drowning in her beatitude like the Duke of Clarence in his butt of Malmsey; or of her love crackling more strongly than a fire abandoned by travellers on the Russian steppes. My inclination would be to see these simply as disastrous attempts at fine writing. But, in any case, they do not predominate; and the simile is quite often used for that lyrical prolongation of the sentence which I have just been discussing. An example is the description of Emma's nostalgia when she receives her father's annual letter, with the turkey, in memory of his mended leg:

> Quel bonheur dans ce temps-là! quel espoir! quelle abondance d'illusions! Il n'en restait plus maintenant! Elle en avait dépensé à toutes les aventures de son âme, par toutes les conditions successives, dans la virginité, dans le mariage et dans l'amour; les perdant ainsi continuellement le long de sa vie, comme un voyageur qui laisse quelque chose de sa richesse à toutes les auberges de la route.

An effective image, this, because there is no inflation, except what the rhythm itself provides – after all (as Léon must have discovered), we all have to pay our hotel bills; though that use of 'richesse' rather than just 'argent' perhaps makes a discreet evaluative point. The exact status of the image in what is a piece of *style indirect libre* might need discussion; but it seems to me undeniable that, for the moment at least, an unironical Flaubert is in action.

I have been selective myself in giving weight to Flaubert's 'straight' use of techniques like the Balzacian 'un de ces', 'ce', 'cette'; but not, I think, distortingly so. Recall, for example, that extraordinary authorial intervention describing Emma's beauty at the height of the affair with Rodolphe: 'Jamais Mme Bovary ne fut aussi belle qu'à cette époque; elle avait cette indéfinissable beauté qui résulte . . .' and then Flaubert goes on to tell us its constituent factors. In some ways this is a more brazen use of the formula than Balzac's: Balzac usually has some sociological intention, or pretension – whereas Flaubert here, while appearing to invoke an existing category, simply tells us what sort of woman he himself considers beautiful. Or we have the Hôtel de la Croix-Rouge at Rouen, 'une de ces auberges comme il y en a dans tous les faubourgs de province . . . bons vieux gîtes à balcons de bois vermoulu . . .' In connection with this one might note that descriptions of journeys and arrivals are very common in Flaubert – one remembers especially the wedding-day in *Madame Bovary* and the return from the races in *L'Education,* with their long, loving lists of the various brands of vehicle on view. Critics of the Richard school would make these episodes reflect a fluid and unstable conception of life; a more old-fashioned approach might see an interested eye for the detail of the animated – especially the regional – scene.

Enough of *Madame Bovary.* I am not going as far as to say that what Flaubert called 'un livre hautain et classique' is in fact a garrulous, sentimental novel, in the Balzac or even the Dickens tradition, full of the bustle of inns and celebrating the last days of the stage-coach. But I would say that, for all the novelty of its aesthetic, it has, in its authorial presence (so often denied), its narrative strategy, its use of simile and description, some pretty close links with its predecessors; and that only a very partial reading could see it as a decisive move towards the abandonment of character and plot, an attack on the novel as institution, a meditation on the inadequacies of language for referential purposes, or a systematic attempt to rout the reader. As we read, the passages of irrelevant or 'irrecuperable' description do not loom large – much more is traditionally relevant; and in giving the former such importance Genette, Culler and others are surely guilty of the very 'recuperative' reading they are concerned to replace. Finally, and most importantly, it seems to me that, whatever problems and unease there may be, they are Flaubert's, and not the reader's. *He* has to get the reader to accept the varying and potentially contradictory styles, and to go on reading without protesting. Nothing is further from Culler's view of the confident trickster playing cat and mouse with his reader than that agonised artist trying to make beauty out of the ordinary without being caught fiddling, trying to reconcile his feeling that 'Madame Bovary, c'est moi' with the drive to demonstrate the nothingness of all things.

* * *

The Conard edition of *L'Education sentimentale*[16] has 612 pages. On p. 375 we read this sentence which, as so often in this novel, is a whole paragraph, calling attention to itself typographically: 'Une lâcheté immense envahit l'amoureux de Mme Arnoux'. The context is an unsuccessful attempt by Deslauriers to make Frédéric admit his love. On p. 429, on the occasion of one of Frédéric's periodic revivals of interest in politics, we are told: 'Frédéric, homme de toutes les faiblesses, fut gagné par la démence universelle'. On p. 449, when Arnoux and Frédéric meet on Rosanette's staircase nd realise that they are now sharing her favours, we hear that, back out in the street, Arnoux talked as naturally as ever; and two tentative explanations are offered: 'Sans doute il n'avait point le caractère jaloux, ou bien il était trop bonhomme pour se fâcher'.

All these sentences seem to me very odd, occurring as they do so late in the book. The oddity of the first can be measured by trying to imagine Flaubert referring to Emma as 'l'amoureuse de Léon'. These periphrases of course abound in Flaubert, as they do in Balzac, and often appropriately: 'le pharmacien' reduces Homais to his true commercial stature, while to call Charles 'le médecin' is perhaps to satirise him by an ironical upgrading. But – 'l'amoureux de Mme Arnoux'? This is to extend stylistically to the main character the detachment shown in the treatment of Regimbart, 'le citoyen', and Hussonnet, 'le bohème'. One also notes that there are similarities between the presentation of Frédéric as lover and Rodolphe in *Madame Bovary* (they both exclaim 'Bah!' and light up a cigarette or pipe when dealing with delicate emotional problems). There would be much to say about this, but let us keep to the narrower stylistic issue. Flaubert could, at a pinch, have referred to the minor characters periphrastically every time they appeared; but that would not have been possible with Frédéric. Why then at one point rather than another? Is he more relevantly, more quintessentially 'l'amoureux de Mme Arnoux' here than elsewhere? I doubt it, and the reminder is in any case hardly necessary after nearly four hundred pages of Frédéric's unpurposeful adoration. Or is there, as one brand of criticism might propose, some superior irony at work, a mocking of the reader or of the conventions of the novel itself? Or is it just a mannerism, a tic, a somewhat unthinking, and here misplaced, use of a favourite device? The proliferation and growing complexity of the periphrases in *L'Education* could support such a reading – Arnoux, in the later part of the book, is 'l'ancien fabricant de faïences' and Deslauriers once, with pedantic specificity, 'l'ex-commissaire de Ledru-Rollin'.

The second sentence, beginning 'Frédéric, homme de toutes les faiblesses', has the same oddity, the same superfluous reminder. Having seen him repeatedly blown by every wind and whim, we hardly need authorial explanation of his present enthusiasm. It is rather as though, fairly late in *Hamlet,* Shakespeare were to remind us by means of a chorus that the Prince is the one plagued with indecision. As to the third example, the tentative explanation of Arnoux's behaviour, we again have the gratuitous gloss, with its postulation of two apparent alternatives, which are not in fact alternatives, but aspects of the same quality – a certain generous *insouciance* – which we have long known Arnoux to have; as too, for all his analytical deficiencies, has Frédéric, so that to read the sentence as *style indirect* does not remove the oddity.

Similar rehearsals of the obvious are frequent in the later part of the novel. In another revolutionary scene we hear that 'Frédéric, *bien qu'il ne fût pas guerrier* [my italics], sentit bondir son sang gaulois' (p. 420). And when he is busy undoing the orders for his marriage with Mme Dambreuse, we have an even flatter authorial comment: 'Les affaires publiques le laissèrent indifférent, tant il était préoccupé des siennes' (p. 596). Sometimes we are not even given the resounding truism, intended as it might be for the newcomer or the forgetful reader; but the cautious, discriminating explanation, which is itself no more than a tautology. Of Rosanette's pregnancy we hear that: 'Sa maternité future la rendait plus sérieuse, même un peu triste, comme si des inquiétudes l'eussent tourmentée' (p. 520). Note the judicious 'même', followed by the near circularity – her 'tristesse' explained by postulated 'inquiétudes'.

All these examples, as I said, come late in the text. They might be more explicable in terms of familiar narrative practice if they were a resolution or synthesis of an evolving fictional account. But this is not the case. On the contrary, if we go back to the beginning of the novel, we find nearly all the characters categorised or devalued immediately and often quite crudely. Cisy is 'une intelligence des plus pauvres' (p. 31); Pellerin believed in 'mille niaiseries' (p. 52); and of Regimbart we hear that 'on aurait dit . . . qu'il roulait le monde dans sa tête. Rien n'en sortait' (pp. 55-56). Minor characters, these, admittedly. But even earlier we learn that Frédéric, at eighteen, 'trouvait que le bonheur mérité par l'excellence de son âme tardait à venir' (p. 3), that his literary heroes were Werther and René, but that 'd'autres plus médiocres encore l'enthousiasmaient presque également' (p. 21); and that, on the whole, he was tiring of literature and thinking of becoming a painter or composer of symphonies. One notes here a certain undisguised irritation with the characters – that petulance which Flaubert tried not to allow into the text of *Madame Bovary*, but worked off, so he tells us, by writing violent sketches not intended for inclusion. (Emma's 'culture' is, of course, no less severely devalued, but not before she has been allowed to build up a substantial capital of interestingness.)

The picture, then, is a puzzling one, starting with an author who does not seem to have much heart for the game. But several hundred pages later he is still playing it – indeed there seems no real reason why he should ever stop; playing it however, one sometimes feels, in an inattentive manner, acting from time to time like a declarer at bridge who leads with a flourish from dummy, but appears to have forgotten that the cards are already face upwards on the table for all to see.

How, then, does the reader fare? Barthes, in *Le Plaisir du texte* (p. 18), says that in Flaubert – and *L'Education* must largely dictate the comment – 'l'asyndète', the grammatical device of omitting connecting words between sentences or phrases, becomes not something 'sporadique, brillante, sertie dans la matière vile d'un énoncé courant', but the mode of the whole text. 'La narrativité est déconstruite, et l'histoire reste cependant lisible.' And no greater pleasure could be offered to the reader, 'si du moins', he adds considerately, 'il a le goût des ruptures surveillées, des conformismes truqués et des destructions indirectes'.

Every reader of *L'Education* will recognise what Barthes is referring to – that flat, laconic style which is the hallmark of the book. The sentences I have discussed above are very short, and have a clipped quality in spite of their superfluous explanations; without these they would be even more typical of a style which recounts, with equal weight and equal lack of logical articulation, indifferent facts and apparently major psychological events.

Here are a few examples of Frédéric in action, though they do not all, technically, exhibit the device asyndeton. When he goes to Pellerin's studio, Pellerin explains his paintings: 'Frédéric les admira' (p. 55). The bric-à-brac in the room included 'une tête de mort sur un prie-Dieu, des yatagans, une robe de moine; Frédéric l'endossa'. When he takes his solitary August walks in Paris: 'De temps à autre il s'arrêtait à l'étalage d'un bouquiniste; un omnibus qui descendait en frôlant le trottoir le faisait se retourner; et, parvenu devant le Luxembourg, il n'allait pas plus loin' (p. 93). His contemplated suicide gets basically the same treatment, though it is filled out with the explanation that his project was foiled by fatigue:

> ... Frédéric se pencha. Le parapet était un peu large, et ce fut par lassitude qu'il n'essaya pas de le franchir.
> Une épouvante le saisit. Il regagna les boulevards et s'affaissa sur un banc.
> Des agents de police le réveillèrent, convaincus qu'il 'avait fait la noce'.
> Il se remit à marcher. (p. 110)

And when Sénécal makes his farewell, 'sa résignation et son air solennel surtout firent rêver Frédéric, qui bientôt n'y pensa plus' (p. 311).

Now, as Barthes genially puts it, this is very pleasurable if you like that sort of thing. But there is a great deal of it, and for an obvious reason. Having landed himself with a character of little depth or interest to him, Flaubert is forced to multiply the number of laconically related episodes: if there is little real action in *L'Education,* there is a vast amount of incident. Rather like Emma and Léon in *their* conversation, Flaubert soon exhausts a subject and moves on. Frédéric did this, then that, went to Nogent and decided to go back to Paris, was revolted by Rosanette's ignorance, then took pity on her, felt a stirring of patriotism and then became absorbed in his own affairs. Incipiently dramatic scenes are frequently interrupted by another character's arrival. Here Mme Arnoux and Frédéric are getting closer to one another:

> Ses bras s'écartèrent; et ils s'étreignirent debout, dans un long baiser.
> Un craquement se fit sur le parquet. Une femme était près d'eux, Rosanette. (p. 514)

Critics may be right in seeing this 'weak register' Frédéric as the perfect mediator for a new, neutral way of writing. But in claiming that *as such* this gives pleasure, they may be underestimating the effects of repetition and the influence of context. Rather than see Frédéric as an *enabling* prop, one might see his character as *dictating* the over-use of a style which has its uses, but which can decline into the tic and call our attention back sharply and unfavourably to the – mediocre – subject-matter. The interruptions of the dramatic scenes, though justifiable in terms of Frédéric's easily interruptible nature, could also point to relief or evasion on

Flaubert's part, an unwillingness, as James put it, to 'fight his case out a little more on the spot'.

My sense is of a Flaubert profoundly ill at ease with his subject-matter. And it is in this way that I would be tempted to account for the gratuitous explanations which I discussed earlier – and which need some accounting for in view of the author's reputed craftsmanship and impersonality. They could represent a loss of grip, of concentration, engendered by distaste; or perhaps a more *positive* dissatisfaction with the laconic, a desire to rejoin for a moment, and without artistic inhibition, the better-aired Balzacian world of meaning. If those monosyllabic exchanges between characters enchant the critics, Flaubert perhaps feels the need to diversify. But, as his world lacks the dynamic qualities of Balzac's, the explanations must be as flat as the things explained. Frédéric here is talking to Louise, who is lonely and wants to marry him:

> 'Votre père vous aime, pourtant!'
> 'Oui; mais...'
> Elle poussa un soupir qui signifiait: 'Cela ne suffit pas à mon bonheur.' (p. 357)

We could have filled *that* in for ourselves.

This intervention – in the event ill-judged – reminds us again that Flaubert's voice (why call it 'the narrator's' when it is so consistent and recognisable?) is more often present, and less easy to get round critically, than some recent admirers of the novel would admit. Often his comments seem to be exasperated intrusions, inviting us to join him in reflecting on the ungratefulness of the subject-matter. In the Dambreuse salon, for example, 'ce qu'on disait' – already castigated as 'la misère de propos' – was, however, 'moins stupide que la manière de causer' (p. 186). But these interventions bring us back to Flaubert's increasing artistic frustrations. He no longer deals with this intellectual and moral poverty by giving it the brilliantly stylised treatment of the *comices agricoles* or the Homais-Bournisien exchanges in *Madame Bovary*. Rather, social and political conversations are presented raw, or recourse is had to a technique we have seen in *Madame Bovary* – that of enumeration:

> [Sénécal] demandait... que l'ouvrier pût devenir capitaliste... Hussonnet, comme poète, regrettait les bannières. Pellerin aussi... Il déclarait Fourier un grand homme. (pp. 197-98)

Lists of uncoordinated impressions are also frequent in the public scenes, and make the general point of random activity, signifying nothing. In the Paris uprising: 'Les marchands de vins étaient ouverts; on allait de temps à autre y fumer une pipe ... puis retournait se battre. Un chien perdu hurlait. Cela faisait rire' (p. 413).

Again, this can give pleasure; and the generalised use of the style produces what, rightly or wrongly, can be enjoyed as delicious bits of self-parody. Thus, as Frédéric's party go to the duel in the Bois: 'De rares passants les croisaient. Le ciel était bleu, et on entendait, par moments, des lapins bondir' (p. 327). But, especially in relation to character, there is again the question of repetition, of the descent into the tic. We saw a creative use of the list in the Yonville inn scene. It has others – to show, for instance, the inability of *things* to fill up the void of life or the absence of individual purpose. Emma's boredom led her to buy 'un buvard, une papeterie, un porte-plumes, des enveloppes, quoiqu'elle n'eût personne à qui écrire'. So we know that, when Frédéric 's'était acheté une boîte de couleurs, des pinceaux, un chevalet' (p. 72), he is unlikely ever to paint. By the time he undertakes the *Histoire de la Renaissance,* the formula is perhaps beginning to wear a bit thin: 'Il entassa pêle-mêle sur la table les humanistes, les philosophes et les poètes; il allait au cabinet des estampes ... il tâchait d'entendre Machiavel' (pp. 265-66).

The tendency of my argument is perhaps becoming clear: I am trying to meet the partisans of *écriture* and its rewards on their own ground, by starting from writing and not from character – but still finding considerable grounds for worry.

Those techniques which were used sparingly and purposefully in *Madame Bovary* become the whole texture of *L'Education.* I have mentioned over-explicitness, but the dominant approach is one of psychological and linguistic caution, a withholding of endorsement for the reality of emotions or perceptions. That had been present, sometimes necessarily, in *Madame Bovary,* as when the delirious Emma 'croyait entendre ... le chant des harpes séraphiques'. In *L'Education* it becomes ubiquitous, to the point where Flaubert seems unable to say that something 'étonna quelqu'un', only that it 'parut l'étonner', where people feel 'une sorte de jalousie', 'une espèce de remords', 'comme un orgueil'. Then there is the attribution of motives. These are sometimes questioned in *Madame Bovary,* and alternatives proposed. But the technique always serves the main theme of homogeneity and recurrence. The attribution of such an important decision as Emma's acceptance of Charles to two possible causes, 'l'anxiété d'un état nouveau, ou peut-être l'irritation causée par la présence de cet homme', might seem to point to randomness or subversion of the novel's conventions; and certainly we are not in the world of delicate psychological analysis. But it reminds us of, and is firmly dictated by, the fact that for Flaubert marriage is the mediocre statistical norm, and that there are only two or three, not very well-differentiated, immediate causes for it.

In *L'Education* these *incertitudes* are pushed to the extreme. As Raitt notes admiringly in his 'Décomposition des personnages', the most consistent and calculating character in the novel, Martinon, is made to act inconsistently at a key moment, when Dambreuse, to test him out, tells him that Cécile has no dowry. He is willing, all the same, to marry her, and three alternative explanations are offered: 'ne croyant pas que cela fût vrai, ou trop avancé pour se dédire, ou par un de ces [*un de ces*] entêtements d'idiot qui sont des actes de génie'. I share Raitt's liking for this, but not as a consummate bit of *incertitude;* rather as the choleric intervention of an unhappy Flaubert, no longer able to hold back the word 'idiot', as a proof that, at p. 524, in spite of all his self-imposed sufferings, there's life in the old novelist yet.

For the rest, in the matter of perception, 'peut-être' and 'sans doute' become the rule of the narrative. And that institutionalised uncertainty is not, I feel, in the service of a new presentation of reality such as we are to find in Proust. Raitt talks of such foreshadowings, but they are no more than that: Frédéric is not equipped for Marcel's sort of *éducation.* His dealings with the puzzling world stop at the stage of the rhetorical question: 'Etait-ce une conjuration?' (p. 336), 'Etait-ce un remords? un désir?' (p. 122), 'Que signifiait cette invitation?' (p. 288). And he rarely stays for an answer.

In fact it is chiefly when passion or irritation overcome Flaubert that the style takes on a refreshing vigour. In the similes for example: in the Dambreuse salon hackneyed theories 'aussi neuves que le jeu d'oie', nevertheless 'épouvantèrent les bourgeois comme une grêle d'aérolithes' (p. 424). But elsewhere, and particularly in the matter of Frédéric's love, Flaubert seems to flounder and lose his grasp: 'Elle souriait quelquefois . . . Alors, il sentait ses regards pénétrer son âme, comme ces rayons de soleil qui descendent jusqu'au fond des eaux' (p. 120). Some critics would claim that this simile is Frédéric's; others might see a willed indeterminacy in its status and relish its parodic flatness; or one might – as I think James would – detect infirmity of purpose, fatigue, automatism.

A last example of recurrent technique: the frequent use of superlative adjectives in this far from superlative world. Seeing Frédéric with Rosanette at the races, Mme Arnoux 'pâlit extraordinairement' (p. 296). Arnoux, at the end, was 'prodigieusement vieilli' (p. 566). Frédéric himself 'pâlit extraordinairement' (p. 582) on hearing of Arnoux's destitution. Rosanette 'bâillait démesurément' (p. 462) while visiting Fontainebleau. A tough task for a critic like Sherrington, needing to explain the adverbs as proceeding from 'points of view'; a windfall, perhaps, for some new critics – 'excessively' used absolutely, without explicit criteria for what is normal; for the seasoned reader of Flaubert, who knows that he likes long adverbs (we remember 'alternativement', the last word of *Hérodias*), a sense perhaps that habit is taking over, linked with a desire to punctuate the mediocre scene, if only with a little facial distortion.

I said of *Madame Bovary* that the problems were all Flaubert's, and not the reader's, and this seems truer still here. Of course he claimed to have been misjudged, but not in the terms proposed by some recent critics. In many ways he both anticipated and endorsed his contemporaries' criticisms, particularly in regard to the lack of action and the relation of the private to the public. His letters suggest no new aesthetic, but rather the same vexations that we hear about during the composition of *Madame Bovary*: recurrent irritation with the subject-matter which, for complex and obscure reasons, he had wished upon himself. He did say, after *L'Education* had failed, that he would like to make a big coup on the Bourse and buy up all the unsold copies of the now vastly popular *Madame Bovary,* implying that in this way his readers' arrested development might be overcome.[17] But that sounds like the cry of a man who by now dislikes success as much as failure. His ambition, while working on *Bouvard et Pécuchet,* to produce a book so monstrous that people will think that it was written by an idiot, perhaps confirms the pathological diagnosis. And *L'Education* seems to me to be an incontrovertible case of a stylistic repertory in search of, or severely suffering from the lack of, a suitable subject-matter.

That the style will still serve is proved by what has been seen by some as the product of a last lucid interval – I mean, of course, *Un Cœur simple.* Nowhere could it be more clearly shown that the impact of techniques is inseparably bound up with the matter they describe. Let us take, for example, the single sentence paragraph:

> Elle avait eu, comme une autre, son histoire d'amour.

This might look like Flaubert on his stylistic last legs, trying yet another formulation of 'l'éternelle monotonie', hoping that the single sentence paragraph may still bring him some mystified applause. Yet in context the effect is completely different. The statement deserves to be set in relief, because it comes at the 'monotonie' from a different and significant angle. Without in the least denying eternal recurrence, it stakes a large claim for Félicité: the 'femme de bois' had a heart like others. This is not a truism or an isolated neutral fact, given spurious typographical interestingness. Similarly with the sentence which describes, in cadences reminiscent of *L'Education,* Félicité's reaction to her mistress's hardheartedness over Félicité's nephew's suspected death: 'Félicité, bien que nourrie dans la rudesse, fut indignée contre Madame, puis oublia'. 'Bien que nourrie dans la rudesse' recalls the 'quoiqu'il ne fût pas guerrier' comment on Frédéric. But though, like that one, it tells us something that we already know, it is justified as a résumé of the moral background to this unique moment of revolt. The brief formula, 'fut indignée, puis oublia' reproduces the cadence of 'firent rêver Frédéric, qui bientôt n'y pensa plus'. But again it is a totally appropriate account of the scope and limits of revolt in a simple soul, rather than, as so often with Frédéric, making us feel that stylistic cleverness is tricking out another short-lived change of heart. In the same way the ubiquitous 'peut-être' and 'sans doute' of *L'Education* come very rarely in *Un Cœur simple,* and, when used in connection with the parrot, they qualify very properly a good-natured bit of anthropomorphism on Flaubert's part: 'La figure de Bourais, sans doute, lui paraissait très drôle'; and he gets excited at the thunderstorm 'se rappelant peut-être les ondées de ses forêts natales'; while the use of 'croire' in the final vision – 'crut voir ... un perroquet gigantesque' – restores the cautious formula to the legitimate use it has in *Madame Bovary,* and which was debased in *L'Education*

This has been a rather bad-tempered essay, unfair perhaps both to the text and to the critics. The 'plaisirs du texte' are very real and, if the reading becomes hard at times, no one will have given up before reaching, on p. 3, that wonderful notation of human daydreams, when the passengers on Frédéric's boat look at the villas on the banks of the Seine:

> Plus d'un, en apercevant ces coquettes résidences, si tranquilles, enviait d'en être le propriétaire, pour vivre là jusqu'à la fin de ses jours, avec un bon billard, une chaloupe, une femme, ou quelque autre rêve.

My excuse for this unfairness will be brief. In the high days of F. R. Leavis, someone said that his orthodoxy operated as though every novel would be *Middlemarch* if it could. I think it an equal pity to suppose that every writer would be a Beckett or a Robbe-Grillet if he could; because this sort of criticism is depressingly reductive, and leads to distorted readings and often perverse valuations. Proust's techniques and conception of the novel are obviously something new. But his work is also a vast repository of social observation and moral reflection, of wit, wisdom, sometimes even warmth: without their intrinsic interest his 'text' would certainly not hold us as it does. So, let us put in a word for mimesis and humanism, and err on the side of *Madame Bovary* and *Un Cœur simple.* Oscar Wilde said that he would rather miss a train by Bradshaw's than catch it by the ABC. Perhaps Flaubert, who at heart felt that there was something very wrong with *L'Education,* would rather have been found deficient in sensibility by Henry James than hailed as a precursor by Nathalie Sarraute. Or perhaps, of course, not.

Notes

[1] H. James, 'Flaubert', in *French Poets and Novelists,* London, 1875, pp. 197-210.

[2] H. James, 'Flaubert (1902)', in *The House of Fiction,* ed. L. Edel, London, 1957, pp. 187-219.

[3] E. Faguet, *Flaubert* (1899), 6th ed., Paris, 1920, pp. 122-26.

[4] D. H. Lawrence, 'Mastro-don Gesualdo by Giovanni Verga' in *Phoenix* (posthumous and uncollected papers), London, 1936, pp. 223-31.

[5] F. Mauriac, *Trois grands hommes devant Dieu,* Paris, 1930, p. 151.

[6] M. Proust, 'A propos du "style" de Flaubert', in *Contre Sainte-Beuve, etc.,* ed. P. Clarac (Bibliothèque de la Pléiade), Paris, 1971, pp. 586-600.

[7] A. Robbe-Grillet, *Pour un nouveau roman,* Paris, 1963, p. 139.

[8] N. Sarraute, 'Flaubert le précurseur', in *Preuves* (February, 1965); quoted in English by Jonathan Culler, *Flaubert. The uses of uncertainty,* London, 1974, p. 134.

[9] L. Bersani, *Balzac to Beckett,* New York, 1970, p. 144.

[10] G. Genette, 'Silences de Flaubert', in *Figures,* Paris, 1966, pp. 223-43.

[11] R. Barthes, *Le Plaisir du texte,* Paris, 1973, p. 44.

[12] P. M. Wetherill (ed.), *Flaubert: la dimension du texte,* Manchester, 1982, pp. 157-74.

[13] op. cit. (note 12), pp. 253-70.

[14] See note 8.

[15] R. Sherrington, *The Novels of Flaubert,* Oxford, 1970, pp. 232-33.

[16] Paris, 1923. Subsequent page references are to this edition.

[17] See the note in the Conard edition, pp. 615-16.

Fromentin's *Dominique*

Norma Rinsler : King's College, London

T H E R E are books which are so familiar that they become invisible.
Dominique has been one of those books for the present writer, remembered, in Empson's phrase, as a 'taste in the head', and offering at a recent
re-reading a profoundly surprising appearance of completely unremem-
bered (or unobserved?) complexity. The 'taste in the head' had been
chiefly elegiac; quite different from the taste of Romantic melancholy or
Baudelairean spleen, it was measured, classical, harmonious and a trifle
vague. I cannot have read it very well. Revisited, it seems not at all vague,
but precise and incisive, and harmonious in quite a different way.

   The critical consensus stresses that *Dominique* is a singular book: it is
Fromentin's only novel, and there is no other novel quite like it.[1] But
since nature abhors a category of one, the next step is generally to show
that it is not in fact alone. At the simplest level, this can be done by
pointing to other 'single' novels, such as Constant's *Adolphe,* or Sainte-
Beuve's *Volupté*; and one can characterise this group still further by
stressing that 'single' novels appear often to be the work of writers who are
chiefly essayists or critics, as if every critic had one novel in his knapsack.
At another level, *Dominique* can be related to recognised types of
nineteenth-century novel: the confessional novel, the novel of psychological analysis, the novel of adulterous passion thwarted or otherwise, the
'roman de l'individu' and the 'roman de la mémoire'.[2] Subjecting the text
to this 'nothing-but' treatment reduces it to familiar and therefore mana-
geable proportions; but it also leaves out of account or obscures precisely
those uncomfortably individual qualities which challenge us in the first
place to find a way of handling them. In taking up that challenge I
recognise that it is doubtful that anything radically new can now be said

about *Dominique,* but it may be possible at least to avoid saying inappropriate things, to clear away some of the accretions and see what remains.

The first notion to examine is the accepted view of *Dominique* as an 'autobiographical novel',[3] a category which may subsume any or all of the types of novel with which this text has been compared. The composite term itself begs a number of questions which are generally ignored, beginning with the relationship between autobiography and fiction. Recent critical studies of texts that present themselves as autobiography or memoirs have radically changed our view of a once unproblematical genre (or no more problematical, at least, than human relations in general). We might however assume that when a writer's 'real' experience is presented as fiction, the problems disappear: we have only to take it as fiction. Unfortunately, the mere fact that we retain a sub-category labelled 'autobiographical fiction' suggests that we do not regard texts which appear to fall into this category in the same way as we regard other fictional works. However limited the measure of 'real' experience contained in a text, it colours the whole, so that we adopt a different receptive stance: instead of waiting to be amused, diverted, provoked or impressed by the skills of the creator of fictional artifice, we expect to be gratified by the author's confidence and to respond in our turn with trust, and preferably with sympathy. Whether we sympathise or not (and we may be antipathetic to what is revealed in the text), our response is primarily moral and emotional, and establishes a relationship between us and the author. I suspect that the confessional atmosphere often leads us to value the text that induces it more highly than we value the 'merely' fictional. In short, we receive autobiographical fiction very much as we receive autobiography, with the added pleasure of believing that we have penetrated a fictional disguise.

It ought to follow that if we are unaware that the experiences recounted in the text have some basis in the experiences of the author himself, we shall read the text differently. This does not seem always to be the case. Something in the text itself may persuade readers that what they are reading about belongs to reality, not fiction. In the case of the first-person narrative, this persuasion may then lead to the conclusion that the story is the story of the author himself: a logical deduction, but not necessarily a true or adequate one. I shall return to that 'something' in due course, but shall first consider what, in reading *Dominique,* we are reading about.

The story, if we attempt to abstract it from the web of language in which it is presented to us, appears remarkably thin. Dominique is brought up on his father's estate at Les Trembles, is tutored by Augustin, then sent away to school in a nearby town where he meets Olivier. He becomes a frequent guest at the house of Olivier's uncle and cousins, and falls in love with the elder girl, Madeleine, who is older than himself. Madeleine becomes engaged to a stranger whom the family had met on holiday. Dominique leaves school and goes to Paris, together with Olivier, for further study. He turns to a casual love affair for consolation when Madeleine is married, but later pursues Madeleine, who at first avoids him, then undertakes to cure him of his hopeless passion. Finally she admits her love for him, and after a single kiss she orders him to go away, and they never meet again. Dominique goes back to Les Trembles, marries some time later, and has two children. Augustin has married too, and has become successful after years of struggle. Olivier rejects the love which Madeleine's sister Julie feels for him; he refuses to marry, and finally attempts to kill himself. The suicide is bungled, and a disfigured Olivier leaves the neighbourhood of Les Trembles. The emotion aroused by this incident leads Dominique to relate the story of his life to an unnamed listener, thus generating the text.

Faced with this story, readers are generally moved to supply an interpretation of its events. This is by no means an invariable reaction to the reading of fiction, and it suggests that the text is felt to be problematical or ambiguous despite (or perhaps because of) the apparent simplicity of the plot. Some such awareness of ambiguity probably dictated the 'improvements' suggested to Fromentin by George Sand, which on the whole he politely ignored. She was particularly worried by the pistol shot which closes the introductory chapters, remarking that 'le coup de pistolet surprend un peu', and qualifying her unease by adding that she did not like the suicide 'là où il est placé'.[4] One may well be puzzled as to Fromentin's intentions in destroying Olivier, while he permits Augustin to climb ever higher and Dominique to achieve a state of equilibrium only momentarily disturbed by echoes from the past. The book was published in 1862, *ergo,* it is felt, it cannot be a straightforward account of Romantic passion. The most tempting conclusion would be to see it as anti-Romantic: Dominique is the man who has learned the futility of the Romantic dissatisfactions that lead Olivier to attempt suicide; putting passion behind him, he has chosen the path of work and will that Augustin had pointed out to him, and has settled for the ordered calm of a gentleman-farmer's life.[5] The ambiguity of the text is not removed by this reading. Dominique's final state may be seen as a proof of moral strength; or it may be interpreted as emotional cowardice, which would allow for an implicitly Romantic view (the reader's, and, if the reader insists, the

author's) of anti-Romanticism (Dominique's). All these readings suppose
that some kind of moral lesson is being offered to the reader, but there are
two possible versions of the moral: the first, that we should all strive for a
sensible resolution like Dominique's; the second, that we should have the
courage of our passions and seize what Dominique allowed himself to lose.
Unless we believe that Fromentin had not made up his mind what he
wanted to say, the apparently equal validity of these two readings suggests
that neither has much to do with the text, and that they are the
conclusions of readers who are reading their own novel.

A clue to Fromentin's intentions is often sought in the fact that
Dominique is accompanied throughout the text by two familiars, Augustin
and Olivier. It is easy to conclude that they are his good and his bad angel,
the one offering an earnest example of will-power, determination, sacrifice
and a serenely saint-like devotion to higher values, the other charmingly
superficial, pleasure-loving, cynical, cruel and unhappy.[6] The contrast
thus established would certainly be important if Dominique appeared
capable of becoming like either the one or the other angel, if they were
indeed merely projections of Dominique's potentialities. I do not believe
however that such is the case. The contrast is too neat, for Augustin is not
a wholly sympathetic character (hence G. Sagnes's regret that 'un pareil
livre s'achève sur son nom'),[7] and Olivier is not shown as wholly bad.
Perhaps only twentieth-century teeth would be set on edge by Augustin's
account of his marriage,[8] but even if one considers this response to be
anachronistic, there are sufficient indications in the text that Augustin is
not a simple allegory of the good life, and indeed is not seen as such even
by Dominique. Similarly, Fromentin presents a complex view of Dominique's friend and contemporary, Olivier, first attracting our interest in his
difficult character by introducing him, at the end of Chapter II, as a visitor
to Dominique's family whose mood is clearly at odds with domestic calm.
Since it is Olivier's attempt to kill himself that precipitates Dominique's
'confession', we are aware of Olivier's lamentable fate, and of his own
judgement on his life, before we meet him as the attractive adolescent
companion of Dominique's schooldays. The same is not true of Augustin,
whose acquaintance we make at the same time as Dominique does, when
he comes to disturb the child's paradise; seeing him first through the eyes
of a child, we remain aware of the distance created by the difference in
their ages, and are made as uncomfortable by his exhortations as if they
were directed at ourselves. Thus Fromentin deliberately counters a simple
view of these two men. Olivier's brutal end prevents us from being
excessively bewitched by his charm, but also from taking his unhappiness

to be a mere pose; it is certainly not intended to make us condemn him. As for Augustin, we meet him as the tutor of an undisciplined, self-consciously sensitive boy, to whom he appears cold and correct and unfeeling; he is seen to be quite incapable of perceiving or understanding, still less of sharing, the life of the sensations that governs the child's existence. His methodical approach to literary creation contrasts sharply with Dominique's ardent effusions, which are foreshadowed in his Latin composition and later channelled into verse. However generously the older Dominique acknowledges Augustin's moral heroism, that first impression – Dominique's own impression – is never completely denied. There is thus good and bad on both sides, or rather, since the yardsticks of good and evil do not seem appropriate here, it would be nearer the truth to say that there is warmth and coldness on both sides; for the judgements that Dominique passes on his two mentors are not based on moral values but on more or less of sympathy and admiration, and these responses fluctuate according to his own development.

The function of Augustin and Olivier in the text appears more central to its meaning than that of Madeleine, who is by contrast a rather shadowy figure. It has been pointed out many times that Dominique falls in love not with Madeleine but with love itself. A diffuse adolescent excitement which initially seeks its release in a wild race through the springtime fields is accidentally crystallised, in Stendhalian fashion, about the image of Madeleine; it is intensified by her absence, and fully realised only at the moment of her betrothal to another man. Dominique's exclamation at that moment: 'Madeleine est perdue, et je l'aime' (p. 445), neatly establishes the prior importance of frustration. What has not been noticed is that Madeleine herself goes through an exactly similar evolution. Her slow awakening to sensuality and self-consciousness does not follow on her marriage, but is triggered by the desire that she perceives in Dominique's eyes. Her mad ride through the woods echoes his adolescent outburst, serving in like fashion to crystallise rather than to sublimate desire. Madeleine, indeed, though shadowy, is not without an active presence in the text. Though we see her almost entirely through the eyes of Dominique (almost, because her quasi-absent husband and her father suggest another view of her), she does react to Dominique's presence and her emotions do evolve. She owes a great deal no doubt, as critics have remarked, to other heroines of literature, offering her sister to Dominique as Madame de Mortsauf offers her daughter to Félix de Vandenesse, and destroying herself through pity like Eloa.[9] I would add that her attempt to cure Dominique of his passion recalls Amélie's role as *guérisseuse* of

René's melancholy. [10] The comparison however also points to the greater complexity of Madeleine, who knows that she is the object of passion as well as its victim, and is consciously playing a very dangerous game. Madeleine's self-styled heroism, accepted by Dominique as heroic despite his temptation to use it to torture her, looks to the reader more like flirting with forbidden emotions, which is exactly the same game as Dominique is playing. It has more than a hint besides of the punishment of Tantalus, keeping Dominique at arm's length and thereby effectively keeping him, which is exactly the manœuvre to which Olivier accuses Dominique of subjecting Madeleine.

It is clear that Dominique does not understand Madeleine, indeed he has never really looked very carefully at her. He spends a good deal of time elaborating hypotheses about the feelings which he thinks may be revealed in her behaviour, for instance at the prize-giving ceremony (p. 458):

> Eprouva-t-elle un peu de confusion elle-même en me voyant là dans l'attitude affreusement gauche que j'essaye de vous peindre? Eut-elle un contre-coup du saisissement qui m'envahit? Son amitié souffrit-elle en me trouvant risible, ou seulement en devinant que je pouvais souffrir? Quels furent au juste ses sentiments pendant cette rapide mais très cuisante épreuve qui sembla nous atteindre tous les deux à la fois et presque dans le même sens? Je l'ignore; mais elle devint très rouge, elle le devint encore davantage quand elle me vit descendre et m'approcher d'elle. [. . .] Il y avait dans ses yeux tout à fait troublés comme une larme ou d'intérêt ou de compassion, ou seulement une larme involontaire de jeune femme timide . . . Qui sait? Je me le suis demandé souvent, et je ne l'ai jamais su.

This passage is typical of many in which Dominique constructs alternative scenarios, striving for the desired significance despite his admitted ignorance of Madeleine's feelings and his patent inability to read the signs. He imagines that he might declare his love to Madeleine, and composes the dialogue: 'Je mettais en scène cette explication fort grave' (p. 503). He constructs such hypotheses (which are never tested) for others too; for instance, during the 'promenade en bateau', he puts together Julie's silence and a view of a departing ship to create a drama: 'Julie, perdue dans je ne sais quelle confuse aspiration, surveillait attentivement le départ du grand navire qui appareillait' (p. 485). Julie is the perfect subject, 'car, avec cette singulière fille clairvoyante et cachée, toutes les suppositions étaient permises, et cependant demeuraient douteuses' (p. 555). The source of all his scenarios is, of course, to be found in other novels.

Fromentin wrote to Du Mesnil while working on *Dominique:* 'L'écueil, c'est de n'être pas du Gessner, ni du Berquin, ni du *René,* ni mille choses'. [11] That he indeed had these and other models in mind is shown by textual reference to literary parallels. The intertextuality operates however on two levels. First, there are the parallels adduced by Dominique himself, as when he refers to *Werther,* to Lamartine's *Le Lac,* or to *Mauprat.* [12] The role of these references is twofold, in that on the one hand they indicate the extent to which Dominique has been moulded by literature, and on the other they allow Dominique himself to draw conclusions about the validity and strength of his emotions. He is fully aware of the power of literature, 'un aliment d'esprit de toute importance', and in a mood of moral uplift he gives up the reading of fiction: 'Je ne me sentais plus aucun besoin d'être éclairé sur les choses du cœur. Me reconnaître dans des livres émouvants, ce n'était pas la peine au moment même où je me fuyais' (p. 538). This moment of renunciation makes it plain that he has habitually turned to fiction for enlightenment about 'les choses du cœur'. He is indeed so steeped in literary images that he suffers some inhibition as a writer in expressing his own feelings, having discovered that what he believed to be the stuff of poetry is only the common currency of prose (p. 485):

> Ce que je vous raconte, jadis quand j'étais jeune, plus d'une fois il m'a passé par la tête de l'écrire, ou, comme on disait alors, de le chanter. A cette époque, il me semblait qu'il n'y avait qu'une langue pour fixer dignement ce que de pareils souvenirs avaient, selon moi, d'inexprimable. Aujourd'hui que j'ai retrouvé mon histoire dans les livres des autres, dont quelques-uns sont immortels, que vous dirais-je?

Spontaneous feelings become problematical as soon as he encounters the literary expression of those feelings: 'je n'eus qu'un regret, ce fut de parodier peut-être en les rapetissant ce que de grands esprits avaient éprouvé avant moi' (p. 420).

On another level, and confirming the impossibility of saying anything new about human experience, the text may suggest to the reader parallels which are not available to Dominique. The influence of literature on the hero may recall, for instance, the case of Emma Bovary, brought to grief five years earlier by being 'plus sentimentale qu'artiste'. But Dominique is not Emma. Not only is he obscurely aware of the role played by literature in his confusions, but he fails both as man of sentiment and as artist. (One is tempted to imagine that he foreshadows Frédéric Moreau.) Similarly, Olivier's suicide, like Emma's, is stripped of Romantic literary convention and presented as physically horrible; but where Emma succeeds in killing herself and thus solves her problems, Olivier is not granted such an easy exit (nor his story such a neat denouement), and has to go on living with the visible mark of his failure. I would suggest that the literary parallels are here being used ironically, though the irony depends of course on the reader's being aware of the existence of the texts – or the sort of texts – at which Fromentin glances. The two kinds of parallel occur together and are thus made explicit in the 'promenade en bateau'. Here Dominique thinks of Elvire and her lover on the waters of Lamartine's lake,[13] while the reader observes a group of disparate individuals, dozing in the heat of the day, and engaged, when awake, in some private interior monologue from which Dominique is excluded. Madeleine, sound asleep, becomes the focus of Dominique's fantasies; awake, she utters banal observations quite unlike Elvire's profundities. In this passage, it is the inappropriateness of the literary allusion that gives it force.

We are warned at the very beginning of the text, by the unnamed listener, that 'il y a tant de nuances dans la sincérité la plus loyale! il y a tant de manières de dire la vérité sans la dire tout entière!' (p. 370). If sincerity is to be judged by spontaneity and candour (though that is debatable), there would be nobody sincere or even truly passionate in this text, were it not for Julie, who is the only character to avoid the keynote of its relationships: calculation. Her essential difference from the other young people is made clear in the extraordinarily powerful episode of the visit to the lighthouse. The *vertige* which overcomes Dominique, and which he senses in his companions, is more than physical (pp. 482-83):

> Il fallait y regarder attentivement pour comprendre où se terminait la mer, où le ciel commençait, tant la limite était douteuse, tant l'un et l'autre avaient la même pâleur incertaine, la même palpitation orageuse et le même infini. [...] ... tous accoudés sur la légère balustrade qui seule nous séparait de l'abîme, sentant très distinctement l'énorme tour osciller sous nos pieds à chaque impulsion du vent, attirés par l'immense danger, et comme sollicités d'en bas par les clameurs de la marée montante, nous restâmes longtemps dans la plus grande stupeur, semblables à des gens qui, le pied posé sur la vie fragile, par miracle, auraient un jour l'aventure inouie de regarder et de voir au-delà.

Dominique waits for one of the group to break under the strain, and it is Julie who faints. He is however wrong in his assumption that of all the companions, Julie is the most 'frêle', but not the most 'ému' (a role which no doubt he reserves for himself). Her feeling for Olivier is not a Romantic preference for frustration, nor a calculated flirtation, but an inveterate passion, profound and lasting, that cohabits, because it must, with genuine despair. Even if Olivier is right in his judgement that 'elle fait son malheur à plaisir', she does so disinterestedly, for she has nothing either to gain or to lose. She is shown indeed as lost from the beginning. Dominique is repeatedly disturbed by her eyes, with their lustreless burning gaze that seems to reflect an inner sickness. She is not weak, compared to Dominique, Olivier and Madeleine, but has a perverse strength and fidelity which only Augustin, in his different way, can match.

It is by such comparison and contrast, rather than by individual analysis, that patterns emerge in the constellation of characters that Fromentin groups and regroups in his novel. None of the individuals is fully 'rounded' in the traditional sense, because none of them needs to be: it is what can be revealed through their dynamic interaction that matters. Thus we learn much of the nature of Olivier and Augustin through each man's assessment of the other, his view of the other's relationship to Dominique, and Dominique's reaction to their views of each other. The moral examples that they offer are, as I suggested above, of no practical use to Dominique, who is no more capable of accepting Augustin's advice than that of Olivier. Nor are they as different as they seem to Dominique. Both are distinguished by their appeal to reason, which Augustin backs up with moral high-mindedness and Olivier with a world-weary pragmatism. But rational principles in either guise do not appeal to Dominique; and perhaps he is right, for reason has led to destructive doubt in Olivier, and to excessive certainty in Augustin. In both men, spontaneous feeling has died, leaving an inner hollowness to which Olivier responds with languid posturing and Augustin with strenuous activity. It is not at all clear that the reader is being asked to approve of the one rather than the other. Olivier has some of the characteristics of Romanticism as Fromentin describes it: 'ce 89 artistique [. . .] qui prit des devises bizarres, affecta très innocemment des tendances farouches, discuta prodigieusement, créa presque autant, se couvrit de ridicule et d'éclat, commit quelques excès, produisit des œuvres admirables, mais au fond ne promulgua rien'.[14] But Olivier is above all a Baudelairean dandy who observes only 'l'horreur de la vie', resolutely rejects the appeal of the transcendent, prefers Paris to the beauties of nature, chooses sterility, fears boredom and hates vulgarity. His refusal to 'épouser la liberté et le bonheur d'une autre' (p. 395) is thought by Dominique to be 'une question de probité' (p. 548); perhaps it is – but it is powerfully supported by his pessimism. Augustin on the other hand has perceived the way of the world, sees Paris as a challenge and sets out to conquer it. Dominique admires his resolution and reflects that he will prove to be no man's slave (p. 521). But though Augustin appears as fiercely independent as Olivier, it is the world that conquers, since he accepts its values; he will be no less subject as a master than he would have been as a slave.

I would suggest – and the book's non-ending seems to confirm this – that Fromentin is not offering a moral lesson or indeed a conclusion of any kind. Though he does have things to say about the business of living, about character, about ideals and ambitions, and about human relationships, conflicting views are constantly expressed on all these topics. Thus Dominique sees Olivier's fear of *ennui* and his hatred of vulgarity as 'd'incurables erreurs' (p. 530); character, in his view, is fate, and he describes Olivier's final act of despair as 'une catastrophe trop facile à prévoir et malheureusement impossible à conjurer' (p. 396). Olivier, on the other hand, having offered a devastatingly acute analysis of Dominique's faults and an accurate prediction of the denouement of his passion for Madeleine, remarks: 'il dépend de toi de me donner tort'; character, in Olivier's view, is not fate. Nothing in the text allows us to choose between these two conceptions. As Olivier explains to Dominique, 'la raison n'est d'aucun côté' (p. 529); it is all a matter of differences.

The Dominique that we meet at the time of his 'confession' cannot be said to have learned very much from either of his mentors. Though he claims to have accepted Augustin's teachings, he is still drawn to Olivier by affection, by shared experience, and by Olivier's links with Madeleine. Their ideas, however, are only superficially alike. Olivier regards happiness as an illusion, and opts for an attainable degree of self-knowledge and for attainable goals: 'Toute la question est là: trouver ce qui convient à sa nature et ne copier le bonheur de personne'. Since he insists that 'l'avenir permet de tout admettre', Olivier is not thinking, when he speaks of 'sa nature', in terms of a fixed personality, but of a malleable and shifting self which we learn to know precisely by finding 'ce qui convient', a discovery which in his view we can only make by rejecting the examples and the conventional wisdom offered us by others, and adopting a sort of Gidean *disponibilité* (pp. 528-29). Dominique's version of 'ce qui convient à sa nature' differs significantly from Olivier's in that Dominique does appear to believe in an essential individual self: 'Je me suis mis d'accord avec moi-même'. He explains that his retreat to his estate is an act of wisdom based on 'l'égalité des désirs et des forces', implying that he has fully measured both (pp. 369-70). Olivier too, on being asked why he has chosen to live on his estate, replies: 'Chacun fait selon ses forces'; but unlike Dominique, he does not claim that this choice is inevitable or definitive: future events for Olivier are only 'possible' or 'probable'. Nor does he present his choice as a virtue: when it is suggested to him that 'C'est de la sagesse', he replies 'Peut-être', adding that 'personne ne peut dire que ce soit une folie de vivre paisiblement sur ses terres et de s'en trouver bien' (pp. 394-95). Dominique insistently reminds his listener that he has chosen the path of modesty because he was clearly not destined for the path of genius. Olivier's grief is not that he is not a great man, but that he is *merely* a man: 'Je suis modeste, profondément humilié de n'être qu'un homme, mais je m'y résigne' (p. 530). This 'modesty' mocks Dominique's pretensions, and Olivier's philosophical position is quite different from Dominique's.

Though it does not make him happy, Olivier has achieved at least a measure of self-knowledge, whereas Dominique's problem is that he has great difficulty in choosing between possible selves. When he compares Augustin with Olivier, Augustin seems to him to show 'des côtés presque vulgaires' (and 'le vulgaire', of course, is one of Olivier's two great aversions). Dominique is at first embarrassed by the 'médiocrités d'existence' of Augustin's domestic life, reacting as Olivier would react; but then, when he begins to help Augustin to cut logs, he rapidly takes an idealised view of their honest labour. Consequently, when Olivier raises an eyebrow at the account of this edifying experience, Dominique feels that Olivier is unjust – yet until he adopted Augustin's persona, that was precisely his own reaction (pp. 516, 522). Olivier's resignation and Dominique's irresolution do have one thing in common: both suggest that since we cannot escape the human condition, a wholly original self is not possible. We have only the freedom to choose what we will resemble. Fromentin says something very similar about art: 'Entre ne plus vouloir imiter et imaginer, il y a renier ses exemples: c'est bien, mais il faut en trouver d'autres, et, quoi qu'on fasse, même avec la souveraine indépendance du génie, s'émanciper n'est que changer de maître'.[15]

If Dominique is unable to make a whole-hearted choice, he will inevitably be unable to effect a whole-hearted renunciation. According to Claude Herzfeld, the retreat to nature is the central theme and justification of the novel. Barthes too claims that *Dominique* is not a 'roman d'amour' but a 'roman de la Campagne', though where Herzfeld sees a Freudian return to the womb, Barthes sees a critique of urban life (of which he approves) and a glorification of patriarchal rural traditions (of which, since they are riddled with the injustices and blindnesses of class-consciousness, he does not).[16] Perhaps we do not need to choose between

these extreme points of view, for I think that although Fromentin's own
love of the countryside in which he grew up informs the text from
beginning to end, it is not the subject of his novel. Nor is love, at least in
the sense in which we generally speak of a 'love story'. Dominique's
feeling for Madeleine is certainly not a tender emotion. When he sees her
'dans la tenue splendide et indiscrète d'une femme en toilette de bal', he
not only learns the meaning of jealousy, but discovers in her 'des attraits
extérieurs qui d'une créature presque angélique faisaient tout simplement
une femme accomplie' (p. 490). Poor Dominique has a very literal mind:
meeting Augustin's wife for the first time, he is surprised to find her
'beaucoup plus jolie que je ne l'avais supposé d'après les opinions
systématiques d'Augustin sur les agréments extérieurs des choses' (p. 519).
Once he has recognised that his ideal love has become a sexual passion, he
is obsessed first with forcing Madeleine to recognise his feelings, then with
extorting from her a confession of her own desire, and at both stages he is
consciously and ruthlessly cruel. As Olivier informs him, he wants
excitement and drama, and does not really want to take possession of
Madeleine. In his long account of his life, he has almost nothing to say
about affection, and does not speak of love at all in relation to his wife and
children, 'trois êtres à qui je me dois et qui me lient par des devoirs précis'
(p. 369). The first paragraph of the novel describes nature as appropriate
rather than central to his existence ('Ma vie est faite et bien faite selon mes
désirs et mes mérites. Elle est rustique, ce qui ne lui messied pas'), does not
mention love, and introduces the key words of the text: 'la certitude et le
repos'; 'un acte de modestie, de prudence et de raison'; 'Ma vie est faite . . .
selon mes désirs et mes mérites'; 'l'égalité des désirs et des forces'; 'la
sagesse'; 'un homme heureux'. Fromentin wrote to George Sand: 'Je ne
suis pas bien sûr d'avoir voulu prouver quelque chose, sinon que le repos
est un des rares bonheurs possibles; et puis que tout irait mieux, les
hommes et les œuvres, si l'on avait la chance de se bien connaître et
l'esprit de se borner' (19 April 1862).[17] But the treatment of this theme is
less simple than that statement might suggest, for where in the novel are
we to find a manifestation of 'le bonheur', or even of 'le repos'? Dominique's peace is easily disturbed, as even his admiring listener can perceive,
by the slightest reference to the past. Olivier's claim to 'vivre paisiblement
sur ses terres' is mocked by his attempted suicide. Augustin has no desire
for the tranquillity that comes from solitude, being prevented by his sense
of duty from isolating himself; the only peace he understands is the quiet
of a clear conscience.

It is this recipe for 'sagesse' that Dominique adopts when he undertakes to devote himself to his family and his estate (showing again his need for a model). But I have already suggested that Augustin is not proposed by the author himself as a model. If Fromentin were really offering a clear moral lesson in 'sagesse', it is unlikely that he would allow Dominique the melancholy pleasure of telling his story in such vividly present detail, or the luxury of his private shrine to the past (from which, it appears, his wife is excluded). Dominique's own reservations about choosing Augustin as a model are revealed in his comment on Augustin's eventual success: 'il est au bout de sa tâche. [. . .] Ce n'est point un grand homme, c'est une grande volonté. Il est aujourd'hui le point de mire de beaucoup de nos contemporains, chose rare qu'une pareille honnêteté parvenant assez haut pour donner aux braves gens l'envie de l'imiter' (p. 562). This remark subtly devalues Augustin's talents, while praising his moral qualities; but since it also suggests that the fame which Augustin has fought so hard to achieve is worthless, it casts an ambiguous light on those moral qualities. Dominique's claim that he has taken Augustin as his example would imply that he has forgotten Olivier's advice to 'n'imiter le bonheur de personne'; for though Augustin does not speak in terms of happiness, Dominique believes him to be happy in his choice of 'des affections sans trouble': 'il disait "ma femme" avec un air de possession tranquille et assurée qui me faisait oublier toutes les duretés de sa carrière, et me représentait la plus parfaite expression du bonheur' (p. 521). For himself, Dominique seems less sure: '*si* le bonheur consiste dans l'égalité des désirs et des forces, [. . .] vous pourrez témoigner que vous avec vu un homme heureux' (pp. 369-70). Once again it is Olivier who is the most pragmatic (pp. 529-30):

> Le bonheur, le vrai bonheur, est un mot de légende. Le paradis de ce monde s'est refermé sur les pas de nos premiers parents; voilà quarante-cinq mille ans qu'on se contente ici-bas de demi-perfections, de demi-bonheurs et de demi-moyens. [. . .] Je suis modeste, profondément humilié de n'être qu'un homme, mais je m'y résigne.

The modulations that Fromentin effects in the meaning of key terms suggest that for human beings there is no such thing as absolute truth. It is not only that, in Olivier's words, 'la raison n'est d'aucun côté' but that 'truth' too is a term whose meaning fluctuates, or more precisely, that there are many kinds of truth. Writing his last Latin exercise for Augustin before leaving Les Trembles to go to school, Dominique composes an account of Hannibal's departure from Italy in which, he says, 'j'essayai d'exprimer ce qui me paraissait être la vérité, sinon historique, au moins lyrique' (p. 408). When he offers his listener an account of his own life, what kind of truth is he telling? The listener is somewhat surprised by the rapid growth of confidence and candour between himself and Dominique. It seems possible that the self-portrait that Dominique offers to his listener is, once more, a version of himself elaborated in response to the character of another: the *cadre* is not merely a narrative device. I suggested at the beginning of this essay that something in the text inclines us nonetheless to read it as truth. If we turn our attention to the structure of the text, it may be possible to see what that 'something' is, remembering that we are not looking for a demonstration of absolute truth, but for the signs of a kind of truth that carries conviction.

The structure of his novel was clear in Fromentin's mind from the earliest stages of its composition: 'Je me suis mis à mon livre depuis cinq ou six jours. J'ai commencé d'écrire une vingtaine de pages à peu près. [. . .] Ce sera une introduction un peu longue, suivie d'un récit'.[18] The introduction occupies in fact two chapters out of eighteen, or almost exactly one-seventh of the total number of pages. Together with the final chapter, it forms the *cadre* of the *récit,* and gives the unnamed listener a substantial presence. The listener acts as a first-person narrator in the first two chapters and the last; he tells us of his friendship with the doctor which led him, one autumn, to visit the village near Dominique's estate, of his encounter with a solitary hunter while out shooting with the doctor, of a brief exchange of courtesies with the hunter, now named as Monsieur Dominique, and of a glimpse of the stranger's house and then of his family as they come to meet him. However, even within the *cadre,* his is not the only narrative voice. The text begins with the voice of Dominique, speaking in the first person to the listener: 'Certainement je n'ai pas à me plaindre, – me disait celui dont je rapporterai les confidences dans le récit très simple et trop peu romanesque qu'on lira tout à l'heure, – car, Dieu merci, je ne suis plus rien, à supposer que j'aie jamais été quelque chose . . .' Only the brief parenthesis ('me disait') establishes the presence of a listener/narrator, and the remainder of the long first paragraph consists of words spoken by Dominique, though transcribed by the listener. The effect of this direct speech is to offer us a first-hand impression of Dominique, but of Dominique *as he wishes to present himself.* Further comments on Dominique's life, made by himself, are reported in indirect speech in the second paragraph of the text. Two further paragraphs explain the listener's reactions to Dominique's presentation of himself, and at this point the notion of relative truth is introduced: 'Etait-il sincère? Je me le suis demandé souvent, [. . .] Mais il y a tant de nuances dans la sincérité la plus loyale! il y a tant de manières de dire la vérité sans la dire tout entière!' It is only after this careful preparation that the listener begins to act as a first-person narrator proper: 'La première fois que je le rencontrai, c'était en automne. Le hasard me le faisait connaître à cette époque de l'année qu'il aime le plus . . .' (p. 371). The present tense here ('il aime', 'il parle', 'toute cette existence modérée qui s'accomplit ou qui s'achève') extends the time scale of the text beyond the narrative of past events, indicating that at the time of writing, the listener is still acquainted with Dominique. The effect of this, together with the immediate sound of Dominique's voice and the reported comments of the doctor, is to persuade us of the reality of Dominique, who is not a figure from a remote past but a man still living in the present, and therefore a man with a future: at the end of the text, Dominique remarks to his listener: 'pour en finir avec le principal personnage de ce récit, je vous dirai que ma vie commence' (p. 563).

There are however not two but three narrative voices in the text. At the beginning of Chapter III, Dominique takes over the role of narrator, speaking in the first person, and only very occasionally reminding us of the presence of his listener. As his narrative proceeds, the voice ceases to be the voice of the forty-year-old man who appears in the first paragraphs, and who reappears at the end of the text; it becomes the voice of his younger self, as if he were recounting recent events and fresh emotions. For the greater part of his *récit*, Dominique does not comment knowingly on the aspirations and errors of his younger self, in the manner of so many fictional self-narrators; he recreates the experiences of the past with an intensity that makes the reader feel that they are happening in the present. If there is irony in this text, it is not perceived by Dominique. The trick is the one that Gide plays with equal skill in *L'Immoraliste*: sympathy for the narrator is the reader's first response, and the irony emerges only slowly and on reflection. The *cadre* is however more highly elaborated in *Dominique* than in *L'Immoraliste,* and the listener's sympathetic view of the protagonist is supported by the doctor's admiration, by our glimpses of a calm and contented wife and of two lively, affectionate children, by the devotion of Dominique's servants and by his popularity on his estate and in the village. The listener however proves to be a less than reliable witness. He too has a tendency to invent scenarios (and borrows Dominique's phrase: 'Je me le suis demandé souvent . . .'). Intrigued by hints of a mystery when he observes that Dominique reacts adversely to reminders of the past, he creates in the reader a sense of expectation and the promise of psychological complexities. These complexities, on the whole, fail to emerge from Dominique's own account. What emerges most clearly is the aspect of his character that he stresses at the beginning of Chapter III, his tendency to be dominated by 'sensations': 'il se formait en moi je ne sais quelle mémoire spéciale assez peu sensible aux faits, mais d'une aptitude singulière à se pénétrer des impressions' (p. 400). That is, Dominique's memory preserves not 'la vérité historique' but 'la vérité lyrique'. The listener resembles him in this also: his careful delineation of the lone hunter in an autumn landscape strikes the note of 'lyrical' truth and of 'impressions' from the beginning. The 'something' that most strongly inclines us to believe Dominique's account of his life is Fromentin's ability to make the reader feel those 'sensations' and receive those 'impressions' as sharply and as clearly as Dominique himself does. We do not learn many facts about Dominique; there is a hiatus of about twenty years in his story, at the point where a *Bildungsroman* would begin to be interesting, and almost everything outside the life of the sensations seems unreal. The stilted rhetoric of Dominique's comments on society, on ambition, even on his friends and family, contrasts strongly with the freshness of perception and phrase when he is describing a landscape or a room, and conveying his response to what he sees.

'L'art', wrote Fromentin, 'n'est pas un récit'.[19] The qualities of his novel are the qualities that he most admired in art, and that he analyses in *Les Maîtres d'autrefois:* sobriety, control, economy of means, subtlety of colouring and gradation; all of these are required by the imagination in its transfiguration of the real, but they are not at the service of a *récit.* Fromentin noted with approval that the Dutch masters, unlike those of the French school, did not look for grandiose or impressive subjects. Anything may become the subject of art, for it is not the thing seen that matters, but the quality of the seeing.[20] Thus the truth that Fromentin himself values most is not 'la vérité historique', the accuracy of the *récit,* but 'la vérité lyrique', the truthfulness of the impression.

But there is a danger in lyricism, and it is a danger that Dominique fails to avoid. The dramatist always generalises, says Fromentin; not so the poet:[21]

> Le propre du poète lyrique, au contraire, c'est de n'admettre les sentiments généraux qu'à leur point de contact et d'union avec ses sentiments particuliers. Il arrive à l'extrémité de ce genre que le poète, n'ayant en vue d'autre objet que lui-même, imprime identiquement à ses créations ce caractère distinctif et particulier qui constitue sa propre individualité.

This passage casts an interesting light on the admiring listener's view of Dominique's qualities: 'Une grande concentration d'esprit, une active et intense observation de lui-même, l'instinct de s'élever plus haut, toujours plus haut, et de se dominer en ne se perdant jamais de vue . . .' (p. 389). The truthful impression can only be achieved by subordinating the self and its busy intellect, its vanities and its desires, and concentrating on the specific nature of the thing seen, felt or heard. Fromentin particularly praises in Rubens 'l'inconscience de lui-même', in Dutch painting as a whole a blend of 'sympathie', 'curiosité attentive' and 'patience': 'Désormais le génie consistera à ne rien préjuger, à ne pas savoir qu'on sait, à se laisser surprendre par son modèle, à ne demander qu'à lui comment il veut qu'on le représente'. [22] Dominique has the sensitivity of an artist, but he can never be a great artist, because he is primarily concerned with himself. Moreover he not only has the literary talents of a second-rate poet, as he readily admits (more 'modestie'): he has also acquired the insights of a third-rate novelist. He is furthest from convincing us when he attempts to construct his historical or psychological scenarios (and psychology as he understands it is structured on the model of a narrative account); but we can fully accept the truth of his sensations and impressions, which must, of course, be those of Fromentin himself. It is usual to praise the quality of the 'description' in *Dominique,* and to see it as an expression of Dominique's nature. Certainly Dominique regards nature as an extension of himself, and certainly description here is not a matter of combining superficial pictorial elements. But nor is the *paysage* merely an *état d'âme*: that would be in complete contradiction of Fromentin's aesthetic of self-subordination. The harmony that one may feel in this novel is the harmony of the physical world, and in that harmony Dominique is at once a sensitive observer and a sadly discordant note. What makes the 'taste in the head' of *Dominique* so lingeringly powerful is its unresolved tension between the implied understanding of human beings as small, undignified and weak, and the presence of a world of mysterious beauty and continuing power. Dominique cannot find a way of expressing that tension, because he believes that the beauty of the world exists only for and in and through his own awareness. But in the story of Dominique's failure, Fromentin has given it definitive expression.

Notes

¹ A. Thibaudet, *Intérieurs: Baudelaire-Fromentin-Amiel*, Plon, 1924, p. 149. *Dominique,*
Gallimard ('Génie de la France'), 1933, p. 7. R. Barthes, 'Fromentin: "Dominique"', *in Le
Degré zéro de l'écriture, suivi de Nouveaux essais critiques,* Seuil ('Points'), 1972, p. 156: 'une
œuvre deux fois solitaire'; '*Dominique* est consacré institutionnellement [. . .] comme un
chef-d'œuvre singulier'.
² M. Cressot, 'Le Sens de *Dominique*', *RHLF*, XXXV (avril-juin 1928), pp. 211-18.
J. Hytier, *Les Romans de l'individu: Constant, Sainte-Beuve, Stendhal, Mérimée, Fromentin,*
Les Arts et le Livre, 1928. S. A. Rhodes, 'Sources of Fromentin's *Dominique*', *PMLA* (1930),
3, pp. 939-49. J. Vier, *Pour l'étude du Dominique de Fromentin, Archives des Lettres
Modernes,* 16-17 (octobre-novembre 1958). Vier states that no precise influence of any
19th-century precursor is visible, but then notes a large number of 'similarities'.
³ Hytier, *Les Romans de l'individu,* p. 140: 'une autobiographie détournée'. C. Reynaud,
La Genèse de "Dominique", Grenoble, Arthaud, 1937, p. 18: 'roman partiellement autobio-
graphique'. M. A. Eckstein, *Le Rôle du souvenir dans l'œuvre d'Eugène Fromentin,* Zurich,
Juris, 1970, p. 3: 'puisque nous savons que Dominique est une espèce d'autre lui-même, nous
nous rendons compte dès notre premier contact avec l'œuvre de Fromentin de l'extrême
importance du souvenir'. Barthes, *Degré zero,* p. 156: 'cette autobiographie discrète'.
A. Fraigneau is almost alone in denying that Dominique is a 'remplaçant' for the author
(*Dominique,* Livre de Poche, 1966, Préface, p. 10).
⁴ Fromentin, *Correspondance et fragments inédits,* ed. P. Blanchon, Plon, 1912, pp.
137-142 (letters from George Sand of 18 April and 24 May 1862).
⁵ See for example M. Cressot, loc. cit.: 'un livre de claire raison et de critique morale',
and C. Herzfeld, *'Dominique' de Fromentin: thèmes et structure,* Nizet, 1977, p. 65: 'le
conteur se juge et condamne le romantisme de sa jeunesse'.
⁶ Thibaudet, *Intérieurs,* p. 179: 'Dominique est placé entre Olivier et Augustin comme
entre deux influences, entre deux choix possibles'. A. R. Evans, Jnr, *The Literary Art of
Eugène Fromentin: a Study in Style and Motif,* Baltimore, Johns Hopkins Press, 1964, pp.
24-25: 'Alternative solutions to the conflict are presented [. . .] first by the blasé and irresolute
Olivier, then by Augustin, the young hero's persevering tutor'. M. Lehtonen, *Essai sur
Dominique de Fromentin,* Suomalainen Tiedeakatemia (Annales Academiae Scientiarum
Fennicae), Helsinki, 1972, p. 11: Fromentin presents Olivier and Augustin schematically as
'projections des différentes tendances psychologiques propres au personnage principal'.
⁷ G. Sagnes, 'Les formes du regard dans *Dominique*', *in Colloque Eugène Fromentin,
Travaux et mémoires de la maison Descartes, Amsterdam,* no. 1 (Publications de l'Université
de Lille III), 1979, p. 93.
⁸ *Œuvres complètes,* ed. G. Sagnes, Gallimard (Bibliothèque de la Pléiade), 1984, p. 517.
All references to *Dominique* are to this edition (hereinafter 'O.C.'), and are given in the text
by page number.
⁹ Fromentin refers to 'cette pauvre Mme de Mortsauf' in a letter to Beltrémieux and his
wife (3 September 1847), *Lettres de jeunesse,* ed. P. Blanchon, Plon, 1909, p. 228.
¹⁰ 'Je m'aperçus qu'Amélie perdait le repos et la santé qu'elle commençait à me rendre'
(*René*).
¹¹ Letter to Armand du Mesnil, n.d. (1859; 'antérieure au 15 octobre': see O.C., pp.
1415-16).
¹² Fromentin's decision to acknowledge the echo of George Sand's novel when she pointed
it out to him did not disadvantage him: the reference is made to play the same role as those
that he had already made explicit in the text. He might have pointed out in his turn that she
had not invented the episode either.

[13] Fromentin is not mocking Lamartine. He deplores the selective and therefore un-comprehending admiration lavished on Lamartine's work: 'Il n'est personne qui ne connaisse [. . .] quelques vers du *Lac,* de *Napoléon* ou du *Poète mourant.* Cherchez combien il y en a [. . .] qui parlent de *Byron,* du *Crucifix,* des *Novissima verba'.* He describes the *Méditations poétiques* as 'un meuble indispensable dans une bibliothèque, surtout chez une femme'. See *A quoi servent les petits poètes,* O.C., p. 914.

[14] *Un programme de critique, III,* O.C., p. 1045.

[15] ibid., pp. 1047-48.

[16] Herzfeld, *'Dominique' de Fromentin,* p. 13 ('ce roman qui dit un retour, un enracine-ment'), and p. 15 ('Le retour à la terre natale est un retour à la mère'); Barthes, *Degré zéro,* pp. 158-60.

[17] *Correspondance,* p. 139.

[18] Letter to Du Mesnil, O.C., p. 1416 (see note 11).

[19] *Correspondance,* p. 195. Blanchon links these unpublished notes with *Un programme de critique,* but they bear a close relation to discussion of 'le sujet' in *Les Maîtres d'autrefois.*

[20] *Les Maîtres d'autrefois,* 'Hollande', IV, O.C., p. 669: 'Une chose vous frappe quand on étudie le fond moral de l'art hollandais, c'est l'absence totale de ce que nous appelons aujourd'hui *un sujet';* and pp. 674-75.

[21] *A quoi servent les petits poètes,* O.C., pp. 910-11.

[22] *Les Maîtres d'autrefois,* 'Hollande', II, O.C., pp. 642, 660. In an essay on Drouineau (1842), Fromentin criticises his tendency to 'ramener la nature à l'homme' (see *Sur un "romantique libre" - Eugène Fromentin et Emile Beltrémieux, "Gustave Drouineau",* texte inédit avec une introduction et des notes par Barbara Wright, *Archives des Lettres Modernes,* no. 97, pp. 315-321, 1969 (1), pp. 42-43). Fromentin had had to combat the same tendency in himself: 'Vous voyez, comme moi, comme nous tous, gens écervelés, les choses en vous plutôt qu'en elles-mêmes' (letter to Du Mesnil (10 August 1843), *Lettres de jeunesse,* p. 94).

The art of *Paul et Virginie:*
articulations and ambiguities

Philip Robinson : University of Kent

I N previous comments on the narrative articulations of Bernardin's tale, I have emphasised poetics. [1] The following pages look briefly at narratology. 'Articulation' means either a segment of text identified by some diegetic discreteness and internal coherence or the manner of linking such segments and making them interact. [2] I shall treat such articulations much as an art critic would the brush strokes and composition of a painter in order to show their expressive function and in particular how they contribute to the establishment of some fundamental poetic ambiguities of the text.

The Narrative Voice

The Old Man, principal narrator of *Paul et Virginie,* has two kinds of authority. His narrative 'privilege' approaches omniscience. [3] And his moral judgment, thanks to his near-omniscience, his age and his dignity, is generally presented to us as law. Both kinds of authority depend on keeping in the foreground three of the Old Man's roles: as narrator, commentator and 'chorus'. [4] His fourth role, as participant in the drama of the doomed families, is played down. The clearest evidence for this is in the second half. Paul's interlocutor in the dialogue (pp. 140-53) and the person who utters the prosopopeia of Virginie (pp. 170-71) can only be middle-aged, yet he is explicitly stated to be identical with the Old Man narrator. This is a particularly graphic example of the ambiguity of all first-person narrative (fictional or not), an ambiguity representing a challenge which the artist using the form must always meet in one way or another: the 'I' refers both to a particular kind of narrating voice (the narrating instance) and to a subject (identifiable with that narrating voice) whose past experiences, deeds or opinions the voice may describe.

The *je* of the Old Man remains for the most part firmly anchored in the narrating instance. The weight of his narrative privilege and moral authority bounces us through the one section of the story which is the exception to the rule, and where he becomes a significant subject of his own narrative, sharing the families' moral doubts and dilemmas; I refer to the events surrounding the adolescents' separation. We accept the narrator-figure's uncertainty in the turmoil of contrary opinions, and we do so because it is attributed to the person he once was and not to the authoritative voice which he is now. He was initially in favour of Paul's departure for India only to be set to rights by the young man himself (pp. 117-18). He opposed the departure of Virginie, only to have events move against him (p. 122). He was wrong, after their emotional moonlight scene, in telling Paul that his sister would not leave (p. 127). By the use of a past tense here I have emphasised a difference between the narrating instance and the *je* subject which the text itself is careful to obscure in the interest of flexible movement between the two. If this blurring of the distinction did not obtain, for example, we might notice that even his moral authority as commentator is called momentarily into question when his poor opinion (as narrator) of Mme de la Tour's motives (p. 122) is belied by her statement, believed by him as subject, that 'Ce malheureux voyage n'aura pas lieu' (p. 127).[5]

The ambiguity of the narratorial *je* is thus artfully masked by the entirely plausible turmoil of plot: it is convincing psychologically that families should react emotionally and with insecure judgment to the devastating threat of disruption. However the ambiguities surrounding the narrator at this point are merely part of a deep-seated and fundamental moral ambiguity: Virginie's departure is both right and wrong. It is right to separate the children for fear of harmfully precocious sexual relations: it is wrong to separate them, since they are meant for each other and since greed and ambition are wicked. And it is correct here to speak of ambiguity rather than ambivalence. As we read, we evaluate the adolescents' separation unequivocally as a disaster. But the critical search for its meaning faces us with two equally plausible, but incompatible, descriptions of events. It is right to protect the children against their own developing sexuality by parting them (pp. 117-18). Their separation also appears as the lamentable result of corrupt European influences. The ambiguity in the presentation of Virginie's departure is nothing less than the ambiguity of Nature itself, particularly as mirrored in sexuality.[6]

Now, to the philosopher ambiguity represents a threat of error; to the poet, if Empson is to be believed, a source of riches.[7] The philosopher tries to avoid being deceived by the mere word or expression into accepting a false logical step. The poet exploits alternative levels of language beyond mere labelling. Novels, I believe, require to be approached from the poet's standpoint and not the philosopher's. Indeed we find a novelist's philosophy by interpreting his work as a poem, not by treating his discourse as philosophical. The point is not infrequently overlooked by critics. Leading eighteenth-century French thinkers characteristically choose fictional forms as a 'vehicle' of social and ethical ideas. The prosaic critic is comfortable with the prevalent satirical forms in the genre: social history discloses the objects of satirical attack; literary history explains the context of literary conventions which ensure that the attacks strike home; and at the end of the interpretative process, the characteristics of an author's 'views' emerge satisfactorily. The poet has become a social commentator, or was one all along.

The writer who makes myth finds less sympathy. Myths by their very nature involve ambiguity, which the prosaic critic has a facile delight in interpreting as contradiction. *Paul et Virginie* is such a case.[8] It is as if the Adam and Eve story were to be ridiculed for presenting knowledge as both God-like and wicked, sexuality as both necessary and guilt-ridden and evil as both inevitable and avoidable. If we forget that the meaning (and truth) of myth is in its affective hold over our imagination, we can easily believe that dismantling Bernardin's story is the same thing as interpreting it. We demand of the poet, quite legitimately, that his ambiguities do not become transparent contradictions requiring our attention as we read. But it is inconsistent to tax him with ambiguities which we have not noticed while reading.

In what follows I deal with passages which, lacking in incident and events, are generally the least appreciated in the tale: the 'idyll' of the first half and the dialogue of the second, each with their adjacent passages. I believe them to be structurally central, and my remarks are intended to help present the structure not as a static shape but as a dynamism in which meaning depends on interaction between one articulation and another.

'Mais' and 'Cependant'

One of the chief ambiguities of the first half of the novel concerns the relationship between the treatment of themes and the treatment of time.

Specifically, the innocent side of adolescence, adolescent love and Nature is presented separately from, and in advance of, the appearance of sexuality and the disruptive aspects of Nature. The succession in narrating conveys the impression of a temporal succession, but at the same time the text explicitly says that the two conflicting aspects of Nature manifest themselves simultaneously.

Bernardin's style, particularly in the first half, has a peculiarity which neatly symbolises this ambiguity. No fewer than fourteen paragraphs of the text, out of some 150 which involve the Old Man speaking as narrator, begin either with *mais* or *cependant*. In itself this is an amusing feature, especially to those of us brought up never to imitate it. Yet it is also, I believe, significant, since the only other initial words of paragraphs (still counting only the Old Man speaking as narrator) which reach, or approach, this level of frequency, fall into unsurprising categories: pronouns (34 times); names or titles (21 times); the definite article (13 times); and the preposition *à* (11 times). But *mais* and *cependant* do stand out, especially considering that ten of the fourteen cases are concentrated between the start of the idyll (p. 99) and the beginning of the second half (p. 128 inclusive), that is, in about one third of the novel. Moreover it is precisely this one third which establishes the ambiguity just mentioned. Nature in its entirety is characterised by these *mais* and *cependant*. It is, for Bernardin, an ordered system of balancing contrasts, a harmony of contradictions. *Cependant,* we shall see, also quite specifically combines the notions of thematic opposition and simultaneity.

First we need to consider the five *mais* and nine *cependant* in relation to articulations of narrative. Half of them mark boundaries between articulations, constituting the hinges, so to speak, which join them together. This is a significantly high proportion. And even of the remainder some are important rhetorically in other ways. *Mais* only once acts as a hinge between articulations, but that one is the most important of all, joining the second half of the text to the first (p. 128). The second half contrasts with the first entirely in terms of the logic of *mais*: Virginie was present, but now she is absent; the adolescents were at one with Nature and with their families, but now they are separated (Virginie is in Europe and Paul more often at the Old Man's habitation than at home); literacy and philosophy were previously redundant, but now they are essential; and so forth.[9] *Mais,* then, is the logical as well as literal hinge of the text at its halfway point. The conjunction also serves twice to mark the culminating development of a major articulation, with a logic of addition rather than of opposition. It introduces the description of the Repos de

Virginie, the *pièce de résistance* of Paul's landscaping (p. 104), and the description of the mothers' name-days, the highlight of idyllic family life (p. 110). The remaining two initial *mais* (pp. 103 and 107) hold no special position in an articulation, but they do help make this feature of Bernardin's style noticeable.

He conspicuously does not vary these two terms of *mais* and *cependant* with equivalents such as *néanmoins, pourtant, par contre,* etc., in the initial position. This choice is artistically right (I do not say consciously made) because such repetition is part of the Old Man's incantatory elegiac voice as narrator, and because it causes the pattern of contrasting articulations to be more strongly felt (I do not say consciously noticed as we read). Their concentration in our designated one third of the novel undoubtedly helps the effect. The first two cases of initial *cependant,* for example, are both major hinges between articulations. The first represents the junction between the two contrasting halves of the 'microcosm' (p. 90), and the second the junction between the idyll (pp. 99-113) and the preparation of the youngsters' separation (pp. 113-28). Both oppose the threat of developing sexuality to the innocence of adolescent love. Both are in that sense the equivalent of *mais.* Yet they each share with most of the other seven cases of the word its alternative meaning of 'meanwhile'.[10] Initial *mais* and *cependant* thus create a kind of ambiguity in themselves: they are not exact equivalents, since *cependant* also conveys the temporal notion of simultaneity and contains, both semantically and by its strategic positions, the principal ambiguity of the first half of the text.

Inflections of time

We realise how thorough-going this principal ambiguity is if we follow it through the text's artful inflections of time.[11] One of the most subtle concerns narrative frequency in the first half, that is, the relation between the repetition (or not) of narrated events and the repetition (or not) of their narrating. It is incontrovertibly true, and generally unnoticed by first-time readers, that the first-half plot is set forth twice, first in the shortened form which I have called the 'microcosm', and then again in a more extended set of articulations (pp. 99-124). I use the word 'plot' in Forster's specific sense of elements indicating causation and motivation, as distinct from the mere events themselves (story).[12] From the plot point of view there is very little in the longer section of narrative which is not already in the 'microcosm' which foreshadows it: innocent adolescent love and the forces which threaten its destruction – sexuality causing Mme de la Tour's concern (p. 90); the great-aunt and her riches and attitudes representative of European corruption; the personal power of La Bourdonnais as governor (pp. 91-92). Practically the only element of plot not already outlined in the 'microcosm' is the influence of Mme de la Tour's confessor (p. 122). This double exposition of plot contributes in a major way to establish a temporal ambiguity. On the one hand, we feel that time moves forward, that segments of narrative which appear later describe events which occur later. On the other hand, because the basic pattern of causation does not change, we feel that time is suspended, or even cancelled: we are made to enter a world of fixed habits in which time has little meaning. The reader experiences what the narrator explicitly states at the end of the idyll: '[Paul et Virginie] ne connaissaient d'autres époques historiques que celle de la vie de leurs mères, d'autre chronologie que celle de leurs vergers...' (p. 111).

Only this once does Bernardin inflect time in the narrative by a repetition of narrating, telling twice a first-half plot which can only occur once.[13] But throughout the articulations which concern us there is a more general manipulation of narrative frequency by cunning juxtapositions of the iterative and the singulative. These can only be appreciated in terms of the text's handling of chronology. In the whole tale there is only one precise date: that of the shipwreck, 24 December 1744.[14] This event is, of course, the imaginative centre of the story, the one which determines the genre.[15] For the rest Bernardin combines an impression of precision in his calendar with a deliberate vagueness over any essential detail which would allow us to pin down the chronology too exactly or encourage us to think of it in too exact terms. Thus we are told that Virginie's father dies shortly after mid-October 1726 (p. 83), but we never learn the children's exact dates of birth. Only painstaking analysis, and some speculation, allow us to conclude that Virginie is probably born in December 1726, that she takes her midnight bathe in December 1738 (p. 114), and probably leaves for France immediately the cyclone season is over, in April 1739. We draw inferences from odd references to months of the year, from occasional specific mentions of the children's ages, and from seasonal phenomena such as the fruiting of mangoes (p. 111).[16]

The lack of a precisely-detailed chronology is not a weakness of the narrative, it is evidence of its particular nature and of Bernardin's deliberate (though not necessarily calculated) art.[17] The iterative is the dominant temporal mode in the parallel central sections of each half, and singulatives are generally subordinate. The iterative imperfect in particular is far more common than the descriptive one, found only in isolated cases like the children's portraits (p. 90). As often as not the iterative quality of the many imperfect tenses is left implicit and not brought prominently to the reader's attention. An excellent example is the celebration of the mothers' name-days (p. 110). Characteristically, we are not given dates and, since we do not know Mme de la Tour's first name, it is impossible to infer one of them: 'Mais il y avait dans l'année des jours qui étaient pour Paul et Virginie des jours de plus grandes réjouissances; c'étaient les fêtes de leurs mères.' When we read 'dans l'année' we understand 'every year', that is, an iterative sense: the celebrations are a long-standing habit. But when we reflect that the adolescent idyll covers at most the calendar year 1738, we realise that only a singulative is logically consistent with the children's portraits: the mothers have only one name-day each. The iterative, impossibly, seems to 'stretch' adolescence back indefinitely into the past.

Descriptive imperfects, as opposed to iterative ones, are so rare in the text that the one extensive picture of wild nature surrounding the Old Man's homestead is, for example, not in the imperfect at all, but in the present tense, drawing the reader into the narrating instance and thus more effectively into the prevailing elegiac emotion (pp. 136-40). The dominant imperfects of the novel are therefore to be distinguished from descriptive pause; they represent a true narrative of habitual actions whereby we become progressively familiar with more and more aspects of the youngsters' affections and their oneness with, or (in the second half) separation from, Nature.[18] Nearly all the singulatives in the novel, apart from those of the exposition (pp. 82-87) and those of the denouement (pp. 153-75), represent striking instances of everyday habit. Thus the famous picture of the two children sheltering from the rain under Virginie's dress is an instance of their inseparability (pp. 88-89). Even a long episode such as the Rivière Noire adventure is an instance of their developing 'bon naturel' (p. 92). Described in another sort of singulative, the great-aunt's first letter and its consequences are the upshot of a series of letters sent to France from the moment of Virginie's birth by Mme de la Tour concerned for her daughter's future (pp. 90-91). Similarly the singulatives leading to the youngsters' separation emerge initially (p. 117) as instances of what might be done in response to a recurrent concern about Virginie's approaching sexual maturity. Paul's landscaping is a retrospect, in the (singulative?) pluperfect, from the iterative imperfect of the idyll (p. 100).

Even in the very different atmosphere of the second half, which examines the reactions of Paul's love to the experience of separation, the narrative, after an account of his immediate responses to Virginie's

departure, and to her letter which arrives after one and a half years, reverts
to the iterative imperfect in order to present his dialogue with the Old
Man. The dialogue is an instance of the many occasions on which the
young man visits the families' neighbour at his homestead beyond the
Montagne Longue (pp. 136 and 140). We thus have the temporal ambiguity of a dialogue, presented in the singulative as the event of one
morning or afternoon, which is actually felt as a picture of Paul's habitual
reading and philosophising during his beloved's absence.

Frequency, however, is not the only sphere in which the reader's sense
of time is manipulated. The ambiguity of *cependant,* already mentioned,
leads us directly to a major point about relationships of order in the
narrative. In both the 'microcosm' of the first half and the corresponding
larger pair of articulations, there is succession in the telling of two
important sets of realities, but simultaneity in their occurrence. In the
'microcosm', the revelation of the existence of the great-aunt comes after
Mme de la Tour's concerns about Virginie's growing up (p. 90). It is
suggested, but not explicitly stated, that this is a reason for turning to her
relative in France, a narratological version of the classic *post hoc ergo
propter hoc.* However, it is also disclosed that she has been writing to her
aunt ever since Virginie's birth, with no response. This repeated writing
must thus be simultaneous with the youngsters' idyllic youth (pp. 87-89).
Its description separately from, and following, that idyllic picture, gives
the impression that European influences briefly intrude to threaten the
idyll from outside. The aunt's eventual reply and its consequences fill two
pages, while the reference to Mme de la Tour's writing is told in a short
paragraph. This presentation plays down the fact that the seeds of
disruption are within, and unavoidable. Narrating order does not conform
to the order of events, and the disparity in this case prompts us to infer
temporal succession from what is actually the outline of two contrasting,
but temporally simultaneous, motifs.

A similar relationship of order is used, on a grander scale, to influence
our view of Virginie's sexual development. This theme, briefly evoked in
the 'microcosm', is reintroduced on p. 113: 'Cependant depuis quelque
temps Virginie se sentait agitée d'un mal inconnu.' By this stage in the
narrative the idyll is complete, including the culminating 'duet' between
the lovers. They have fallen in love and expressed that love in numerous
ways, all in an atmosphere of the utmost innocence and the closest
communion with Nature. The reader has appreciated their love and
innocence in a world of indeterminate and suspended time. Now it is
revealed (in iterative form) that Virginie has 'for some time' been disturbed

by her sexual symptoms. We realise, after critical reflexion (which comes only once the reading experience is over), that this 'for some time' must largely overlap with all the events described from the Rivière Noire adventure onwards, a period of around a year at most. The two contradictory (and simultaneous) aspects of sexual growth are thus presented as if they were successive. It is the thematic opposition, and not chronological order, which determines the narrating order. We are explicitly told that the two sequences of events are practically simultaneous, but our impression as we read is that they are in succession, because their narration is in succession. The order of narrating therefore performs an important expressive function, in that it permits the idyll to exist at all: negative aspects are isolated and gathered together to be narrated immediately before the final decisive intrusion of the surrounding world. The establishment of this version of the myth of natural innocence depends on a contradiction, by the narrating order, of what the text, considered analytically, actually states. It depends on a strong form of ambiguity.

Disparities between the order of events and the order of narrating do more than sustain the illusion that thematically contrasting material is also temporally in succession: they contribute in their own way to the impression that time has been suspended. The narrative retraces its steps, while the point of temporal focus, provided by the portraits of Virginie and Paul in the first half, remains constantly the same (p. 90). They are aged twelve and thirteen years respectively, and these are still their ages at their ultimate separation at the end of the first half (cf. p. 111). The chronology therefore does not progress between p. 90 and p. 128, it is only made to seem to progress. The arrival of the great-aunt's first letter (p. 91), which in the narrating order is after the double portrait, happens when Virginie is eleven years old, that is, earlier. We have seen already how the account of Virginie's sexual maturation (pp. 113-16) is a retracing of practically the identical time occupied by the idyll, and indeed a reversion to Mme de la Tour's maternal concerns as sketched on p. 90.

The idyll itself is a retracing of steps. After the crisis of the great-aunt's first letter (when Virginie is eleven), the narrative reverts, for one sentence, to a general iterative imperfect, the precise reference of which is not specified. It then proceeds with the Rivière Noire adventure, after which that same imperfect returns to describe the families' happy life (pp. 99-100) and begin the idyll. It quickly changes, however, to a pluperfect, continued into Paul's landscaping (pp. 100-02). Since Paul is twelve when he gardens, this pluperfect retraces steps not merely in terms of the immediately preceding imperfects, but also in relation to the lad's portrait at 13 (p. 90). The description of the two coconut trees over the Repos de Virginie is the most thorough retracing of steps of all, since it projects us back again to the times of their planting in commemoration of the children's births.

In the second half of the novel, by contrast with the first, diegetic order and narrating order are essentially the same. It is a difference which more than any other brings out the contrast between two experiences of time. Whereas time hardly exists for the children on their island, it weighs heavily upon them (and on the reader through Paul) once they are separated. The difference provides the context for a few remarks concerning inflections of duration.

The idyll is seemingly durable. By inflections of order and frequency it is 'spread' back into the past or made to appear as a picture of unremitting habit in an atmosphere where time has little significance, where time is suspended. The sense that the suspended time is also durable time is created chiefly by the amount of text which the idyll occupies relative to the whole. Taken together with the Rivière Noire adventure, which it incorporates diegetically and to which it is juxtaposed, it represents nearly one quarter of the entire novel. There is a kind of temporal ambiguity here in which time is on the one hand 'cancelled' and on the other hand made to feel full and extensive. The details of family life and blissful adolescence occupying the calendar year 1738 are felt as a permanent form of existence and the normal condition of Nature. Largely by the volume of text, the fleeting moment is made to seem without end.

The major articulation which balances the idyll in the second half, namely the dialogue, is a more clear-cut, and artistically less subtle, case of the use of narrating duration to generate a feeling of diegetic duration. The dialogue is actually introduced in the Past Historic tense as a singulative event. In strict diegetic terms it could take only as long as the words require for utterance: something less than a day, indeed probably less than a morning or afternoon. And yet it 'represents' by its duration of narrating (together with the description of wild nature around the Old Man's homestead (pp. 136-40)) a period of some four years, between the receipt (after eighteen months or more) of Virginie's letter from France and her reappearance on the doomed ship, the *Saint-Géran*. Details of story occurring between these events are given only the most cursory mention: Paul's reply to her and the unsuccessful planting of seeds (p. 135); six months during which ships arrive with no news of her (p. 136); Paul's habitual visits to the Old Man's homestead (p. 140); and finally Paul's resumptions of the tilling of the land, presented iteratively in the imperfect

(p. 153). All the rest of the intervening 20 pages of text is description or dialogue. But the presence of this body of material means that the narrative speed of these four years is anything but an ellipsis, that is, an exclusion of some story time from the narrating. On the contrary, they feel far longer than the idyll and with a completely different quality of time. Nearly all readers experience the dialogue as boring, but not many realise that this experience is very nearly aesthetically right. It is entirely appropriate that Virginie's absence should weigh heavily and the philosophising is only necessary at all because the world of innocence has been lost and because the principal characters now know what time is.[19]

The object of the foregoing remarks has been to add further to an aesthetic apologia for some of the least appreciated parts of Bernardin's famous novel. The dimensions of voice, frequency, order, and duration in narrating, as far as these pivotal articulations are concerned, establish and sustain a nexus of ambiguities which is at the heart of the text's affective and mythic power. These ambiguities are poetic in that, for as long as the tale grips our imagination, we accept their contrary propositions as legitimate descriptions of a single fictional universe; we accept them, that is, as cumulative rather than contradictory. Adolescent innocence is no less convincing than its disruption by the guilts of sexuality. Death is at once outrageous and acceptable, and so forth. There is clearly scope for more detailed classification of the ambiguities than I have had space for, but I have largely pointed to Empson's seventh type, that is, to ambiguity at the extreme of logical incoherence. I have not discussed at all (and the subject is treated quite cursorily by Empson)[20] the degree to which our apprehension of the ambiguities is conscious, the important question raised by distinctions between reading experience and critical reflexion. I have also not striven to prove the work's complex psychological effects; I have, in such phrases as 'affective and mythic power', assumed them as the context for critical description. I believe that the demonstration of Bernardin's intelligence as a craftsman, an intelligence sometimes contested, is an essential first step to carry the recalcitrant modern reader past his ethical and ideological prejudices and into lasting enjoyment of the tale.

Notes

[1] See P. Robinson, *Bernardin de Saint-Pierre: Paul et Virginie* (London, 1986), whose fifth chapter, using a musical analogy, attributes a lyric function to the text's structure. References to *Paul et Virginie* are to the edition presented by R. Mauzi (Paris, Garnier-Flammarion, 1966).

[2] The term 'articulation' is used in this sense by G. Genette, *Figures III, Discours du récit* (Paris, 1972), p. 124. My discussion is throughout underpinned by other concepts from this basic narratological study. Marie-Thérèse Veyrenc, *Edition critique du manuscrit de Paul et Virginie de Bernardin de Saint-Pierre intitulée Histoire de Melle Virginie de la Tour* (Paris, 1975), reveals that an important part of Bernardin's creative activity is the arrangement and placing of already existing segments or articulations of text (pp. 34-45).

[3] The term 'privilege' is employed for this purpose by Wayne C. Booth, *The Rhetoric of Fiction* (University of Chicago Press, 1961), p. 160. For a specific discussion of the Old Man's near-omniscience, see Vivienne G. Mylne, *The Eighteenth-Century French Novel, Techniques of Illusion,* second edition (Cambridge University Press, 1981), pp. 246-49. The Old Man's 'privilege' means that we accept that he may tell us, on authority, things which 'realistically' he cannot possibly know, for example, Virginie's midnight bathe (p. 114) or Mme de la Tour's conversation with La Bourdonnais (p. 120). It is hard to take seriously those critics who have treated this 'privilege' as a flaw.

[4] The late Jean Fabre, in a historic study, 'Paul et Virginie, pastorale', in his *Lumières et Romantisme* (Paris, 1963), pp. 167-99, identifies this three-fold role of the Old Man narrator (p. 230). The term 'chorus' translates his more felicitous expression: *coryphée,* which justly points to the lyric quality of Bernardin's text.

[5] In Genette's terms, the Old Man narrator is in this part of the text both 'homodiegetic' and 'heterodiegetic', both inside and outside his own story, with different views according to each of these positions (op. cit., p. 252).

[6] See F. Flahaut, *'Paul et Virginie* lu comme un mythe', *Revue philosophique* (1968), pp. 361-79, and in particular pp. 376-77 with diagram. The only reservation to make is that education has precisely not, according to the text, made any contribution to Virginie's refusal to disrobe on the doomed ship: cf. P. Robinson, op. cit., p. 56.

[7] W. Empson, *Seven Types of Ambiguity* (London, 1930), esp. chap. 1. It is particularly apt to cite a critic who deals chiefly with verse literature, since Bernardin deserves parallel treatment with the lyric poet.

[8] Valuable studies of *Paul et Virginie* as myth include Flahaut (see note 6) and J. Dunkley, *'Paul et Virginie:* aesthetic appeal and archetypal structures', *Trivium,* 13 (1978), pp. 95-112 (see p. 106). G. Michaut, *Bernardin de Saint-Pierre: Paul et Virginie,* Cours de Sorbonne (Paris, 1941), cited by H. Hudde, *Bernardin de Saint-Pierre: Paul et Virginie. Studien zum Roman und seiner Wirkung* (Munich, 1975), p. 27, note 30, is an extreme example of prosaic criticism, commenting thus on the children's freedom from intemperance (p. 112): 'On peut être intempérant en se gorgeant de mets très simples' (p. 39).

[9] H. Hudde, op. cit., pp. 24-25, citing D. Tahhan-Bittar, 'Bernardin de Saint-Pierre romancier', *doctorat d'état* thesis (Paris, 1970), shows just how all-pervasive the thematic contrasts are.

[10] While nowadays the word is principally an expression of opposition or restriction, the *Dictionnaire de Trévoux* (1752) makes clear the possibilities open to Bernardin: 'CEPEN-DANT, adv. de temps.... *Cependant* a deux significations, 1° Il veut dire, *Pendant ce temps-là, Interea.* 2° Il signifie *pourtant, tamen, nihilominus.'* The article in the *Trésor de la langue française* (Paris, 1977), cites examples from the early nineteenth century in the temporal meaning.

[11] The temporal framework of the novel has been set out by D. Tahhan-Bittar (see note 9), p. 408, cited by H. Hudde, op. cit., pp. 23-24. I hope to show that Hudde is unnecessarily dismissive of Tahhan-Bittar's descriptive commentary: 'Es überrascht weiterhin nicht besonders, dass die Darstellung der Kindheit Raffungen, Zeitsprünge and Rückgriffe aufweist' (p. 24).

[12] E. M. Forster, *Aspects of the Novel* (London, 1927).

[13] The wholesale repetition of structure in the second half is, of course, of a different order both from this twofold narrating of plot and from the multifarious thematic contrasts (see note 9).

[14] This is not the historical date of the *Saint-Géran* disaster (17 August 1744). Bernardin ignores historical fact here in order to establish correspondences between the summer solstice and crucial dramatic moments of his narrative such as Virginie's midnight bathe and the shipwreck (cf. Hudde, op. cit., p. 29). Nowhere in the text, for example, is there any allusion to the fact that few ships in the early eighteenth century ventured at all into the southern Indian Ocean in the cyclone season (December to April). See J.-M. Filliot, *La Traite des esclaves vers les Mascareignes au XVIIIe siècle* (Paris, 1974), pp. 86-94.

[15] Veyrenc, op. cit., p. 50, notes that the event was even more dominant in the earliest complete draft than in the definitive published version.

[16] Bernardin tells us in the *Voyage à l'île de France* (Paris, 1983), p. 133, that mangoes fruit in the cyclone season, and the *Oxford English Dictionary,* article MANGO, with a sixteenth-century quotation, refers more specifically to Lent, hence March.

[17] For example he suppresses the dating of La Bourdonnais's visit to the families (p. 119) as 10 November 1747, equivalent to 10 November 1738, in the definitive chronology (see Veyrenc, op. cit., p. 267). Such a date would suggest too clearly that the visit is before Virginie's midnight bathe, which precedes it in the narrative. Compare, later in this section, my remarks on order.

[18] Flahaut is for this reason misguided in suggesting that *Paul et Virginie* should not be read as a novel (op. cit., p. 361). The genre, even before the twentieth century, embraces far more types than such a view would imply. Cf. P. Robinson, op. cit., p. 24 sqq.

[19] It is the socio-critical, or satirical, aspects of the dialogue, principally, which make it hard to take. Something like the dialogue is necessary structurally, but Bernardin indulges a tendency to preach which is inessential to the human situation portrayed and inimical to the prevailing elegiac emotion of the novel as a whole.

[20] Empson, op. cit., p. 62 and pp. 301-25.

Les figures de *Manon Lescaut* en 1753

Jean Sgard : University of Grenoble

P E R S O N N E ne doute qu'en 1753, Prévost n'ait voulu donner à l'*Histoire du chevalier des Grieux et de Manon Lescaut* un lustre tout particulier. Détaché des *Mémoires et aventures d'un homme de qualité,* le 'petit ouvrage', purgé des 'fautes grossières qui le défiguraient', réapparaît sous la forme de deux élégants volumes de 303 et 252 pages, parfaitement composées, tirées sur papier bleuté. On sait que le texte, corrigé en plus de 860 endroits, est en outre augmenté de l'épisode du Prince italien. L'édition, donnée sous adresse d'Amsterdam, mais certainement réalisée par François Didot, s'adresse visiblement à des amateurs fortunés. Le libraire écrit dans le *Mercure de France* en mai 1753:

> L'auteur de *Manon Lescaut,* ouvrage si original, si bien écrit et si intéressant, sollicité depuis longtemps de donner une édition correcte de ce roman, s'est déterminé à ne rien épargner pour la rendre telle qu'on la désire: papier, caractères, figures, tout y est digne de l'attention du public. Elle a paru dans le courant d'avril avec des additions considérables. On en a tiré peu d'exemplaires afin que la beauté des figures et des caractères ne reçût aucune diminution. Ce livre se vend chez Didot, Quai des Augustins, à la Bible d'Or.

Prévost lui-même précisait dans le 'Nota' liminaire: 'Les vignettes et les figures portent en elles-mêmes leur recommandation et leur éloge'. Ce sont ces figures que je me propose d'étudier: comment ont-elles été choisies? dans quel style ont-elles été conçues? Vingt ans après avoir donné ce qui est resté son chef d'œuvre, Prévost l'a relu; il le modernise et l'adapte aux goûts, aux exigences d'un nouveau public; il en propose une nouvelle lecture. Or les figures nous suggèrent elles-mêmes un parcours de lecture, sur lequel il vaut la peine de s'interroger.

Le choix

Le commentaire illustratif de *Manon Lescaut* se présente en 1753 sous la forme d'une séquence de huit 'figures':

I) 1ère Partie, p. 29 [la rencontre d'Amiens] par J. J. Pasquier
II)   p. 97 [la scène de Saint-Sulpice] par Gravelot, gravée par Le Bas
III)   p. 186 [la comédie chez le vieux G.M.] par Gravelot, gravée par Le Bas
IV)   p. 262 [la rencontre à l'Hôpital-Général] par Pasquier
V) 2ème Partie, p. 20 [la scène du Prince italien] par Pasquier
VI)   p. 115 [l'arrestation chez G.M.] par Pasquier
VII)   p. 183 [sur la route de Passy] par Pasquier
VIII)   p. 241 [la mort de Manon] par Pasquier

Deux des figures sont dessinées par Hubert-François Gravelot (1699-1773) et gravées par Jacques-Philippe Le Bas (1707-1783); les autres sont dessinées et gravées ('inv. et sc.') par Jacques-Jean Pasquier (1718-1785). Soit donc huit figures, quatre pour chaque partie, mais inégalement réparties: rien ne vient illustrer l'épisode de la rue V . . . , le séjour à Chaillot, l'épisode de l'Hôtel de Transylvanie, la liaison avec le jeune G.M. ou le séjour au Nouvel Orléans. Quelques grandes scènes ont été retenues, comme si l'on s'acheminait vers une vision théâtrale de l'œuvre. Dans chacune de ces scènes, les amants sont au premier plan, et leur histoire se déroule en une courbe d'une belle simplicité. La scène de Passy, que l'on attendait au début, disparaît au profit d'une scène pénultième qui annonce la catastrophe: la belle passion et la terrible punition s'opposent terme à terme, avec un infléchissement certain vers le pathétique.

Une seconde observation s'impose d'emblée: le rapport entre l'image et le texte a été voulu et souligné: chaque gravure porte en haut et à droite l'indication de la page qu'elle illustre. On peut constater dans l'exemplaire de la Bibliothèque Nationale (Rés. Y²3274-3275) que ces indications ont été suivies à la lettre: chaque figure commente la page de vis-à-vis; la gravure a été placée tantôt à droite, tantôt à gauche pour faciliter le parallélisme. S'agissant de pages courtes et très aérées (20 lignes par page, correspondant à 11 lignes dans l'édition des Classiques Garnier), cette mise en rapport dut exiger beaucoup de soins. Peut-être les artistes ont-ils disposé d'un exemplaire de base, comme l'édition de 1742, qui leur permettait de savoir, de manière sensiblement comparable, ce que contenait la page à illustrer; mais dans le tome II figurait l'épisode nouveau du Prince italien, décrit avec précision dans la figure correspondante: Pasquier a-t-il disposé du manuscrit, ou travaillé d'après un texte déjà composé? Cette dernière hypothèse expliquerait le caractère un peu hâtif des illustrations, et le recours à trois artistes différents. On ne possède malheureusement aucune trace d'un contrat éventuel entre Didot et ses graveurs: le Minutier Central des notaires parisiens ne mentionne pas leurs noms, qui sont absents du dépouillement systématique effectué pour l'année 1752. Si l'on observe de près les illustrations, on constatera simplement qu'elles commentent la page entière, et qu'elles supposent une parfaite connaissance du roman.

I) *La rencontre d'Amiens* (éd. de 1753, t. I, p. 29; éd. des Classiques Garnier, p. 21): la page commentée va de 'Son vieil Argus étant venu nous rejoindre . . .' à 'je lui proposai de se loger . . .' Manon a usé d'un petit subterfuge en nommant le chevalier son 'cousin'; celui-ci entre dans le sens de la ruse et lui propose de se loger dans une hôtellerie, que visiblement il montre de la main. On est tenté de croire que le 'vieil Argus', qui, un instant plus tôt 's'empressait pour faire tirer son équipage des paniers', est maintenant le vieil homme à gauche, qui apporte à Manon ses bagages. Dans ce cas, le personnage de droite, vu de profil arrière, assez jeune et élégant, en perruque à catogan, mais en habit foncé et sans épée, représente Tiberge, dont on nous dira un peu plus tard qu'il ne comprend rien à la scène et suit son ami 'sans prononcer une parole'. Cette figure, tout en reposant sur une réplique ('je lui proposai de se loger'), regroupe en fait toutes sortes d'informations sur le cours du récit. C'est une figure d'exposition: la cour de l'hôtellerie, les équipages qu'on tire des paniers de la voiture, le vieil Argus qui s'approche en maugréant, Manon qui s'évente délicatement dans la chaleur de juillet, Des Grieux qui s'enhardit, qui d'un pas en avant sépare Manon de Tiberge et engage un mouvement dans une autre direction, tout suggère l'importance de l'instant, du tournant qui se dessine. Pasquier n'a pas cédé à la tentation du théâtre; il représente une transition, une modification. La scène n'est pas anecdotique ni réaliste, malgré les arrière-plans rustiques à la manière de Boucher; elle esquisse de façon poétique un suspens, un je-ne-sais-quoi qui se décide à travers deux pas de danse et une auréole de lumière.

II) *La scène de Saint-Sulpice* (éd. de 1753, t. I, p. 97; éd. Deloffre, p. 44): la page à illustrer comporte quatre répliques et un moment d'intense émotion, marqué par des larmes. Gravelot semble d'abord isoler la phrase introductive: 'Elle s'assit. Je demeurai debout, le corps à demi tourné, n'osant l'envisager directement'. Comme Pasquier dans la scène précédente il a donc focalisé sur un instant de suspens et de transition: le jeune abbé pivote sur le pied gauche, une main tendue vers les calmes couloirs du séminaire, qu'on aperçoit par la porte entrebaillée; le regard, lui, est tourné vers les yeux de Manon, un peu plombés (rougis de larmes?). Manon va parler; comme souvent chez Gravelot, toute l'action est dans les mains, mains de Manon qui plaident, s'entrouvrent, et mains du chevalier qui ne savent où se poser. Rien ou presque rien n'est dit du lieu, aussi impersonnel qu'une antichambre de tragédie classique; toute la description porte sur le contraste entre la soutane de soutenance de l'abbé, riche, soyeuse, sombre et mobile, et le luxe provoquant de la robe et des bijoux de Manon; tout ceci dessiné un peu vite, sans ornements, mais tendu, mouvementé, inquiet. Le graveur a parfaitement réparti les valeurs; une grande diagonale soulignée par l'arrivée de la lumière suffit à dramatiser la scène, à opposer un territoire du sacré et un territoire du profane. Du corps 'à demi tourné' du chevalier, Gravelot a saisi toute la signification.

III) *La comédie chez le vieux G.M.* (éd. de 1753, t. I, p. 187; éd. Deloffre, p. 77): ici encore, le commentaire illustré repose en premier lieu sur une réplique, la première qui apparaisse en haut de la page 187: 'Je lui trouve l'air de Manon, reprit le vieillard en me haussant le menton avec la main'. Mais une fois encore, toute la scène de comédie est suggérée, et d'abord par le jeu des mains: main protectrice de G.M. sur l'épaule de Manon, et main badine sous le menton de Des Grieux, mains timides que Manon avance vers son amant, mains appliquées du chevalier, bien posées comme il faut sur le bord du chapeau, et main démonstrative de Lescaut, l'impresario, le metteur en scène de la comédie. L'expression des visages est elle-même rendue avec un souci de psychologie qu'on ne retrouvera guère par la suite: niaiserie affectée du chevalier, suffisance un peu attendrie de G.M., 'morbidezza' de Manon. Pour une fois, le décor de la scène est richement gravé et suggère tout le déroulement de la scène: entrée à droite et présentation du chevalier devant les paravents, vaisselier luxueux d'où un serviteur impalpable sort le plat qui ornera la table, toute prête à gauche; une fête s'annonce discrètement, dont G.M. sera le payeur et la dupe. Il faudrait dire encore le mouvement des gilets entrouverts, les ronds de jambes qui préparent le ballet comique, les falbalas de Manon, plus irrésistibles que jamais, et puis encore ce miroitement des surfaces, ce luxe fascinant, parfaitement obtenus par le graveur: c'est le chef d'œuvre!

IV) *La rencontre à l'Hôpital-Général* (éd. de 1753, t. I, p. 262; éd. Deloffre, p. 103): avec la figure suivante, de Pasquier, la chute est brusque. La page 262 évoquait la réunion des amants dans la cellule de la prison: 'J'entrai, lorsqu'elle y accourait avec précipitation. Nous nous embrassâmes avec cette effusion de tendresse, qu'une absence de trois mois fait trouver si charmante à de parfaits amants'. Pasquier, à l'accoutumé, tente de rendre la totalité de la scène: l'entrée du chevalier, la précipitation de Manon, l'attendrissement de M. de T., qui doit durer 'un quart d'heure', et jusqu'à la présence de Marcel, dont on saura, quelques pages plus loin, qu'il a été témoin de cette entrevue, et que 'ce tendre spectacle' l'a beaucoup touché; pour le moment, il en reste la bouche ouverte. Pasquier ne pèche que par excès de fidélité; rien ne manque au tableau: les barreaux de la prison, les pelottes et les aiguilles de Manon, le chapeau tombé; mais l'embrassade est manquée; les corps sont raides et étirés; le témoin attendri, M. de T., diminué exagérément pour créer un arrière-plan, est bonnement ridicule. Ce médiocre 'happy end' clôt pauvrement la première partie du roman.

V) *La scène du Prince italien* (éd. de 1753, t. II, p. 20; éd. Deloffre, p. 123): la page 20 commence effectivement par la scène décrite: 'Manon ne lui laissa pas le temps d'ouvrir la bouche. Elle lui présenta son miroir...' Pas plus que Gravelot en pareil cas, Pasquier ne tente de représenter la parole, mais il suggère au moins la conclusion de la folle harangue de Manon, car celle-ci tient les cheveux de son amant: '...tous les princes d'Italie ne valent pas un seul des cheveux que je tiens'. La figure repose donc, une fois encore, sur un enjambement, sur le début et sur la fin du discours de Manon. Elle vise surtout à représenter les amants au temps de leur apogée: Manon, plus gracieuse que jamais, le chevalier chez lui, parfaitement élégant dans un drapé improvisé, tandis que le Prince fait figure de repoussoir. C'est le temps du triomphe; l'Amour, ce 'bon maître', règne dans la décoration; les amants sont comme encadrés dans une image-souvenir. On peut croire que Prévost a donné ici des instructions précises au graveur, car la figure contribue à la 'plénitude d'un des principaux caractères', pour reprendre l'expression du 'Nota' liminaire. Pasquier, très consciencieusement, a exécuté la commande; l'essentiel est dit, non sans grâce.

VI) *L'arrestation chez G.M.* (éd. de 1753, t. II, p. 115; éd. Deloffre, p. 155): la gravure s'accorde parfaitement au contenu entier de la page 115: 'Après cette découverte, le vieillard emporté...' jusqu'à 'les reconnaissez-vous? lui dit-il avec un sourire moqueur'. Pasquier, ici encore, s'impose par son honnêteté et sa fidélité au modèle littéraire. La scène est totalement rendue et assez bien composée: Des Grieux, en bonnet de nuit, va se mettre au lit, sur lequel Manon est déjà 'assise'; G.M., avec un sourire moqueur (bien proche, à vrai-dire, de la grimace) fait voir 'de près' à Manon le collier de perles et la bourse contenant les dix-mille francs. Si Des Grieux n'est pas représenté 'crevant de rage', comme le voudrait le texte, du moins faut-il le maintenir assis. Le décor, celui de la petite maison du jeune G.M., est résolument galant et moderne: trumeau encadré de rocaille Louis XV, pendule rococo marquant l'heure exacte de la scène – 'quoiqu'il fût au moins dix heures et demie' –, lit à baldaquin et à pompons, etc. La scène, très dramatique, est saisie dans le contraste violent de l'ombre et de la lumière: le halo de lumière des candélabres encercle les trois protagonistes, tandis que bougent dans la pénombre les figurants, les spectateurs: trois gardes à la fois inquiets et sceptiques. Comme souvent chez Pasquier, la scène s'immobilise dans une sorte d'instantané, mais la composition reste éloquente, et l'animation des mains, prises dans une sorte d'ellipse centrale, rappelle assez bien la manière de Gravelot.

VII) *Sur la route de Passy* (éd. de 1753, t. II, p. 183; éd. Deloffre, p. 179: la page 183 évoque dans ses vingt lignes deux mouvements différents; Manon reconnaît Des Grieux et tente de se précipiter vers lui, Des Grieux quitte son cheval pour s'asseoir auprès d'elle. Pasquier représente l'intervalle de ces deux moments: Des Grieux a quitté son cheval, qui reste là au premier plan, et il se hisse – on se demande un peu comment – vers Manon qui se penche en avant. Les visages des amants se rejoignent ainsi au centre parfait du tableau, et se détachent sur un fond mouvementé de chevaux, de voitures; il y faut encore une église dans le lointain, des claquements de fouet et un chien qui se gratte au premier plan, on se demande pourquoi. Dans cette composition très anecdotique, l'accessoire l'emporte sur l'essentiel, au point qu'on hésite à identifier Manon dans la femme qui se penche (la main du chevalier semble plutôt aller vers la femme de gauche). Il y a là, il faut en convenir, beaucoup de bavardage.

VIII) *L'enterrement de Manon* (éd. de 1753, t. II, p. 241; éd. Deloffre, p. 200): comme dans la plupart des cas, le texte de la page 241 contient tous les détails repris par le graveur: les vêtements étendus sous le corps de Manon, l'épée rompue, et le chevalier qui se sert de ses mains; la scène de l'ensevelissement est naturellement éludée, quoique le geste du chevalier l'annonce. En tout ceci, Pasquier reste parfaitement fidèle à Prévost, et sa scène est imposante, même si l'on ne peut éviter de compter les boutons de l'habit, ou de dénombrer au premier plan le chapeau, le baudrier et le fourreau. Le dessin est rapide, la gravure aussi: d'horribles rochers sont restés à l'état d'ébauches nuageuses; sable et broussailles sont réduits à de simples pointillés. Du moins le graveur a-t-il réussi à suggérer l'espace désert qui entoure les amants, et donné une image ultime du couple parfait. Pour donner un tableau unique en son genre, il suffisait de suivre littéralement le texte de Prévost, et c'est ce que Pasquier a fait.

Au vu de cette séquence de huit figures, quelques réflexions viennent à l'esprit. Ces huit scènes dessinent, de façon purement linéaire, la courbe d'une existence, de la radieuse rencontre à la catastrophe finale; les scènes graves ont tendance à l'emporter sur les scènes enjouées; le pathétique tend à s'imposer, surtout dans la seconde partie, où l'apparition lumineuse de Manon en V est suivie des étapes successives de son malheur. On notera en outre une constante focalisation sur les deux amants. Il s'agissait bien sûr de 'figures', et par conséquent de portraits des principaux personnages; mais on a à peine deviné Tiberge; on ne voit ni M. de B., ni le jeune G.M., ni le père du chevalier. Comme dans les versions pour opéra d'Auber, de Massenet ou de Puccini, la morale s'estompe, le nombre des amants de Manon se réduit à un seul, les scènes de réconciliation disparaissent. Seul l'amour est mis en scène. Si Prévost avait voulu, comme on est porté à le croire, ôter à son roman tout parfum de scandale et provoquer la pitié ou l'attendrissement, rien ne pouvait mieux l'y aider que ce commentaire gravé. Lorsque des témoins figurent dans le tableau, ils anticipent la réaction du lecteur: M. de T. est pénétré d'admiration pour ces parfaits amants et Marcel en est tout ému (IV); les trois gardes s'interrogent, mais traitent visiblement le chevalier avec douceur (VI); les archers contemplent les amants avec quelque étonnement, et l'on voit le palefrenier esquisser un geste d'admiration (VII). Les deux héros bénéficient désormais d'une indulgence plénière.

On ne saurait affirmer que Prévost a guidé constamment le graveur; mais il est certainement intervenu pour mettre en relief l'épisode du Prince italien. On serait tenté de croire que l'égale répartition des huit figures sur deux parties lui doit aussi quelque chose. La division du roman en deux parties, consacrée par la publication en deux volumes, trouve ici sa justification: l'épisode moral de la prison clôt la première partie comme la mort de Manon clôt la seconde. Mais le trait le plus original de cette suite de gravures est leur fidélité scrupuleuse au texte. Les graveurs semblent avoir eu devant eux la page qu'ils devaient illustrer, et se sont attachés à regrouper, à la ligne près, tous les détails qu'elle renfermait. On est ainsi invité à procéder à deux lectures parallèles: l'image devient discours, le texte devient légende. Les figures illustrent des moments plus que des répliques; elles cernent le texte dans son développement et invitent à rêver sur la totalité du récit qui nous est présenté. Il y a là une conception relativement nouvelle de l'illustration, qu'il nous faut tenter d'éclairer.

Le style

Nous ne savons rien des rapports de Prévost et de Gravelot. Ils ont pu se rencontrer en Angleterre: Prévost a eu l'occasion, dès 1733, de voir les vignettes de l'*Astrée,* car il donne un compte rendu de cette édition dans *Le Pour et Contre* (t. I, pp. 260-61), sans toutefois parler des gravures. Gravelot, entre 1741 et 1748, semble avoir fait de nombreux voyages entre l'Angleterre et la France, avant de se fixer à Paris, vers 1750-1753. Après avoir collaboré avec Hogarth, il s'était spécialisé dans l'illustration du roman anglais: *Pamela* en 1742, *Tom Jones* en 1750; mais il ne conquiert la célébrité en France qu'avec l'illustration du *Decameron* en 1757-1761. Didot eut sans doute plus d'occasions de connaître Jacques-Jean Pasquier, honnête artisan qui avait donné à divers éditeurs nombre de vignettes, de portraits et d'illustrations. En 1750, nous le trouvons associé à Gravelot pour le *Tom Jones*; il collabore encore avec lui pour le *Decameron*. Mais il a surtout gravé, avec Eisen, dès 1751-1752, la suite de figures de *Clarisse Harlowe* dans la traduction française de Prévost, et c'est par là qu'il a pu intéresser notre romancier. Sans doute existait-il, avant cette date, de nombreuses suites de figures, en général composées pour des rééditions soignées; c'est le cas de l'édition de 1726 du *Diable boîteux,* dont les douze figures illustrent de façon précise autant de passages du texte; *Gil Blas, La Vie de Marianne, Les Aventures de Télémaque* ont fait l'objet également d'un commentaire illustré. Ce que l'on découvre avec la *Clarisse* d'Eisen et Pasquier, c'est une sorte de commentaire littéral du roman, en vis-à-vis du texte, avec un luxe de connotations visuelles qui permettent d'envisager l'ensemble de la scène. On retrouvera aisément dans le dessin de Pasquier la raideur, le pathétique immobilisé qui sont sa marque, mais aussi le goût de l'ornementation rocaille, la pendule ciselée qui marque l'heure exacte, ce caractère anecdotique qui est son faible. Mais l'ensemble de ces illustrations forme véritablement un discours en images dont l'influence fut certainement décisive pour l'illustration de *Manon Lescaut* et pour celle de *La Nouvelle Héloïse*.

Deux tendances semblaient alors diviser les illustrateurs: l'illustration allégorique ou emblématique, qui avait régné au XVIe et au XVIIe siècle, commençait à perdre du terrain; l'illustration pathétique ou dramatique, directement appliquée à un épisode du texte, ne s'était pas encore imposée. Une nouvelle génération de graveurs (Gillot, Oudry, Boucher, etc.) s'applique à restaurer l'autonomie du discours illustratif, mais le renouveau du livre illustré n'apparaît vraiment qu'après 1750. Les gravures de *Clarisse* inclinent vers le pathétique; celles de *Manon* obéissent à un idéal plus subtil et en partie contradictoire: elles marquent une transition.

Ce qui fait le charme de ces figures, c'est assurément leur accent poétique et emblématique. La page entière est commentée, et par là même la démarche du récit. On a vu comment le dessin tendait à fixer un double mouvement, une modification; l'instant précis de la parole, du baiser, de l'arrestation ou de l'ensevelissement est comme éludé. C'est cet entre-deux qui permet d'introduire dans le récit une pause, un suspens, un temps de réflexion ou de rêverie. Il arrive aussi que l'illustration colle littéralement à une réplique du texte: 'Je lui trouve l'air de Manon . . .' (III), 'Nous nous embrassâmes . . .' (IV), 'Les reconnaissez-vous?' (VI). Et l'on est tout près alors du style d'illustration dénotative qui dominera vers 1770, en particulier dans le *Cleveland* de 1777 ou dans les *Œuvres choisies* de 1783, illustrées par Marillier dans un style néo-classique et théâtral. Ici, la phrase même est portée par un cartouche, gravée sur une sorte de pierre lapidaire qui immobilise la réplique tout juste sortie de la bouche ouverte du héros. Pourtant, si la réplique citée est toute proche dans certaines gravures de *Manon,* elle ne donne pas à elle seule le sens de la scène, et jamais nous n'y trouvons de bouche ouverte. Si le commentaire visible épouse la forme du texte, il n'en suit pas moins ses propres règles. Tout se passe comme si Gravelot avait retenu Pasquier sur la pente où l'entraînait Eisen.

Si l'on tente de caractériser le style propre de Gravelot et de Pasquier, on se heurte en fait à des interférences de styles. Dans les deux dessins de Gravelot se manifeste un coup de crayon original: on admire la clarté de la composition, un sens aigu des valeurs et des fonds brillantés, parfaitement rendus par Le Bas (III), l'exquise sinuosité des lignes du vêtement, l'arabesque souple qui développe une sorte de discours des mains, l'éloquence des gestes, le jeu des jambes dans un ballet esquissé. Dans ce dessin nerveux, vivant, fuselé, on croirait retrouver parfois la trace de Gillot et de Watteau, une manière très française et qui, curieusement, ne doit rien à

Hogarth. Mais peut-être Gravelot doit-il à ce dernier son sens du commentaire visuel, cet esprit de la 'Suite' qui s'était imposé avec *A Harlot's Progress* en 1732, et *The Rake's Progress* en 1735. Rappelons que dans la *Carrière d'une prostituée,* Hogarth avait représenté l'arrivée en diligence de la jeune étourdie, sa liaison avec un riche financier, son internement à Bridewell et son enterrement, le tout dans un style haut en couleurs, souvent burlesque, réaliste jusqu'au sordide. Prévost a sans doute apprécié Hogarth, dont il a commenté, dans *Le Pour et Contre,* le portrait de Sara Malcolm (t. I, pp. 19-21), tout en sachant que ce goût était inacceptable en France. En rêvant un peu, on pourrait imaginer qu'il ait discuté avec Gravelot de ce modèle du discours en images, et de sa transcription dans le goût français . . .

Le Bas et Pasquier sont d'honnêtes graveurs à l'apogée de leur carrière. Le Bas semble avoir suivi, autant qu'on peut le supposer, les indications de Gravelot. Pasquier, lui, exécute sans génie la commande du libraire. Il travaille sans doute comme le faisaient nombre d'illustrateurs, à partir de marionnettes de bois, sans réussir à s'abstraire de ces silhouettes maigres, raides et légèrement déséquilibrées (IV, VIII). Mais il lui arrive, au moins à deux reprises, de s'inspirer de la manière de Gravelot: la scène d'Amiens (I) et la scène de l'arrestation (VI) sont relativement convaincantes. Son domaine préféré était celui de la vignette, et il n'est pas étonnant que Didot lui ait confié le soin de la vignette initiale, donnée en tête des tomes I et II. Ce qui surprend plus, c'est la médiocrité de son travail: la composition est confuse, les détails sont oiseux, l'allégorie démodée tranche curieusement avec l'esprit des autres figures. On ne serait pas surpris, à vrai-dire, qu'il ait emprunté sa vignette à un ouvrage plus ancien. Cela nous conduit à revenir, en conclusion, sur la lecture qui nous est proposée.

Le choix des épisodes, on l'a vu, est très explicite: des Grieux et Manon, avec leur jeunesse, leur insouciance, leur amour, forment le centre de chaque composition, du premier pas sur la place d'Amiens à la scène finale. Les trahisons de Manon sont à peine suggérées. Les représentants de la morale n'interviennent pas. La religion est absente, même dans le parloir de Saint-Sulpice – là où, au dix-neuvième siècle, on placera au moins un crucifix. Nous nous trouvons devant une sorte de plaidoyer pour l'amour et la jeunesse; à ce point de vue, l'œuvre s'est modernisée. Le décor lui-même s'est renouvelé: les meubles, les trumeaux, les ornements, tout jusqu'à la pendule, jusqu'aux assiettes d'argent est en rococo Louis XV. Cette adaptation va naturellement dans le sens de la modernisation du texte en 1753: si Prévost n'a pas guidé ses illustrateurs, du moins devait-il les approuver. Mais comment croire qu'il n'a pas choisi lui-même de mettre en valeur dès le début la rencontre d'Amiens, et en tête de la seconde partie l'épisode tout nouveau du Prince italien? Dans cette nouvelle version, que le romancier défend dans son 'Nota' de 1753, et qu'il reprend intégralement en 1756, l'*Histoire du chevalier* a soudain rajeuni; elle s'est accordée aux temps nouveaux; elle ne montre plus que deux jeunes amants, leurs plaisirs et leur malheur. Elle ne met en scène que 'des peintures vraies et des sentiments naturels': c'est ainsi que dès 1734, Prévost avait défendu son roman dans le *Pour et Contre* (t. III, p. 139). Sur les suggestions de l'auteur, ou peut-être parce qu'ils aimaient *Manon Lescaut,* deux artistes ont développé leur propre lecture, peint le monde nouveau qu'ils avaient sous les yeux, suggéré la tendresse, la complicité, l'insouciance des amants, et parfois marqué l'émotion qui pouvait gagner un public étonné. Leurs illustrations ne sont pas simplement dénotatives; elles témoignent d'une lecture personnelle, de pauses réflexives ou sentimentales dans le cours du récit. Ces figures ne sont assurément pas des chefs d'œuvre, et tout porte à croire qu'elles ont été réalisées dans la hâte. Gravelot fera beaucoup mieux avec Boccace, Marmontel ou Rousseau, Cochin avec Fénelon, Eisen, Gravelot et Moreau avec *La Nouvelle Héloïse*. La suite des figures de *Manon Lescaut* reste pourtant, par sa conception à la fois poétique et dramatique, par le libre rapport qu'elle entretient avec le texte, un moment de l'histoire du livre illustré. D'une certaine façon, elle mène à la suite parfaitement réussie des illustrations de *La Nouvelle Héloïse*.

Narration and experience in Genet's
Journal du Voleur

Michael Sheringham : University of Kent

A man sits writing in a luxury hotel somewhere in a European resort shortly after the Second World War. He had spent much of the war in prison, mainly for burglary, but there he had begun to write. His verbally luxuriant embroiderings on his experiences in prison, and as a child, have earned him the admiration of Cocteau, Gide, and Sartre. What will he write now that he is free, relatively successful and respectable? 'De nauséabondes bouffées de mon Espagne remontent à mes narines' (p. 180).[1] He had spent much of the period from 1932 to 1940 in Barcelona and other parts of Spain, living amongst the lowest of the low, making a living as a prostitute, a beggar, and a thief. He had also wandered through most other European countries, and had lived for a time in Antwerp. Somehow he became someone who writes. Perhaps he should now write about this transformation? He takes a first plunge into his memories of Barcelona: the Barrio Chino, Stilitano with his stump, the Carolinas, the day Pépé killed a man . . . Why did he live in all this squalor, even choose it, and revel in it? The incidents, the sights, sounds and smells, the picaresque and the picturesque, do not seem to contain the explanation. What counted was what the man made of them in his head, the ways he transformed his experience imaginatively. He made 'Barcelona', his own Barcelona, as much as it made him. It is part of 'cette contrée de moi que j'ai nommée l'Espagne' (p. 306). A bare narrative of his Barcelona days would be futile, but to trace the geography and history of his imaginary Spain is no easy task. The process of imaginative transformation did not cease when he left the country, and indeed as he writes now, after the war, he is perpetuating it: it is not the past he is reanimating but a whole dimension of himself, and a latent imaginative dynamism.

As we read *Journal du voleur,* we are never firmly back there in Spain. We never lose sight for long of the contexts in which the man, Jean Genet, writes: the sumptuous hotel which contrasts so ironically with his earlier *misère*; his newfound notoriety; his current lovers. He proceeds by plunges back into the past, many of very brief duration, and resurfacings, often abrupt, to the time and place of writing. When we plunge again we are often uncertain if we are back where we were a moment before, or if this time another period, earlier or later; another place, Antwerp instead of Barcelona; another person, Armand rather than Stilitano, is involved. Nor can we be quite sure, as we zoom back and forth, of distinguishing remembered fact from past or present fantasy. One thing that remains fairly constant, however, is the way we, the readers, are openly allotted an important function in this performance. 'Pour me comprendre une complicité du lecteur sera nécessaire' (p. 17), we are warned early on. The reader's putative opinions, responses and judgements are repeatedly invoked, offering him a role which cannot easily be declined. These devices and strategies produce a difficult, uneven, sometimes rebarbative reading experience. Often, however, they give rise to sequences of dazzling complexity and power which, as they exploit to the full the extraordinary capacities of narrative discourse, cast light not only on the particularities of a rare individual but also on the interplay of narrative structures and personal identity.

Despite the title, and sporadic references in the text, *Journal du voleur* has none of the obvious features of a journal. There are no dated entries, or units corresponding to specific days or periods, nor is the principal focus ostensibly on the period contemporary with the writing. Given this, the word 'journal' emphasises the paradox whereby two sets of day-to-day experiences – wanderings in Spain and Belgium, and writing a book based on them – are made to interpenetrate and suffuse one another. There is no suggestion that Genet kept any sort of diary during the thirties – he is writing about a time when he did not write – but it is implied once or twice that he began taking notes in 1945, amassed material, and then, in 1947-48, organised and composed the book which was published in 1949. At one point Genet refers to being thirty-five, which implies 1945, and portions of the text appeared in *Les Temps Modernes* in 1946 when it was clearly work in progress. From time to time Genet refers to the 'journal' as something pre-existing the narration we are reading, and he twice refers to having lost considerable portions of it (pp. 172, 233). About three-quarters of the way through he tells us that this will be his last book, that writing has now served any function it had for him, and that the 'chapitres' which follow will be delivered 'en vrac' (p. 233).

The book is divided into four un-numbered and uneven sections separated by blank space, the only other typographical division being an asterisk (p. 44). The opening section is a short preamble (pp. 9-13). Next comes the first of the two longer sections (pp. 14-161). It concerns: Barcelona and Genet's relationships with Stilitano and others; wanderings in Spain and, after a brief return to France, central Europe after being abandoned by Stilitano; a chance reunion with Stilitano in Antwerp and Genet's first meeting with Armand. Within this overall sequence there are quite long detours into other periods, earlier and later, as well as a good deal of 'intercutting' between, for example, Barcelona and Antwerp (the arrival in Antwerp is anticipated several times), while particular episodes, rather than being narrated chronologically in one go, sometimes need to be reconstructed retrospectively by the reader from a series of partial accounts. The brief third section (pp. 162-80) largely concerns Genet's relationship with a younger man named Lucien in the period during which the book is being composed. This is made to link with the recollection of Spain because Genet wonders how Lucien will react to the disclosures about his abject past. And when the fourth section (pp. 181-306) opens we are plunged back into the past, not to Antwerp however, but to Barcelona again as Genet tries to fuse his image of Lucien with his own imagined past self. This is followed by a return to Genet's solitary wanderings in Spain after leaving Barcelona and it is only after an interval of some forty pages that the account of Antwerp is resumed, only to be interrupted by a long digression concerning an affair with Bernardini, a Marseilles policeman (pp. 213-27). In fact Genet's recollections of the Antwerp phase, involving Stilitano, his girl-friend Sylvia, Robert, Roger and Armand, are never gripped closely by the narration. These are the portions referred to as 'en vrac' and, with the exception of the account of Armand, the Antwerp material is subordinated to the abstract discussions of 'sainteté' and related concepts which come to dominate the book. (There are also long digressions concerning theft, primarily with Guy during the Occupation.)

As *Journal du voleur* moves from past to present, from reality to fantasy, and from description to lyrical flights or abstract meditation, no consistent relationship is established between remembered incidents, anecdotes, portrayals of character, and the narrator's discourse through which they are filtered. In fact it is the quest for such a relationship – for a clear sense of how a past which can only be apprehended through the distortions of the present might relate to a present which can only be understood in terms of the past that produced it – which seems to generate the narration and to engender its vertiginous, lurching progress. In the course of this search the relation between events and narration, *Histoire* and *Discours,* becomes crucial as the process of narration establishes, and then rapidly disestablishes, a series of provisional alliances between them. It is these which must now be examined.

At some points the standard motives of autobiography are adduced by Genet in connection with the re-enactment of his past. He refers, for example, to his 'aventures . . . érotiques, dont je veux maintenant découvrir le sens' (p. 112), and affirms further on that his reasons for returning to France were not apparent to him at the time but become evident to him as he writes (p. 128). Moreover, it becomes progressively clearer that Genet's fascination with his time in Spain has to do with his sense that it holds the key both to the identity he forged in childhood and adolescence, and to his later identity as a writer. By wilfully making himself abject in Spain – materially, sexually, sociologically, morally – he transformed his relative social alienation into an essential and absolute condition. In doing so he was repeating the fundamental choice he claims to have made in childhood (pp. 50, 198, 277): that of deciding to be what others accused him of being, turning the tables on his accusers by actively assuming rather than passively resisting the role they foisted on him. (Sartre will make this declaration the cornerstone of his *Saint-Genet: comédien et martyr*).[2] But in Spain Genet was also initiating mental procedures, habitual reflexes, analogies and transformations, which will be crucial when, in prison in the forties, he puts pen to paper and transforms himself into a writer. In a long passage (pp. 95-101) where he makes the links between childhood, Spain, and writing, Genet takes as his starting-point two photographs of himself taken when he was sixteen and thirty respectively. They stake out a period in which, as he now sees it, in the solitude of prisons and slums, he applied the imaginative energies of his solitary childhood to the art of transmuting prisons into palaces, misery into glory, humiliation into humility:

> c'est l'imagination amoureuse des fastes royaux, du gamin abandonné, qui me permit de dorer ma honte, de la ciseler, d'en faire un travail d'orfévrerie dans le sens habituel de ce mot, jusqu'à ce que, par l'usage peut-être et l'usure des mots la voilant, s'en dégageât l'humilité. Mon amour pour Stilitano me remettait au fait d'une si exceptionelle disposition. Par lui si j'avais connu quelque noblesse voici que je retrouvais le

véritable sens de ma vie – comme on dit le sens du bois – et que la mienne se devrait signifier hors de votre monde. (p. 100)

Looked at this way Genet's experience seems to be a continuous chain whose inherent links are revealed and clarified but not created by writing. Indeed writing is seen as a way of perpetuating what had happened in Spain; even the consequences of his decision to write, his literary fame and financial security, merely extended the chain: 'j'écris ce livre dans un palace de l'une des villes les plus luxueuses du monde où je suis riche cependant que je ne puis plaindre les pauvres: je les suis' (p. 100). If the sleazy bars where Genet transformed himself imaginatively prefigured the prisons where he began to write, so the 'palace' in which he now writes is a prison in which Genet risks being trapped by the audience which reads his books: as we shall see later Genet's life only makes sense 'hors de votre monde' as he puts it in the passage quoted, that is to say outside the structures of bourgeois culture; yet it can only be made to manifest this sense in a discourse produced and understood within the framework of that culture.

The notion that Genet's narrative manifests a continuity of past and present by uncovering lost or virtual meaning does not, however, survive for long periods in the *Journal.* Even at points where the book is regarded as directly self-revealing, another view, that the self revealed is that of the man who writes in the present rather than the one who experienced in the past, often prevails. In the opening of the second section (pp. 14-16) Genet offers a paradoxical definition of violence, in terms of calm audacity, the willingness to accept risks and so forth, and then observes: 'j'utiliserai les mots non afin qu'ils dépeignent mieux un événement ou son héros mais qu'ils vous instruisent sur moi-même' (p. 17). When he recollects his *coup de foudre* for Stilitano he compares it to a bird of prey swooping on a dove, but he acknowledges that this may not be what he felt at the time: 'ce qu'alors j'éprouvai je l'ignore, mais il me suffit d'évoquer l'apparition de Stilitano pour que ma détresse aussitôt se traduise aujourd'hui par un rapport d'oiseau cruel à sa victime' (p. 39). Genet does not claim to be depicting past events as they were but, through the way he writes, to register his current feelings about events in the past. This is formulated more explicitly in a significant passage where Genet asserts that 'recomposer mon attitude d'alors' is not his aim since he acknowledges that language cannot catch so much as a gleam of 'ces états défunts, étrangers'. Hence the aim of the *Journal* is not 'la notation de qui je fus':

> il doit renseigner sur qui je suis, aujourd'hui que je l'écris. Il n'est pas une
> recherche du temps passé, mais une œuvre d'art dont la matière-prétexte
> est ma vie d'autrefois. Il sera un présent fixé à l'aide du passé, non
> l'inverse. Qu'on sache donc que les faits furent ce que je les dis, mais
> l'interprétation que j'en tire c'est ce que je suis – devenu. (p. 80)

'Un présent fixé à l'aide du passé' is an excellent definition of a certain
form of lucid autobiographical writing, and there is much in the *Journal*
that seems to conform to it. (Later Genet will employ another striking
formula to describe his book: 'Il aura servi à préciser les indications que
me *présente le passé'*, p. 305.) Yet the rest of the passage reveals a tension
which is just as crucial to the book: against the assurance that the facts are
genuine ('ce que je les dis') must be set the assertion that the book is 'une
œuvre d'art' for which the raw materials – Genet's life-history – are no
more than a 'matière-prétexte'.

At its most triumphal the *Journal du voleur* is indeed the assertion of
just this sovereignty of the aesthetic. It is in the act of writing that Genet
transmutes his past *misère*: 'Je veux réhabiliter cette époque en l'écrivant
avec les noms des choses les plus nobles. Ma victoire est verbale et je la
dois à la somptuosité des termes' (p. 65). But Genet's victory goes beyond
the merely aesthetic, or rather the aesthetic is seen to encompass wider
values. As he progresses, 'ordonnant ce que ma vie passée me propose, à
mesure que je m'obstine dans les rigueurs de la composition [. . .] je me
sens m'affermir dans la volonté d'utiliser, à des fins de vertus, mes misères
d'autrefois' (p. 69). 'Vertus' are seen to inhere not in the past experiences
of humiliation but in the beauty which can be derived from them:

> (Le but de ce récit, c'est d'embellir mes aventures révolues, c'est à dire
> obtenir d'elles la beauté, découvrir en elles ce qui aujourd'hui suscitera le
> chant, seule preuve de cette beauté) (p. 230)

It is in this atmosphere that the notion of 'sainteté' emerges, and it will
occur frequently in the last third of the *Journal*. Although he ventures at
least one definition ('la sainteté c'est de faire servir la douleur', p. 232) the
notion remains enigmatic. This is partly by design since Genet asserts
(pp. 237, 243) that it is above all a *word*, signifier rather than signified, for
a state to which he aspires but which he does not fully comprehend. The
word seems to encompass the willing espousal of abjection, the verbal
transmutation of such a choice, the 'chant' which consecrates this, and the
ultimate state of the person who engages in the whole process.

> Par l'écriture j'ai obtenu ce que je cherchais. Ce qui m'étant un enseigne-
> ment, me guidera, ce n'est pas ce que j'ai vécu mais le ton sur lequel je
> le rapporte. Non les anecdotes mais l'œuvre d'art. Non ma vie mais son
> interprétation. C'est ce que m'offre le langage pour l'évoquer, pour parler
> d'elle, la traduire. Réussir ma légende [. . .] pas l'idée plus ou moins
> décorative que le public connaissant mon nom se fera de moi, mais
> l'identité de ma vie future avec l'idée la plus audacieuse que moi-même
> et les autres, après ce récit, s'en puissent former. (pp. 234-35)

In this connection Genet at times gives a rather garish portrait or myth of the artist as a redeemer who takes on the sufferings of his fellow creatures, but in doing so becomes a living work of art himself. The idea of an aesthetic transfiguration and redemption of personal experience, and the possible implications of this for the artist-protagonist, is prominent in the *Journal* but there are also points at which it is given short shrift. At times Genet recognises the risk of embellishing what is ignoble simply on principle, in a purely automatic way: 'je refuse d'être le prisonnier d'un automatisme verbal mais il faut encore une fois que j'aie recours à une image religieuse: ce postérieur était un Reposoir' (p. 67). And more than once he looks askance at his 'volonté de réhabilitation de sentiments réputés vils' acknowledging that simply to apply to them words customar-ily reserved for what is worthy may be no more than a childish way of reversing consecrated norms (p. 122). To glorify homosexuality, theft, betrayal or fear may be to miss the point which is not to shock people but to crystallise an individual's subjective responses. Indeed, running through Genet's paeans to the redemptive power of the poet's 'chant' over his abject experience, and through his own doubts on this score, is a theme which is of greater interest and importance in the *Journal.*

Genet knows very well how powerful some of the images and identities he deploys are, and he consciously works with the 'aura', the dark glamour, which surrounds the thief, the pimp, the male prostitute. But he is also aware that to hallow these figures and their lives is to risk dealing in mere stereotypes. An important aspect of the *Journal* is therefore the way Genet attempts to extricate his relation to his own past from the reductive opposition between moral censure and camp glamour. What from time to time he tries, often vainly, to express is the way the experiences he writes about exist in his own private mental space: 'en moi' as he repeatedly and obsessively puts it (the phrase occurs at least a hundred times). Here Genet's quest is not so much for a new image of himself, a new hypostasis as the Thief, or the Poet, but for a flight or at least a distancing from all images.

> ce que j'ai recherché surtout c'est d'être la conscience du vol dont j'écris
> le poème, c'est-à-dire: refusant d'énumérer mes exploits, je montre ce que
> je leur dois dans l'ordre moral, ce qu'à partir d'eux je construis, ce
> qu'obscurément recherchent peut-être les voleurs plus simples, ce qu'eux-
> mêmes pourraient obtenir. (pp. 105-06)

The refusal to enumerate the thief's exploits which would provide a
spurious local colour is linked to the desire to reveal Genet's sense of
having partaken, in these experiences, of the essence of Theft as a
metaphysical experience. But at this level his book is not an autobiography, nor an aesthete's album, but a spiritual exercise in its own right:
'Ce livre, "Journal du voleur": poursuite de l'Impossible Nullité' (p. 106).
To achieve 'Nullité' would be to coincide utterly, to dissolve entirely into
the essences which we can apprehend through what we build, in word and
thought, out of our past deeds. This sense of a negative experience of
identity, like a photographic portrait of oneself in negative, or in which
the self is apprehended not as an entity but as the vanishing point of
various perspectives, is communicated in an interpolated passage which
enlarges on Genet's disinclination to try and describe Michaelis or his
other male lovers:

> (Prétextes à mon irisation – puis à ma transparence – à mon absence
> enfin –, ces garçons dont je parle s'évaporent. Il ne demeure d'eux que
> ce qui de moi demeure: je ne suis que par eux qui ne sont rien, n'étant
> que par moi. Ils m'éclairent, mais je suis la zone d'interférence. Les
> garçons: ma Garde crépusculaire.) (p. 106)

The 'crepuscular' self – or sense of self – has no identity: it flickers at the
edge of consciousness as Genet imagines existing only in the gaze of beings
who are of his own invention but who retain a tangible sense of otherness.
    Genet's strictures (already noted) against assigning specific meanings to
his past experiences sometimes lead him in a similar direction. Even when
he does use words to try and uncover or explain the past, what count are
not the facts or the explanations but what happens in and through the
words: 'le chant':

> ce rapport sur ma vie intime ou ce qu'elle suggère ne sera qu'un chant
> d'amour. [. . .] Ce que j'écris fut-il vrai? Faux? Seul ce livre d'amour sera
> réel. Les faits qui lui servirent de prétexte? Je dois en être le dépositaire.
> Ce n'est pas eux que je restitue. (pp. 112-13)

Genet's interpolations about the process of composing the *Journal* frequently serve to break up the narrative at points where it seems to be coagulating into a fixed representation. For example, he interrupts (pp. 131-33) an account of his travels in Central Europe with reflections which develop in a remarkable fashion. Facts and events, he writes, however subtly enumerated or formed into patterns, or interpreted (the activity of interpretation, he observes, simply creates additional facts) cannot provide 'ma propre clé' (p. 132). One's experience, he suggests, is inextricably bound up with a global intuitive sense of existence, and this is inseparable from the language and the idiolect through which we apprehend it, as well as our fantasies:

> J'ai parcouru [as a child] la campagne, ravi de découvrir dans les blés ou sous les sapins des noyés à qui j'accordais d'invraisemblables funérailles. Puis-je dire que c'était le passé – ou que c'était le futur? Tout est déjà pris, jusqu'à ma mort, dans une banquise de *étant* . . . (p. 132)

The child's imaginary ceremonies are past but they are also in the future which echoes, repeats, sustains, and is sustained by them. All one's experiences are, as it were, suspended in an essentially timeless medium, translucent as an iceberg. As soon as we pick on a moment, singling it out from the inchoate welter of second-by-second experience, we freeze it. Genet, in this passage, lists a dozen such moments:

> mon tremblement quand un malabar me demande d'être son épouse (je découvre que son désir c'est mon tremblement) un soir de Carnaval; au crépuscule, d'une colline de sable la vue des guerriers arabes faisant leur reddition aux généraux français; le dos de ma main posée sur la braguette d'un soldat mais surtout sur elle le regard narquois du soldat; la mer soudaine entre deux maisons m'apparaît à Biarritz [. . .] Des nègres me donnent à manger sur les quais de Bordeaux; un poète illustre porte à son front mes mains . . . (pp. 132-33)

Of each of these moments he would say: 'il faut que cet instant douloureux concoure à la beauté de ma vie, cet instant et tous les autres je refuse qu'ils soient des déchets'. But he recognises that, conserved in this way, these moments do not constitute living experience; the life they make up is not the one that was lived:

> je parle de quelqu'un – et dans cela le temps de respirer des roses, en prison d'entendre un soir chanter le convoi pour le bagne, m'éprendre d'un acrobate ganté de blanc – mort depuis toujours, c'est-à-dire fixé, car

> je refuse de vivre pour une autre fin que celle même que je trouvais
> contenir le premier malheur: que ma vie doit être légende c'est-à-dire
> lisible et sa lecture donner naissance à quelque émotion nouvelle que je
> nomme poésie. Je ne suis plus rien, qu'un prétexte. (p. 133)

To render one's life legendary, legible, poetic is to sever oneself from one's
experience (even as, at the fringes of consciousness, it carries on prolifer-
ating all the while), to fix it, and thereby to kill it. And yet the process
Genet defines here differs markedly from the deliberate attempts to trans-
mute abject experience into poetic prose. Here the experiences are presented without embellishment, in a clipped, sober, direct style; they are
without antecedents or consequences. Their sovereignty lies precisely in
their resistance to narrative. Their legendary quality, and extreme legibi-
lity, are inherent; they require no adornment. But for *whom* do they
constitute the elements of a legendary Genet? Not for the man himself
who – in the very act of referring to his *alter ego,* 'quelqu'un [. . .] mort
depuis toujours' – shows himself to be very much alive, smelling roses,
hearing a prisoner's song, falling for an acrobat. If 'Genet' becomes 'plus
rien, qu'un prétexte', he is, so to speak, shut out from the 'poésie' of his
own experience which can only communicate an 'émotion nouvelle' to
someone looking at it from the outside. To become 'poésie', to make
oneself 'lisible', one needs a reader.

> Quand pourrai-je enfin bondir au cœur de l'image, être moi-même la
> lumière qui la porte jusqu'à vos yeux? Quand serai-je au cœur de la
> poésie? [. . .] Cette recherche de la transparence est peut-être vaine.
> Atteinte elle serait le repos. Cessant d'être 'je', cessant d'être 'vous', le
> sourire subsistant c'est un sourire égal posé sur les choses. (p. 245)

What Genet seems to recognise here is that the 'démarche' (p. 244) he calls
'sainteté', which should enable him to be fully incarnate in the legendary
image he seeks to project, and allow him to fuse with his utterance ('au
cœur de la poésie') must fail. This is because, inherent in its structure, is
the postulation of another who sees and listens. The act of utterance
includes an anticipation of its own reception. The utterer is *ipso facto* his
own addressee. He cannot become transparent, immanent in the experience of saying or writing, he must remain not only a 'je', that is to say a
transcendent origin, but also a 'vous', a hypothetical interpreter. It is in
this connection, then, that the crucial question of Genet's insistent relation
to an imagined reader, a 'vous', in the *Journal* may be broached. First,
however, it should be stressed that the various attitudes we have seen

Genet taking towards his project in composing the *Journal* – from straight autobiography to the achievement of 'sainteté' and 'Nullité' – must now be envisaged in the context of the interaction between events and discourse. Genet does not move definitively from one stance to another but back and forth between them and around them. The activity of narration juxtaposes the reconstruction of past events with discursive meditations on them or on the process of writing; or it allows the two to interpenetrate, to punctuate and puncture one another in innumerable ways. And Genet uses many stylistic devices, particularly in the area of syntax, as well as parentheses, italics, footnotes, and so forth, to keep the reader constantly aware of the process of writing. There is nonetheless perhaps an overall movement, as the various major avenues turn into impasses, and as Genet exhausts the Spanish material, having saturated it with various blends of sense, for the discussion to become more abstract and confused, and also strangely desultory, as he comes to recognise the fundamental impossibility of his project. More than once, in the *Journal,* Genet announces that this will be his last book, 'Ce livre est le dernier' (p. 232): Genet has exhausted the uses literature has for him.

Few works are as insistently reader-oriented as the *Journal du voleur.* Repeatedly, a hundred times or more, the reader is directly invoked, sometimes several times a page. Rather than being apostrophised (and thus left free to judge and as it were to 'answer back') the reader is habitually represented as the embodiment of norms, values, and presuppositions which can be taken for granted, a fixed point of reference against which Genet can trace his deviations. The reader supposedly inhabits, and so represents, a world of fixed moral, psychological, and metaphysical bearings, which are his possession. And so we are presented *ad nauseam* with references to 'votre monde', 'votre sol' (p. 55), 'votre langage' (p. 29), 'vos règles' (p. 94), 'votre salut' (p. 94), 'votre beauté' (p. 110), 'votre morale' (p. 111). This 'dummy reader', defined and trapped by the author, is the reverse image of Genet. In other words, by arranging the lamps in this way, Genet can turn the spotlight on a clearly defined persona: the criminal, pimp, thief, etc. who, in all he does, is an infringement and subversion of the 'reader's' world-view. But if it involves trapping the reader, this arrangement is supposed to guarantee Genet his freedom: *he* knows that he does not coincide with the image he has foisted on the reader: 'Enfin plus ma culpabilité serait grande, à vos yeux, entière, totalement assumée, plus grande sera ma liberté' (p. 94). Genet's freedom, brilliantly analysed by Sartre, lies in the knowledge that he is other than the way others define him. His strategy is to use the other's defining gaze in order, ideally, to deflect it. The reader is forced to become Genet's accomplice. And so, as Georges Bataille stressed, in his important response to Sartre's book, Genet refuses communication with his readers. [3] His purposes are solitary and involve the desire to remain trapped within his own mental space.

This remains essentially true even when Genet adopts a different stance towards the reader, partly as a result of the acknowledgement of his own change of status in becoming an admired writer, 'riche mais las', denizen of luxury hotels. It is in this new situation that Genet, reviewing his past activity as a writer – as he does throughout the *Journal* – adopts the strategy of 'la sainteté', a project which involves the reader in a somewhat different way. In an extraordinary passage (p. 233) Genet proclaims his ability, when afraid of the police, to shrink into a hidden recess of himself, evacuating his outer appearance which is left as a kind of decoy to divert attention from his true hiding-place. Once the danger has passed, the 'flame' of selfhood flickers up again. Yet this desire to escape definition, and to remain free (literally and metaphorically) is countered by the desire to be apprehended, to become utterly the object of another's gaze. Genet's writing, and his goal of 'sainteté', is a witness to the ambition which asserts itself here when Genet first admits his inclination to take flagrant risks with the police, and then interprets this as a sign of his desire to 'm'accomplir en une destinée des plus rares', to become an object, a beautiful artefact whose qualities depend on the eyes of the beholder:

> Je détruirai les apparences, les bâches tomberont brûlées et j'apparaîtrai là, un soir, sur la paume de votre main, tranquille et pur comme une statuette de verre. Vous me verrez. Autour de moi, il n'y aura plus rien. (p. 234)

This weird apotheosis in which Genet pictures himself as a statuette in the reader's hand shows how badly he needs the reader he constantly shuns. Yet, as was suggested earlier, Genet's need for the reader is in fact a recognition of his entrapment within his own psyche. The 'reader' Genet desires is a fictional entity entailed by the act of attempting to achieve a distinctive form of selfhood through writing. When Genet notes that to depict a brute like Armand in terms of images of tenderness is to express his love not for Armand but for us, the readers ('pour vous', p. 289), he wryly recognises that his machinations only make sense to him, only have a hope of efficacy, in terms of something laid on for an imaginary audience. It is a spectacle put on by and for the benefit of a man who in lucid moments acknowledges that he is 'un homme monstrueusement enlisé en lui-même' (p. 235):

> A la gravité des moyens que j'exige pour vous écarter de moi, mesurez la tendresse que je vous porte. Jugez à quel point je vous aime par ces barricades que j'élève dans ma vie et dans mon œuvre (l'œuvre d'art ne devant être que la preuve de ma sainteté [. . .]) [. . .] afin que votre haleine (je suis corruptible à l'extrême), ne me puisse pourrir. (p. 235)

By seeming to exclude the reader (to distance himself from 'votre monde') Genet woos him. But in seeking to make the reader party to his canonisation, putting himself out of reach of the reader's corrupting breath, Genet not only fictionalises himself but fictionalises the reader too, removing what he writes from any communicative circuit. Yet Genet knows that from the standpoint of real readers there is a real writer, the ex-prisoner in the luxury hotel, who, come what may, remains dangerously exposed and for whom the only sure remedy would be to cease writing altogether.

Narration in *Journal du Voleur,* in its deployment of narrative situation, in the interplay of discourse and event, and in the relation with readers, produces sequences of extraordinary intricacy. Only one instance can be examined in detail here, but a few others stand out as requiring mention. For example the elaborate treatment of Genet's first encounter with Stilitano (pp. 36-44), or the passage (pp. 20-23) singled out for analysis by Sartre concerning the tube of vaseline which, as it lies among Genet's confiscated possessions in a police-station, attracting the disgust of the officers, becomes the embodiment of his alienation and also – in terms of the mechanism we have described – his freedom. Much could be said about Genet's treatment of the figure of Armand, not least that nearly all Genet does say about him consciously flies in the face of any straightforward assessment of a man whose brutishness and lack of charm are made evident throughout. There had been a point in Genet's account of Stilitano when he had recognised that the real man he remembered was dissolving into an imaginary creation, a fabrication of his retrospective desires. In the case of Armand Genet gives even clearer evidence that any attempt to evade self-entrapment by rejoining the past is doomed to failure as past events are annihilated by the self's present energies.

Perhaps the most extraordinary sequences in the *Journal* are, however, to be found in the short third section and at the beginning of the fourth (pp. 162-88). The third section (pp. 162-80) constitutes a parenthesis in which Genet decides to incorporate into the book another set of notes made while he has been resurrecting his life in the thirties. These concern a recent love affair with a younger man called Lucien. Various connections are made between Lucien and Spain. The affair may still be going on but it has reached a critical point (we gather intermittently throughout the *Journal* that there is another current lover in Genet's life: Java), and writing about it may play a role in determining what course it will now take: 'Mon amour finira par sortir peut-être, me dis-je, de moi, emporté par ces mots, comme un toxique l'est du corps par le lait ou la purge' (p. 165). Part of Genet seems to want to abandon Lucien, or at any rate a recent desire of this sort is recollected. But another part of him recognises that like Stilitano or Armand Lucien has become an imaginary creation as much as a creature of flesh and blood, and that to end the relationship is impossible. Another interpolation, following a remembered conversation, confronts the past with the present (Genet writing) and with the anticipation of Lucien's immediate physical presence which will be situated in a wholly different dimension: 'je resterai là, mon visage enfoui dans son cou. Il ne bougera pas. Je serai pris dans l'amour, comme on l'est dans la glace, ou la boue, ou la peur' (p. 178). Part of Genet's suffering relates to his inability to imagine what would happen to Lucien if they separated, and this leads to an identification between Genet's sense of Lucien's waif-like innocence and his own abject past self in Spain. Three strands – associating Lucien abandoned with his own past self, the desire to disclose his past to Lucien, and the acute sense that 'Lucien' is no more than an extension of his own imagination – intertwine to produce an extraordinary sequence at the beginning of section four.

Fusing his memories of Spain with his anxieties about Lucien Genet announces (p. 181) that he intends to recount one of the most humiliating experiences which ever befell him *as if it had happened to Lucien.* The incident turns out to involve images, and the experience of being looked at. Genet-Lucien accepts to be photographed by wealthy foreign tourists whose visit to Barcelona would be incomplete without a look at the famous beggars' quarter. For the tourists in their gabardene raincoats the beggars and pimps in their picturesque rags are no more than 'local colour', living bits of Goya:

> 'L'accord est parfait', says one tourist, 'entre la tonalité des ciels et les teintes un peu verdâtres des loques.
>   –. . . ce côté Goya . . .

>   –Le groupe de gauche est très curieux à observer. Il y a des scènes de
>   Gustave Doré dont la composition . . .
>   –Ils sont plus heureux que nous. (p. 185)

As the object of the 'objectif cruel des appareils photographiques' Genet-
Lucien found himself 'd'un coup, vertigineusement, précipité au fond de
l'innommable' (p. 186). By the extraordinary device of narrating one of his
own experiences as if it had happened to someone else, Genet contrives to
make a confession to his lover about his own past, warning him of a
degradation he hopes he will be spared, but simultaneously desecrating
Lucien's image, drawing him into the world from which he claims to wish
to preserve him. Just as tellingly, though, Genet's tactic shifts the reader's
alignment to the text. While he still addresses the reader, describing and
commenting on the 'operation' he is performing, he also implicates Lucien
as an implied reader of the *Journal.* The *Journal* is revealed to be, in part,
a 'Letter to Lucien', a performance laid on for his benefit, and this
performative dimension of the text displaces the reader, giving him
another role, not as moral arbiter but as voyeur, complicit third party. The
reader is, in other words, placed in the role of the tourists with their
cameras. In consenting to be photographed, Genet had accepted to
become no more than an image, a 'reflet', an extra in someone else's
fantasy of Spain. In the text he subjects Lucien to a comparable manipulation. In doing so he lays bare a central preoccupation of the *Journal*: the
relationship in Genet's imaginative processes beween the roles of witness
and 'reflet', seer and seen, and, in addition, the relationship of both these
roles to a third: that of controller and manipulator of images.

These issues come to the fore fairly explicitly in the last part of the
book. Chronologically, the last 'event' to be narrated (p. 232) is Genet's
precipitate departure from Antwerp, extricating himself from the complex
emotional power struggles with Armand, Robert, and Stilitano. Genet
twice evokes a moment on his journey back to France, as the train went
through forests near Maubeuge (pp. 232, 289), when his mental image of
Armand underwent a crucial transformation so that it came to encapsulate
the paradoxes and tensions in Genet's imaginative relation to his experience. Henceforth the figure of Armand, plastic and malleable, will serve
Genet as raw material for his attempts to find some kind of resolution to
the divisions which his writing sets out to explore (or create), and perpe-
tuate. Even more prominent than before, as the dominant context, the
baseline, of the narration is Genet's post-war situation as a writer, and his

affairs with Lucien and Java. At one level the image of Armand can serve as a refuge from current emotional turmoil: 'maintenant [. . .] j'ose, désespéré, m'y engloutir' (p. 287). Yet there is a price to be paid for seeking gratification at a purely imaginary level: one may succeed only in annihilating one's own experience, transforming the elements of one's past into polymorphous and arbitrary images: 'Au lieu de se préciser et réduire à des limites observables Armand se déforme à mesure que je le poursuis' (p. 292). All Genet's 'heroes', his 'garçons', are in any case confined to a shadow-world of images and reflections because the qualities Genet finds in them cannot be understood in 'our' terms. Thus, the flatness of Armand's nose is not due to a man's fist but his constant bumping against the 'glaces qui nous coupent de votre monde' (p. 287). Their status is wholly dependent on Genet's imaginative vision and ultimately on the activity of writing. Yet if in writing Genet deploys his fantasies and desires it is also here that he engages with 'our' world, with 'our' words and meanings. Writing, then, places Genet both inside his fantasies, so to speak, and outside them, in a kind of no man's land. He is torn between the world of Armand – as transformed, redeemed, by his imagination, and hence always at risk of veering off into the wholly fanciful – and our world which he would like to repudiate but which he still needs since it is only by 'showing' his friends to us, by adopting but subverting our norms, that he can give them any existence.

This feeling of being shut out, of a separation entailed by his ambiguous position, is superbly enacted near the end of the book in a scene where Genet recalls witnessing Stilitano trapped in a fairground 'Palais des Miroirs'. This is interpolated in a longer sequence concerned with a key incident in the drama of control and mastery played out between Armand, Stilitano, and Genet. Someone reports that Armand has in the past been reduced to earning money through his skill at making lace-work patterns out of paper (this is first mentioned on p. 251). For Genet this surprising hint of femininity adds a new dimension to Armand which will play a significant role in subsequent fantasies as he writes. For Stilitano and the other 'durs' it is a weapon. Armand gives Genet the cue to return home together. They leave the café with Stilitano ('Près d'eux', observes Genet, 'je les contenais, contenant l'idée d'eux-mêmes, j'étais leur conscience réfléchissante', p. 195), who then prompts Genet to accompany him instead and, taking advantage of the evening's revelations, seeks to enlist his aid in robbing Armand. Genet's account of how he came to accept involves a moral dialectic dizzyingly complex even by his usual standards (p. 298). At a key moment Stilitano had demonstrated his utter control and self-containedness by manipulating a lighted cigarette with his tongue, holding it in his mouth without releasing any smoke. But this triggers in Genet a recollection of a then recent incident when Stilitano had, like Armand, been seen in a humiliating light. Having entered the 'Palais des Miroirs', and visible to the spectators outside, he had been unable to find his way out: 'C'est alors qu'on bute désespérément contre sa propre image [. . .] Stilitano était pris, *visiblement* égaré dans les couloirs de verre' (p. 302). Genet had come on the scene from a distance and, uncertain how to act, had watched Robert, ashen-faced, take the decision to rescue Stilitano, stepping resolutely into the 'Palais' and extricating him without difficulty. Genet's sense of solitude and exclusion (he creeps away without revealing his presence) underlines the scene's symbolic status as a *mise en abyme* of his ambiguous and marginal position. Genet can invest the scene with symbolic power, can identify (and identify with) Stilitano's anger at the proliferation of self-images, or Robert's stricken, tragic look, but only by remaining outside, as a witness. Reverting to the initial context, of his responses to Stilitano's invitation to betray Armand, Genet recalls his consent – a response to Stilitano's sexuality and power, but also a recognition of his love for Armand without which betrayal would have been meaningless. Yet if the narration stops here, it is because it is in the aftermath of this incident that Genet's decision to leave Antwerp is taken.

By this point Genet's principal 'heroes' have come to symbolise alternative poles: in Armand's case 'engloutissement' in the imaginary, in the 'Palais des Miroirs', femininity; while Stilitano represents lucidity, clarity of outline and purpose, ruthlessness, masculinity. They have come to symbolise, in other words, warring forces in Genet's existence: should the luxury 'palace' where he writes be a haven of the purely subjective and asocial, or should it be a place of negotiation with society? Will Genet remain a tourist in 'our' world, or will he stay?

In this latter part of the book the ambition of 'sainteté' is identified in terms of a union with God, but a God defined as 'mon tribunal intime', the inner voice of self-judgement which prevents us from being unified with ourselves. Union with God, 'sainteté', would annihilate the split of self-consciousness: 'Je cesserai d'être le juge et l'accusé' (p. 279). A more potent symbol of this desire, however, is the image of 'La Guyane'. The former prison colony, both feminine through its name, and masculine through its connotations (p. 288), whose recent closure had been noted at the beginning of the *Journal* and which is therefore now an imaginary place, becomes for Genet an image of reconciliation associated with luxuriance and maternity as well as aridity and corruption. To transpose his 'garçons' from the dust of Spain or the squalor of Antwerp's *bas-quartiers* to 'Guyane', as criminals were once transported there in reality, is to offer them the apotheosis, as archetypes, which his imagination wishes to confer on them. And it is to pitch himself utterly into 'ces fêtes d'un bagne intime que je découvre en moi après la traversée de cette contrée de moi que j'ai nommée l'Espagne' (p. 306). But if the *Journal* ends with these words, heralding a sequel Genet was never to write, the preceding paragraphs of the book's brief coda (pp. 305-06) reveal clearly Genet's awareness that the real issues – for instance reconciling his private world with the public one – remain unresolved:

> Le bagne – nommons cet endroit du monde et de l'esprit – où je me dirige m'offre plus de joies que vos honneurs et vos fêtes. Cependant ce sont ceux-ci que je rechercherai. J'aspire à votre reconnaissance, à votre sacre. (pp. 305-06)

Despite what Sartre will have to say, Genet is far from having found 'la sainteté'. His contradictions are still alive and for some years after the publication of the *Journal* – which was to be his last main narrative work – they will commit him to silence.

Notes

[1] References, incorporated in the text, are to the Gallimard 'Folio' edition (1982).

[2] Sartre's *Saint-Genet: comédien et martyr,* Gallimard, 1952, remains fundamental for any study of *Journal du voleur.* The standard works by C. Bonnefoy, R. Coe, and P. Thody are still useful. Certain significant insights may be gleaned from J. Derrida, *Glas,* Galilée, 1978, and J. Kristeva, *Polylogue,* Seuil, 1980. See also: Elaine Marks, 'The Dream of Love: a Study of three Autobiographies', in G. Stambolian (ed.), *Twentieth Century French Fiction: Essays for Germaine Brée,* Rutgers University Press, 1975, pp. 72-88. Serge Meitinger, 'L'Irréel de jouissance dans le *Journal du voleur* de Genet', *Littérature,* April 1986, pp. 65-74.

[3] Georges Bataille, *La Littérature et le Mal,* Gallimard 'Idées', 1967, pp. 199-244.

Body language in *La Religieuse*

Philip Stewart : Duke University, North Carolina

S T Y L I S T I C S has long been interested in the identification of objectively consistent grammatical features within a given corpus; and for the
principal literary monuments, concordances have made it possible not
only to confirm readers' intuitions on this level but at the same time to
pursue thematic developments through constellations of semantically
related lexical items. With the growing availability of on-line literary data
bases, this possibility is expanded to hundreds of works for which extensive hand-counting has never been practical; once the text is digitalized,
the concordance becomes the most ordinary of tools.

What this can mean is illustrated in the following pages with a very
limited example, drawing on the textual data base established for the
Trésor de la langue française and now available for on-line use in
America at the University of Chicago.[1] It is by no means a systematic
exploration even of its limited target, but simply an attempt to show,
thanks especially to the distribution charts furnished by its search program, how an intuitively identified phenomenon can be pursued with
complete accuracy leading to further nuances as one proceeds. Short of a
rigorously thorough lexical and quantitative study (and doubtless we will
in time see many dissertations of this kind), it is reading which must
always supply the starting point for the inquiry and continue to guide its
pursuit.

Suzanne Simonin's education in lesbian ways takes place via an erotic
repertory of exterior anatomy; her own apt metaphor for her initiation to
the personnel in the convent of Sainte-Eutrope is: 'on vous tâte partout'
(p. 143). That the body is an object of desire is evident enough, but the
physical suffering which is another major element of the plot equally
evokes bodily representation. Both the dominant erotic function and this
thematic distinction between the two 'bodies' at issue can be illuminated

in revealing ways by examining the distribution of particular terms referring to the body as the novel progresses.

There are several passages which essentially follow a pattern which Leo Spitzer has no doubt rightfully assimilated to the literary tradition of the *blason:* parts of the body are enumerated and each in turn poetically extolled. This practice appears in the first descriptive section on Mme ***, mother superior of Sainte-Eutrope, in one of the generalized, representative scenes which occur so frequently in *La Religieuse,* sometimes as here in the present tense: 'la supérieure . . . se met à pleurer, dit qu'elle est bien malheureuse d'avoir à punir, lui baise le front, les yeux, la bouche, les épaules, la caresse, la loue: mais qu'elle a la peau blanche et douce! le bel embonpoint! le beau cou! le beau chignon!' (p. 140) In this example, *récit* and indirect discourse, in succession grammatically, thematically are parallel. The possibility of Suzanne's serving as eventual object of such an exercise is first merely sketched: 'Ce fut elle qui m'ôta mon voile et ma guimpe et qui me coiffa de nuit, ce fut elle qui me déshabilla' (p. 144); the 'blason' aspects of the progression are displaced, being expressed as articles of clothing rather than members of the body. It is then extended, in a passage which figures, through anaphora, the character's mechanical reflex by which the erotic repertory is developed:

> En vérité, je serais bien belle si je méritais la plus petite partie des éloges qu'elle me donnait; si c'était mon front, il était blanc, uni et d'une forme charmante; si c'étaient mes yeux, ils étaient brillants; si c'étaient mes joues, elles étaient vermeilles et douces; si c'étaient mes mains, elles étaient petites et potelées; si c'était ma gorge, elle était d'une fermeté de pierre et d'une forme admirable; si c'était mes bras, il était impossible de les avoir mieux tournés et plus ronds; si c'était mon cou, aucune des sœurs ne l'avait mieux fait et d'une beauté plus exquise et plus rare: que sais-je tout ce qu'elle me disait. (p. 151)

And, finally, in the passage on which Spitzer specifically commented, the style is based on alternation, extended anaphora being reinforced this time with an additional, rhythmic matching of gesture in diegetic *récit* (right column below) to the 'blason' in direct discourse (left column). [2] The better to emphasize the anaphoric structure, the passage here is parsed as if in verse:

> Comment tous ces petits membres n'ont-ils pas été brisés?
> Comment toute cette machine délicate n'a-t-elle pas été détruite?
> Comment l'éclat de ces yeux ne s'est-il pas éteint dans les larmes? Les
>   cruelles!

serrer ces bras avec des cordes!...
>> et elle me prenait les bras,
>> et elle les baisait...

Noyer de larmes ces yeux!...
>> et elle les baisait...

Arracher la plainte et les gémissements de cette bouche!...
>> et elle la baisait...

Condamner ce visage charmant et serein à se couvrir sans cesse des
nuages de la tristesse!...
>> et elle le baisait...

Faner les roses de ces joues!...
>> et elle les flattait de la main
>> et elle les baisait...

Déparer cette tête!
arracher ces cheveux!
charger ce front de souci!...
>> et elle baisait ma tête, mon
>>> front, mes cheveux..

Oser entourer ce cou d'une corde,
et déchirer ces épaules avec des pointes aiguës!...
>> et elle écartait mon linge de
>> cou et de tête,
>> elle entr'ouvrait le haut de ma robe,

>> mes cheveux tombaient épars sur
>> mes épaules découvertes, ma
>> poitrine était à demi nue,

>> et ses baisers se répandaient
>> sur mon cou, sur mes épaules
>> découvertes et sur ma poitrine
>> à demi nue. (p. 160)

However, the fundamental essence of the *blason,* a sort of literary sublima-
tion metamorphosing flesh into literary figure, is in effect here reversed, as
the Mother Superior methodically transforms text (the story of tribulation
which Suzanne has just related to her) into a tactile itinerary, with the
syntax ritually patterning the obsessive gesture.

The lexicon of the Sainte-Eutrope section of the novel naturally
reflects the frequency of such episodes. The language of the body was not
absent – far from it – from the earlier parts of the book, but it had a certain
insistent sameness reflecting, for the most part, a topology of suffering.[3]
Now, however, it proliferates not only in frequency but in variety,
deploying an extensive panoply of erotic foci. Still all possible, or even
conjecturally relevant, corporal terms will not be equally manifest.

Corps itself, an extremely general term, is as would be expected relatively neutral in distribution: of 19 occurrences in the text, 10 are in the Ste-E (Sainte-Eutrope)[4] section, which hardly amounts to a high concentration. *Chair,* though, proves quite different; of its four occurrences, only one falls into the Ste-E category, yet it is highly erotic: 'Jamais vous n'avez pensé à promener vos mains sur cette gorge, sur ces cuisses, sur ce ventre, sur *ces chairs si fermes, si douces et si blanches?*' (p. 165). Of the three remaining, one is purely metaphoric ('j'avais un *cœur de chair* et les autres un cœur de pierre', p. 89) and the other two depict physical suffering ('la corde . . . m'était entré presque entièrement *dans les chairs*', p. 111; 'mes bras livides et sans *chair*', p. 116).

The other examples to be explored here do not quite add up to an exhaustive repertory of body-related expressions, but there should be enough of them to suggest the most apposite inferences to be drawn. The graphs used to illustrate the distributions are the on-line ones furnished by the search program by which the data base was accessed.[5] They represent a percentage distribution of the text which is not easily, on this small scale, plotted with respect to page references. For purposes of the graph, the text is divided into segments representing 2 % of its length, marked by the '+' sign along the base; single occurrences of the word (or of items in a group) within a given 2 % segment are indicated by an 'X' on the graph. In the reference edition, the text of the novel runs from p. 39 to p. 208 and its midpoint is p. 124.[6] Three critical points are indicated below, to help shape the visual sense of the graphic for the reader: the range of the Longchamp episode (beginning p. 62), the death of Mme de Moni (p. 71), and the placement of the Sainte-Eutrope episode (pp. 139-203) which is critical to this study:

TABLE 1

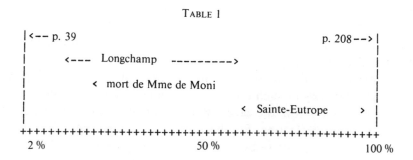

Let us take as a first example the word *visage,* whose frequency in fact reveals little:

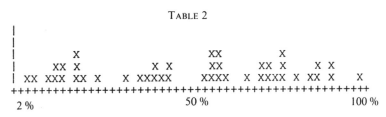

TABLE 2

DISTRIBUTION: VISAGE

In other words, *visage* is simply not a distributionally marked word; it is about as likely to appear anywhere in the text as in those sections of it specifically concerned with erotic exploitation of the body. The obvious explanation for this is that although the first half of the text is also extremely physical, particularly the Longchamp part which dominates it, the sense of that physicality is radically different from what happens at Sainte-Eutrope. The possible range of terms designating the body throughout the text is likely to include some which are more or less equally pertinent to either of these two contrasting registers, and others, on the contrary, which are much more likely to occur in the Sainte-Eutrope context than at Longchamp. But *visage,* like *corps,* is indifferent to this particular polarization.

Similarly, if we take a large group of words denoting features of the head (category HEAD = *bouche, cheveux, dents, face, figure, lèvres, œil, yeux, oreille(s), tête(s), visage, joues, mentons, sourcils),*[7] its distribution, somewhat heavier in the last half of the text yet not greatly lopsided, is the following:

TABLE 3

```
Freq. 20 |                                           X
         |                                           X
         |                                           X
         |                                          XXX
         |                                          XXX    X
         |                                          XXX    X
         |                               X          XXX    X
         |                               X          XXX    X
         |                      X         X          XXX    X
         |                      X        X X         XXX    X
Freq. 10 |                      X         XXX       XXXXX X
         |                      X         XXX       XXXXX X
         |       XX   X   X     XX        XXX       XXXXX X           X
         |       XX   X   X     XX X     XXXX X   XXXXX X          XX
         |    X  XX   X   X     XX X     XXXX X   XXXXX X   X       XX
         |    X  XX   X  XX     XX X     XXXXXX   XXXXX   XXXXX    XXX
         |    X  XXX XXXX X     X XXX XXXXXXXXXXXXXXXX  XXXXXX  XXX
         |   XX XXXXXXXX X    XXXXXX XXXXXXXXXXXXXXXX  XXXXX XXX
         |XXXXXXXXXXXX XXXXXXXXX XXXXXXXXXXXXXXXXX XXXXXXXXXX
         |XXXXXXXXXXXXXXXXXXXXXXXXXXXXXXXXXXXXXXXXXXXXXXXXXXXXX
         +++++++++++++++++++++++++++++++++++++++++++++++++++++++++
          2 %                         50 %                   100 %
```

DISTRIBUTION: HEAD

This particular combination of items results from some empirical experiments not worth going into in detail (they involve in part the elimination of terms or variations not present at all in the text), and of course its representation here in the aggregate hides some significant distinctions between the dissimilar distributions of particular terms comprising the group. There is, for example, no instance of the substantive *joue* in the singular, yet all but three of the 13 *joues* in the plural are Ste-E. Of the two *sourcils,* one is Ste-E and the other is not; six *lèvres* are Ste-E but six are not; on the other hand, only nine of 21 *bouche* are non-Ste-E. The word *tête* is itself only very slightly tilted toward the Ste-E zone:

TABLE 4

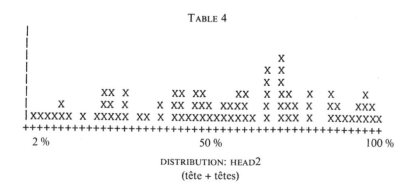

```
         |                                    X
         |                                  X X
         |                                  X X
         |            XX X        XX XX       XX   X XX   X   X      X
         |    X       XX X     X XX XXX XXXX   X XXX X   XX   XXX
         |XXXXXX X XXXXX XX X XXXXXXXXXXXX X XXX X   XXXXXXXX
         +++++++++++++++++++++++++++++++++++++++++++++++++++++++++
          2 %                         50 %                   100 %
```

DISTRIBUTION: HEAD2

(tête + têtes)

The evident explanation for the relatively flat distribution of certain words in contrast to the highly focused occurrence of others designating approximately the same region of the body is the erotic potential of the latter category. The body is not a uniform surface but a semiotically charted map with highly varied local connotations. *Sourcils* may be on the head but they are not sexually charged, and about all they ever do in a literary text is *froncer* (such is the context for both occurrences in *La Religieuse*). The same is true of *menton,* which occurs only once, in a portrait and in the plural at that: '... avec *deux mentons* qu'elle portait d'assez bonne grâce' (p. 171); and of *nez,* which occurs only thrice: twice in one page, when Suzanne's bleeds inopportunely on the dress of her mother (p. 52), and once when she seems to be dying and the sentence is: 'Son nez est froid...' (p. 130). Hardly an erogenous zone. *Oreille* (4 occurrences), which on the contrary *is* erogenous by twentieth-century sensibilities, is not so here; ears serve only to hear, and in the one instance where they denote an external appendage it is to suggest madness and not sexual excitement ('les mains posées sur ses oreilles', p. 200).

For the same reason, one is not surprised to find that *coude* occurs only twice (and in the same scene). It does nonetheless have a langorous context ('... avec de petits coussins sous les coudes pour les soutenir', p. 172); and even if it is not valorized as an erotic object in itself it is not devoid of erotic potential ('... le coude appuyé entre ses deux cuisses...' p. 173). Surprisingly enough, *doigt* is remarkably concentrated in the Ste-E region:

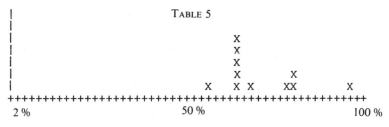

DISTRIBUTION: FINGER

– although the whole arm as a category (ARM = *main, bras, coude, doigt*) appears rather uninteresting:

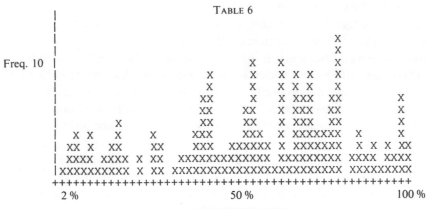

DISTRIBUTION: ARM

Similarly, a leg category (LEG1 = *pied, cuisse, jambe*: it bears noting, though, that neither *cuisse* nor *jambe* occurs in the singular, and there are no toes) is completely uninspiring:

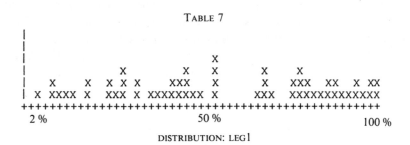

DISTRIBUTION: LEG1

Indeed, if *genou* is added to the previous category, there is a little less symmetry but the overall pattern is no more striking (LEG2 = LEG1 + *genou*):

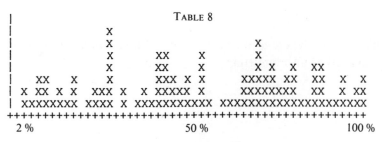

DISTRIBUTION: LEG2

Now in one sense, accounting for this fairly equal spread appears quite easy, for knees should be an active anatomical feature in a convent; but its frequency throughout this text does not relate alone to the amount of time spent praying – which in any event was not great at Sainte-Eutrope. In fact, the distribution of just the singular *genou:*

TABLE 9

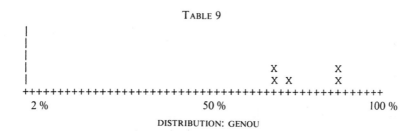

DISTRIBUTION: GENOU

immediately suggests that it is more erotic than the plural.

But it is the trunk of the body from the neck to the belly – precisely that portion which usually, one assumes, would have virtually no place in a description of convent life – which receives the most attention at Sainte-Eutrope. Indeed a constellation of words in that area (BODY3 = *ceinture, cou, épaule, gorge, poitrine, taille, ventre*) is textually highly concentrated:

TABLE 10

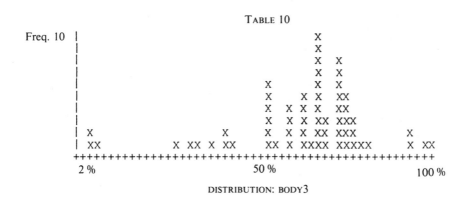

DISTRIBUTION: BODY3

Fourteen out of 20 *cou* are Ste-E, 6 of 7 *gorge,* and all 6 *épaule* in the singular as well as 7 of 11 plural *épaules.*

To a certain extent these terms are selected for inclusion *because* they are concentrated in this manner; that is, they appear massively in the kind of well-known tactile passages quoted earlier. Yet in the process of

research, heuristic groupings of this sort emerge from findings specific to
the way particular items behave *semantically* in the text; concordance
printouts too lengthy to reproduce here made it quite feasible to check the
context for each and every occurrence. *Embonpoint* is an intriguing case
in point, since it refers to an area of the body without being the name for
any specific part. As it happens, all five of its occurrences are Ste-E, and
two are 'blason'-related:

> Mais, qu'elle a la peau blanche et douce! *Le bel embonpoint*! Le beau
> cou! (p. 140);
> Elle me baisa le cou, les épaules, les bras; elle *loua mon embonpoint* et
> ma taille . . . (p. 144);

but the others relate to health only (e.g., 'elle avait *perdu son embonpoint*',
p. 188). In fact, sometimes groups of single words are quite inadequate as
guides to semantic clusters. Erotically, *le milieu du corps* figures more
prominently than does *embonpoint*: four times in *La Religieuse,* of which
three are Ste-E. Were this a modern text, one would certainly expect to
find *sein* a markedly tactile term, but here it plays no such role; there is
not a single instance of the plural *seins*; and of the eight *sein* in the
singular, three are purely abstract (e.g., 'Je portai . . . mes peines dans le
sein du nouveau directeur'), two refer to the womb (pp. 57-58), and the
three that do refer to the female breast do so only vaguely (e.g., 'je tirai
doucement le papier *de mon sein*', p. 79); indeed, the two occurrences
which are Ste-E are among the abstract ones (pp. 191-92).

   Another instance of significant syntactic context – in terms both of the
body's own 'syntax' and that of the prose describing it – is the preponder-
ant role already mentioned of the upper torso: for *cou, gorge* and *épaule*
are all liminal areas of the nun's habit where the margin between the
veiled and exposed regions of the body is in play. Four of the 14 *cou* which
are Ste-E are part of the expression *linge de cou*:

> . . . cependant elle avait *levé mon linge de cou, sa main était placée* sur
> mon épaule nue, et l'extrémité de ses doigts posé sur ma gorge. (p. 152)
> Cependant elle avait *levé son linge de cou* et elle avait *mis une de mes
> mains* sur sa gorge . . . (p. 155)
> Et elle *écartait mon linge de cou* et de tête; elle *entrouvrait* le haut de ma
> robe . . . (p. 160)
> . . . elle se promenait autour de la table, *posant sa main sur la tête* de
> l'une, la renversant doucement en arrière et lui baisant le front, *levant le
> linge de cou* à une autre, plaçant sa main dessus . . . (p. 174)

It can readily be seen that each instance associates *linge de cou* with the verbs *écarter* or *lever* and the placing of hands: *linge de cou* is important precisely because it is there to be lifted. The same configuration may govern *linge* without qualifiers: 'tu es folle d'être honteuse, *laisse tomber ce linge*' (p. 140); 'Je m'étais retournée, elle avait *écarté son linge*, et j'allais *écarter le mien* . . .' (p. 169). Six of the 20 *linge* in the text function in this precise way, and thus relate intimately to our subject, but one would never locate them in a purely mechanical search of corporal vocabulary.

Just this sort of contextualization is necessary to lend proper relief to the semic texture of some words. As the preceding examples suggest, hands have a major erotic function in the text, but one would not easily identify it simply by surveying the distribution of *main,* which is only slightly bunched on the right:

TABLE 11

```
|
|                             X
|                             X        XXX
|                     X       XX       XXX      X
|         X           X       XXX    X XXX      X               X
|   X X  XX      X          XX       XXX    X XXXXXXX       X    X
|   X X  XXX    X  XX    X  XXX       XXX    XXXXXXXXX    XXX X XX
| XXXXXXXX  X  XX  XXXXXXXX  XXXXXXXXXXXXXXX  XXXX  XXXX
+++++++++++++++++++++++++++++++++++++++++++++++++++++++++++++
   2 %                      50 %                     100 %
```

DISTRIBUTION: HANDS

But if a search is done for *main* in combination with one of the terms in the torso (BODY3) category above, seven of its occurrences are found to belong to the particular sensual context of a hand being placed upon a part of the mid-body.[8] Others may fit the body-syntactic mould but in ways wholly unrelated to sensual petting: 'celles qui m'avaient saisie par le bras me courbèrent comme de force, et les autres m'appuyaient *les mains sur les épaules*' (p. 110); this example is a 'tableau' indeed strongly conditioned by interrelation of the particular parts depicted, but in a 'syntax' referring rather to persecution and torture.

Some terms inherently imply some such contact. *Embrasser* is one which can have many kinds of relatively unsensual applications, and accordingly it occurs 22 times (TOUCH4 = all forms of *embrasser*) in a spread quite independent of the Ste-E nexus:

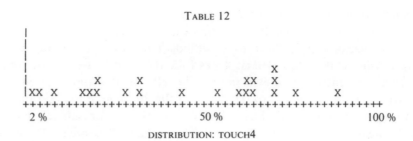

TABLE 12

DISTRIBUTION: TOUCH4

On the other hand, uses of *caresser* are typically much more topologically focused than are those of *embrasser*; we find twenty occurrences of its forms along with those of the substantive *caresse,* and they concentrate in this way (TOUCH3 = *caresse* noun + all forms of *caresser*):

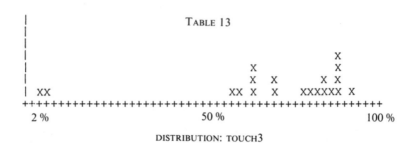

TABLE 13

DISTRIBUTION: TOUCH3

By comparison with the two tables above, *baiser* can easily be shown to function semantically in the text in a manner much more similar to *caresser* than to *embrasser* (TOUCH5 = *baiser* noun + *baiser* verb):

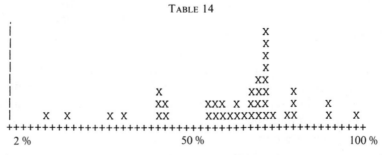

TABLE 14

DISTRIBUTION: TOUCH5

(Of the eleven *baiser* in the text, only three are substantives – which the graphic distribution program cannot distinguish from the infinitive – and there is one plural *baisers*.) The conflation of these two similar families thus yields a high concentration in the Ste-E passage (KISS = TOUCH3 + TOUCH5):

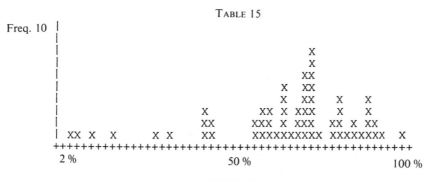

TABLE 15

DISTRIBUTION: KISS

Thus, though the physical aspects of Sainte-Eutrope are obvious enough not to need demonstrating, significant discriminations can be made among the varying signifying functions of semantically related items. It may appear uselessly redundant to assert that occurrences of a certain group of terms tend to accumulate in the very passages where one would intuitively and thematically expect them. One does not read by word counts, and common sense probably dictates a limit beyond which one need not venture in attempting to correlate statistics with generation of meaning. On the other hand, the reader does perceive the persistence of signifieds, at least above a certain threshold, and to some degree of signifiers as well. He may thus quite well assimilate the gist of the Sainte-Eutrope episode without paying particular attention to whether the female breast is *gorge, poitrine* or *sein(s),* and he may detect the non-contemporary aspect of its diction without consciously noticing either the relative absence of *sein* or the quite fundamental distinction between *embrasser* and *baiser.* Nor would he be too surprised, without thinking on it, to hear that little is made of noses, elbows or toes.

Yet for literary study these factors unquestionably add up. What distinguishes one text (or one style) from another is best approached in terms of objectively identifiable criteria, because otherwise one is misled by everyday assumptions about meaning. There is an enormous vocabulary of the body which figures in no way in *La Religieuse.* The most

evident category is scientific Latin terminology: of course, it would not
readily come to mind in discussion of a novel, but it makes the point all
the same. Even if we pared the overall list down to genuinely quotidian
usage, we would find that not all of our words for the 'body', even the
represented body in its predominantly sensuous functions, play a role in a
given physical or erotic text. Looked at microscopically, in fact only a
small vocabulary will emerge, and it will likely be polarized in highly
specific ways. Yet even those words will not reliably index the sexual
phenomenon: they will be susceptible of use in many rather unrelated
ways, and they will by themselves fail to take into account a whole
panoply of related periphrases, allusions, and perhaps metonomies and
catachresis. The substance of Sainte-Eutrope could theoretically be treated
either in a roundabout way or with massive substitution of other signifiers
for the ones we have been discussing. But of course we would then no
longer be talking about *La Religieuse*: and that is just the point.

A further remark, finally, about this application of the computer. The
proof would be even more *probant* (as the French puts it nicely) if it were
based upon a more massive text where time-honoured techniques such as
counting by hand would be, or nearly so, out of the question. As it
happens, I have done some exploration of *La Nouvelle Héloïse,* which
certainly meets that criterion, but the data base in question could at this
time serve up that text only in separate chunks for each of the six books:
therefore an overall graphic was not possible. That is only a temporary
limitation. As for *La Religieuse,* these explorations were done to corrobor-
ate, if possible, some tallies I had indeed first done manually, based upon
a readerly inference. This tool was of course faster, but also much more
accurate; my empirical lists were in fact far from complete.

Nevertheless I would be interested in invoking its use only where I had
some sort of critical intuition to test, and even then not all critical notions
would necessarily gain from lexical statistics. What distinguishes this
medium from the traditional concordance is that the data can be interro-
gated in almost any order as long as the question can be formulated with
some precision. Thus syntax and other aspects of style should ultimately
yield also to investigative techniques. Critical intuition in any case takes
many forms and feeds on many subtle inklings, and it is possible that the
sheer possibility of unlimited manipulative inquiries will nourish and
intrigue – I do not quite say inspire – the indispensible critical intelligence
behind the keyboard.

Notes

[1] The ARTFL database (American and French Research on the Treasury of the French Language) is a joint project of the Centre National de la Recherche Scientifique and the University of Chicago. Further information may be obtained from the Department of Romance Languages and Literatures, University of Chicago, 1050 East 59th St., Chicago, IL 60637. For additional background on this type of study and the basic research tools, see the acts of the round table 'Traitements informatiques de textes du xvIIIe siècle' at the Sixth International Enlightenment Congress, 1983, published by the C.N.R.S. (Institut National de la Langue Française, Textes et documents, série VII, 1984).

[2] Leo Spitzer, 'The Style of Diderot', in *Linguistics and Literary History,* Princeton, 1967. Besides those quoted here, many other examples of anaphora can be cited in *La Religieuse,* often compounded with other repetition/parallelism devices: cf. for example 'je ... je ... on ... on ... on ...' p. 43; 'on ... on ...', etc., p. 78; 'comme si ...' p. 110; 'Où ...' p. 120; 'on ...' p. 143; 'elle ... elle ... je ... je ...' p. 146; 'elle ...' p. 159; 'l'histoire ...' p. 193. A sign of her assimilation at Sainte-Eutrope: Suzanne herself vaguely imitates a *blason* technique in her portrayal of Mme***'s *salon* on p. 172: 'Les unes étaient blondes, d'autres brunes', etc.

[3] Related to the wounds of Christ, indirectly; as Spitzer has pointed out, the *blason* itself derives from a worshipful recital of those sufferings (op. cit., p. 149).

[4] For convenience, I shall continue to use 'Ste-E' adjectively to designate occurrences within this range of text.

[5] The Archive Retrieval and Analysis System (ARRAS) was developed by John B. Smith of the University of North Carolina and adapted for use on the ARTFL database by the ARTFL Project.

[6] The edition cited here is Denis Diderot, *La Religieuse,* Garnier-Flammarion, 1968. The actual text of the data base is that of the Robert Mauzi edition, Paris: Armand Colin, 1961.

[7] Categories of words in this project have English rubrics, to distinguish them from specific French words searched in the text. Singular and plural of nouns are combined unless a specific distinction between their functions is pointed out.

[8] One of the powerful ARRAS search functions, called 'configuration', allows great flexibility in specifying such parameters: in this instance, *main* was to be located within ten words of one of the other terms being searched. Each example rendered must, however, be read to see whether it matches the intention. In this case, the following was one of the spurious results: 'j'avais les deux *mains* dans l'eau, la tête penchée sur la *poitrine,* et je poussais une plainte inarticulée' (p. 109).

The English Proust

Philip Thody : University of Leeds

I

PROUST would have liked Wittgenstein's duck-rabbit. As the first major imaginative writer to give pride of place to the idea that what we see depends upon what we believe to be the case, he would have enjoyed the diagram in *Philosophical Investigations*[1] illustrating what philosophers call the intentionalist theory of perception. Indeed, he might even have found that Wittgenstein had not gone far enough. One of the themes which recurs most insistently in *A la recherche du temps perdu* is that what we see depends on what we feel. When the eye of love is absent, and Marcel catches sight of his grandmother at a moment when he is not expecting to do so, all that he sees 'sous la lampe, rouge, lourde et vulgaire, rêvassant, promenant au-dessus d'un livre des yeux un peu fous' is, as he says, 'une vieille femme accablée que je ne connaissais pas'.[2]

A comparably important theme in *A la recherche du temps perdu* is the way in which the artist can change the perception which we have both of objects and of human beings. A cousin of la Princesse de Luxembourg, for example, described as 'une des beautés les plus altières', commissions a portrait of herself from a leading naturalist painter. Instead of the flattering vision which she expects, that of 'une grande dame', what she is given is that of a little shop girl, 'un trottin', behind whom there is 'un vaste décor incliné et violet qui faisait penser à la place Pigalle'.[3] However hard her more charitably minded friends may try, they will always in the future see her potential sisterhood with Judy O'Grady not very far beneath this society lady's elegant skin.

The knowledge we acquire of the possible similarities between imaginative writers can have a comparably irreversible effect on the way we see them. Once suggest that Somerset Maugham is the English Maupassant, and you can never see either of them in quite the same light again. The deliberate ironies and conscious over-simplifications which seem inseparable from the commercial short story leap at you even more disconcertingly from the page, at the same time as your gratitude is renewed at the possibility of yet another escape into a world brought totally under artistic control. The remark that Aldous Huxley is the nearest thing the English-speaking peoples have to Jean-Paul Sartre makes you similarly conscious of the tendency of writers with ideas to become left-bank pundits or Californian bores, and there is a similar if more dramatic change in your perception when you hear somebody speak of Anthony Powell as 'the English Proust'. Whole sections of *A Dance to the Music of Time* immediately take on additional implications, just as you begin to see the characters, construction and world view of *A la recherche du temps perdu* in a different light. Indeed, your idea of both authors undergoes something of the metamorphosis which comes over the Narrator's vision of Madame de Villeparisis when it is suddenly revealed to him that this rather starchy old lady is in fact a Guermantes. [4]

There is, nevertheless, an important difference. For while a closer look at Maugham and Maupassant may reduce the importance of the similarities between them, it does not make them disappear. The two authors remain in the same tradition of middle-brow fiction, just as Huxley and Sartre continue to be primarily ideological writers in spite of the pacifism of the first and the increasingly indiscriminate cult of violence in the later works of the second. The collocation of *A la recherche du temps perdu* and *A Dance to the Music of Time* gives, in contrast, much more of a duck-rabbit type of picture of literary parallels and resemblances. Now you see them and now you don't, so much so that you sometimes wonder whether the demon of analogy has not taken your reason prisoner in order to make you an object lesson in the folly of making comparisons where no genuine similarities are to be found.

The parallels are there, of course, even if the most immediately obvious of them turns out to be an illusion. For in spite of the apparently striking similarity, the title of Anthony Powell's twelve volume series, *A Dance to the Music of Time* (some 1,130,000 words, as against Proust's 1,240,000), is not specifically derived from *A la recherche du temps perdu.* As Nicholas Jenkins tells us on almost the first page of the first volume, it is taken from 'Poussin's scene in which the Seasons, hand in hand and facing outward, tread in rhythm to the notes of the lyre that the greybeard plays', and we are reminded of the image in the very last volume, *Hearing Secret Harmonies.*[5] The use which Powell makes of the associations of the dance also has no real parallel in Proust. Odette de Crécy may change partners as she moves from Swann to de Forcheville before ending up as mistress of the ageing Basin de Guermantes. But there is nothing comparable to Jean Templer's gyrations as she moves from Bob Duport to Nicholas Jenkins to Colonel Flores, or to the intricate threestep which she executes at another point in the novel between her husband, Bob Duport, Jimmy Stripling and Jimmy Brent. Odette may have cleaned out Pierre de Verjus, comte de Crécy, to his last farthing. But she causes nothing of the misery and destruction which Pamela Flitton leaves behind her as she spins from Bob Duport to Peter Templer or from Kenneth Widmerpool to Xavier Trapnel. Both male and female characters in *A Dance to the Music of Time* are caught up in a complicated pattern of sexual exchanges which sometimes leaves the reader with his head spinning as he tries to work out who is dancing – or sleeping – with whom. Indeed, there is even a sense in which you feel that the hints which Powell drops in *The Military Philosophers* about a possible similarity to Proust are put there almost as a kind of a joke, as a reminder of how very different a picture he is in fact giving of the nature of human relations. For while Proust insists on how long it takes the emotional traumas of Marcel's childhood to work themselves out just in his one relationship with Albertine, Powell offers us a world in which only death or old age can put an end to the apparently insatiable appetite for sexual change which inhabits a particular group of human beings.

But no sooner have you thus convinced yourself that the duck of the initial resemblance is really a rabbit of ironic contrasts than you remember how similar Proust and Powell nevertheless are in their continual use of the visual arts. For, like Proust, Powell has a constant tendency to describe his characters in terms of their similarity to paintings. Charles Stringham, for example, is compared to Alexander the Great receiving the children of Darius after the battle of Issus in the Veronese canvas in the National Gallery. Gypsy Jones looks like Goya's Maja Desnuda or Monet's Olympia. Jean Flores, *ci-devant* Jean Duport, née Jean Templer, looks in old age 'like one of those sad Goya duchesses', and the egregious Scorpio Murtlock is described as being 'not unlike the younger of the two torturers in Mr Deacon's *By the Will of Diocletian*'.[6] It is by reference to Tiepolo's rendering of the Candaules and Cyges legend that Powell brings out the peculiarities of Widmerpool's masochistic voyeurism, and there is considerable retrospective irony in the fact that we are first introduced to Jean Templer as 'a young and virginal saint as depicted by an old Flemish master'.[7] As her subsequent behaviour reveals, it is much more appropriate that she and Nicholas Jenkins should have first dined together sitting directly opposite the depiction of Luxuria in the tapestry illustrating the seven deadly sins at Stourwater Castle.[8]

It is when you visit an art gallery after reading either Powell or Proust that you particularly appreciate how similar the two authors are in the impact which they have made upon you. For you realize that you cannot now look at pictures or portraits without automatically noticing how much the people in them do or do not resemble your friends. Both authors thus modify the way in which we see the artistic as well as the real world, and this again reminds you of the importance which the act of seeing has in *A la recherche du temps perdu.* There is also, in a more literary context, a similarity in the attitude which both authors have towards the real people who have supposedly sat as models for their characters. For although some of the people and incidents in the ninth volume of the series, *The Military Philosophers,* are, as Anthony Powell himself says, 'drawn directly from life' or 'described more or less word for word', he is as reluctant as Proust himself to encourage any attempt to find a one to one relationship between people he knew and the characters he has created. 'To the novelist', writes Powell in the first volume of his autobiography, *Infants of the Spring,* 'the characters in his novel are known as those in a dream are known, the texture too complicated to be explained', and Proust's remark that 'un livre est un grand cimetière où sur la plupart des tombes on ne peut plus lire les noms effacés'[9] shows a comparable recognition of the complicated process of reduction, replacement and substitution whereby the often disappointing real world is transmuted into an imaginary one which is both more coherent and more convincing. Indeed, another of Powell's comments in the first volume of *Keep the Ball Rolling* on what he calls 'the projection of Anatole France as Bergotte' helps us to see how Proust produces some of his best effects. For this projection works, as Powell observes, in *Infants of the Spring,* precisely because Proust omits 'all sorts of comic aspects of Anatole France's true character that might have been included in an unfriendly portrait'.[10]

One reason why we are so often tempted to see Anthony Powell as 'the English Proust' does of course lie in remarks of this kind. Powell is clearly a very enthusiastic Proustian. He has written with wit and knowledge about Proust as a soldier,[11] and Proustian comparisons come so readily to

him that he is not averse to inventing them if he cannot find a suitable one
to hand. As Hilary Spurling has observed, the supposed extract describing
the appearance of Prince Odoacer at a party given by la Princesse de
Guermantes, which takes up at least four pages in *The Military Philosophers,* does not form part of the text of *A la recherche du temps perdu* at
all.[12] Neither have I been able to find textual evidence in Proust's own
description of Saint Loup for the remark in *The Valley of Bones* that
Bithel's military cap resembled that of the Marquis in being 'cut higher
than normal',[13] and inventions like these do rather strengthen the impression that Powell is deliberately drawing your attention to a series of
resemblances between his work and that of Proust in order to lead you up
the garden path. No sooner have you adjusted your sights to bring into
focus the parallels that do exist – both writers describe the upper classes
and the aristocracy, both talk about writers and artists, neither has any
sympathy for the commercial or industrial world, both are interested in
the impact of time on individuals and on society, both give you a good,
long read, both are aware that heterosexuality is not necessarily the
statistical norm – than you become aware of how differently it is possible
to see and interpret any genuine similarities which might happen to exist.
For just as the rapidity with which Powell's characters change partners as
they dance makes you more aware of how slowly human emotions evolve
in *A la recherche du temps perdu,* so the use of the first person narrative
in *A Dance to the Music of Time* brings home to you how differently two
apparently similar novelists can exploit what might at first sight seem very
much the same device.

This difference has even led one of Powell's critics to discount the
possibility of any useful comparison being made between the two novelists. 'I do not think', writes James Tucker in *The Novels of Anthony
Powell,* 'that any useful purpose can be learned from putting *A Dance to
the Music of Time* alongside Proust's *A la recherche du temps perdu.*
Proust's eye is on his narrator's development ('the goal is my heart' as
Swann's Way has it); Powell's is not: the goal is in social patterns'. This is
fair comment, even though one may not agree with the remark later on
that there is 'a gap, an emptiness, or even a wetness, at the centre of the
novel' because of the 'passivity and self-effacement'[14] of the Nicholas
Jenkins who tells the story. Nicholas may not have Marcel's gift for
sustained jealousy. But he is very conscious of what he calls – in a phrase
which reminds you of how often Proust assimilates love to an illness –
'those spasms of frustrated passion that sometimes, like an uncured
disease, break out with renewed virulence at a date when treatment

seemed no longer necessary'.[15] Unlike Marcel, and in another contrast which might be suspected of being deliberate, he is also granted full and detailed knowledge of his mistress's infidelities. Jean Duport tells him that she has had an affair with Jimmy Stripling and he is 'suddenly overwhelmed with a horrible feeling of nausea, as if one had suddenly awoken from sleep and found oneself chained to a corpse'.[16] Later on, in *The Kindly Ones,* Bob Duport tells him of how Jean had deliberately arranged to share her favours simultaneously with Jimmy Strickland and with that 'fat slob' Jimmy Brent, and Jenkins feels as though his legs had been suddenly kicked from under him so that he 'lands on the other side of the room'.[17] The violence of the physical comparisons stands out all the more sharply in Powell's normally restrained style, and we are again reminded of the intensity of Jenkins's feelings when the thought of Jean 'united to Duport had brought to the heart a touch of the red-hot pincers'.[18] But the essential quality of Nicholas Jenkins is that he does not dwell on his feelings, and he is so different in this as in other respects from the Marcel of *A la recherche du temps perdu* that it is again hard to read *A Dance to the Music of Time* without feeling that the contrast is a deliberate one. It is almost as though Powell is telling us that he is indeed a kind of Proust, but a Proust of a very different kind from the anguished, neurotic, half-gentile, guilt-ridden, mother-fixated Marcel – a Proust so English, in fact that he is almost the opposite of the author whom in other respects he so much admires.

II

This is especially the case when one goes against the precepts of *Contre Sainte-Beuve* and looks at the relationship between Powell the man and Powell the creative writer. 'One learns in due course (without ever achieving the aim in practice)', writes Powell in *Infants of the Spring,* 'that, more often than not, it is better to keep deeply felt views about oneself to oneself',[19] and the discretion which Nicholas Jenkins shows in telling us about his marriage or his artistic ambitions seems at times to be aimed at reminding us, in the nicest possible way, that Marcel really does make rather a fuss. For when Powell tells us, in *A Buyer's Market,* that 'this matter of writing was beginning to occupy an increasing amount of attention in my own mind',[20] it is hard to forget the very much more detailed account which the Marcel of *A la recherche du temps perdu* gives us about the nature and scope of his literary ambitions. It is as though

Jenkins were reminding the reader that a gentleman – especially if he happens to be English – does not give more than the absolute minimum of information about his own ambitions or feelings.

This rather curious impression that *A Dance to the Music of Time* offers a kind of parody by contrast to *A la recherche du temps perdu* is strengthened when one turns from Nicholas himself to the artists and writers whose work and personality he chooses to describe. There is Mr Deacon, for example, who benefits in *Hearing Secret Harmonies* from a change in artistic fashions similar in a number of respects to the one which leads le Duc de Guermantes, long after Elstir's death, to bring down from his upstairs study the two sketches which Marcel had earlier seen only by chance and put them on public display.[21] But Mr Deacon, as Ralph Barnby remarks, is an artist who 'as a bad painter, carries all before him',[22] and his posthumous rehabilitation – unlike Elstir's – is in no way the product of a previously unrecognized genius. It is merely the effect of a change in artistic fashion, and Powell's description of it has nothing of Proust's insistence on how long it takes for a truly original artist to be appreciated. It is merely part of the account which *A Dance to the Music of Time* provides of the evolution of English society between the early twenties and the early nineteen-seventies. The revival in popularity of artists such as Edgar Deacon, whose canvases sound rather like a mixture of Puvis de Chavanne and Edward Landseer, was a marked feature of the sixties and seventies. Powell's acknowledgement of the growth of neo-Victorianism is very much part of his notation in other parts of *Hearing Secret Harmonies* of the social atmosphere of the period which also, and rather paradoxically, witnessed what Ken Widmerpool greets as the 'uprooting of bourgeois values relating to morality'.[23]

Any echoes in the character of Mr Deacon of the role played by Elstir in *A la recherche du temps perdu* cannot therefore be taken very seriously. In his own development as a writer, Nicholas Jenkins also needs none of the mentors who help to guide Marcel towards his vocation, and the account of St John Clarke's defects as a novelist reads at times like an ironic echo of the praise bestowed upon Bergotte. Even before he has written any novels himself, Nicholas is scathing about St John Clarke's 'windy descriptive passages' and 'two dimensional characterisation' as well as about the 'emptiness of the writing's inner content'.[24] Any youthful admiration which he might have experienced for St John Clarke's artistic achievement gives way to the impatience which he now feels towards him as towards 'an older person practising the arts in an inept and outworn manner'.[25] It is a characteristic of the inadequate and drunken Bithel in

The Soldier's Art that he should like *Match Me Such Marvel* and describe it as 'something serious that takes a long time to get through',[26] and equally significant that the desirable and sophisticated Jean Duport should have grown out of a liking for St John Clarke's fiction. The artists whom Nicholas likes and admires are his near contemporaries, though it is perhaps significant that none of them creates an abiding masterpiece. Ralph Barnby's murals in the new Donners-Brebner building are destroyed by a direct hit. The manuscript of X. Trapnel's *Profiles in String* is thrown into the Maida Vale canal by Pamela Widmerpool, and the performance of Moreland's symphony in *Temporary Kings* leaves a slight taste of disappointment. It is almost as though Powell were inviting his reader to think more critically both about Marcel's need for the leadership and example of older artists and about the immense importance played by art and artists in the general value system of *A la recherche du temps perdu.* Indeed, there is even a rhetorical question at the end of the fourth volume of Powell's autobiography, *The Strangers are All Gone,* which suggests that this might indeed be his intention. For when he asks 'But if the consolation for life is art, what may the artist expect from life?'[27] it is hard not to feel that he is calling into question Proust's view that 'la vraie vie, la vie enfin découverte et éclaircie, la seule vie par conséquent réellement vécue, c'est la littérature' and that 'la vérité suprême de la vie est dans l'art'.[28] Unlike the Marcel whose capacity to love is totally destroyed by the failure of his relationship with Albertine, Nicholas Jenkins recovers from the jealousy which serves as a leitmotif to his affair with Jean Duport and makes one of the very few happy marriages in modern fiction. Both in its attitude to art and in the general value system which it proposes to the reader, *A Dance to the Music of Time* is a work that seems to belong to a totally different world from *A la recherche du temps perdu.* Not only is it true that now you see the similarities between the two works and now you don't. The similarities which are undoubtedly there seem increasingly to have been deliberately invented in order to make you conscious of how differently human experience can be presented.

For not only is Nicholas Jenkins a self-effacing narrator and an adult who needs no artistic foster parents to enable him to discover his vocation as a writer. He is also a cool and neutral observer of the peculiarities of the sexual world whose easy-going tolerance again underlines what a very anguished narrator we have in *A la recherche du temps perdu.* Nothing can really shock Nicholas Jenkins – unless, of course, it happens to be connected with Jean Duport. Mr Deacon is a homosexual, Eleanor Walpole-

Wilson and Norah Tolland set up what is obviously a lesbian *ménage,* Sir
Magnus Donners combines an interest in bondage with the occasional dip
into voyeurism, Widmerpool has masochistic tendencies which blend
appropriately enough into his Candaules complex, Pamela Flitton is a
frigid nymphomaniac whose interest in death is not unlinked with necrophilia, and Louis Glober has a most unusual if effective way of providing
himself with a memento of the various women he has enjoyed: he takes a
clipping from their pubic hair with a pair of nail scissors which he carries
round with him in 'a small real leather case', and acquires enough to stuff
'a charming little cushion' with these recollections of his triumphs. [29] But
the presentation of these eccentricities reflects nothing of the horror which
Proust's Narrator feels for the very idea of lesbianism, nothing of the
almost morbid fascination inspired in him by le Baron de Charlus's sado-
masochism, nothing of the anguished struggle to come to terms with the
phenomenon of homosexuality which gives rise to the long passage in 'La
race des hommes-femmes' at the beginning of *Sodome et Gomorrhe.*

A story often told in philosophical seminars relates how two school-
boys are required to write a description of their favourite dog. When the
teacher accuses them of plagiarism, on the initially convincing grounds
that the similarity between the two essays extends to the spelling mistakes
and misplaced apostrophes, they justify themselves with one voice by
pointing out that it is the same dog. The similarity of content between *A
la recherche du temps perdu* and *A Dance to the Music of Time* reminds
us that the material available for inclusion in a work of fiction is often
remarkably uniform. If, like Powell, you move between Bohemia, Blooms-
bury, and the English equivalent of the Faubourg Saint-Germain, you are
bound to come across very much the same things that Proust did in the
Paris of the *belle époque.* It is how you react towards them that makes the
difference, and there is again something particularly English in the fact
that Powell's attitude should be more tolerant than that of Proust in
literary as well as in sexual matters. While Nicholas Jenkins is prepared to
accept that the novels of St John Clarke have given a great deal of pleasure
to a number of people, [30] the Narrator in *A la recherche du temps perdu*
has a far more absolutist vision of the nature of literature. Indeed, there
are so many literary styles that he doesn't like – realism and naturalism,
patriotic and committed literature, authors who do not write from inner
experience – that you begin to wonder what cakes and ale are going to be
allowed in the literary feasts of the Proustian future. The recognition by
Nicholas Jenkins that there is room in the literary world for St John
Clarke as well as for X. Trapnel provides a reassuring contrast. At the

same time, it reminds us of how very eclectic English intellectual life so often seems when you compare it with the ferocious battlefields surrounding St Germain-des-Prés. At no point in *A la recherche du temps perdu* is there any acknowledgement that you might want to read a book merely for the fun of it rather than as an exercise in increased perception or spiritual improvement. Both in actual content and explicit philosophy, *A Dance to the Music of Time* offers a different view.

In this respect, of course, both *A la recherche du temps perdu* and *A Dance to the Music of Time* are novels which read the reader almost as much as he reads them. Just as a long exposure to Proust makes you more aware of whether or not you do regard the doctrine of life for art's sake as a satisfactory way of making sense of your experience, so the repeated indulgence in Anthony Powell brings out the extent to which you regard tolerance and clubability as the most important qualities to be cultivated by the late twentieth century urban European. For the characters whom Nicholas Jenkins presents most sympathetically – Ted Jeavons, Sunny Farebrother, Charles Stringham, Odo Stevens, General Conyers, Ralph Barnby, Dicky Umfraville – would obviously be highly acceptable in a Powellian equivalent of Wodehouse's Drones or of Evelyn Waugh's Bellamy's. Uncle Giles, Kenneth Widmerpool or Scorpio Murtlock, on the other hand, would not, and although it may be true that the most interesting characters in Powell's novel are writers – X. Trapnel chief among them – the final values in *A Dance to the Music of Time* are not really those of the artistic life. Nicholas Jenkins, it is true, ends up as the author of a large number of books. But his most endearing characteristic is not his literary creativity, which is almost never discussed. It is his tolerance of other people's foibles, his freedom from the egotism which dominates Uncle Giles and Widmerpool as it does Erridge and X. Trapnel. What makes Jenkins attractive, and what enables you to understand both the success of his marriage and his popularity with so many different people, is the tireless and sympathetic curiosity which he has about his fellow men. It is this which leads him to define himself most accurately when he says 'I always enjoy hearing the details of other people's lives, whether imaginary or not',[31] and which makes you feel how much you would like to meet him.

At first sight, the contrast in this respect between Proust's Marcel and Powell's narrator is absolute. Marcel speaks in *A l'ombre des jeunes filles en fleurs* of his 'total égoisme'[32] and there is little reason to suspect him of exaggeration. Except perhaps in his relationship with his grandmother, he is interested in other people primarily for what he can get out of them.

This is one of the reasons why he goes out of his way to call into question the value of friendship: it tends to lead the artist to waste on company and conversation the time and energy which he ought to be devoting to his work. If time were going backwards, and *A la recherche du temps perdu* happened to have been written after *A Dance to the Music of Time,* you would suspect that Proust was putting Powell right about the nature of the artist's priorities. He certainly had strong enough views on the question for us to imagine him wishing to make the situation quite clear.

III

One of the advantages of comparing Proust to an author who is often so unlike him in a number of respects as Anthony Powell is nevertheless that it can show up aspects of *A la recherche du temps perdu* which a more direct reading might not illuminate. When the violinist Morel turns out to be none other than the son of the Narrator's great-uncle's manservant, we feel that we are in a world whose social unity is expressing itself in a very Anthony Powell-like coincidence, and the same is true of the occasion in *La Fugitive* when the Narrator and his mother come across Mme de Villeparisis in Venice. This is very much an example of what Powell calls in the second volume of his autobiography, *Messengers of Day,* 'the inexorable law of coincidence',[33] as well as an incident which links Proust's ideas on the relationship between what we see and what we know to his consciousness of the passage of time. Madame Sazerat completely fails to recognize in this 'petite bossue, rougeaude et affreuse' old lady the glamorous adventuress who, when she was la Duchesse d'Havré, reduced her father to penury.[34] It is equally instructive, when your recollections of J. G. Quiggin are of the keen Marxist of the twenties and thirties, to visualize him as the now respectable publisher appalled by the revolutionary behaviour of his twin daughters when they let off a stink bomb at the dinner held to celebrate the award of the Magnus Donners Memorial Prize to Russell Gwynnett's *Death's-head Swordsman* in the final volume.

There is also another incident, earlier in the novel, which takes on some additional implications when you read Proust with Powell-like eyes. It takes place in *Sodome et Gomorrhe* at a reception given by the Guermantes for the King and Queen of England. The Duke and Duchess espy the Narrator from afar off, just as the royal party is approaching the buffet, and make what seem like the most enthusiastic gestures inviting him to join them. But he does nothing of the kind, and wins their undying admiration by contenting himself with a deep but distant bow before continuing on his way. It is, when you think of it, a very Anthony Powell thing to do, and highlights a truth about social behaviour which runs through the whole of Proust's analysis of society in *A la recherche du temps perdu.* For if Marcel had judged solely by appearances, he would have ruined his social career for ever. By responding to the invitation, he would not only have become a *terzio incommodo* at the royal table and caused great embarrassment to Oriane and Basin de Guermantes by joining them at the very moment when they did not at all want to see him. He would also have shown a total failure to understand that the social behaviour of human beings is dominated by two contradictory desires: the ambition to be polite; and the equally devout wish to give complete rein to one's egotism. When, in *The Military Philosophers,* Nicholas Jenkins shows a comparable understanding of the prima donna type egoism of high-ranking generals, he is acting in exactly the same way as Proust's Narrator in *Sodome et Gomorrhe.*

What both writers are offering us, in this respect, is a kind of guide to correct social behaviour which it would be very foolish to neglect, for example, when coming into contact with senior members of the British civil service. For if you were to take literally the apparently open and enthusiastic invitation to 'drop in and have lunch next time you are in Whitehall', you would very soon find yourself dropping out of the ranks of the Great and the Good and relegated to the outer darkness reserved for those who do not understand what Proust calls 'l'extension et les limites de certaines formes de l'amabilité aristocratique'.[35] On occasions such as these, the rabbit of the resemblance takes over almost completely, with the duck of difference falling quite a long way out of sight. For Nicholas Jenkins, you may be sure, would have a very keen appreciation of the allowances you must make for the apparent tempering of egotism by good manners in contemporary English society, just as the Marcel of *A la recherche du temps perdu* did in the France of the *belle époque.*

For when you look at the two novels together, you realize that it is no accident that both *A la recherche du temps perdu* and *A Dance to the Music of Time* deal with aristocratic societies which have reached a high though not excessive degree of sophistication. To be acceptable, as Nicholas Jenkins is instinctively acceptable and as Marcel eventually learns to be, you have to learn to bring your own egotism under complete control. As Nicholas Jenkins observes after lunching with Widmerpool in *A Buyer's Market,* 'the illusion that egotists will be pleased, or flattered, by interest taken in their habits persists throughout life',[36] but it is an illusion and should be treated as such. On the one hand, you must forget it is there, and that it rules everybody's conduct; but, on the other, you must join in the universal pretence that it does not exist and therefore plays no part at all. You make yourself what the seventeenth century would have called 'un honnête homme' by diligently repressing your own egotism while at the same time recognizing that other people will still be primarily, if unofficially, motivated by theirs. Neither the Marcel of *Le Côté de Guermantes* nor the Nicholas Jenkins of *A Dance to the Music of Time* see any reason to enter into fits of Alceste-like indignation when confronted by this fact and by the price you have to pay in order to perform your part of the dance without treading on other people's toes. But it is surprising, when you think of it, how like each other the two narrators do then become in their perception of how human beings expect their fellows to behave, and of how essential it is to read the social signs correctly.

G. K. Chesterton once said that the aim of literary criticism should be to tell the author something which would make him jump out of his boots. Marcel Proust would certainly have evinced more than a mild surprise at the suggestion that any part of *A la recherche du temps perdu* could be read as a guide to correct social behaviour, just as he might well have found that some of Anthony Powell's other attitudes verged on the flippant. For it is indeed a far cry from the virtual sanctification of the writer's function in *Le Temps retrouvé* to Anthony Powell's comment that 'I don't think you've got to take yourself too seriously ... you've got to work exceedingly hard, but I don't think an enormous solemnity about it is the right way to get it done'. [37] There is also a remark in *Messengers of Day* which could well have made Proust feel that a tragic subject was not being given its proper importance. 'I don't mind the boys doing it', Rosa Lewis is quoted as saying, 'if they do it with their own class, but I won't have the girls doing it, because they've nothing to do it with'. [38] If the duck of the resemblance between Proust and Powell does so often shift to the rabbit of their difference, it is because of a fundamental contrast in attitudes which makes Proust an obsessed and tragic writer and Powell a detached and comic one. But you can then correct this vision by reminding yourself of how many parallels still remain to be explored. For both authors write about time, but prefer to eschew precise historical dates. Events both in *A la recherche du temps perdu* and in *A Dance to the Music of Time* are situated by reference to what is happening in the world outside the novel, and the only date in Powell's twelve volume series occurs in the very first book to be published, *A Question of Upbringing.*

After that, it is as though he consciously decided to use the Abdication Crisis of 1938 or the events of the Second World War in the same way that Proust used the Dreyfus case or the resignation of MacMahon: as events clear enough in the reader's mind for him to do the dating without any further intervention by the author. The greater control which he had over his material enabled Powell to be far more systematic than Proust ever was, and this again emphasizes the gap between an author who sets his readers only problems they can solve and a writer who, like Proust, still seems to be working on the frontiers of literature. But the ultimate comparison between Powell and Proust, and the one which perhaps fixes itself most permanently in the reader's mind, is that of two authors whose characters grow old. It is so rare a feature of the novel that it deserves to remain as the ultimate justification for bringing together two writers whose books do, above everything else, make us conscious of the passage of time.

Notes

A la recherche du temps perdu is quoted throughout in the 1954 Pléiade edition.
A Dance to the Music of Time is quoted in the standard Heinemann edition, and the following abbreviations are used:

QB	A Question of Upbringing, 1951
BM	A Buyer's Market, 1952
AW	The Acceptance World, 1955
ALM	At Lady Molly's, 1957
CCR	Casanova's Chinese Restaurant, 1960
KO	The Kindly Ones, 1962
VB	The Valley of Bones, 1964
SA	The Soldier's Art, 1966
MP	The Military Philosophers, 1968
BR	Book Do Furnish a Room, 1971
TK	Temporary Kings, 1973
HSH	Hearing Secret Harmonies, 1975.

[1] Basil Blackwell, Oxford, 1953, p. 194.
[2] Pléiade II, p. 141.
[3] Pléiade I, p. 862.
[4] Pléiade I, p. 754.
[5] QB, p. 5 and HSH, p. 32.
[6] Stringham: QB, p. 5; Gypsy Jones: BM, p. 258; Jean Templer: HSH, p. 230; Murtlock: HSH, p. 231.
[7] Jean Templer: QB, p. 73; Candaules and Cyges – see TK, *passim.*

[8] Luxuria: KO, p. 117.
[9] Pléiade III, p. 903. *Infants of the Spring,* Heinemann, p. 52.
[10] *Infants,* p. 53.
[11] In *Marcel Proust. A Centenary Volume 1871-1922,* Weidenfeld and Nicolson, 1971.
[12] Spurling, *A Handbook to Anthony Powell's 'A Dance to the Music of Time',* Heinemann, London, 1977, p. 246.
[13] Bithel/Saint-Loup: VB, p. 32.
[14] James Tucker. *The Novels of Anthony Powell,* Macmillan, 1976, pp. 4 and 103.
[15] Jealousy: BM, p. 207.
[16] Corpse: AW, p. 142.
[17] KO, p. 178.
[18] ALM, p. 68.
[19] *Infants,* p. 189.
[20] BM, p. 242.
[21] Pléiade III, pp. 582-83.
[22] BM, p. 167.
[23] HSH, p. 128.
[24] BM, p. 244.
[25] AW, p. 20.
[26] Bithel: SA, p. 13; Jean Duport: AW, p. 61.
[27] *The Strangers are All Gone,* Heinemann, 1982, p. 201.
[28] Pléiade III, pp. 895 and 902.
[29] TK, pp. 72 and 258.
[30] CCR, p. 82.
[31] ALM, p. 212.
[32] Pléiade I, p. 852.
[33] *Messengers of Day,* Heinemann, 1978, p. 160.
[34] Pléiade III, p. 634.
[35] Pléiade II, p. 663.
[36] BM, p. 32.
[37] *Times Educational Supplement,* 7/3/86.
[38] *Messengers of Day,* p. 138.

The sense of unending

George Watson : St John's College, Cambridge

S O M E stories – most bar-room anecdotes, for instance – are only good for one telling, at least to the same audience.

Others, like Homer's, go on and on. They can be retold to the same listeners, re-read, imitated or extended, and yet remain endlessly new in themselves. No end, apparently, to the variations that can be worked upon them, or to the translations made of them. They are 'unending' stories, so to speak.

In the world's opinion, these are the world's best. I want to ask what is good about them; and out of deference to the dedicatee, and in timorous awareness of my own competence and its limits, I shall consider them less in the realms of ancient epic or medieval romance than in modern prose fiction.

In modern Europe alone, there are half-a-dozen and more stories which, in the sense I have just described, look unending. Drama and poetry long since gave us Faust and Don Juan. In modern prose fiction, the first such instances were surely Spanish – the *picaro,* quickly followed by Cervantes's *Don Quixote* (1605-15), itself a parody of romance; and that comical duo of innocent master and shrewd servant was imitated by Fielding in *Joseph Andrews,* by Dickens in *Pickwick,* and by P. G. Wodehouse in the Jeeves stories. Another was Defoe's *Robinson Crusoe* (1719), based on an existing literature of voyages, real or imaginary – and there the shipwrecked solitary can expand into a group, as in Wyss's *Der schweizerische Robinson,* Ballantyne's *Coral Island* or William Golding's *Lord of the Flies.* Again, there is Mary Shelley's *Frankenstein* (1818) and its legend of the invented monster. And one could go on: in the 1880s Conan Doyle established the whodunit, dominated by a detective of superior intellect; and if film adaptations are to be believed, Dracula and Tarzan may need to be added as candidates for immortality, though only time will tell.

Realistic, here at the outset, to dismiss as naïve and illusory any demand for a common denominator of qualities that make a good story good, or an unending story unending. That very demand, as we have recently been shown, can all too easily lead to convenient falsifications of evidence.[1] On the other hand, the humanistic doctrine of the unchanging human heart looks none the worse for such long-lasting tales, and philosophers are surely right in trying to revive it. 'Après la mort de Dieu, la mort de l'homme', Foucault once triumphantly announced. But the announcement was premature; and after the death of Foucault, it is now tempting to suggest we are witnessing the death of anti-humanism, at least in its wilder literary aspects. Mankind after all is not altogether a product of conditioning: nature as well as nurture has a part to play. 'The notion that we "have a nature"', as Mary Midgley has sagely remarked of the human condition in her *Beast and Man* (1978) – a neo-humanistic study by a professional philosopher –

> far from threatening the concept of freedom, is absolutely essential to it. If we were genuinely plastic and indeterminate at birth, there could be no reason why society should not stamp us into any shape that might suit it. (p. xviii)

adding that the humanistic doctrine of an unchanging human condition is far stronger, on reflection, than anthropology has encouraged us by its habitual assumptions to suppose:

> We take things for granted just because they are constant ... Our business is always for the mutable ... (p. 326)

and if we only *look* for the mutable, whether as South Sea anthropologists or as literary historians – for unlikenesses and never likenesses – then it is the mutable, and only that, that we shall find and report on. Our perceptions are filtered, then, our conclusions partial or false.

The immutable or unending, by contrast – that heartland of the humanistic consciousness, whether in Erasmus, Montaigne, Shakespeare, or Samuel Johnson – is what till recently we did not and dared not study. The very nature of an unchanging human reality was taboo among most French critical theorists of the Sixties and their Anglo-American admirers.

'No text means by itself', as a British disciple of *La Nouvelle Critique* has ventured confidently to put it:

> We *make* texts mean, and the positions from which we do so constitute a major aspect of the meanings we produce ... There is no essential text 'itself', ... any more than there can be ... 'unchanging' reality itself ... [2]

The simplest revenge against that extreme of folly from a professor of English is to turn the argument back on itself. If individual readers, not authors, make texts mean, will the author of that passage licence us to attribute any meaning we please to what he has written? Presumably not; but if not, we may fairly ask, then why not?

But then the arguments of 'narratology' in recent years have been notoriously less than rigorous, and few disciplines are by now so urgently in need of a new broom to sweep clean as the theory of fiction. The dust is mounting. Any old argument, one is inclined to think, has lately been good enough for our mid-century theorists of narrative; any old nonsense will do, provided only it is tricked out with a terminology to look new. When Gérard Genette, in *Figures III* (1972), remarked of Proust that a novelist can tell a story without a place but not without a time, the tenses of verbs necessarily defining temporality – a 'dissymmetry', as he called it, of which 'the deep causes escape us' – his argument was hailed by a Yale admirer as 'valid';[3] though central European critics have long since demonstrated that past and present tenses need reflect nothing as to past and present time – just as we none of us expect science-fiction to be composed in the future tense. The past tense may be nothing more than the conventional mode for telling stories in, whether in fiction or in fact; and such usages are subject in themselves to certain marked exceptions such as the Historic Present. Tenses do not necessarily define temporality, then; Genette's dissymmetry is simply not there; and the search for its 'deep causes', like Roland Barthes's earlier search for 'le principe de la narrativité', may be as indefinitely postponed as Swift's imaginary project for extracting sunbeams out of cucumbers.

But if the humanistic doctrine of the unchanging human heart – nature as well as nurture – is now soundly back, then its first proof of literary excellence is likely to lie in what Samuel Johnson, in his Shakespeare preface of 1765, memorably called 'continuance of esteem'; and there can be no doubt that Quixote and Crusoe have long since earned that. What mankind has loved for generations, as Johnson argued, is unlikely to be slight or trivial. And such continuing esteem seems plainly based on intriguing regularities of design: the shrewd servant saves his innocent master, whether Don Quixote or Bertie Wooster, from his worst follies; the marooned hero survives to be rescued; the monster innocently created turns fiendish, and so on. These are unending, as narrative themes; they work for ever and ever.

To the humanist-critic, that spectacle presents no paradox at all. Why should human beings not be interested in the same stories down the ages, or find them all the more seductive for being utterly familiar? Small children can insist that stories should be repeated identically at bedtime, even word for word; and they do not seem to differ much, in what they relish, from one generation to another. And if adults come to prefer variations of pace and incident, their palates having grown jaded with the years, the variations they sanction remain severely and significantly limited. No reader of a James Bond thriller, for example, and no film-goer, would countenance the death of Bond.

The case of Bond is classic. It seems impossible, on a long view, to suppose that we read stories to discover how they will end, in the larger sense, since in the larger sense we commonly know or guess how they will end; and on re-reading, if we have memories at all, we always know. Even the first-time reader of whodunits knows that a crime will be committed and the criminal unmasked; and the best written of them, like Raymond Chandler's, can be profitably re-read even in the recollected knowledge of who the criminal was. It is not the destination that counts, but the scenery glimpsed along the way. Even alternative endings, when offered, are severely limited in their scope, and John Fowles's final device in *The French Lieutenant's Woman* (1969) was by no means new. In *Villette* (1853), for example, Charlotte Brontë had openly offered her readers, on her last page, the choice of a happy ending or an unhappy. The hero returns from across the seas to marry the heroine, when a storm blows up:

> Here pause: pause at once. There is enough said. Trouble no quiet, kind heart; leave sunny imaginations hope . . . Let them picture union, and a happy succeeding life

plainly implying that the novelist, for herself, regretfully believed her novel to end tragically with a dead hero. And eight years later Dickens was to alter the ending of *Great Expectations* (1861) from a sad to a serene one – '. . . I saw no shadow of another parting from her' – at Bulwer Lytton's suggestion, but as conscious as Charlotte Brontë that a traditional expectation could be satisfied one way or the other.

If humanism were false, it would be hard to explain why, across epochs and continents, we should be interested at all in stories we know to be fictional, and why we should continue to be interested in them even after hearing them once or often. But if, as the great humanists proclaim, the human mind is naturally given to studying likenesses and unlikenesses as a single continuous process – how individuals or communities at once resemble one another and differ – then there is nothing surprising in the view that stories offer ways of studying both, and that by reading and re-reading we enlarge an understanding of humanity that is already in some measure possessed. Any expedition starts from one's own front door, into territory however unknown; and fictions, like other kinds of explanation, naturally move from the familiar to the unfamiliar. The reader starts from somewhere – never from a total ignorance, that is – in order to get anywhere with his reading at all.

Recent theorists have made heavy weather of this, and imagine there is something problematical and unexplainable about caring for worlds that never existed, or about feeling suspense over an ending already known or guessed at. They can be unaware of the wealth and cogency of the long-standing humanist case for such stories, from Erasmus down to the Enlightment. But Sir Philip Sidney has long since summarized Aristotelian mimesis, in his *Apology for Poetry* (1595), with the claims of early modern fiction in mind – whether as prose romances or as Italian-style epics; and among eighteenth-century critics we can find apt solutions to critical problems that the twentieth century has found hard to explain, or has explained wrongly.

One recent critic, for example, has spoken of the 'gap or division within reading', as he calls it, notably in 'our appreciation of the suspense of a story whose ending, in fact, we already know.'[4] But that is to create a problem that is not there, and to answer it in ignorance of what is already known. The 'gap or division' does not exist. Suspense flourishes not in spite of our knowledge of a story, but because of it. It is because we know how a story will end, at least in outline, that we care; and if we did not know, we would not care.

The point can be seized by story-tellers with minds more critical than some critics. In *Betrayal* (1978), for example, Harold Pinter has illustrated it ingeniously by telling a story of adultery in reverse order, starting his play with the bored estrangement of the two lovers and tracing their affair backwards, scene by scene, to end with the initial moment when the wife is seduced by her husband's best friend. That is to underline something that all readers and audiences, though not all critics, easily understand: it is only because a story is going somewhere, and somewhere we want to go, that we are willing to go with it at all. That does not look like a paradox when we take a train or a bus, and it is odd that literary theorists have made a puzzle of it in fiction.

Out of the freedom conferred by the sheer familiarity of story, I suggest, great fictions are born. Every reader of Homer knows that Troy will fall; of Virgil, that Aeneas will survive to found Rome. In *Beowulf,* the hero slays a monster and a dragon and then dies, so that the poem does not even need narrative pace to convince. As J.R.R. Tolkien teasingly remarked long ago, 'the poem was not meant to advance, steadily or unsteadily',[5] so well do we know where it is going. To the ancient and medieval mind, it seems likely, stories were in any case true histories. They had already happened, that is to say; and their endings, though highly interpretable, were known to historians and even, as with Cressida's infidelity, to common proverb. And when the flood of written stories began in Europe, no earlier than the twelfth century, it arose without any theory of fiction to justify it, and needed none, since it was neither offered nor received as fiction – flourishing, as seems likely, in the new conditions of settled town-and-court existence.[6]

There is no 'gap or division', then, in fictional suspense, and we do not suspend belief or knowledge when we cherish and re-read stories whose endings we already know, whether in history, in novels, or in that enormous overlap of the two called historical fiction. The real puzzle would be there if it were otherwise. It would be more than odd – indeed all but incredible – to say that one was interested in the Napoleonic Wars without already knowing that Napoleon eventually lost them. A survivor of a Japanese prisoner-of-war camp once told me that he would find it difficult or impossible to describe his experiences there, whether as fact or fiction, because they were dominated at the time by a deep fear he shared with his fellow-P.O.W.s that the war would drag on and on, and they would never survive it. The same objection, it might be said, if it is one, applies to writing or reading *Robinson Crusoe*: it is a necessary conclusion from the fact that the book exists at all in the first person to suppose that Crusoe was eventually rescued from his island. The problem of the camp-survivor, which is mind-stretching in its implications for fiction and historiography alike, suggests how remote must remain the prospect of telling stories, whether real or imaginary, that are totally unpredictable in their outcome. If such stories exist at all, they exist only exceptionally. For good or ill, we are accustomed as readers to knowing early and soon, in outline at least, how matters will turn out.

Knowing, as usual, means knowing a little or even a good deal, and seeking for just that reason to know more. 'If a lion could talk,' said Wittgenstein, 'we could not understand him.' A non-human consciousness might be so remote as to be meaningless. Even a human consciousness, in a total stranger, can embarrasssingly approach meaninglessness; but in any society one is familiar with, dress and accent offer instant clues to be rapidly and efficiently interpreted and built upon. To read fiction efficiently, then, may be like listening to the gossip of friends: you know, or know about, the characters already; and the stories you hear will help you to know them better. They are not uncommonly told in reverse order, though not usually in the methodical stage-by-stage order of Pinter's *Betrayal.* 'X is in hospital.' 'What's the matter with him?' 'He was knocked down in the street. You see . . .' It would be exceptional, and highly annoying, to be told about X's broken leg strictly in the order in which the events occurred; and pointless to be told about it at all if we did not know X, or know something about him. When the Princess of Wales had a baby in 1982, a London journalist charged with having given wider coverage to the birth of Prince William than to a simultaneous change in Soviet leadership remarked in self-defence that his readers demanded nothing less of him. The ruler of the Soviet Union may be a more important being than an eventual heir to the British throne, at least for the time being. But people *know* Diana Princess of Wales, from photos and press-reports, in a way they do not know the faceless men of the Kremlin. Wanting to know more means knowing something already. No paradox, then, if the stories we know already are more interesting than the stories we do not know.

What is the force of narrative familiarity and repetition – whether re-reading the same old story, as we re-read Homer, or reading new variants of an old story, and perceiving Quixote in Fielding's Parson Adams or in Wodehouse's Bertie Wooster?

Not a damaging force, plainly. Literature is not subject to the commonplace challenge of the anecdotal bore, 'Stop me if you've heard this one before.' As Ezra Pound once remarked, literature is news that stays news. We do not tire of revisiting *Hamlet* or *Faust.* At the start of *Romeo and Juliet,* Shakespeare boldly announces his entire plot in miniature:

> From forth the fatal loins of these two foes
> A pair of star-crossed lovers take their lives

but nobody is meant to leave his theatre-seat on hearing that, two minutes after curtain up. On the contrary, Shakespeare's opening chorus draws one irresistibly, as it is meant to do, into the vaster action of the play. We take delight in the total logic of stories, it seems clear, when perceived singly and at a glance, much as we take delight in the total logic of a great painting at first sight and before entering into its details. In order to take an interest in its details, indeed, we often prefer to know, or to be able to guess, how in broad terms a story will be concluded. When Kipling finished writing *Kim* (1900) he told his father, expecting congratulations. But his father, an intelligent man, asked him searchingly: 'Did *it* stop, or did you?'; and only when Kipling replied that *it* did, would his father concede 'Then it oughtn't to be too bad.'[7]

In the best stories, I suggest, the end is seen in the beginning, if only by parallels. We guess at an early stage, as we are meant to guess, that Viola will marry Orsino at the end of *Twelfth Night* or that Elizabeth Bennet, in *Pride and Prejudice,* will eventually marry Darcy. Faced with a variation or a surprise – we do not know, for example, and are not meant to guess, that Fabrice will become a *chartreux* at the end of Stendhal's *La Chartreuse de Parme,* or that Dorothea Brooke will marry Ladislaw at the end of George Eliot's *Middlemarch* – we are all the more conscious of a norm for having seen it defied. A surprise is relative to an expectation; a variation cannot forget what it varies. Modern fiction has not abandoned the humanistic demand that stories should speak to something permanent in the human heart, and it is hardly possible to see how it ever could.

Stories offer certainties, then, though not only that; and great stories offer certainties we abidingly want. When an infant insists that his bedtime story should be undeviatingly repeated, he is so far from stopping you because he has heard it before that he might be said to want it performed for no reason but that. Perhaps early audiences of the Homeric poems were something like that; and it seems certain that many early readers of the Authorized Version of the Bible or of Milton's *Paradise Lost* were like that, adult as well as childish. The humanistic way of reading is the child's way, though it is not only children who relish repetition, and though it is not just childish to do so. It is by our acceptance of repetition that we recognize great fiction to be that.

The case for the known or predictable ending, whether varied or plain, is essential to the humanistic case for story-telling. When Sir Philip Sidney speaks of stories that hold children from play, in the *Apology for Poetry,* as well as old men from the chimney corner, it is surely known or predictable stories that he has in mind. The Middle Ages, like the early modern era of Sidney, scarcely knew of stories where endings were radically contrary to expectation – the fourteenth-century poem *Sir Gawain and the Green Knight* is a rare and startling exception here – and Sidney did not need to labour the point that the stories of literature are familiar as material, unfamiliar only as to style and treatment. Centuries later a modern scholar was to endorse the same point. 'The romance is the cathedral', wrote C. S. Lewis, 'and the anthropological material the rubble that was used by the builders.'[8] Literary stories are shaped; and their shapes, like those of great architecture, are formally predictable.

It has been all too characteristic of twentieth-century narratology that so much of it has been conducted as if the problem of narrative interest or suspense were a recent and unexplained discovery. But the Enlightenment, in some neglected passages, has long since given us the right explanatory clues, if only we would attend to them. In 1758 Diderot wrote an essay on drama to accompany his play *Le Père de famille*. Called 'Discours sur la poésie dramatique', its eleventh section is devoted to the problem of how to hold the attention of an audience. Diderot may not have read *Romeo and Juliet,* but like Shakespeare he seems to believe that an audience should ideally be told the plot at the start:

> Je ne croirais pas me proposer une tâche fort au-dessus de mes forces, si j'entreprenais un drame où le dénouement serait annoncé dès la première scène, et où je ferais sortir l'intérêt le plus violent de cette circonstance même.

Far from being a make-believe convention between author and audience, then, suspense depends altogether on knowing or guessing what the end must be.

> Le poète me ménage par le secret un instant de surprise; il m'eût exposé par la confidence à une longue inquiétude.

And that leads Diderot to a resounding conclusion about drama that is fully in the long tradition of ancient, medieval and Renaissance story-telling, but somehow lost sight of in twentieth-century criticism: that for the highest dramatic interest, characters themselves may well be ignorant of the story, but the audience should in outline know everything from the start. A few years later, Lessing was to applaud Diderot's doctrine in the *Hamburgische Dramaturgie* (1767-68): 'What a poor pleasure surprise is! And why, in any case, does the poet *need* to surprise us? . . . Our share will

be stronger and livelier, the longer and the more reliably we have
predicted it.'

Great stories have endings, then – preferably predictable and expected
endings.

Story, by contrast, does not, or rather need not. There is no compelling reason why *Quixote* should ever end, as a saga; and Defoe seems to
have left the first part of *Crusoe* deliberately open, in 1719, to see if it
would sell:

> All these things, with some very surprising incidents in some new
> adventures of my own, for ten years more, I may perhaps give a farther
> account of hereafter.

That is how he concludes his first part; and his public duly responding,
Defoe wrote his sequel, *The Farther Adventures of Robinson Crusoe,*
ending with an undeniable conclusion that smacks of authorial fatigue.
'Here resolving to harass myself no more...', though spoken by the
character Crusoe, presumably reflects Defoe's own sense of impatience
with desert islands. In a similar way, Trollope in his *Autobiography* (1883)
has told how he overheard two clergyman in the Athenaeum Club
complaining about his habit of reintroducing the same characters into
each successive Barchester novel, and promised them he would kill off
Mrs Proudie within a week. A given story may have a closure; the great
unending stories do not. In 1931, Wodehouse prefaced his *Jeeves Omnibus* with a categorical undertaking that there would be more stories: 'the
end is not yet'. Authors may grow tired; even readers, for a time, may long
for a change. But the great story-sequences like Quixote and Crusoe still
look inexhaustible in themselves, in principle – infinitely extensible in the
instances they can endlessly accommodate, whether by the same author or
by a succession of authors, whether with characters of the same names or
with different names. Though stories stop, as Kipling's father put it, story
itself does not. There are themes, and echoes of themes, that every
generation wants.

What is it, then, in such great unending stories, that the human race
does not tire of?

If we do not read such stories in order to discover how they will end,
then we must read them for another reason. And that reason, it seems
plain, has to do with what they show us along the way.

Consider, as illustration, the same journey made by two travellers for different reasons. The first, a commuter, performs the journey for no purpose but to get to his destination; and he may not even notice the scenery, since he has travelled that way a hundred times before. The other traveller, by contrast, is travelling for the sake of the journey itself. He may not even want to get to his destination, at least not too quickly; he is there in order to look out of the window. Anyone who has ever travelled on a Swiss mountain railway can tell the difference between these two travellers at a glance: it is usually the difference between a native Swiss and a foreigner. The Swiss is impassive, and probably content to read a newspaper. The foreigner looks awestruck by what he sees from his window. And yet the two men are making the same journey.

I suggest that the rewards of story, in its classic form, are like the rewards of the traveller in a foreign land. There can be no point in travelling towards an unnamed destination – a ticket is always a ticket to somewhere – and Diderot and Lessing were surely right to suggest that one should be told where the train is going before getting on. In *The Faerie Queene,* a poem which in the event he never finished, Spenser tells us in the preface that his twelve books will eventually end with King Arthur finding the Queen of Faery and winning her for himself, having fallen in love with her in a dream. Now we can sit back and look at the scenery: a world of knights and giants, not of ordinary men; of castles, not of cottages; of magic, not of common events.

That may help to explain why some stories are worth re-reading and some are not; some worth extending and some not. Even the most ordinary journey, after all, may be interesting for the first time, and a bar-room anecdote is like that ordinary journey: we are happy to hear it once but no more than once, and it may take an effort in politeness to pretend that we do. Great fiction is something else. A Czech Anglophile once told me how, at the height of the Stalinist oppression of his native land after 1948, when frontiers were closed, he would solace himself by reading and re-reading the novels of Jane Austen; and that effect of internal emigration, as he called it, would presumably have worked far more feebly had he been living in Hampshire or in Bath. The real power of story, surely, lies in its coherence of atmosphere, and not least when that atmosphere is as fresh and as alien as Swiss mountain scenery to a visitor from a lowland plain. The stories we read most, and value most, we read and value less for what they narrate than for their power to build and project worlds other than our own.

The point was seized on by one of the livelier theorists of narrative in our times, C. S. Lewis, in a posthumous collection of essays called *Of This and Other Worlds* (1982) – a group of essays mainly composed in the sixteen years before his death in 1963. The essays were widely hailed, as they appeared, as an expression of a late romantic temperament, in their passion for the otherness of other worlds – whether of *The Faerie Queene,* or of the great Italian epics, or of his friend Tolkien's *Lord of the Rings;* and certainly Lewis and Tolkien were late romantics. But classic and romantic are not opposing terms here, and the demand that a world of story should be something other than our own is a Renaissance critical demand – Sidney called it a 'second Nature' – and it embraces the worlds of Homer and Virgil, of medieval romance, of Malory and Ariosto. To revive all that, as theory or practice, is to revive an ancient and classical idea. 'Tollers', Lewis once remarked to his friend, 'there is too little of what we really like in stories; I am afraid we shall have to write some ourselves.'

Lewis's most potent critical point lies in his attempt to explain why it is that we love stories when we already know or guess how matters will end in them. Story-teller and reader alike, he suggests, are 'trying to catch in a net of successive moments something that is not successive'. It is not the sequence of events we care for, as such, but watching them build and cohere into a total world, and one not our own. For instance: an American pupil once told Lewis he admired the novels of Fenimore Cooper for the excitement of events themselves.

> But I, remembering the great moments of my own early reading, felt quite sure that my friend was misinterpreting his experience, and indeed leaving out the real point. Surely, surely, I thought, the sheer excitement, the suspense, was not what had kept him going back to Fenimore Cooper... I knew that what I wanted from them was not merely 'excitement'. Dangers, of course... But they must... be Redskin dangers. The Redskinnery was what really mattered. (pp. 26-27)

In other words, a coherent other world: feathers, high cheek-bones, whiskered trousers, snow and snow-shoes, beavers and canoes...

Redskinnery, or the atmosphere of otherness, may seem perilous as a general explanation of why we love fiction. And perhaps it is, if it lays too heavy an emphasis on the element of otherness, too little on the issue of sheer coherence of detail. A Frenchman reading a novel by Lesage in the eighteenth century, or an Englishman reading one by Iris Murdoch now, might be thought to belong, as instances, outside the range of the Redskin principle altogether. Such readers might be supposed to be reading for the Here-and-Now.

But are they? Much of the potency of a Murdoch novel, it is true, as of many a compelling radio or TV series, lies in the thousand threads that connect it to one's own life, dreaming or waking: so much so, indeed, that readers have been known to confuse their characters with people they know. Such fictions can easily have a clarity and an urgency that life itself lacks, for some; and it can take an effort of will to pull oneself out of such fictions and back into domestic realities. In Anita Brookner's *Look at Me* (1983), for example, the heroine drops in on friends who are watching the tragic end of a TV film. A beautiful, heart-broken woman rushes out of a building and into her car, and is driven away. The hosts switch off; but for the next few moments, they cannot fully attend to their visitor:

> Nick and Alix stirred like sleepers ... They sipped their coffee almost wordlessly, still contemplating the blank screen. (ch. 9)

Parents who took their children to cinemas to see *The Railway Children,* similarly, have been known to report that it took those children several days to become fully conscious once more of the world around them. It is no exaggeration to say that fiction can be more real than life, and not least to the very young.

The Redskin principle may survive such evidence, however, if we recall that our Here-and-Now has its own Redskinnery. By that I mean that it hangs together: the foods we eat, the clothes we wear, the conversational signs we make to one another, the moral issues we face or funk. The beautiful, heart-broken woman in a Hollywood film, or the brave family of *The Railway Children,* are twentieth-century and Anglo-Saxon: not very exotic, in fact; and we need no subtitles, so to speak. And yet their worlds are not literally our worlds. Their costumes belong to an earlier generation: recognizable, and yet not our own. Their values are similar but not the same. Their choices are lucid, where ours are mostly smudged and fudged. Such worlds are simultaneously both 'this' and 'other'. But then nothing, in fiction, is ever likely to be purely this or purely other. Reading and watching fiction means watching likenesses and differences between our own world and another at the same time.

If Redskinnery can be widened beyond the strictly exotic, I suggest, then as a fictional principle it may do. What it would need to emphasize, that is, is at once the otherness of fictional worlds and their internal coherence. That coherence may be verified against a real world, indeed, but it must also convince on its own terms. Novelists, in that sense, can get it right or wrong; they can even generously admit to having got it wrong. Alison Lurie, questioned on her Anglo-American novel *Foreign Affairs* (1984), has engagingly admitted on radio that she made one or two mistakes, as an American novelist, about British social life – she had not known, for example, that a melodic front-door bell, though U in the United States, is non-U in England – and fully intended to correct those minor errors in a paperback edition. A British reader may be startled to know that he is himself an instance of Redskinnery. But why not? A social texture hangs together – whether real, as in Lurie, or imaginary as in Tolkien. And it begins to fall apart when a mistake is made.

If the story does not depend for its interest on events, why are there events at all?

Lewis dismisses that as a mere technical difficulty: 'Dangers, of course, there must be: how else can you keep a story going?' But that does not answer the question why what you want to keep going should be a story – as opposed to an exposition, perhaps, or an argument. There are other ways of progressing in literature besides narrative. When Sidney wrote the *Apology for Poetry,* he meant by 'poetry' fiction; and it is surely clear that we once again need an apology for fiction, specifically and in the sense of an *apologia.* It needs to be explained, above all, why stories can be so compelling even when no one believes them true.

Sidney's explanation was Aristotle's, or the theory of mimesis. But mimesis, or the lucid representation of eternal verities by imagined instances, is more like a brilliant description of the problem than an explanation of it. Why should we accept that an instance is an instance of anything – the more so since (in modern fiction at least) the instance is usually an invented one? No need to quarrel with Aristotle's account in the *Poetics,* or with Sidney's summary of it. The trouble is, notoriously, that it does not begin to show us how cases relate to generalities, or by what strange and devious routes a child can identify the events of *The Railway Children* with his own mental life.

Some critics have harked back hopefully here to a theory of parable. 'You cannot tell people what to do', W. H. Auden once wrote as a revolutionary young man,

> you can only tell them parables; and that is what art really is, particular stories of particular people and experiences, from which each . . . may draw his own conclusions,

and he calls art – including the art of fiction – 'parable-art'.[9] But that is no more than a place to start an argument, and nothing like the end of it. It may do for the teachings of certain great religious teachers who are precise in the moral lesson they wish to impart, and who translate them into stories to make them the more memorable and the more palatable. 'A sower went forth to sow . . .' But a modern novel is not much like that. It would seem odd, perhaps even crazy, to attempt to squeeze Proust's great novel into a single moral injunction, or even into a series of interconnected injunctions. For one thing, it tells far more, as moral fable, than Proust consciously knows or clearly articulates. For another, the parable-view leaves out the Redskinnery of a great fiction: it suits the thin-blooded clarities of some of Auden's Thirties dramas, that is to say, or of Brecht's theatre, but not the full-blooded life of social fiction. As a concept, it is bloodless.

To put the blood back into modern theory, I suggest we need an admixture of humanism and of Redskinnery.

If humanism is the doctrine that the human heart is unchanging – that there exists, in us all, a nature that can fairly be called human – then it is good news from our schools of philosophy that a such a claim, so strenuously underrated in a century of anthropology and nationalism, is now being seriously considered afresh. Hard to see how the power of the unending, in stories, could ever be explained without such a hypothesis. Redskinnery, by contrast, is not a humanistic doctrine in any classic sense that would have been understood by Erasmus or Montaigne. Its concern is with nurture rather than nature. It sees human worlds as distinctive rather than of a kind. At first blush, it looks contemptuous of the whole principle of the unending in human affairs, whether in fiction or in fact.

It is possible to believe, none the less, that the contempt of Redskinnery for the unending and the commonplace is more apparent than real. And some of the greatest of modern fictions illustrate that paradox in full measure.

This and other worlds . . . But do we not, in the nature of things, need the 'this' to see the 'other' at all, and vice versa? A musicologist once remarked that the only kinds of music he found totally uninteresting were the utterly familiar and the utterly unfamilar; and the literary arts too, it seems likely, flourish best in that 'Middle Earth' between the known and the unknown. When Marguerite Yourcenar was writing the *Mémoires d'Hadrien* (1951), as she has recently told, she was inspired to resume her task soon after the war by a resemblance between the Emperor Hadrian and Winston Churchill, whose memoirs she had just read:

> Je me suis dit: un homme d'Etat peut donc s'expliquer jusqu'à un certain
> point, même en tenant compte de certaines falsifications ou de certaines
> omissions. Mais je ne compare pas Hadrien à Churchill...

meaning that she refused to equate Hadrian with Churchill – if only
because Churchill smoked cigars.[10] (Compare she plainly does.) The
Emperor's family, too, was like and unlike her own family, as twentieth-
century families are like those of the second century and unlike them too.
In fact it is only because they are like that the question of being unlike
arises at all or can be answered at all.

What great fictions offer, then, are worlds like and unlike ours at the
same time. That must seem an unresolvable paradox to whose who, like
critical theorists in the Sixties style, were baffled by anything fuzzier than
lucid symmetries in human understanding. Less baffling, however, to
those who have grasped the humanistic truth that to perceive likeness and
unlikeness is by its nature a single mental operation, whether in literature
or in life; and that if we could not perceive the unchanging elements in
what mankind thinks and feels, the transient and the occasional could
hardly be recognized, in their turn, for what they are, or relished and
revisited like great stories for what they unfailingly have to give.

Notes

[1] See Claude Brémond, *Logique du récit* (Paris, 1973), pp. 11-47, attacking Vladimir
Propp's attempted taxonomy of Russian folk-tales as subject to convenient distortions.

[2] Terence Hawkes, *TLS* (8 June 1984).

[3] Peter Brooks, *Reading for the Plot* (Oxford, 1984), p. 21. On narrative tense see Harald
Weinrich, *Tempus: besprochene und erzählte Welt* (Stuttgart, 1964) and C. P. Casparis,
Tense without Time (Berne, 1975).

[4] Jonathan Culler, *On Deconstruction* (London, 1982), pp. 67-68.

[5] J.R.R. Tolkien, 'Beowulf: the monsters and the critics', *Proceedings of the British
Academy*, 22 (1936), p. 271.

[6] G.T. Shepherd, 'The emancipation of story in the twelfth century', in *Medieval
Narrative: a Symposium*, ed. Hans Bekker-Nielson *et al.*, (Odense, 1979).

[7] Rudyard Kipling, *Something of Myself* (London, 1937), p. 140. On fictional endings
see *Nineteenth-Century Fiction*, 33 (1978); D.L. Higdon, 'Endgames in John Fowles's *The
French Lieutenant's Woman'*, *English Studies*, 65 (1984), based on manuscripts in the
University of Tulsa.

[8] C.S. Lewis, 'The anthropological approach', in *English and Medieval Studies Presented
to J.R.R. Tolkien* (London, 1962), p. 233; reprinted in Lewis, *Selected Essays* (Cambridge,
1969), p. 306, echoing an article by Eugène Vinaver. See also Vinaver, *The Rise of Romance*
(Oxford, 1971), pp. 53 f.

⁹ W.H. Auden, 'Psychology and art today', in *The Arts Today,* ed. Geoffrey Grigson (London, 1935).

¹⁰ Marguerite Yourcenar, *Les Yeux ouverts: entretiens avec Matthieu Galey* (Paris, 1980), p. 159.

'The education of the heart': the moral and social dimensions of George Sand's *Mauprat*[1]

Keith Wren : University of Kent

> 'Crois-tu qu'il y ait autre chose
> dans la vie que l'amour?'[2]

I T is doubtless something of a truism to say that George Sand's reputation as an author has been harmed in the eyes of posterity by her literary facility. Musset's cruel but witty parody of her capacity for over-production in his *Histoire d'un merle blanc* is echoed by the writer herself: 'Je reconnus que j'écrivais vite, facilement, longtemps'.[3] As a result, then, until quite recently, she could be numbered amongst the more neglected representatives of French literary Romanticism. The past few years have, however, witnessed an extraordinary recrudescence of critical activity. It may be argued, nevertheless, that the enormous diversity of her output, not only in terms of the different genres she essayed, but within those genres themselves, makes it feasible to interpret her work from a multiplicity of viewpoints, and it is in this context that I propose to re-evaluate *Mauprat,* published in 1837, with a view to suggesting that in one respect at least it stands at the crossroads of George Sand's early novelistic output, at one and the same time a lapidary reassertion of her views on marriage, as previously exemplified in the cycle of novels from *Indiana* to *Simon,* and in the uncompleted *Lettres à Marcie,* and a precursor of those broader social and political concerns which were to predominate in the subsequent novels of the 1830s and the 1840s.

Such a reading undoubtedly subsumes the interpretations of recent critics, such as C. Sicard and J.-P. Lacassagne in their respective editions of the novel, but ultimately makes wider and more far-reaching claims for *Mauprat* as a pivotal work in George Sand's world-view.[4] P. Vermeylen sees it as prototypical of numerous novels of education for marriage, but I would argue that it is much more than this.[5] It is, I think, the first novel in which George Sand integrates a theory of personal development within the context of the marriage-bond into a theory of human socio-political development. It is, moreover, to my mind the only novel in which she so succinctly achieves an equilibrium between the two, as well as contriving to avoid an excess of overt didacticism. This equilibrium George Sand had tried, but failed, to strike in her novel of 1836, *Simon,* of which *Mauprat* is in a number of respects a more successful reworking. In *Simon* we have the familiar situation of love transcending social class, in the shape of the peasant Simon Féline's aspirations to the hand of Fiamma, the daughter of the comte de Fougères, but we have also the first significant attempt to integrate a political dimension into the fiction, not merely in terms of the satire of the *ancien régime* nobility (in itself not new), but more specifically in the embodiment in one character – Simon's mother Jeanne – of the essential redemptive virtue of the *peuple.* Unfortunately the attempted integration does not really work: Jeanne's role remains largely peripheral, and the plot focuses on the relationship between Fiamma and Simon. In many ways, however, Jeanne does prefigure the more powerful figure of Patience in *Mauprat,* and other similarities are marked. The openings of the novels, emphasising the symbolism of demolished castles formerly inhabited by feudal tyrants are closely parallel; the characters of Fiamma's father and her unsuccessful suitor are essentially reproduced in those of Hubert and M. de la Marche in *Mauprat,* although the satire of the former is considerably and felicitously toned down; the notion of *épreuve* is present, with the woman's apparent coldness very much to the fore in both novels, although in *Simon* the problem is primarily a social rather than a moral one; and, on a more trivial note, each novel features a favourite domestic animal (the hawk Italia in *Simon,* the terrier Blaireau in *Mauprat*) which dies at a great age as a consequence of over-indulgence!

In *Histoire de ma vie* George Sand wrote: 'Quiconque observe le développement de l'enfant, le passage à l'adolescence, à la virilité et toutes nos transformations jusqu'à l'âge mûr, assiste a l'histoire abrégée de la race humaine, laquelle a eu aussi son enfance, sa jeunesse et sa virilité'.[6] In *Mauprat* she makes it clear that her study of the development of Bernard must be seen on these two levels, the literal and the symbolic. Bernard is both the individual, growing up in physical and moral terms, preparing himself for the most testing and significant of human relationships, marriage; and a representative of humanity in general – Everyman – being educated to take his place as a denizen of a new, idealised family of Man, a point which makes the concentration of the action within the Mauprat family so pertinent and symbolic. If the emphasis of the novel seems in the last analysis to fall in the latter category, this is in keeping with preoccupations expressed contemporaneously in the *Lettres à Marcie* and the *Lettres d'un voyageur,* with their stress on the oppression of humanity in general as a consequence of an ill-constructed social order, rather than on the oppression of women by men.[7] This idea is most succinctly expressed in the preface to *Le Compagnon du Tour de France* (1840): 'Tant que la société officielle ne sera pas construite en vue de l'égalité humaine, la société officielle sera caste'.[8] The 1851 *notice* to *Mauprat* confirms the broadening base of George Sand's field of enquiry in the novel – 'ce qui manque au mariage, ce sont des éléments de bonheur et d'équité d'un ordre trop élevé pour que la société actuelle s'en occupe' (p. 29) – and the peroration of the novel, added for this edition, with its insistence on the transformation of humanity, individually and collectively, through love, clearly indicates that for George Sand the problem of interpersonal relations has been absorbed into the wider context of the reform of society: in this respect the historical setting of the main action of the novel in the 1770s and its anticipatory references to the coming of the French Revolution are undeniably significant.

For the purposes of her demonstration, George Sand sets much store by placing Bernard in an atmosphere that is both socially and personally retrogressive. His grandfather Tristan (the name, with its echoes of Arthurian chivalry, is profoundly ironic) is characterised as 'le dernier débris que notre province eût conservé de cette race de petits tyrans féodaux dont la France avait été couverte et infestée pendant tant de siècles' (p. 38). Tristan's idea of his exalted station goes hand in hand with a pervasive nostalgia for the past: 'mon grand-père ne parlait que de sa généalogie et des prouesses de ses ancêtres; il regrettait le bon temps où les châtelains avaient chez eux des instruments pour la torture, des oubliettes et surtout des canons' (pp. 40-41). In fact he is endeavouring to resurrect those times when the aristocracy ruled absolutely as autonomous sovereigns over their terrified vassals. Even in the extremely backward area of France where he holds sway, however, his notion of the principles of power is becoming an anachronism as 1789 approaches: 'Même dans nos provinces du centre, les plus arriérées par leur situation, le sentiment de l'équité sociale l'emportait déjà sur la coutume barbare' (p. 38), and Tristan's attempt to turn the clock back is ultimately doomed to failure.[9] Nonetheless, the personal prestige of the old renegade enables him temporarily to impose his will on his peasants, 'de sorte que, tandis qu'à une faible distance de ce pays la France marchait à grands pas vers l'affranchissement des classes pauvres, la Varenne suivait une marche rétrograde, et retournait à plein collier vers l'ancienne tyrannie des hobereaux' (p. 40). And George Sand insists that 'Mauprat et ses enfants rompirent avec les

lois civiles comme ils avaient rompu avec les lois morales' (p. 38), thus
equating political oppression with moral inadequacy.

Bernard's situation in his formative years is thus both morally and
socially primitive and retrograde, declining further on the death of Tristan,
whose only superiority was over his sons: 'il est certain qu'il y avait en lui
quelque chose de plus cruel et de moins vil que dans ses fils ... De
brigands nous devînmes filous, et notre nom détesté s'avilit de plus en
plus' (p. 67). The insistence on the idea of baseness clearly makes the
point that for George Sand nobility is not dependent on lineage: the
Mauprat brothers are 'de vrais coquins, capables de tout mal, et complètement idiots devant une noble idée, ou devant un bon sentiment' (pp.
43-44). Bernard is potentially less beyond redemption than such a description would imply, for he is not quintessentially vicious, as his uncles are,
though if, as he says, 'je grandis ... sans concevoir aucun attrait pour le
vice' (p. 45), he admits that 'j'avais le caractère aussi mal fait que mes
compagnons; et si mon cœur valait mieux, mes manières n'étaient pas
moins arrogantes ni mes plaisanteries de meilleur goût' (p. 47). Significantly his relative superiority in this respect is ascribed to the only woman
in his early life, his mother, although she dies (symbolically murdered by
Tristan) before her beneficial influence can be translated into anything
more specific: 'j'avais reçu de ma mere de bonnes notions sans avoir
peut-être naturellement de bonnes qualités ... J'étais d'une opiniâtreté
révoltante; pourtant ma mère seule réussissait à me vaincre ... Avec ce
seul ascendant, dont je me souviens, et celui d'une autre femme que j'ai
subi par la suite, il y avait et il y a eu de quoi me mener à bien' (p. 44). As
a consequence of this, he stands aloof from the barbaric and brutal
treatment of women captives by his uncles, since his own sexual arousal
cannot obliterate a sense of the grotesque indignity of what they suffer:
'Tout ce que je sais, c'est que j'éprouvais un affreux malaise en présence
de ces actions iniques; mon sang se figeait dans mes veines, ma gorge se
serrait, et je m'enfuyais pour ne pas répéter les cris qui frappaient mon
oreille' (p. 47). This marginally more evolved view, as much as anything
else, marks him out from his uncles since 'les femmes n'étaient qu'un objet
de mépris pour tout ce qui m'entourait' (p. 47).

In this way George Sand sets the scene for Bernard's rehabilitation at
the hands of Edmée: paradoxically, although *he* appears to rescue *her* from
his uncles' depredations, it is in fact *she* who rescues *him,* not only from
the besieging soldiery, but from succumbing without reprieve to his baser
instincts. The surface symbolism is, however, telling: Edmée, trapped on
alien ground, where the unjust and inequitable conventions of a 'feudal'

past prevail, can only escape by selling herself to Bernard on the latter's terms, even though pardonable sophistry enables her to convert Bernard's determination to pre-empt the marital rights of M. de la Marche – 'Jurez que vous serez à moi d'abord' (p. 84) – to the subtly different 'je jure de n'être à personne avant d'être à vous' (p. 84). The château of La Roche-Mauprat, a microcosm of the values (if such they can be called) of the old world, is thus the setting for a promise exacted by force, whereby man's power over woman, a social relationship typifying such values, is perpetuated. As the price of her freedom, Edmée must yield herself to Bernard. A key theme of the novel, the replacement of compulsion by consent, is here adumbrated.

The escape from the castle permits Bernard literally to emerge into a new world. Himself in fee to the values of the past, he encounters those who have kept pace with the times, and those who have moved ahead of them. Amongst the former are the chevalier Hubert de Mauprat, Edmée's father, 'un homme sage et juste, parce qu'il était éclairé, parce que son père n'avait pas repoussé l'esprit de son siècle et lui avait fait donner de l'éducation' (p. 36), and her fiancé, M. de la Marche, 'grand voltairien, grand admirateur de Franklin, plus honnête qu'intelligent' (p. 111). Amongst the latter are Edmée herself and her tutor, the abbé Aubert; and George Sand rather systematically characterises the division: 'Le fait est que le chevalier était imbu de beaucoup de préjugés. Il avait recu une très bonne éducation pour son temps et pour un noble campagnard; mais le siècle avait marché plus vite que lui. Edmée, ardente et romanesque; l'abbé, sentimental et systématique, avaient marché plus vite encore que le siècle' (p. 157). A similar division exists between Edmée and her fiancé: 'Il avait développé la pale intelligence dont il était doué à la froide école de Voltaire et d'Helvétius. Edmée avait allumé sa vaste intelligence aux brûlantes déclamations de Jean-Jacques' (p. 116). Hence Bernard's attachment to Edmée posits a relationship between the product of the retrogressive feudal order and the representative of the progressive revolutionary one. His personal and social education could hardly be more thoroughgoing.

In a profound sense, the social education is a consequence of the personal, for Bernard's learning to understand the nature of the only relationship Edmée will accept, a contract between equals, implies his learning to understand that the nature of the only genuine social bond is similar. Bernard's attempts to assert over Edmée the rights that he considers her promise to have given him, 'la criminelle résolution de la posséder par la force' (p. 123), get short shrift: 'Je ne vous appartiendrai jamais, répondit-elle avec une froideur de plus en plus glaciale, si vous ne changez pas de langage, de manières et de sentiments' (p. 123). As these words indicate, a complete overhaul is necessitated. Edmée cannot agree to the purely physical release of casual sex which is what Bernard originally had in mind. 'Vos sentiments et vos idées sont comme vos manières', she tells him, 'et c'est là ce que je ne puis souffrir . . . L'affection ne se commande pas, elle se demande ou s'inspire; faites que je vous aime toujours' (pp. 125-26). Relationships between the sexes cannot be conducted purely on the grounds of appetite, neither can they be made to order on the basis of society's (and Hubert's) habitual understanding of what constitutes a 'suitable' marriage: the 'beauté morale de son principe' (p. 29) does not lie here. From now on, Bernard *intellectually* understands the basis of a future relationship, 'ces lois de la pudeur et de la liberté sainte que mon ignorance avait outragées et blasphémées jusque-là' (p. 147), to the extent that he now feels humiliated by Edmée's entirely justified mistrust: but the implementation of this intellectual awareness is another matter, and Bernard fails to rise to the challenge posed by M. de la Marche's renewed offer of marriage after he has learned of Edmée's compromising sojourn at La Roche-Mauprat. Here George Sand makes the position perfectly plain. If indeed Edmée were to decline M. de la Marche's offer, would Bernard release her from her promise, thus rendering her freedom absolute? As she observes, Bernard 'se prévaut d'un engagement que mon cœur n'a peut-être pas ratifié' (p. 174): does he possess the moral stature to release her *without preconditions* – 'sans savoir ce que je prétends faire, comprenez-vous que vous devez me rendre ma liberté et renoncer à des droits barbares?' (p. 175)? Bernard fails the test – 'Je ne me sentais pas la force de renoncer à elle de bonne grâce' (p. 174) – and his subsequent attempt to retrieve the position is still not quite good enough. He enlists with Lafayette's volunteer force to fight for the Americans in the War of Independence, only writing to Edmée prior to his embarcation at Cadiz 'qu'elle était libre et que je ne contrarierais aucune de ses résolutions, mais qu'il m'était impossible d'être témoin du triomphe de mon rival' (p. 178). Significantly it is easier for Bernard to commit himself to supporting political freedom than it is for him to accept the consequences of such egalitarian principles in the realm of personal relationships, despite the fact that it is Edmée who has first fired him with the love of liberty. We can surely see this as a fictional exemplification of George Sand's argument that universal political emancipation will (and must) precede that of the so-called weaker sex.[10] The American expedition, however, brings him into providential contact with Arthur, whose therapeutic conversation suggests to Bernard 'de telles réflexions, que je parvins à déduire logiquement de tous mes souvenirs les motifs de la conduite d'Edmée' (p. 182).[11] It is Arthur who keeps Bernard up to the mark: 'sans lui je fusse redevenu peut-être, sinon le coupe-jarret de la Roche-Mauprat, du moins le sauvage de la Varenne' (p. 182). Such moral reinforcement enables Bernard to be in a position, after his return to France, to tell Hubert in his daughter's presence that 'Edmée ne doit pas m'épouser; ce serait accepter la honte de l'injure que j'ai attirée sur elle' (p. 223). This renunciation of sorts, however, is *still* not quite good enough, and George Sand spins the process out (arguably somewhat overplaying her hand) until Hubert's fox-hunt. Here Bernard confronts Edmée at La Tour Gazeau, site of her previous escape from his clutches, and, despite the fact that she is now even more completely at his mercy than on the former occasion, summons the requisite strength of character to abjure the gratification of his desires:

> J'étais pâle, mes poings se contractaient; je n'avais qu'à vouloir, et la plus faible de mes étreintes l'eût arrachée de son cheval, terrassée, livrée à mes désirs. Un moment d'abandon à mes instincts farouches, et je pouvais assouvir, éteindre, par la possession d'un instant, le feu qui me dévorait depuis sept années! Edmée n'a jamais su quel péril son honneur a couru dans cette minute d'angoisses; j'en garde un éternel remords; mais Dieu seul en sera juge, car je triomphai, et cette pensée de mal fut la dernière de ma vie. (pp. 251-52)

Only now can Edmée acclaim him in the courtroom as 'le premier des hommes par la sagesse et l'intelligence, comme tu en es le premier par le cœur' (p. 299).[12]

But if George Sand offers us in *Mauprat* an image of the development of the perfect relationship, she no less importantly provides an image of the new society in which that relationship can flourish. In this respect it is significant that the setting of the novel is a historical one, for there can be little doubt that the new society is to be based on the principles of the Revolution. Bernard must be led from the values of feudal tyranny to those enshrining the equality of all human beings. Instrumental in this task is the figure of Patience, whom George Sand pointedly depicts as at odds with the old social order, in consequence of which he has become a recluse. The analogies between this rustic philosopher, 'une nature éminemment contemplative' (p. 48), and J.-J. Rousseau are perhaps a trifle too obvious: not only does Patience announce that 'je m'en vais vivre dans les bois à la manière des hommes primitifs' (p. 51), he develops an unbounded enthusiasm for the works of Jean-Jacques, especially for *Du Contrat social,* which becomes his preferred bedside reading. Like the Rousseau of *Les Rêveries du promeneur solitaire,* therefore, Patience is leading an isolated existence away from the rest of humanity which has rejected him, and which he rejects, when he comes into contact with Bernard, whose social education he is to be instrumental in forwarding, just as Edmée promotes his moral and emotional education.

The first encounter between Bernard and Patience is, as befits their essential function in the novel, profoundly symbolic. Patience has no love for the elder branch of the Mauprat family to which Bernard belongs, as one of Bernard's companions warns him: 'Ce vieux *chétif* n'aime pas les *monsieu,* et il dit qu'il voudrait voir M. Tristan et tous ses enfants pendus au bout de la même branche' (p. 50). Bernard, apparently aspiring to play David to Patience's Goliath, endeavours to fell the old man with a shot from his sling. Inadequate marksmanship causes the stone to miss its target, and kill instead Patience's pet owl. The death of this somewhat improbable domestic beast infuriates Patience, although its demise and the subsequent punishment inflicted on Bernard are more germane to George Sand's allegorical purposes than to any attempt at realism. The beating which Bernard receives inverts the social scale as a foretaste of the coming Revolution: when Bernard subsequently threatens retribution by docking Patience's ears, the rustic (with remarkable historical prescience) replies that 'un temps n'est peut-être pas loin où les manants ne couperont aux nobles ni les jarrets ni les oreilles, mais la tête et la bourse' (p. 65). It also points to the abuse of intellectual capacity by the *ancien régime* nobility, who fail to use their gifts for the betterment of their fellows – 'un Mauprat, vois-tu, ça sait lire et écrire, et ça n'en est que plus méchant' (p. 58). But his approach to his quarrels is less sanguinary than the Mauprats' to theirs – the case of Tristan and the *greffier* comes to mind – and Bernard's punishment is less painful than humiliating: Patience 'accrocha la chouette à une branche au-dessus de ma tête, et le sang de l'oiseau, s'égouttant sur moi, me pénétrait d'horreur' (p. 58). Now the owl in Greek mythology was sacred to Pallas Athene, goddess of wisdom, which suggests that George Sand may well wish to make the point that Bernard, as a consequence of his punishment, is 'penetrated' not only with horror, but ultimately with wisdom: dimly he perceives the justice of Patience's beating, and eschews the possibility of easy revenge carried out by his uncles: 'je fus retenu par je ne sais quel instinct de loyauté que je ne me connaissais pas, et que je ne pus guère m'expliquer à moi-même' (p. 62).[13] What is more, Pallas Athene may equally be seen to epitomise the female principle, in which sense the punishment not only prefigures the subsequent influence of Edmée in Bernard's life, but also obscurely inculcates the first seeds of an awareness of an empathy with the condition of women; it is noticeable that Bernard's plight vis-à-vis Patience is an exact parallel of the plight of the female prisoners in his uncles' den.

Clearly, therefore, George Sand intends us to understand Bernard's moral and social education as proceeding hand in hand. Not only are Edmée's political proclivities very much geared towards the people, rather than her own class, as exemplified by her treatment of Patience – 'c'était la première fois que j'entendais parler d'un paysan comme un homme . . . voilà qu'Edmée prenait parti pour lui contre la noblesse' (p. 110) – but the turning-point in Bernard's own development, the evening of which he says 'je n'étais déjà plus l'homme de la veille, et je ne devais jamais redevenir complètement celui de la Roche-Mauprat' (p. 135), comprises two long interviews, of which the first, with Edmée, posits, as we have seen, the notion of individual equality between the sexes, and is followed by an interview with Patience, signalling the concept of equality between the classes. This gospel of liberation in favour of the oppressed – 'le peuple vaut mieux que la noblesse, parce que la noblesse l'écrase et qu'il le souffre!' (p. 133) once again becomes an apocalyptic prefiguration of the Revolution: 'Le pauvre a assez souffert; il se tournera contre le riche, et les châteaux tomberont, et les terres seront dépecées . . . Les étoiles vivent en paix, et rien ne dérange leur ordre éternel . . . Or, un temps viendra où le même ordre régnera parmi les hommes. Les méchants seront balayés par le vent du Seigneur' (p. 133).[14] The mythopoetic impression conveyed by Patience's words serves to transcend historical contingency and to underline the continuing validity of his vision. Not for nothing does he remind Bernard of an Old Testament prophet, or us of the Rousseau of the second *promenade* of the *Rêveries*.

This symbolic social renewal is also exemplified in the physical displacements of Patience. He abandons the ruins of La Tour Gazeau for 'une cabane voisine du château' (p. 115), the chateau being Hubert's estate at Sainte-Sévère where his friend and mentor, the abbé Aubert, has been installed. He does have misgivings about this. 'Tant d'années passées dans la solitude l'avaient tellement attaché à sa tour Gazeau qu'il hésitait à lui préférer la société de son ami. En outre, il disait que l'abbé allait se corrompre dans le *commerce des grands,* que bientôt il subirait à son insu l'influence des vieilles idées, et qu'il se refroidirait à l'égard de la *cause sainte*' (p. 115). In fact, what we see here is the beginning of the reintegration of the Rousseau-figure into a regenerated social order. The misgivings prove groundless, and when Bernard returns from America, he notices that Patience has now gone in for home improvements: flowers, vegetables and fruit-trees abound, all of which 'trahissaient dans Patience un singulier retour à des idées d'ordre social et des habitudes de luxe' (p. 198). Patience himself is discovered in this 'nouvel Eden' (p. 198) counting his money. He has become Edmée's almoner, administering her charitable works much more efficiently than she herself and the abbé have been able to do, for he tells her that 'il faudrait que les personnes qui font comme vous beaucoup de charités particulières les fissent sans consulter la fantaisie de celui qui demande, mais bien après avoir reconnu ses véritables besoins' (p. 201). This aptly makes the point that there *is* a role for the Rousseau-style misanthropist in a rejuvenated social order: as Patience declares, 'Je n'avais pas voulu vivre avec les hommes, mais je les aimais; je les savais plus malheureux que méchants' (p. 201).

However, if Patience appears to take control of Sainte-Sévère after the attempt on Edmée's life (Hubert's increasing senility rendering him incapable of so doing), it is significant that he goes to ground when the corrupt combination of the Church and the legal system reasserts the worst aspects of the *ancien régime* in the manipulation of Bernard's trial: 'il avait repris sa vie errante dans les bois, et sans se cacher, il était insaisissable' (p. 269). His reappearance, to testify in favour of Bernard, whose condemnation is otherwise assured thanks to an unsavoury mixture of clerical skullduggery and personal rancour, is thus to be seen as a redemptive act, underlining the fact that Bernard is now ready to take his place amongst the élite of the new social order: his support for the American republicans in the War of Independence has gained him the right to be considered as an embodiment of the ideals of revolutionary democracy, and the old order, symbolically personified in Jean de Mauprat, must not be allowed to reclaim or to destroy him. His trial is therefore a test case, justifying Patience's appeal over the heads of the corrupt legal establishment directly to the people: 'vous qui m'entendez, hommes du peuple . . . vous dont on appelle la voix la voix de Dieu, joignez-vous à moi, embrassez la défense de la vérité . . . c'est vous qu'on insulte et qu'on menace quand on viole les lois' (p. 281). Moreover, to underline the divorce between him and the prevailing criminal code, he refuses to give evidence unless he is allowed to remove his formal dress: 'il attendit à peine un signe d'adhésion . . . pour jeter à terre ces insignes de la civilisation' (p. 287). Apprehended as a fugitive witness, it is nonetheless he who puts his captors on trial.

Edmée's appearance in the courtroom completes the picture. Bernard, on trial before a court embodying the corrupt values of the past, is symbolically reclaimed by the two figures who have effected his rehabilitation and who represent the libertarian values of the future. The delegates of the old order betray and destroy each other, for Jean de Mauprat's denunciation of Antoine exposes and invalidates the judicial system that has called Bernard to trial and reveals the machinations of the Catholic church that has masterminded it. On the other hand, Edmée – whose presence in law is surely entirely superfluous – at last recognises and exalts Bernard's full potential. Her role here may well represent George Sand's attempt to rework the Isis myth, in which the unveiling of the goddess symbolises a destruction of the prevailing order of things. [15] Significantly it is Bernard's American friend Arthur who physically supports Edmée and who removes her veil: thus political and moral transformation are again seen to go hand in hand and are revealed together.

With Bernard acquitted and the old order defeated, George Sand can indulge herself in a slightly improbable epilogue, in which the chosen harbingers of a utopian future – Bernard, Edmée, Patience, Marcasse, Arthur and the abbé – go off to visit Switzerland, land of equality. All distinctions of rank are abolished between them: 'nous montâmes tous dans la même voiture de voyage' (p. 307), and although Patience and Marcasse travel on the outside, being more accustomed to the vagaries of the climatic conditions, 'nous les traitâmes sur le pied de la plus parfaite égalité' (p. 307). It is perhaps superfluous to say that Rousseau's homeland has a dramatic effect on Patience, although he is persuaded not to retire there, but to return to Sainte-Sévère. This is necessitated as much by the author's wish to show the protagonists' reaction to the coming of the Revolution as by the needs of the plot. For if the novel deals essentially with the inadequacy of the old social and moral order, then the Revolution should logically represent its demolition on a global scale, just as Bernard's education had represented it on an individual scale. In fact George Sand makes it perfectly clear that the principles of the Revolution embody a philosophy that its practice signally fails to put into effect. Certainly, Bernard and Edmée hand over the larger part of their lands to the state 'de grand cœur, et en les considérant comme de justes sacrifices' (p. 312), and Patience, in defiance of historical veracity, is unanimously named as district judge, with exceptionally positive consequences. But there is no doubt that the 'orages' and the 'passions' of the period are viewed as regrettable, not only by the abbé, 'effrayé du sang versé' (p. 312), but by Edmée herself: 'femme et compatissante, elle souffrit profondément des misères de tous les partis, elle pleura tous les malheurs de son siècle mais elle n'en méconnut jamais la grandeur saintement fanatique'

(p. 312).[16] If the Revolution has failed, for whatever reason, to implement the new society, then it is clear that the burden of this historical novel's message must be aimed at the author's contemporaries.

For George Sand, therefore, the purport of her novel was one of actuality and immediacy. On the last page, Bernard, in his role as narrator, reverts to a mode of overt didacticism which effectively summarises the implications of the narrative.[17] George Sand opts for a form of relative, rather than absolute, social and moral determinism: 'Ne croyez à aucune fatalité absolue et nécessaire, mes enfants, et cependant admettez une part d'entraînement dans nos instincts, dans nos facultés, dans les impressions qui ont entouré notre berceau, dans les premiers spectacles qui ont frappé notre enfance; en un mot, dans tout ce monde extérieur qui a présidé au développement de notre âme' (p. 314). In this way we can accept Bernard's basic decency and cast the blame on to the corroding effects of his inevitably misspent youth at La Roche-Mauprat. How then are the positive qualities of *each* individual to be elicited? By education, certainly and definitely: 'l'éducation peut et doit trouver remède à tout' (p. 314), but 'l'éducation générale et en commun semble nécessaire, s'ensuit-il qu'elle doive être la même pour tous?' (p. 314). And, George Sand exhorts us, 'en attendant qu'on ait résolu le problème d'une éducation commune à tous, et cependant appropriée à chacun, attachez-vous à vous corriger les uns les autres ... en vous aimant beaucoup les uns les autres' (p. 314).[18]

This secularised version of the commandment to 'love thy neighbour as thyself' surely offers a key to George Sand's social thought as exemplified in the didactic import of the novel. If she has chosen to focus on the rehabilitation of a brute, 'un vieux rameau heureusement détaché d'un méchant tronc et transplanté dans la bonne terre' (p. 33), to render her message more striking, we must remember that the novel is also about the social re-education of Patience. Since we are told of Patience that, during the Revolution, 'son intégrité, son impartialité entre le château et la chaumière, sa fermeté et sa sagesse, ont laissé des souvenirs ineffaçables dans la Varenne' (p. 313), it becomes clear that the *ancien régime*'s ostracism of him is, in effect, self-defeating, and that persons such as he have a major social contribution to make. Bernard's education, if fraught with difficulties, is at least relatively straightforward. Patience poses a different problem. Unschooled and unacademic, practically unable to read, he confounds the abbé with his 'intelligence inculte' (p. 50): 'ces idées abstraites étaient en lui, on les pressentait en le voyant, en l'écoutant; et c'était merveille que la manière dont il parvenait à les rendre dans son langage rustique, animé d'une poésie barbare' (p. 50). He it is, as we have seen, who points out Bernard's abuse of the talents conveyed by literacy, yet he himself has talents which bear no relation to literacy, a finer feeling illustrated by his appreciation of poetry, which so inspires him that in his imagination 'il combattit, il aima, il vainquit, il éclaira les peuples, pacifia le monde, redressa les torts du genre humain et bâtit des temples au grand esprit de l'univers' (p. 111). In the novel we see a fair proportion of such fantastic aspirations realised, yet only in the utopian universe of Bernard and Edmée is his potential recognised.

So the novel, in effect, closes on a question, aptly posed by the beneficiary of education, Bernard himself. How can the talents of the people, who comprise the vast majority of society, be channelled to benefit that society? Bernard implies that education cannot be 'la même pour tous', and the novel's achievement in demonstrating the fruitful consequences of two very different 'educations', Bernard's and Patience's, both widely at variance with the norm, conveys the necessity for a comprehensive *redefinition* of the nature and purpose of education. Humanity, after all, is not, or should not be an endless series of clones: 'Dieu eût départi à tous les hommes une égale dose d'intelligence et de vertu s'il eût voulu fonder le principe d'égalité parmi eux ... mais il fait les grands hommes pour commander aux petits hommes, comme il a fait un cèdre pour protéger l'hysope'.[19] We see here the implication of a rejection of the principle of equality that would sit ill with the doctrine of *Mauprat,* were it not possible to gloss it with a further quotation from the same source: 'je te dirai bien que la grande loi d'égalité ... est la première et la seule invariable loi de morale et d'équité qui se présente à mon esprit dans tous les temps'.[20] These mutually contradictory statements can however be reconciled, and so to do is to cast light on the question posed on the closing page of *Mauprat.* In the persons of Bernard and Patience, George Sand depicts two individuals, who in their total personal dissimilarity are nonetheless *complementary* in terms of her social vision. It seems clear that what she envisages is a *society* built in the image of the ideal *marriage,* a society based on contractual understanding and an acceptance of individual differences. Each individual must be educated in such a way as to elicit from him or her the best that he or she has to offer. Only in this way can an 'égalité' based on 'équité' foster utopia. For it is 'équité' that corresponds to that love advocated by Bernard in the novel's epilogue, which, in its turn, looks forward to the clarion call of Yseult de Villepreux: 'Aime, crois, travaille, et tu seras ange dans ce monde des anges'.[21]

Notes

[1] I am grateful to the French Government, whose generous financial assistance enabled me to complete this essay, and to my friend and colleague, Dr Susan Taylor-Horrex, whose helpful and perceptive comments have materially improved the finished product.

[2] G. Sand, *Leone Leoni* (Plan de la Tour, 1976), p. 127.

[3] G. Sand, *Œuvres autobiographiques,* edited by G. Lubin (Paris, 1970-71), II, p. 101.

[4] G. Sand, *Mauprat,* edited by C. Sicard (Paris, 1969), pp. 11-24; edited by J.-P. Lacassagne (Paris, 1981), pp. 7-29. All ensuing page references are to the Sicard edition.

[5] P. Vermeylen, *Les Idées politiques et sociales de George Sand* (Brussels, 1984), p. 20.

[6] Sand, *Œuvres,* I, p. 535.

[7] The ninth of the *Lettres d'un voyageur* contains the following elaboration of the *fonction du poète*: 'Les abus du monde lui arrachent des cris de détresse; le spectacle de l'hypocrisie brûle ses yeux d'un feu rouge; les souffrances de l'opprimé allument son courage; des sympathies audacieuses bouillonnent dans son sein. Le poète élève la voix et dit aux hommes des vérités qui les irritent' (*Œuvres,* II, p. 873). The third of the *Lettres à Marcie* stresses the soberly realistic limits to George Sand's feminism: 'Les femmes crient à l'esclavage: qu'elles attendent que l'homme soit libre, car l'esclavage ne peut donner la liberté' (G. Sand, *Les Sept cordes de la lyre* (Paris, 1869), p. 194).

[8] G. Sand, *Le Compagnon du Tour de France,* edited by R. Bourgeois (Grenoble, 1979), p. 37.

[9] The backwardness of Berry was genuine, and not invented by George Sand for the symbolic purposes of the novel. It is mentioned in *Valentine* – 'Le Berry ayant moins souffert que toute autre province des envahissements de la civilisation' (G. Sand, *Valentine,* edited by G. Lubin (Plan de la Tour, 1976), pp. 5-6).

[10] On this point, see the quotation from the *Lettres à Marcie* in note 7.

[11] The stress on Arthur's providentiality cannot be coincidental, for the point is made three times: he is 'un jeune homme de mérite que la Providence me donna pour compagnon' (p. 180); 'il fut pour moi l'envoyé du ciel' (p. 182); and his remarkably opportune arrival in time to salvage Bernard from the clutches of the law is 'cette marque d'amour de la Providence' (p. 282). As we shall subsequently see in *Spiridion,* God is clearly colluding in the work of redemption.

[12] The whole concept of split personality is echoed in a letter to Eugène Pelletan (13-14 May 1837): 'Nous avons tous deux hommes à gouverner, celui que nous sommes et celui que nous voudrions être' (G. Sand, *Correspondance,* ed. G. Lubin, Paris, 1964-   , IV, p. 51).

[13] We learn later in the novel (p. 269) that Patience has the capacity more or less to disappear at will, and thus would presumably have been able to evade the Mauprat uncles, but there is no reason to suppose that Bernard's decision is invalidated by any such knowledge.

[14] The second of the *Lettres à Marcie* reveals a similar preoccupation: 'Autour de nous, sous le voile d'une humble obscurité, dans les conditions les plus pauvres, sous notre main, sous nos pieds, en apparence, il y a des hommes meilleurs que nous, des hommes plus forts, plus intelligents, plus patients que nous. De grossiers habits et de rudes manières couvrent des trésors de bonté ou de sagesse que nous méconnaissons ou que nous dédaignons d'apercevoir' (*Sept cordes,* pp. 179-80).

[15] The most familiar recurrence of this myth with a similar connotation is in Hugo's 'Plein ciel' – 'C'est Isis qui déchire éperdument son voile!' See V. Hugo, *Œuvres complètes,* ed. J. Massin (Paris, 1967-79), X, p. 647.

[16] A letter from George Sand to her son (6 November 1835) reinforces the point that the Revolution *has* failed, not through the inadequacy of its principles, but because 'ceux qui y

ont travaillé avec le plus de générosité ont été vaincus par ceux qui, aimant les richesses et les plaisirs, ne se servaient du grand mot de République que pour être des espèces de princes pleins de vices et de fantaisies' (*Correspondance,* III, pp. 108-09). This letter is particularly interesting because, in stressing the need for education, it also warns against the trap of vanity, a point George Sand takes up in *Mauprat.* The fourth of the *Lettres à Marcie,* however, illustrates her confidence that the vital spark can never be extinguished, and that humanity still has the opportunity to construct its own future: 'L'humanité procède historiquement, en vertu de son libre arbitre; et la souveraine intelligence qui la gouverne l'abandonne à toutes ses chances d'erreur et d'infortune, parce qu'elle l'a douée d'un principe vital qui ne périt point, parce qu'elle sait que la vérité renaît toujours de ses propres cendres et que l'on ne l'enterre pas sous des ruines' (*Sept cordes,* pp. 209-10).

[17] This impressively eloquent page was, it seems, written to order against a commission from her publisher, Hetzel. See *Correspondance,* X, p. 539.

[18] This again echoes a theme from the fourth of the *Lettres à Marcie*: 'Du jour où nous aimons, nous serons religieux et Dieu nous visitera' (*Sept cordes,* p. 217).

[19] Sand, *Œuvres,* II, p. 780.

[20] Sand, *Œuvres,* II, p. 790.

[21] Sand, *Compagnon,* p. 256.

Tabula gratulatoria

Aberdeen University Library
Alberta University Library, Edmonton
Janet Gurkin Altman, University of Iowa
Professor L. J. Austin, Cambridge
Dr Richard Bales, Queen's University, Belfast
Dr Sheila M. Bell, Rutherford College, University of Kent
Institut für Romanische Philologie, Freie Universität Berlin
Birmingham University Library
Barbara Boland, Canterbury
Bristol University Library
Brock University Library, St Catharines, Ontario
Mr Andrew Brown, Oxford
Modern and Medieval Languages Libraries, Cambridge
Romansk Bibliotek, University of Copenhagen
Boole Library, University College, Cork
Dr Simon Davies, Queen's University, Belfast
Professor Robert Dawson, University of Texas at Austin
Durham University Library
University of East Anglia Library
Institut für Romanistik, Universität Erlangen-Nürnberg
Mr George Evans, University College of Swansea
Exeter University Library
Professor Alison Fairlie, Cambridge
Professor Graham Falconer, University of Toronto
Dr Patrick L-M. Fein, University of Zimbabwe
Fitzwilliam College, Cambridge
Bibliothèque Publique et Universitaire, Geneva
Professor F. W. A. George, Swansea
Institut für Romanische Philologie, Justus-Liebig-Universität, Giessen
Glasgow University Library
Goldsmiths College, London
Dr Josephine Grieder, New York

Bibliotheek der Rijksuniversiteit, Groningen
Dr Patricia M. Harry, Royal Holloway and Bedford New College
Bibliothèque de l'Université de Haute Alsace
Romanisches Seminar der Universität Heidelberg
Professor W. D. Howarth, Bristol
Kent University Library
Department of French, King's College, London
Library, King's College, London
Professor Wallace Kirsop, Monash University
Professor R. C. Knight, Swansea
Dr Ulla Kölving, Oxford
Saint David's University College, Lampeter
Brotherton Library, University of Leeds
Leicester University Library
Bibliotheek der Rijksuniversiteit te Leiden
Liverpool University Library
University of London Library
Olivia Lowe, London
Centre Universitaire de Luxembourg
Angus Martin, Macquarie University
Georges May, New Haven
Merton College, Oxford
Professor Valerie Minogue, Swansea
Newcastle upon Tyne University Library
Brian L. Nicholas, University of Sussex
Professor Robert Niklaus, Exeter
Modern Languages Faculty Library, Oxford
Dr. Norma Perry, University of Exeter
Reading University Library
Professor Norma Rinsler, King's College, London
Rutgers University Libraries, New Brunswick
St Andrews University Library
St Edmund Hall, Oxford
Bibliothèque des Facultés Universitaires Saint-Louis, Brussels
Dr Naomi Segal, St John's College, Cambridge
Selwyn College, Cambridge
Catriona Seth, Paris
Dr D. J. Shaw, Darwin College, University of Kent
Dr. Marjorie Shaw, Sheffield

Sheffield University Library
University of South Africa Library
Stanford University Library, California
Philip Stewart, Duke University
Stirling University Library
Sussex University Library
University College of Swansea
Sydney University Library
Taylor Institution Library, Oxford
University of Texas at Austin
Professor P. M. W. Thody, University of Leeds
London Borough of Tower Hamlets
University of Waterloo, Ontario
Whitelands College, London
Yale University Library, New Haven

Trade

B. H. Blackwell Ltd, Oxford
Erasmus bv, Amsterdam
Galloway Ltd, Aberystwyth
Dr Ludwig Häntzschel GmbH, Göttingen
John Smith & Son Ltd, Glasgow
Starkmann Library Services, Ltd, London
Stevens & Brown Ltd, Godalming